VIRAL JUSTICE

VIRAL JUSTICE

HOW WE GROW
THE WORLD WE WANT

RUHA BENJAMIN

PRINCETON UNIVERSITY PRESS

PRINCETON AND OXFORD

Published by Princeton University Press
41 William Street, Princeton, New Jersey 08540
99 Banbury Road, Oxford OX2 6JX

press.princeton.edu

All Rights Reserved

Library of Congress Control Number: 2022932477

ISBN 9780691222882
ISBN (e-book) 9780691222899

British Library Cataloging-in-Publication Data is available

Editorial: Meagan Levinson, Jacqueline Delaney
Jacket Design: Henry Sene Yee
Production: Erin Suydam
Publicity: Maria Whelan, Kate Farquhar-Thomson
Copyeditor: Ashley Moore

Jacket Credit: Cyndi Shattuck

Printed on acid-free paper. ∞

Printed in the United States of America

10 9 8 7 6 5 4 3 2 1

CONTENTS

All that you touch
You Change.

All that you Change
Changes you.

—OCTAVIA E. BUTLER

AUTHOR'S NOTE

In order to maintain the flow of the text, I have opted to use keywords instead of superscript numeric callouts for the endnotes. To look up reference material, refer to the notes section at the back of the book or use the last three words of the sentence to digitally access a note.

Many of the endnotes expand on the topic in question from the main text. Other notes contain source material for further research if you choose to pursue the topic.

The Siamese crocodiles (*Funtunfunefu Denkyemfunefu*), which mark new sections within each chapter, are one of the Adinkra symbols that represent concepts and aphorisms, originally created by the Gyaaman people of the Bono region (Ghana and Ivory Coast): "The Siamese crocodiles share one stomach, yet they fight over food." Like a chorus repeating throughout the text, they remind us of our interconnectedness and our foolishness as human beings.

VIRAL JUSTICE

The White House

I grew up in the White House. At least that's what the gold-plated sign hanging on the front door announced. In the 1950s, my grandparents bought a two-story Craftsman house just off Crenshaw Boulevard in Los Angeles. They were children of the Great Migration, the era between 1915 and 1970 when millions of African Americans left the Jim Crow South to search for better futures in the northern and western United States. They sprang from Arkansas and Texas by way of Georgia, then made their way west, first to Watts, and eventually to the Leimert Park area, a little corner of the city where they finally put down roots. These "acts of flight" would later be recognized as a *general strike*—fugitives escaping the newfangled forms of servitude that evolved out of slavery. My grandparents, if you hadn't guessed, were "the Whites."

They raised my father and my four aunts in that Craftsman on Fourth Avenue. By the early '80s, I also found refuge in the White House along with my parents and brother, Jamal. Although this was the side of LA where even the palm trees looked exhausted, in my mind, the entire world revolved around our block: school bells ringing, police helicopters circling, music vibrating from the apartments next door, and my grandma holding court in the kitchen.

Grandma, perched on a tall chair within arm's length of her mustard-yellow rotary phone, seemed to be always on call. As a former social worker and the retired director of the South Central office of the County of Los Angeles Department of Adoptions, Grandma's bible was a large calendar book inked with meticulous notes and reminders about church weddings and family counseling.

The book was always sprawled open on the counter, beside her daily pillbox stuffed with colorful contents that never ran out: blue to offset the side effects of the green, and to counteract the symptoms of the yellow. Grandma's voice was the center of our record—steady, soothing, never raised as she reminded us, "This, too, shall pass." The only good reason to venture out was to play tag with kids on the block or buy sunflower seeds and Now and Later candy at the corner store a couple of blocks east on Second Avenue. Everything else I could ever want was within reach.

The White House must have been the center of the universe, I thought, since even my public elementary school stood across the street, at the far end of the block. Inexplicably, my dad would make us walk *back* to the corner closest to the house to cross the street, then walk in the direction of Angeles Mesa Elementary, passing the White House from across the street. We were deep in the hood, but *no jaywalking.* Day after day, first backward, then forward.

This is when I learned to roll my eyes so no one could see. It is also where my abiding admiration of rule breakers was seeded, especially when the rules seemed arbitrary and controlling. Of course now, as a parent, I get it. Dad's rules were an invisible web meant to protect, not entrap, so that when he wasn't there to watch us cross, the light at the corner could watch over us instead.

The playground was where I let loose. I was a beast at kickball, tetherball, and handball. Or so I imagined. One day, as I rounded the kickball field, one of the boys I liked on the other team was blocking my access to second base, so I pushed him to the ground and kept running. This landed me in the principal's office, a truly foreign experience that I approached as an alien might, detached but interested, observing some strange rite of punishment. Stranger still, it seemed to be happening to someone who looked exactly like me but wasn't me. With my parents at work, my grandma was the one to pick me up. Driving the short distance home in her gold Chrysler, there was no disappointed speech, no grounding, no punishment. Clearly, from her point of view, whoever had branded me with this suspension was not in possession of all the facts.

Sure, suspension was designed to teach me a lesson, and it worked. It just didn't teach me the one they intended. In the world my grandmother had built, suspension meant time to decompress, space to reflect, a chance to bond, and most importantly, plentiful access to my favorite snacks.

Grandma White, it turns out, was an undercover abolitionist, replacing castigation with care, suspension with connection, shame with encouragement. Rather than making me feel small and bad, she showered me with tenderness, making me want to do better. It was what she *didn't* say, what she chose *not* to shine a light on, that imprinted on me with such force. Rather than parrot the school's reprimand, she chose a different poetics, one guided by the credo that *what you water grows*. And in her unassuming subversion of school punishment, she gave me my first lesson in abolitionist world-making.

Before and after that day, I spent an inordinate amount of time ruminating about fights and was dogged by a constant and nagging expectation of imminent conflict. I'm not exactly sure how common fights were at Angeles Mesa, but they felt routine—like ritual eruptions, exploding on the playground or in the open-air cafeteria at lunchtime. *What if she comes up to me and says this? What if he walks past me and does that?* So much energy preparing for different scenarios, mentally sparring imagined foes. Stay *ready so you don't have to* get *ready*, was our unspoken code. But except for pushing down that boy I liked, my moment in the ring never materialized. I wasted hours upon hours preparing—hours that might have been spent otherwise.

In the afternoons, I raced home to play hide-and-seek, hopscotch, and foursquare with our neighbors, the Martinez kids, using chalk to outline games on our shared driveway. In front of the White House stood a magnificent magnolia tree, lush and extravagant, offering us a place to shelter ourselves from the blazing sun.

Even then I sensed that the magnificent tree with its perfumed white flowers was a luxury on a block with very little shade and in a neighborhood with little foliage. My favorite game was playing "school" on our huge stone porch, which was covered with a layer of faux grass carpet that was good for sitting on and "instructing" my friends.

The front window that ran the length of the porch gave us a great view of all the passersby on Fourth Avenue—kids chasing down the ice cream truck, neighbors playing hopscotch in the driveway, motorists speeding by—but it also forced me into a state of constant vigilance. Lined with burglar bars like all the other houses in the neighborhood, ours stood out thanks to a jagged hole in the window—a small, cone-shaped opening almost exactly in the center that rippled outward, stubbornly refusing to break. Created by a bullet, BB gun, or rock, it must've been too expensive to fix. And so the crack in the window broke into my imagination and, as a result, I spent most of my childhood sleeping defensively.

It was the mid-'80s, the era of routine drive-by shootings popularized in films like *Boyz n the Hood*, and a girl just a little older than me was gunned down right across from Angeles Mesa. Although my bed was on the second floor, up against a window facing a completely different direction, I forced myself to lie as flat as possible, "just in case." My flesh was spared, but imaginary bullets interrupted my dreams night after night. This is why Breonna's death at the hands of police in the middle of the night hit me so hard.

On March 13, 2020, Breonna Taylor and her boyfriend, Kenny, were asleep in their apartment in Louisville, Kentucky, when, just before 1:00 a.m., they heard a thunderous noise at the door. Kenny was a postal worker, and Breonna, an aspiring nurse, was an emergency medical technician (EMT) covering two hospitals in the city. Kenny and Breonna were two of the millions of "essential workers" who supported Americans during the COVID-19 pandemic, until their sleep was violently interrupted.

Imagine pulling a double shift, putting your life in jeopardy transporting people to the hospital, getting home, showering off the fearful energy of the day, eating dinner while studying, perhaps snuggling with your partner until both of you fall asleep, only to be jolted awake by a terrifying sound coming from outside your home.

Kenny, a licensed gun owner, grabbed his weapon and crept down the hallway. Only later would he learn that three plainclothes officers had a no-knock warrant to enter the home without identifying themselves. The police used a battering ram to break down the front door. Not knowing who it was and fearing for his and Breonna's lives, Kenny shot one of the intruders in the leg. In response, the police unloaded thirty-two rounds of ammunition, several rounds of which also sprayed into a neighbor's apartment where a young child and mother slept.

The officers' bullets ripped into Breonna's flesh, striking her eight times and savagely stealing her life. According to neighbors, the officers made no attempt to identify themselves, as they initially claimed. It turned out that one of the people whom police were investigating and looking for—someone who had a prior relationship with Breonna—was already in custody at the time they burst into Breonna's apartment. Officers said they were searching her place for suspected drugs, which they didn't find.

Breonna was killed in March 2020, but her story didn't receive widespread attention until mid-May after her mother filed a lawsuit against the Louisville Metro Police Department. Breonna had been killed the same week that many Americans finally started grappling with the seriousness of COVID-19 and states started issuing stay-at-home orders to "flatten the curve."

The irony of this timing was not lost on Breonna's mother, Tamika Palmer, who "gets emotional when she considers that she was more concerned with her daughter's safety as a health-care worker than she was about her being safe in her own home." The ultimate threat to Breonna's life was never COVID-19, but brutality at the hands of the police, licensed by the claim of upholding law and order.

For family and friends, whose hearts are broken apart, the shattering is not only emotional but physiological; the trauma gets under the skin, into the bloodstream, making collective forms of healing and protest—from hashtags like #SayHerName to street-corner altars with flowers and photos—so vital. But also never enough. Rage and grief, when borne alone, would surely crush us under the weight, and so our only hope to survive—if not transmute—heartache is to do for each other what surgeons do when they take a patient's heart in their hands and manually pump it until it begins to beat on its own again.

Breonna's murder stands out in part because she was an EMT. She would have been among the millions of first responders on the front lines during the pandemic lauded for putting their lives at risk. But deadly police violence got Breonna before COVID-19 could.

Whether swift and violent or slow and subtle, racism uses multiple paths to get under our skin. The violent interruption of sleep by police is one, and the list of victims is long. With such a steady stream of hash-tagged names in our newsfeed, it may be easy to grow numb.

On May 16, 2010, seven-year-old Aiyana Mo'Nay Stanley-Jones was asleep on her grandmother's couch when, in the middle of the night, a Detroit SWAT team raided their home looking for a murder suspect. In the process, an officer threw a flash-bang grenade—a war weapon—through the window and killed Aiyana with a single bullet to the head. What's more, a reality TV crew was filming the raid outside for the A&E cable network show *The First 48*. Recording be damned, the case against Joseph Weekley, the officer who shot Aiyana, was dismissed due to a lack of evidence.

Even as she dreamed, Aiyana was forced into a nightmare not of her making, her body snatched into a Sunken Place from which there is no return. Still, while swift and deadly forms of state-sanctioned violence may elicit collective rage, the subtler, everyday harms that interrupt sleep can be easy to dismiss. A Chicago-based study conducted in the early 2000s, entitled "'Every Shut Eye, Ain't Sleep,'" explores the relationship between sleep difficulty and *racism-related vigilance*, which entails the ongoing "preparation for and anticipation of discrimination."

In short, racism and chronic stress also make us restless and, like me, unable to dream with ease. But like a defiant Nina Simone, who recorded "Feeling Good" in 1965—the same year civil rights marchers were brutally beaten by state troopers in Selma, and thousands of U.S. troops arrived in Vietnam, and the Watts rebellion popped off, and antiwar protests spread far and wide, and the world was burning then like it is now—I wail willfully:

Sleep in peace when day is done, that's what I mean
It's a new dawn
It's a new day
It's a new life
For me

The White House eventually killed my father at age sixty-three. On January 5, 2014, he had been feeling under the weather for several days but still decided to go to work. He wasn't there long. He called my mother to drive him to Cedars-Sinai hospital, where he deteriorated quickly. I was on a plane from San Francisco to Boston, after a retreat with friends and family in California's Santa Cruz Mountains. As soon as I landed, I received the dreaded call from my mom, her voice breaking in disbelief, and I got back on a flight to Los Angeles to bury my dad. He had been infected with the H1N1 virus, widely known as the "swine flu."

My dad, a former college athlete, was one of those tolerable vegans who didn't try to convince you to stop eating meat. He also had a sweet tooth, which he often satiated with one of his go-to smoothies containing a mix of berries, bananas, nondairy milk, and a smidge of kale. He was the kind of person who recovered from a stroke at fifty-nine and celebrated by jogging a 5K.

Still, his sleep was erratic, especially in the years leading up to his death. As a dutiful daughter, I emailed him articles with titles like "Yes. Your Sleep Schedule Is Making You Sick" and "Study Ties 6–7 Hours of Sleep to Longer Life," even though I knew sleep isn't simply a matter of willpower when the broader climate conspires to make you ill. He was, in a word, *weathered.*

"Weathering" is a concept first coined in 1992 by public health researcher Arline Geronimus. With the term, Geronimus draws attention to the ways in which people absorb stressors and oppressors in the broader environment, and how this causes preventable illness and premature death.

In my dad's case, weathering wore down his immune system, making him more vulnerable to viruses and less able to fight off infection or endure aggressive treatment. In a society that fetishizes individual responsibility—where even the scientific establishment prefers to focus on genetic rather than social or political explanations for racial health disparities—the concept of weathering is battling its own version of (antiblack) climate denial.

In 1978, the year I was born, Black families in the U.S. earned fifty-nine cents for every dollar of income whites received. In 2015, the year my dad died, Black families *still* earned only fifty-nine cents for every dollar of income whites received, and today the racial wage gap has actually increased. The wealth gap is even larger, driven largely by racial discrimination in the real estate industry. Progress, it seems, is a tear-soaked mirage.

When the housing bubble burst in 2007, hitting Black homeowners especially hard, the financial fallout became a death sentence as predatory loans poisoned people's lives like radioactive debris. "Mortgage" literally means *death pledge*—born from the same Latin root that gives us "mortuary," "mortal," and "postmortem."

Although it might make you think of the borrower's demise, the "death" in "mortgage" actually refers to the fact that debt becomes void once it's paid off, and the fact that the pledge, too, becomes null if the borrower fails to pay. But here, too, Black debt and white debt do not carry the same burden. Sociologist Louise Seamster explains, "Debt's role in your life depends on who you are . . . Racial discrimination shapes who feels debt as crushing and who experiences it as an opportunity." When it comes to the predatory loans that precipitated the 2008 housing crash, "high-income Black borrowers were *more* likely than low-income White borrowers to get these subprime loans."

In the end, the burden of Black debt turned the White House upside down, and our family yoke began weighing heavier and heavier, leaving my dad exposed . . . So H1N1 killed my dad. But no, I don't blame the virus.

Viral Justice grows out of my contention that viruses are not our ultimate foe. In the same way that COVID-19 kills, so too ableism, racism, sexism, classism, and colonialism work to eliminate unwanted people. Ours is a eugenicist society: from the funding of school districts to the triaging of patients, "privilege" is a euphemism for tyranny. Any attempt at spreading justice, then, entails not simply "including" those who've been disposed of but fundamentally transforming the societies into which they're included.

In the words of James Baldwin, "We are living in a world in which everybody and everything is interdependent." It is not something we must strive to be. We *are*. Opposing everyday eugenics requires that we acknowledge and foster a *deep-rooted interdependence*, not as some cheery platitude but as a guiding ethos for regenerating life on this planet. This is what disability justice organizers have been trying to tell us, and what Indigenous peoples have long asserted—that whether we want to accept it or not, we are connected, not just to other living things but to those yet born. Our decisions today ripple across time . . . seven generations, according to the Haudenosaunee Confederacy's Great Law of Peace. Interdependence is not only part of a sacred philosophy but also a guiding ethos for refashioning social and political structures.

Consider what began with mass protests over social and environmental injustices in Chile in 2019, where Indigenous communities led the charge for a nationwide "reinvention." Hundreds of thousands of Chileans mobilized, and in late 2021, they elected 155 representatives to completely rewrite their dictatorship-era constitution amid a "climate and ecological emergency." An Indigenous language and literature professor, Elisa Loncon Antileo, a member of the Mapuche community, was elected president of the constitutional convention. She and the other participants posed fundamental questions that citizens of most nations have probably never considered: "Should the country retain a presidential system? Should nature have rights? How about future generations?" This is world-building on a grand scale with local communities and Indigenous values guiding the process. It is a process of *reworlding* that doesn't try to smother differences, one that envisions a "pluriverse" rather than a universe, welcoming heterogeneity rather than enforcing a singularity.

As professor of Africana studies Greg Carr tweeted at the time, "The fight to rewrite Chile's national constitution should be leading global conversations & everyday talk alike. The people have forced a social structure confrontation, with structural inequities and our planetary environmental emergency at the center. We should all be watching." Watching, yes, and asking how we might rewrite our own constitutions; how we might even reconstitute the outworn political imagination that carved up the planet into nation-states to begin with, and refashion the failed economic ideology that treats the earth like one giant mine despite our collective demise.

Alas, it is not my mission in this book to answer these questions exactly but, rather, to remind each of us that they can and should be asked at all. As you'll see, while many of the examples to follow tend to come from the North American context, this is not because we, here, have *any* business holding ourselves up as examples to the rest of the world. Instead, in seeking examples of viral justice, I turned mostly to people and projects in my own backyard, as I encourage each of us to start right where we are. But make no mistake—individuals, communities, and movements across the planet, like what we witnessed in Chile, are lighting the way. They remind us that even things that seem hardened in stone can be shed, *should* be shed, when they run counter to human and ecological interdependence.

Racism, inequality, and indifference are a juvenile rebellion against the reality of this interconnection, microscopically and sociopolitically. "I want to grow up and so should you," exclaimed an exasperated Baldwin, addressing an audience at the National Press Club on December 10, 1986, a year before he died. Perhaps, then, COVID-19 is forcing us all to grow up, exposing that vulnerability and interdependence are our lot, whether we like it or not.

COVID-19 is a social disease and, as sociologist Eric Klinenberg insists, solidarity is an "essential tool for combatting infectious disease and other collective threats. Solidarity motivates us to promote public health, not just our own personal security." But, he cautions, "It's an open question whether Americans have enough social solidarity to stave off the worst possibilities of the coronavirus pandemic." Vaccines, in turn, are no magical fix for the kind of pathological self-interest that masquerades as independence. When we look worldwide, access to a COVID-19 vaccine has widened the gap between those whose lives matter and those deemed disposable. But we don't have to resign ourselves to this infantile individualism-cum-vaccine nationalism.

What if, instead, we reimagined virality as something we might learn from? What if the virus is not something simply to be feared and eliminated, but a microscopic model of what it could look like to spread justice and joy in small but perceptible ways? Little by little, day by day, starting in our own backyards, let's identify our plots, get to the root cause of what's ailing us, accept our interconnectedness, and finally grow the fuck up.

To that end, I propose a microvision of social change, much like Grandma White's everyday abolitionism, which we seed in the present as alternatives to our fracturing system. But where should we start? Sleep deprived, let's start with our *dreams*.

Dreaming is a luxury. Many people have spent their lives being forced to live inside other people's dreams. And we must come to terms with the fact that the nightmares that people endure represent the underside of elite fantasies about efficiency, profit, and social control. For those who want to construct a different social reality, one grounded in justice and joy, we can't only critique the world as it is. We have to build the world as it should be to make justice irresistible.

That many of us have a hard time imagining a world with universal healthcare or a world without prisons is a clear sign that even our dreams are weathered. To dream bigger, we no doubt have to start redistributing wealth and creating a much stronger social safety net where everyone has access to *the goods*—material and social—that are essential to lead a flourishing life. There's just no getting around it. As geographer and abolitionist Ruth Wilson Gilmore insists, "Capitalism requires inequality and racism enshrines it."

In March 2020, when the pandemic forced schools to close, many people were surprised to learn how many students are homeless. In New York City, the largest public school system in the United States, roughly 111,000 students—1 in 10 children—were homeless during the 2019–20 school year. As more people bear witness to the shameful social inequities that have been right under our noses, we must demand bolder forms of wealth redistribution: Universal Basic Income, universal healthcare, and free college tuition, for starters. *Impossible. Inconceivable. Pie in the sky*! people will say. Two words for them: police budgets. More specifically, diverting budgets such as the $100 billion spent on policing in the U.S. to public goods that people actually need.

Despite how inequality is made to seem natural, scarcity is manufactured. We no doubt have the means to guarantee that everyone has jobs, healthcare, education, housing, and the ability to ensure millions of children do not go hungry. But we must demand a permanent divestment from policing, prisons, and the entire carceral apparatus, and a radical reinvestment in public goods that reflect our interdependence as people. Legendary civil rights activist Bayard Rustin put it plainly: "We are all one—and if we don't know it, we will learn it the hard way."

So how do we go about materializing a more expansive commitment to the Common Good? The late sociologist Erik Olin Wright offers a wonderfully lucid vision for this transition in *How to Be an Anticapitalist in the Twenty-First Century*, which he completed after being diagnosed with acute myeloid leukemia. In describing how we can grow the world we want, Wright likens society to the ecosystem of a lake, in which we find an intricate web of many kinds of life-forms: bacteria, aquatic plants and algae, and fish, among other vertebrates. Despite this heterogeneity, a dominant species of capitalism (and I would add racism, ableism, sexism, and imperialism) reigns in this ecosystem. He suggests that transforming our current system will require a gradual process of introducing "alien species" that can survive the environment—nurturing their niches, protecting their habitats until, eventually, they spill into the mainstream and displace the dominant species.

"Viral justice" as an approach to social change seeks to nurture alienated species—all the forms of life and living that are routinely cast out and rendered worthless in our current system. These are the species of behavior that embody interdependence and, in the old ecosystem, would be judged as weak: non-carceral responses to harm, non-capitalist approaches to healthcare, and mutual aid of all kinds. Look closely, and you'll find these alienated life-forms already taking root under the atomized and stratified habitats that have been slowly killing us. The pandemic has allowed these life-forms to grow beyond their niches, and with more of us fostering them, they could eventually transform our entire ecosystem.

Many of these life-forms are not new but build on past efforts that are easy to overlook, such as the volunteer-based Freedom Schools organized by civil rights activists throughout Mississippi in the mid-1960s. These schools were student-centered and culturally relevant, combining political education with more traditional academic skills and serving everyone from small children to the elderly.

During the COVID-19 pandemic, similar alternatives started sprouting up in many places, with neighbors offering each other basic provisions and planning for the long haul. Within the first ten weeks of the stay-at-home orders, over ninety mutual aid groups and over 550 resource groups registered under the banner of Mutual Aid NYC. Mutual aid groups are not charities but voluntary associations that are part of a long tradition of radical change focused on meeting people's immediate needs *and* transforming the underlying conditions that produce those needs in the first place.

Viral justice takes many forms.

As an individual, it could look like Ruhel Islam, a Bangladeshi immigrant and the owner of Gandhi Mahal, an Indian restaurant in Minneapolis. When Islam's eatery was damaged in a fire apparently started by a right-wing extremist during the Black Lives Matter protests in 2020—after the murder of George Floyd—he thanked his neighbors for trying to stand guard but said, "Let my building burn. Justice needs to be served." His daughter Hafsa Islam posted on the restaurant's Facebook page, "Gandhi Mahal may have felt the flames last night, but our fiery drive to help protect and stand with our community will never die! Peace be with everyone." This kind of solidarity is contagious, no doubt inspiring the rest of us to consider how we, too, can stoke the flames of justice.

As collectives, viral justice could look like the youths at South End Technology Center in Boston creating masks for frontline workers and other vulnerable groups. For their "PPE for the People" campaign, young people in the community used sewing machines, 3-D printers, and laser cutters to create everything from 3-D-printed N95-style masks and clear face shields to hand-sewn personal masks for everyday use by the elderly, low-income folks, and essential workers. This initiative is just one of many making social change irresistible.

Longtime organizers such as Mariame Kaba insist that mutual aid is a practice that entails meeting people's immediate needs through food donation, grocery delivery, bail funds, transportation, and childcare, in the spirit of "solidarity not charity." But mutual aid is also an opportunity for political education—an "on-ramp" for people to get involved in social movements, according to Dean Spade, a Seattle-based organizer and founder of the mutual aid resource website Big Door Brigade.

To that end, Spade points to three types of movement work: *dismantling* harmful systems, *providing* for people's immediate needs, and *creating* alternative structures that can meet those needs based on values of care, democratic participation, and solidarity. Take Ecuador, which, in 2007, began a bold experiment that didn't cost a lot of money. Rather than continuing to criminalize street gangs, the country legalized them. And as sociologist David Brotherton documents, gangs were able to "remake themselves as cultural associations that could register with the government, which in turn allowed them to qualify for grants and benefit from social programming, just like everybody else."

Some members went to school, started businesses like and graphic design companies, or took advantage of grants training or setting up community centers. As a result, homici dropped dramatically, and gangs began operating more like social movements, even collaborating with their rivals on cultural events.

Of course, change didn't happen overnight, but as Brotherton reminds us, little by little over ten years, "trust and long-term relationships had a chance to build up." It wasn't the policy alone but how people used the legalization of gangs as an opportunity to transform how they related to one another. That's viral justice at work.

In the pages ahead, we'll come across examples of these kinds of movements, with an eye to how everyday people choose to get involved in the nitty-gritty work of world-building. But in every case, before we can really appreciate the stubborn audacity and courage this takes, we have to look squarely, soberly at what we're up against. I warn you now, it ain't pretty. Each time you find yourself staring at the page thinking, *I thought this was a hopeful manifesto about change!* I urge you to recollect the words of poet Mary Oliver:

> I tell you this
> to break your heart,
> by which I mean only
> that it break open and never close again
> to the rest of the world

This is what we call *witnessing*. The surge of sorrow, rage, and weariness that comes each time we learn anew of the never-ending cruelties that surround us, that is our hearts breaking, each piece of our insides offering up a new surface—fresh understanding, greater resolve—connecting to our outsides.

Only then can we truly grasp the mettle it takes for people to bear witness to this burning world, their clothes reeking of soot, their eyes itching from smoke, and yet turning one to another to plot a world where they can take off the masks and breathe easy. They are, in the words of Kaba, "pre-figuring the world in which we want to live." Again, it may be tempting to dismiss these efforts as small, fleeting, and inconsequential, as we're still taught to only appreciate that which is big and grand, official, and codified. But a microscopic virus has news for us: a microvision of justice and generosity, love, and solidarity can have exponential effects.

At the end of the day, I am a student of the late-great Octavia E. Butler, writer and builder of speculative worlds. To the question, *What is there to do?* she once responded, "I mean there's no single answer that will solve all our future problems. There's no magic bullet. Instead, there are thousands of answers—at least. You can be one of them if you choose to be."

We can be one of them, if we choose: vectors of justice, spreaders of joy, transforming our world so that everyone has the chance to thrive.

This book is for everyone who, deep down, knows our fates are linked, even when our antisocial system tries to convince us otherwise. We have healthcare policies neglecting the needy, education policies breeding ignorance, labor policies producing disposable employees, housing policies building scarcity, tech policies encoding inequity, environmental policies ensuring our extinction—all by design. We can and must design otherwise.

Viral Justice offers a vision of change that requires each of us to individually confront how we participate in unjust systems, even when "in theory" we stand for justice. Whether you're the explicit target or not, inequality makes us *all* sick. The dirty secret of antisocial policies is that even those who demand cuts to public education, healthcare, and housing—demands animated by anti-Blackness—are suffering. Namely, the relative life expectancy of white Americans, along with other groups, has been on the decline compared with other nations. As it turns out, few can shelter from the weathering effects of a fraying social system, even those who happen to be "privileged."

My work is fueled by an atypical upbringing—born in India, I moved to South Central Los Angeles, then Conway, South Carolina, . . .

Majuro, South Pacific, . . . and Eswatani, Southern Africa, all before I was eighteen. My parents were educators who worked on different projects that had us moving every few years after their particular positions ran their course. I come from many *Souths*, and I tend to bring this perspective of looking at the world from its underbelly to my thinking. My fascination with world-building grows out of the fact that I have lived in many different worlds—big cities, small towns, remote islands, even a real-life kingdom.

For the first time, in *Viral Justice*, I explore the connections between my personal life and public commitments. I was born in a small clinic in the town of Wai (pronounced "why"), India, to an Indian-born mother of Persian descent and a Black American father hailing from Houston and raised in Los Angeles. My parents' stories of my birth—the one-size-fits-all stirrups, a stainless-steel bed around which resident chickens squawked, and nurses waiting on my mom day and night—ignite my imagination about the places where cold tools and warm humans meet. My work as a writer, researcher, and teacher takes shape in the borderlands between mainstream institutions and the messiness of everyday life.

The way we classify and are classified as different human kinds is another enduring fascination that grows out of the social boundary crossing of my family, who raised me with the Bahá'í teachings that place justice at their core. The central principle of the Bahá'í faith is the *oneness of humanity*: "Know ye not why We created you all from the same dust, that no one should exalt himself over the other." And then there is my favorite passage, the one I memorized as a teen and grew up reciting: "The best beloved of all things in My sight is Justice; turn not away therefrom if thou desirest Me, and neglect it not that I may confide in thee. By its aid thou shalt see with thine own eyes and not through the eyes of others, and shalt know of thine own knowledge and not through the knowledge of thy neighbor. Ponder this in thy heart; how it behooveth thee to be. Verily justice is My gift to thee and the sign of My loving-kindness. Set it then before thine eyes." Only much later, as an adult, did it really hit me that this vision of justice wasn't something granted by governments "out there," but something people express "in here," by how we each see, know, and move in the world.

In their own way, my parents were "seeing with their own eyes and not through the eyes of others" by deciding to marry. In July 1973 my dad, Truitt, boarded a plane at LAX with three other Bahá'ís from the U.S. to attend the second Western Asia Youth Conference in Bangalore, the capital city of the state of Karnataka in southern India, where my mom, Behin, happened to be giving a presentation. It must have been one hell of a talk because the next day—after several hours of conversation, so the story goes—my dad asked her if she would marry him. And on September 19, after my dad traveled to the town of Panchgani to meet my mom's family, and after they sent a telegram to my grandmother in Los Angeles asking for her blessing, they tied the knot.

And so, my family and faith were my first classroom, where I became a student of race, ethnicity, gender, class, and citizenship—an ongoing touchstone for questioning the established order of things. They helped me appreciate that experimentation doesn't just happen in sterile laboratories. People experiment all the time in their daily lives, challenging how things have always been done.

In the following pages, I'll shine a light on the patterns of inequity we perpetuate by just doing our jobs, clocking in and out, making small talk with our neighbors, avoiding uncomfortable conversations, all while the machinery of our everyday lives hums along. I won't ignore the big, macro changes that need to happen. Rather, we're going to question the distinction between macro and micro, big and small, because all the great transformations that societies undergo rely on the low-key scheming of everyday people. Even now, behind each grand headline and pronouncement, we'll find individuals and groups who've decided to disrupt the status quo.

Whether people are tearing down concrete monuments or overturning racist symbols and policies, it's hard to deny that something different is in the air, and it seems to be contagious. To that end, viral justice elaborates a practical and principled approach to spreading solidarity and justice, drawing on historical and ongoing examples of mutual aid, community organizing, and collective healing.

But viral justice is not a new academic theory or a novel organizing strategy, nor does it name a newfangled phenomenon. Instead, it is an orientation, a way of looking at, or looking *again* at (i.e., respecting), all the ways people are working, little by little, day by day, to combat unjust systems and build alternatives to the oppressive status quo.

Viral justice orients us differently toward small-scale, often localized, actions. It invites us to witness how an idea or action that sprouts in one place may be adopted, adapted, and diffused elsewhere. But it also counters the assumption that "scaling up" should always be the goal.

Viral justice directs our attention to how groups seek to embody and experiment with new ways of relating—"networks of mutual aid, maroon communities, survival programs, and circles of care." It shines a light on individuals' "self-conscious effort to direct energy into practising in the present the future that is sought."

Viral justice rejects false dichotomies and either-or options when it comes to our goals and dispositions: idealistic or pragmatic, experimental or enduring, spontaneous or strategic, fiery or cool, romantic or gritty, creative or cerebral, joyful or enraged. Yes, and . . .

Viral justice is a parable of the sower *and* of the uprooter.

Viral justice is invested not only in our material welfare but also our spiritual well-being: "It is to acknowledge that *we were never meant to survive*, and yet we are still here."

Viral justice is an admission: I am, *we are*, exhausted, discouraged, grieving, and, sometimes, even too exhausted to grieve. It is a recognition that even the most resolute and hopeful among us worry that our efforts are futile, and we need encouragement to see another day.

In its attention to everyday insurrections and *beautiful experiments*—"radical designs for living . . . seeking, venturing, testing, trying, speculating, discovering, exploring new avenues, breaking with traditions, defying law, and making it"—viral justice expresses a deep longing that animates Black life.

Viral justice is not about dystopia, or utopia, but *u*stopia.

As a world-building rubric, it is anticipatory and inventive— asking *what if?*—while stubbornly invested in the here and now— demanding *why wait?*

What if we can architect a radically different existence? *Why wait* for these brutal, death-making structures to completely collapse before we start truly living?

Although mutual aid involves people meeting one another's basic needs in the short term, it's predicated on a shared belief that we must reimagine social systems over the long haul. The lens of viral justice encourages us to amplify, as a microscope would, these seemingly small efforts and entices us to spread them, like a life-sustaining virus. Visionary writer adrienne maree brown invites this kind of attention to the microscopic when she observes, "The crisis is everywhere, massive massive massive. And we are small. But emergence notices the way small actions and connections create complex systems, patterns that become ecosystems and societies . . . How we are at the small scale is how we are at the large scale . . . what we practice at the small scale sets the pattern for the whole system."

Viral justice, in this way, is attentive to the large, looming crises and the many caring connections that people form despite, amid, and because of injustice. This book is a rallying cry that scraps the bogus idea that you're *just* one person. As *just* one person, let's band together with all the other *just people* who are equally hungry for change.

If anti-Black racism is the soundtrack of our lives, buzzing so low in the background that we don't even hear it—that we don't realize we're humming along with it even though we hate the lyrics—then this book turns up the volume.

Viral justice is an invitation to listen anew to the white noise that is killing us softly, so that we can then make something soulful together, so that we can then compose harmonies that give us life.

In the midst of multiple ongoing calamities, this work of crafting more caring social relations isn't charity work—work to be done on behalf of others. Falling from a burning building, I might hit the ground first, but you won't be far behind. My well-being is intimately bound up with yours. I don't need an ally; I need you to smell the smoke. So come. We'll start at the White House and, brick by brick, build a world where, eventually, we can lower our defenses because the weather won't be so goddamn lethal.

If the COVID-19 pandemic has taught us anything, it's that something almost undetectable can be deadly, and that we can transmit it without even knowing. Doesn't this imply that *small* things, seemingly minor actions, decisions, and habits could have exponential effects in the other direction, tipping the scales toward justice: *affirming* life, *fostering* well-being, and *invigorating* society? The pages that follow answer, *yes, yes, yes*. Though, like some of you perhaps, I've sometimes found myself thinking, *no, no way, no chance*.

Trained as a sociologist, I've always been more disposed toward structural, *macro* change targeting policies and institutions over more diffuse cultural transformation that directly engages individuals. I tend to wince at self-help-style books, trainings, and gurus. But in trying so hard to push back on individualistic approaches to empowerment, I went to the other extreme for a while, losing touch with the importance of everyday decisions and actions—what my colleague Imani Perry calls "practices of inequality"—as an essential part of social transformation. Commenting on the many forms of racism that resurfaced during the pandemic, Imani tweeted, "That white male doctor who strangled and assaulted a black girl child for 'not social distancing' is also a sign of what African Americans confront in the health care system. It's not just 'structural' racism folks." This was a needed punch to my disciplinary gut, as I had been trained to critique "the system" and "systemic inequality," as if these were divorced from everyday human decisions and actions. After all, the doctor, not "the system," made a choice to violently assault a Black girl child. Yet at the same time, we can uphold unjust systems without physically attacking another person; that, for me, is the risk in highlighting the most obvious cases of brutality: it can let us off the hook.

Ultimately, then, this is not a book for those interested primarily in policy, however important policy remains. Rather, this is a call to action for individuals to reclaim power over how our thoughts, habits, and actions shape—as much as they are shaped by—the larger environment.

As disability justice activist Mia Mingus puts it, "If we cannot handle the small things between us, how will we be able to handle the big things? Learning how to address these smaller hurts or breaks in trust can help us learn the basic skills we need to address large harms. It can also help to reduce and prevent larger forms of ha and violence."

This book seeks to not only redress harms but also enact all its variety. Each of us is called on to put our hand to the p do the work that is ours, a saying commonly passed down amo Black women. Indeed, many of the world-changers we'll learn from in the pages ahead literally till and seed the soil.

Philadelphia-based prison abolitionist Stephanie Keene says people often ask her, "How can I get involved?" Her response is, "'Do what it is you're good at'—that is, if your thing is data, figure out how to contribute those skills to a cause. If you're a writer, lend your words to the struggle. If you're good at cooking, feed the people. Revolutionaries certainly need full bellies to keep up the fight. I say this to emphasize everyone isn't skilled at the same things, and the work wouldn't be dynamic or sustainable if we were. We each can and should offer our particular skills to the collective pursuit of liberty and justice for all." So, hand to the plow, where is your plot?

My primary plot is the classroom. I remember the moment it dawned on me. It was summer, and I was with my family at a beach in Santa Monica, California, about a week before we were scheduled to fly to Boston, where I was starting my first job as an assistant professor at Boston University. Lying there on the sand, watching my kids chase each other in and out of the water, I cracked open a new-at-the-time book titled *The New Jim Crow* by Michelle Alexander.

Turning each page and getting pulled deeper and deeper into her analysis of how mass incarceration is an institution of social and racial control, an epiphany occurred to me like a massive wave knocking me off my feet: *I could assign this book, and any others I deem important, to all my students and no one could stop me!* I admit, this realization was followed by a witchy cackle. At that moment, it felt magical. Powerful. That the design of my classes, the seemingly small choices of what I assigned my students to read and reflect on, could have exponential effects.

That day on the beach was a turning point for me, and from my first day in the classroom at BU all the way to my present position as professor of African American studies at Princeton University, I've tended to teach like my life depends on it. Although my commitment has been recognized officially, what matter much more are the messages I receive from students long after they've graduated.

They share how the lessons, discussions, and texts we've read stick with them, influencing their work in courtrooms, hospitals, tech companies, community organizations, and classrooms of their design. There's nothing in the world more satisfying. The energy we pour into our plot is not charitable if only because the fruits flow back to us, sometimes immediately, but more often circuitously over time.

I've also come to realize that spaces of learning are not confined to the classroom, and that tilling my plot often requires scaling the constrictive walls of the university. In rejecting the tired script of what it means to be a professor, my plot is the Brooklyn Public Library, speaking with patrons about algorithmic discrimination in their everyday lives. It is the artist-run School for Poetic Computation, scheming with students about how to create a different ecosystem for tech design that prioritizes people over profits. My plot is an LA community center, collaborating with Black Women for Wellness around health advocacy in my old neighborhood. And one of my favorite plots is sharing stories with swimsuit-clad kids at a summer reading program at the community pool in my town. Plotting, for me, is learning alongside young and old, rich and poor, those with an alphabet soup after their names and those who graduated from the School of Hard Knocks. This book, too, is my plot.

Rather than confining me, plotting frees me up to see the potential for learning everywhere with anyone, not simply those who register for my classes. Plotting, like learning, is about "invention and re-invention . . . the restless, impatient, continuing, hopeful inquiry human beings pursue in the world, with the world, and with each other," says Brazilian educator Paulo Freire. Your plot, too, doesn't have to mean committing to only one thing.

Whether digging deep or sowing seeds far and wide, plotting is about questioning the scripts you've been handed and scheming with others to do and be otherwise for the collective good of all.

Once we've discovered our plots, the next step is to reflect on the roles and narratives we've inherited, and how patterns of injustice have infected the way people think and act. For me, this meant understanding how many sociology classes are taught—what texts are assigned, what paradigms are centered, what (dead, white, male) authors are canonized, how professors perform their authority, and so many other micro-ways of doing and being—and how these add up to reproduce a harmful status quo.

In most cases, we inherit established patterns without questioning. In the context of higher education, that looks quite literally like getting handed a syllabus that others have used time and time again.

In this quiet passing down of canonical knowledge year after year, inequality is reproduced—reading German sociologist Émile Durkheim but not Black sociologist W.E.B. Du Bois, learning about the "race relations" paradigm (a framework that downplays, if not totally ignores, the role of white supremacy and colonialism in shaping "relations" between groups), assigning Talcott Parsons's functionalist theory of social systems but not Patricia Hill Collins's Black feminist thought, regurgitating academic concepts that grew out of the Jim Crow era without ever engaging the *new* Jim Crow à la Alexander. An entire world of thought passed down to students, generation after generation, bleeding into their work as lawyers, artists, politicians, doctors, and parents.

Racism, I have long contended, is not born out of "ignorance," or *not* knowing. Rather, it's a distorted form of knowledge: a way of seeing and thus being in the world. In the classroom, I can either reproduce authoritative distortions or incubate alternatives to the status quo in the minds and hearts of students.

Your plot, too, is a potential incubator. If, in most cases, we inherit established patterns of thought and action without question, then questioning dominant narratives—the established order of things—is a powerful starting point for plotting a different future. Many people want a full-fledged alternative to materialize before they're willing to act. But it's in our daily actions and shifts in thinking that new worlds are first conceived. Every living thing goes through stages of growth. So, too, should be our expectation for growing new worlds—not something that will float down from above (*Don't look up!*), but something we are tending right under our feet.

As community organizer Kali Akuno will remind us in chapter 4, "We are trying to learn how to be democratic. We don't know how to do that. I've never lived in a democratic society. I really don't know what that looks like."

Ultimately, we change the world by changing it. Remember that the first time someone hung up a For Whites Only sign outside a storefront, that represented change. The first time someone placed an electronic monitor around a person's ankle, that represented change. The first time a bank drew up a redlining map to restrict home loans to Black homebuyers, that represented change.

That means "change" is neither inherently good nor synonymous with social progress. As we work to engender more just and equitable patterns of thought and action, let's be prepared to admit when the changes we make do not turn out as intended. In fact, we may find that we inadvertently spread more of the status quo wrapped in the rhetoric of justice.

I begin this book the same way I begin teaching my freshman course, Race is Socially Constructed: Now What? Standing in front of a buzzing lecture hall on the first day, I always caution, "We are not the 'good guys' *in here*, railing against the 'bad guys' *out there*. We are all in this fishbowl together. Taking this class (or reading this book) does not confer on you a badge, licensing you to lecture your peers or scold your relatives."

It is, after all, possible to become so intoxicated with new knowledge, so zealous with righteous indignation that we become the

Antiracism Police. Without vigilance, our attempts to incubate anti-racist forms of knowledge and action could reproduce the same logics of policing and harassment, albeit in a more enlightened guise. But this doesn't mean we'll tiptoe around or cater to the feigned fragility of those for whom even a sigh is construed as a roaring rebuke. While they get over themselves, we will press on, learning, connecting, and seeding "a world where many worlds fit."

ONE

Weather

At twenty-four years old, Erica Garner-Snipes was the "spitting image" of her father. The day her aunt called to say her father had stopped breathing, she was riding the train, on her way from Queens in New York City to Staten Island. But it wasn't clear at first what had happened. *He had asthma, so was he still alive . . . in the hospital? Or worse?* The train went through a tunnel, so she lost the connection, and passengers who witnessed Erica's confusion and tears held space for her: "They prayed for me right there and then," she said. Although distraught, she was not alone.

In the weeks and months to come, tens of thousands of people who learned about the killing of Eric Garner at the hands of New York Police Department officers would hold Erica's grief as their own. She described the protests as her "support group," and observers noted how she came alive—her voice more animated and stride more energized—when leading the crowd. Erica was the eldest of four full siblings, so the fact that she picked up a bullhorn and led chants with her father's last words, "I can't breathe!" should not come as a surprise. She was used to leading a group. In the end, though, her heartbreak would prove to be too much to bear.

Eric Garner was a hands-on dad who participated in school drop-offs and pickups and helped with homework before chasing Erica and her siblings around the house. He was also a gushing grandad who splurged on his granddaughter so she'd have a brand-new stroller and crib. He was one of those dads whose love was "thick." That's the word Toni Morrison uses to describe a love that's vast, unwavering, and swollen with affection. What happens when that thick, gushing love is suddenly taken from you, and your body cannot contain the grief?

"All I can see on that video is my Dad just trying to live for his kids, just fighting for us," Erica said. "You can hear his voice get muffled and high-pitched. It sounds like he was scared. Really scared. He wasn't fighting the police. He was fighting to breathe."

On December 30, 2017, after three years of demanding justice for her father, Erica's heart broke apart. At twenty-seven years old, it was her second heart attack; the first was just three months earlier after she had given birth to her son. This time she fell into a coma and suffered significant brain damage. One week later, at Woodhull Hospital, the same Brooklyn facility where she was born, Erica died.

In the months and years leading up to her death, Erica visited the scene of her father's killing repeatedly, leading twice-weekly protests. She supported other families whose loved ones had been killed. And she was in the process of starting an organization to support political candidates committed to police reform. This became Erica's plot. In all the ways we might imagine, she seemed to metabolize her anguish through activism. But as writer Bruce Britt observed, Erica was taking serious risks in publicly agitating against a powerful and routinely violent organization like the New York Police Department: "To have any hope of earning sympathy from her reflexively unsympathetic critics, she suppressed whatever rage she must have been feeling, opting instead to coolly advocate for due process." But what does it take for our bodies to remain cool when our spirits are burning with rage and grief?

When journalist Elizabeth Day visited Erica on the sixteenth floor of her Brooklyn high-rise, she asked Erica about her experience with racism before Officer Daniel Pantaleo choked her father to death. Erica described customers verbally harassing her, and others insisting on being served by white staff. She remembered being called a "slave" by a teenage boy—all while she worked at a

Dunkin Donuts in a predominantly non-Black area of Queens. But Erica did not sound angry: "Her voice is resigned, her shoulders slumped. At 24, her face is young but her eyes are tired and seem to belong to a much older woman. A crooked half-smile plays around her lips as she speaks. The smile sits a little oddly with the gravity of what she is saying, but then it strikes me that this is an expression of someone who copes with injustice on a daily basis." Shoulders slumped, perhaps, because of all she was carrying; a crooked smile that could not mask her sorrow. Even Erica's daughter saw through her strength, asking, "What's the matter Mommy, are you thinking about Pop-pop?" Pop-pop is what Erica called her dad.

Erica Garner-Snipes, no doubt, was weathered. Not only by the senseless loss of her father, but by a lifetime of economic precarity and everyday racism.

Arline Geronimus coined "weathering" as a public health concept in 1992 to underscore how we embody stressors and oppressors in the broader environment and how this process causes preventable illness and premature death. While the scientific establishment prefers to focus on genetic rather than sociopolitical explanations for racial health disparities, proponents of weathering and other kindred concepts are fighting to get us to consider the structural determinants of health—the institutions and processes that cause health disparities. Instead of taking the weather for granted, we must engage in our own fight against (anti-Black) climate denial. If weathering wears our bodies down, like the weather wears away even the oldest of cliff faces, how can we protect ourselves from it?

In this chapter, I focus on weathering as both a public health idea and a framework for understanding and challenging how everyone's lives and futures are affected by anti-Black racism. Here I draw from both Geronimus's public health approach and scholar Christina Sharpe's emphasis on the weather as "the totality of our environments." Sharpe makes an important point about the racism that is part of that total environment: "The weather is the total climate;

and that climate is antiblack." Taken together, weathering is one way of explaining the often devastating, yet preventable, health outcomes of Black folks because of living day in and day out in a hostile environment.

In the United Kingdom, they just call it what it is. Former prime minister Theresa May's "hostile environment policy" was rolled out in 2012 as a set of legal requirements and administrative practices designed to make living in Britain for a subset of immigrants as burdensome as possible so that they "voluntarily leave."

It led to the 2018 Windrush scandal, in which British subjects, mainly those of Caribbean descent, were made to jump through ridiculous bureaucratic hoops, were wrongly detained, lost their jobs, were deported, and were refused reentry despite being citizens of and longtime residents of the United Kingdom. But even in places without an explicit policy, hostile environments are made and remade daily through the machinations of institutions and individuals alike.

In tracing the relationship between weathering and the storm of police violence exposed in 2020, this chapter calls bullshit on the language of "preexisting conditions," which is often used to describe Black vulnerability to illness and violence. Whether we find it at political press conferences or in autopsy reports, the accusation that Black people have prior poor health places responsibility on those harmed by a sick social order rather than on harmful social conditions themselves.

Weathering includes the sudden storms that flood our lives *and* the slow droughts that create famine—a reminder that the weather comes in many forms. Acute crises like eviction, job loss, and death in the family are like hurricanes that swoop in, engulfing us with pain and heartache. But when it comes to chronic stress—watching rents creep higher and higher, job hunting with nary a callback, worrying the police will harass your child—it's like dry, hot winds scraping slowly across your face. Sure, violent storms bring us periodically to our knees, but the arid austerity of everyday life can be fatal. What is there to do when the forecast is always precarious and even the air seems out to get us? Ration our energy, breathe shallower, *wear a mask.*

This chapter also weaves together the multiple vulnerabilities that correspond to the converging pandemics of COVID-19 and racist policing to consider how social stressors and oppressors get under our skin and into our bloodstream, burdening our organs, overloading our systems, and wearing us down over time.

We will consider how people seek to protect themselves and each other from weathering using individual practices and collective care. We will also bear witness to the weight of individual and communal protective acts and consider how all of us can be involved in sheltering one another from the rain and sun by cultivating relationships, trust, skills, accountability, and healing—starting in our own front yards. All around us there are also rainmakers showering support, planting solidarity, and creating refuge so that, ultimately, we can transform the weather.

Social epidemiologist Nancy Krieger argues that "bodies tell stories that people cannot or will not tell": bodies can confirm stories on which other people cast doubt, and bodies tell stories that people can't bear to reveal. And embodied stories, at times, can run against our collective "common sense." Socioeconomic class, for instance, is not always protective. Highly educated Black women, for example, have higher rates of preterm birth than white women with high school diplomas. Living in a rich country is not automatically good for your health. Black teen boys living in Harlem are less likely to reach age sixty-five than their counterparts in Bangladesh. In a similar vein, immigration to the U.S. does not automatically promise a "better life." Research shows many Latinx immigrants see a progressive decline in health with each subsequent generation.

Focusing only on race can sometimes hide other essential determinants of health. *Intraracial* disparities based on skin tone (i.e., colorism) are even more pronounced than many differences across racial groups. Likewise, the "model minority myth" would lead many to expect that Asian Americans have better overall health than even whites. But when researchers disaggregate the data, they find deadly disparities between Filipino, Vietnamese, Chinese, Japanese, and Korean adults. And perhaps most surprising of all, whiteness is toxic even to its supposed beneficiaries—a matter we will return to in the pages ahead. Yet, complexity notwithstanding, we are sold simplified stories about social mobility, assimilation, racial progress, and white privilege that flatten social reality.

A few years ago, I was at the Moscone Center in San Francisco to speak at a national conference for K–12 educators. Since it was my first time at this convention, I wanted to sit in on a few sessions to soak in the conversation before it was my turn to take the stage the next day. I chose a talk in the same hall that I would be presenting in, listening in on a workshop about how teachers could better relate to their students by understanding more about generational cohorts: X, Y, Z, Millennials.

I admit that I've always been skeptical about the idea of coherent identities built around age. Born in 1978, I am technically a Gen Xer (1965–80). Generation X is described as a demographic of latchkey kids with high debt, also known as the "MTV generation." Deemed cynical and alienated slackers in our younger years, we are turning out to be happy, active adults who are heavily into Facebook, according to researchers. But more recently, those of us born at the tail of the '70s and early '80s have been dubbed a "micro generation" by the powers that be, a bridge between disaffected Gen Xers and overly optimistic Millennials, known best for our savvy uptake of technology.

Sitting at the back of that cold, airy hall, I grew irritated as I soaked up the marketing fluff presented to educators as a basis for improving pedagogy. *OK, Boomer*, I thought to myself. Naturally, I pulled out my phone to look up the speaker and, as I had guessed, she was from a firm whose entire business was to advise marketers on how to best sell products to young people. Never mind the ways in which racism, classism, sexism, or ableism carve up young people's lives into nothing that resembles the glossy pie chart on the slides. Bubbly and with broad strokes, she was selling a story about age as a primary identity and basis of shared personality that papers over the many fault lines that shape students' experiences in and out of the classroom. As a *Washington Post* headline put it, "Your Generational Identity Is a Lie." Speaking on generational labels, sociologist Philip N. Cohen states, "Worse than irrelevant, such baseless categories drive people toward stereotyping and rash character judgment." In 2021 he and 150 demographers and social scientists wrote to the Pew Research Center urging it to ditch the labels in its surveys. This was not only because of the sweeping assumptions about a shared experience that those generational identities presume but, more pressingly, because racism, in tandem with other axes of power and difference, creates divergent climates—sheltering some while weathering others.

Two people can share a chronological age but have different biological ages due to chronic stress and persistent environmental threats. According to developmental psychologist Virginia Huynh, "Years of being followed around in a grocery store or liquor market—subtle everyday slight insults—convey to people of color and marginalized communities that they don't belong, don't fit in." And "it's often cumulative, a lifetime of experiences" that affect multiple systems in the body.

Huynh's lab at California State University, Northridge, has measured this phenomenon by collecting saliva from three hundred teenagers to assess their cortisol levels. The researchers found that those who reported experiencing discrimination had higher cortisol levels, which didn't decrease over the course of the day. In another study, the lab found that even when teenagers merely witness or overhear a racist comment, they experience spikes in cortisol, "indicating that vicarious discrimination can create a physiological response."

When it comes to measuring biological age, some researchers have been focusing on telomere length. Telomeres are DNA sequences on the ends of our chromosomes that keep them from fraying. They are like the plastic caps at the ends of shoelaces. As we age, those protective caps become shorter, and this shortening is linked to chronic conditions like diabetes, heart disease, and strokes. In an Auburn University study on coronary artery risk development in young adults, researchers examined telomere data from nearly four hundred African Americans who were forty years old on average when the study began in 2000. Ten years later, researchers collected follow-up data, and people who reported experiences of discrimination showed a faster rate of telomere shortening, otherwise known as cellular aging.

Likewise, Geronimus and colleagues analyzed data from the Study of Women's Health across the Nation. They estimated that for women between forty-nine and fifty-five years old, Black women have a cellular age that is biologically seven and a half years "older" than white women's. Thus, the popular adage "Black don't crack" may hide the reality of weathering beneath the smooth, shea-butter-glistening surface of Black women's skin.

The nerd in me can geek out on this research all day. My inner public health advocate appreciates its utility in demonstrating the tangible harm caused by everyday racism. But the grumpy and impatient scalawag in me feels vexed that we must keep making a case for tangible harm.

Who exactly needs convincing that racism and other stressors are deadly? Whose skepticism requires that we pour more time and resources into pinpointing exactly how it erodes *our fuckin' telomeres*? Don't get me started on the headlines: "New Study Shows Racism May Shorten Black Americans' Lifespans," "Perceived Racism in Relation to Telomere Length among African American Women," "Racism Might Hurt Your Cells." I read the headlines, and then I hear the voice of writer Toni Cade Bambara asking, "What are we pretending not to know today?"

Too often, the point of studying health disparities seems to be to conduct another study that begets more funding to carry out another study, rather than to do what we can in the here and now to eliminate the sources of harm. Take the 2017 study by a team of social science and life science researchers that concluded that "father loss harms DNA."

The team conceded that when children lose a father due to death, incarceration, divorce, or separation, it affects their health and behaviors. But *the underlying biological processes are not well understood*. And the researchers wanted to drill down and understand the precise mechanisms by which trauma gets under the skin. So they examined data produced by the Fragile Families and Child Wellbeing Study—a sample of 2,420 young people across twenty large U.S. cities who were enrolled at birth and followed throughout their lives. They set out to measure stress-induced cellular aging using telomere length and found that, indeed, adverse life events get under our skin. The team concluded, "This underscores the important role of fathers in the care and development of children." Surely we know this. The study also "supplements evidence of the strong negative effects of parental incarceration." Again, no dispute here.

But how does understanding the biological impact of father loss upend the punitive policies that create father loss in the first place? Will knowledge of their shorter telomeres engender greater public empathy for the 2.7 million children in the U.S. who have a parent serving time and the over 5 million who, at some point in their lives, have had an incarcerated parent? Or might it just solidify the popular view of "urban and disadvantaged" children as damaged, socially, culturally, and *now* biologically? We should ask ourselves whether research is serving as a stall tactic so we never collectively act on what we already know when it comes to engendering health and well-being.

I refer to this as the *datafication of injustice*—the hunt for more and more data about things we already know much about. Next thing you know, researchers will be measuring the telomeres from a blood sample of Erica Garner-Snipes.

Although technically she was a Millennial, with all that *that's* supposed to mean, Erica's body told a different story. Who exactly needs to know Erica's cellular age to verify that racism maybe, *just maybe*, shortened her life? The research community needs to reckon with how our work contributes to *structural gaslighting*—misattributing the causes of premature death to biological factors—whether we intend to conceal them or not. And rather than simply studying "race" as a safe and convenient variable in our regression analyses, we need to call out and organize against *racism* and interlocking systems of oppression. No more euphemisms, no more feigned uncertainty, no more publications pretending we don't know why people are perishing.

I'll say it again: *the facts alone will not save us.*

What's even worse is that those in positions of authority too often use the language of science to distort the truth or flat-out lie about what has happened to people's bodies. New York Police Department chief surgeon Eli J. Kleinman concluded that Eric Garner's preexisting poor health, not the chokehold, contributed to his death.

While bullets tend to have a clear point of origin, asthma, hypertension, and other chronic illnesses have a more diffuse set of causes in the physical and social structures that we take as fixed. Garner's suffocation may have been exacerbated by his asthma, but his asthma itself was a result of environmental racism. Urban planners locate highways, trash transfer stations, and other toxic structures near Black and Latinx communities. It was *already* hard to breathe. This longer chain of connections is harder to narrate and so rarely captures the public imagination, much less a viral hashtag, except when the two converge. In Garner's death, we see how direct and indirect forms of racial violence are, and have always been, connected.

Fortunately, there is growing attention to these life-and-death connections. Led by the new Office of Resilience created in June 2020, my current home state of New Jersey has created an action plan focused on "adverse childhood experiences" (ACEs), or traumatic events that negatively affect the brain, causing lifelong, "even generational[,] emotional, physical and economic challenges." The goal of this initiative is for New Jersey to become a "trauma informed/ healing centered state." Currently about 40 percent of children in the Garden State—more than 782,000—have experienced at least one ACE, and about 18 percent have experienced multiple traumas. The action plan notes that ACEs are concentrated among children of color and those living in poverty, and part of the justification for the program is that the economic burden in healthcare and social services across the nation is in the billions.

To its credit, the initiative attempts to counter the idea that ACEs cause irreparable damage, by reminding us that they do not determine the destiny of a child, nor are they inevitable: "ACEs can be prevented, and when they do occur, concrete steps can be taken to help children, families, and communities heal from their effects. Intervening early, supporting resilience in individuals, and building resilient communities are key to mitigating the impacts of childhood trauma." The Office of Resilience aims to build statewide capacity across state and nongovernmental agencies, and communities to address the root causes of ACEs.

When I saw that the action plan mentioned "racialized violence, institutionalized racism, and white supremacy" as sites of intervention, I thought, *Word. OK, maybe this isn't another exercise in pathologizing the victims of unjust systems.* It's still too early to tell where those implementing this plan will focus. And I also wonder whether a state initiative focused on resilience can ever fully reckon with the state's central role—via police, prosecutors, and agents of the "family regulation system"—in creating the hostile weather that requires so much resilience in the first place. I don't think so, unless the most affected communities are the ones really driving the interventions. Otherwise, viral justice ends up being more like viral *tweaks* to the status quo, viral *veneer* to business as usual, and viral *rhetoric* that begins and ends with words.

While the world became accustomed to wearing physical masks during the COVID-19 pandemic, for Black folks, wearing a mask is nothing new. Long before the pandemic, Black people had to shield themselves from a hostile world as a survival strategy. Legal scholar Cheryl I. Harris begins her classic 1993 essay "Whiteness as Property" with a story from the 1930s about her white-passing grandma moving back and forth across the color line to work in a whites-only department store:

"Every day my grandmother rose from her bed in her house in a Black enclave on the south side of Chicago, sent her children off to a Black school, boarded a bus full of Black passengers, and rode to work . . . Each evening, my grandmother, tired and worn, retraced her steps home, laid aside her mask, and reentered herself. Day in and day out, she made herself invisible, then visible again . . . She left the job some years later, finding the strain too much to bear."

Harris recalls conversations with her grandmother in which, on rare occasions, she admitted overhearing some racist comment her coworkers had made because they assumed she was white. She swallowed any response that might've been warranted, since silence was the price of opportunity. "Accepting the risk of self-annihilation was the only way to survive," as Harris puts it.

Today the color line may not be as rigid, but masking and suppression are still too often required for survival. Sixty years after Harris's grandmother risked self-annihilation, sociologist Joe Feagin found a similar pattern of racism-related vigilance in interviews with Black respondents. One older woman described having to put on her "shield" every morning: "She said that for more than six decades, as she leaves her home, she has tried to be prepared for insults and discrimination in public places, even if nothing happens that day." Although Whites Only signs don't hang in store windows at the local mall, white spaces are a social reality produced repeatedly through subtle forms of exclusion and derision.

This is why, I think, Grandma White was vigilant when it came to self-presentation. When I was going through my grunge phase as a teenager in Los Angeles—ripped jeans, oversize T-shirts, and black combat boots from the army and navy surplus supply store—our sensibilities clashed. *What was the big deal?* I thought. *Everyone does it! Why were my clothes so offensive?*

"But *you* are not 'everyone,'" she replied. Especially when it came time for me to board a bus, train, or plane, the stakes were raised. My grandma would take me to Fox Hills Mall—now known as Westfield Culver City—on a mission to purchase new outfits. And without her saying so, I knew what I was looking for: more "respectable" garb. Later that evening, she would wait in the sitting room adjacent to her bedroom where she had a special closet just for her wigs, and I'd put on a fashion show, parading in and out to a soundtrack of *oohs* and *aahs*.

Only when I became a mother did it hit me that self-presentation was my grandma's tactic for self-preservation. A few years ago, I was folding laundry and came across my eldest son's holey jeans. I'll admit, I've hidden my children's tattered clothes in the far reaches of a closet so they couldn't find them easily. This time, however, I froze, seeing the jeans through Grandma White's eyes.

Clothes are a kind of armor, however feeble, against the snap judgments of people looking for any reason to ignore, dismiss, or harm my child. I can hardly imagine how much more clothes would've meant for my grandmother's generation. I pictured her riding the bus from Little Rock, Arkansas, to Atlanta University in the 1940s, a time when looking like a student might offer some small protection against the everyday slights and savagery of Jim Crow racism.

A starched collar, a creased skirt or trouser, white gloves—all signs that this person *belongs to someone*. A mother, an aunty, or a grandma woke up early to press that outfit. These visual indicators of care served as warnings that if she went missing, an entire community would come looking for her. My hole-ridden jeans spat in the face of that loving and terrified attempt at self-preservation.

As historian Tanisha Ford explains in her work on the politics of Black women's dress, "Possessing, embodying, and performing the brand of womanhood that institutions like Spelman and other black colleges across the South espoused became a way for black women to publicly articulate their moral aptitude in order to lift African Americans and women out of the depths of racist and sexist stereotypes." Ford points to an old photograph of four women on the steps of Atlanta University, noting how their clothes and accessory choices "lent a sense of refinement and sartorial elegance." Clothing was one more tool to protect oneself from the plague of white supremacy.

Truth be told, having my teenage sons close to me during the pandemic was a relief; there were fewer chances, it seemed, of them being harmed by those dreadful creatures feigning fear while wielding badges and bitterness. Shelter-in-place policies have their perks when a constant menace to Black folks is still on the hunt.

Anthropologist Dána-Ain Davis explains, "To be sure Black mothering can be sorrowful when we lose our children but also just the threat of losing our children can precipitate an almost constant state of sorrow. We have been losing our children for centuries: through the slave trade, the plantation system, and as a result of infant mortality. We have lost our children as a consequence of the 'war' on drugs, stop and frisk policies, and to the prison industrial complex."

And so, every day, when my sons go out for a run or to get some air, I ask them to *please* be careful. They respond with polite exasperation. And sometimes I'll catch their eye, willing them to stay safe. But I know, and they know, it's not really up to them.

Just ask Ahmaud Arbery's mother. After her twenty-five-year-old son was chased down and murdered while out jogging, she was forced to listen to the defense attorney depict Ahmaud as the *real* menace. After all, explained the defense attorney, Ahmaud had on "khaki shorts with no socks to cover his long, dirty toenails."

These are the lengths to which defenders of white violence will go to fabricate a deviant image of the slain. Imagine that attorney clawing her way through the coroner's report, casting aside all signs of victimhood, scanning head to toe, from Ahmaud's fresh haircut to his calloused runner's soles, from his bullet-grazed wrist to his shattered ribs, hunting for any whiff of deviance until finally . . . "long, dirty toenails."

For civil rights attorney and legal analyst Charles Coleman Jr., the toenail comment was the defense's attempt to portray Ahmaud as a "runaway slave," a way to "trigger some of the racial tropes and stereotypes that may be deeply embedded in the psyche of some of the jurors." Out of the nine jurors asked to determine the fate of the three white men who chased and killed Ahmaud, only one was Black in a county where Black residents form 27 percent of the population.

For some Black parents, talk of dirty toenails at a murder trial is also why our plea to *please be safe* is often accompanied by anxiety over grooming. We know that even when our grownish kids go out for a casual jog, they might end up on the run. And that their bodies, their sun-kissed, perspiring, pulsing bodies, could be conscripted to testify against them. That if they are found in the wrong place at the wrong time, every single hair on their head will be scrutinized as defenders of white violence hunt for signs of deviance. Hence, many of us end up scrutinizing them first—lovingly, fearfully, *preventively*.

This is perhaps the most sickening part of white supremacy, that to survive, we must inhabit it, know its logics, adopt its vision, if only to evade it.

Such, too, is the inexplicable cruelty of this world. In the very act of doing something that is "good for your health," Black lives are still at risk. And not only because a violent vigilante could be on the hunt, but also because of the chronic stress of remaining vigilant. Protecting oneself from the weather can take its toll. Adrenaline and cortisol released. Blood pressure raised. Immune system suppressed.

The absurdity of healthful activity precipitating decay is enough to make even the most stubbornly hopeful among us grow weary. When it comes to racism-related vigilance, our caution may feel protective in the short term, but chronic stress slowly destroys us in the long term. When our body gets ready for "fight or flight," it becomes flooded with hormones, which is great in short bursts. But when we're *always* on edge, it can lead to hypertension and an enlarged heart, and can overstimulate our immune system to begin attacking normal cells and tissues—causing "cytokine storms," which have been linked to some of the most severe cases of COVID-19.

In his essay "The White Space," sociologist Elijah Anderson notes that white people perceive many neighborhoods, workplaces, schools, and other public places as "diverse," whereas Black people view those same places as homogeneously white. To gain provisional acceptance in such spaces, Black people have to "pass inspection" in their speech and dress. Using interviews with five hundred college-educated Black men, sociologist Rashawn Ray documented the lengths respondents go to just to exercise: running in well-lit, densely populated areas, wearing college alumni T-shirts, waving and smiling at neighbors, carrying an ID on them. Just like Grandma White—just like every Black person trying to survive the assault of everyday racism—those men are signaling, *I am not a threat*.

Anderson, who is Black, tells a story of vacationing with his family in Cape Cod, Massachusetts. The setting is idyllic: two weeks

in a beautiful cottage about a mile from town. One morning at about
six o'clock, he's going for a run, enjoying the clear blue skies, and
taking in the sounds of nature when a middle-aged white man in
a red pickup truck stops in the middle of the road. The white man
begins gesticulating and yelling for the professor to "Go home! Go
home!" Two simple words, uttered with disdain, turning a healthy
activity into one more leg of a dangerous race Black folks have been
running for centuries.

But if such a simple exchange can suddenly transform the weather
from calming and regenerative to blustery and corrosive, doesn't this
mean a simple exchange could transmute the weather in the other
direction if we choose?

Before my family officially moved to Princeton, Principal Jason
Burr walked us around the boys' soon-to-be public middle school.
I was initially caught by surprise when students chatting at their
lockers in between classes—most of them white and Asian—greeted
us warmly as we passed, pausing their conversations to ask Malachi
and Khalil, "Hey! Where are you from?" and "When are you starting?" Before we had even unpacked our bags, these small gestures
seemed to call, *Welcome home!* . . . cliquey and angsty stereotypes
of tweens be damned.

Perhaps even more telling, in my eyes, was that Principal Burr
himself greeted the janitorial staff mopping up a spill in the cafeteria
with the same respect he did the teachers and students we passed in
the halls. And over the years, those initial observations bore out—
here was a school leader who did not ration respect, one who was
deeply committed to making *everyone* feel welcome, and he did this
less with grand gestures and more in the genuine regard he showed
to each person he encountered. I'm not sure whether the students
"caught it" from Principal Burr, or they inspired him, but the con-
viviality was contagious.

While the weather envelops all of us, as Christina Sharpe underscores, it is decisively anti-Black. We can see this in the literal masks

we wore during the pandemic, which came with an added catch for Black people. "I don't feel safe wearing a handkerchief or something else that isn't CLEARLY a protective mask covering my face to the store because I am a Black man living in this world. I want to stay alive but I also want to stay alive," tweeted Ohio resident Aaron Thomas. The goal of staying alive but also *stayin' alive* represents the longing to survive a biological threat and the multiple social threats that make it hard to rest. But how else, I wonder, could Black people use all that energy currently expended on self-preservation?

A week before Thomas's tweet, two Black men wearing hospital masks recorded themselves being followed around and kicked out of Walmart by an officer. The fact that you could endanger yourself by acting in solidarity with everyone else is surely a symptom of an ailing society. Around the same time, a Black man was dragged off a Philadelphia bus by a group of officers for allegedly not wearing a mask. The mask, it appears, was never the issue. Covered or exposed, it was always Blackness. With pandemics and police threatening us, how do we stay alive and *stay alive*?

Meanwhile, in what may seem like a parallel universe produced by white supremacy, throngs of mostly maskless white protesters staged Reopen America rallies across the country. No, COVID-19 hadn't been eradicated, but these white people exhibited an entitlement and indifference that makes us all sick, themselves included.

That's the thing about hostile weather. It can't be neatly contained. As psychiatrist and historian Jonathan Metzl describes in *Dying of Whiteness: How the Politics of Racial Resentment Is Killing America's Heartland,* many lower- and middle-class white Americans are suffering from their support of policies that cut funding for healthcare, schools, and social services. To the extent that public funding is thought to benefit racialized groups, these white folks want none of it, even if it could save their lives, too.

Racial capitalism serves up a potent cocktail of corrosive individualism, persistent anti-Blackness, and relentless grind that means many white people, too, stagger early to their graves. The violent history of settler colonialism in the U.S. required a romantic figure, the Rugged Individual, to help distract from the atrocities of scalping, stolen children, concentration camps, broken treaties, and mass genocide. To manifest his destiny, the Rugged Individual had to declare his (alleged) independence over and over.

"All I'm for is the liberty of the individual . . . I'd like to know why the well-educated idiots keep apologizing for *lazing and complaining* people who think the world owes them a living," so lamented Hollywood film star John Wayne, an exemplar of this distorted outlook.

Now take this settler mythology and stir it up with the specter of slavery—the master who benevolently feeds, shelters, and trains his property to work. Their "childlike" dependence on him is a sign, nay *proof*, of their inferiority. The Rugged Individual finds his foil in the Helpless Horde. In our cultural imagination, Blackness is derided as the epitome of slothful dependence. For the Rugged Individual, any whiff of dependence on the state is reviled because of its association with Blackness.

"Ain't no way I would ever support Obamacare or sign up for it. I would rather die," a white former cab driver, Trevor, told Metzl during an interview. When asked the reason for his policy position, Trevor, who was suffering from an inflamed liver and having difficulty breathing—he came to the interview with an oxygen mask—responded with, "We don't need any more government in our lives. And in any case, no way I want my tax dollars paying for Mexicans and welfare queens." One starts to grasp the deep-seated contempt in America for a *Black* president who created "handouts" for *Blacks*. It appears hardworking white people can only know themselves by creating a foil: lazy, good-for-nothing n*ggers.

Never mind that this nation nursed itself on the scarred breasts of Black women and was made rich by the toiling of enslaved men, women, and children drenched in salty sweat. Never mind that the United States continues to be nourished by weathered farmhands, almost half of whom are undocumented immigrants deemed "essential." *Who* is dependent on *whom*, exactly?

It's not paradoxical so much as hypocritical and pathological. This is how the funhouse mirror of white supremacy has always worked—depicting as "needy" those whom our society needs most. But there's more. Ours is a nation that was erected on the powerful idea that *all men are created equal, that they are endowed by their Creator with certain unalienable Rights,* even as the founders held people in bondage. Rather than face up to that original sin, those drunken with patriotism today project what should be their own shame onto others.

Blackness, in brief, is a mirror reflecting America's hypocrisy, threatening the idealized story patriots want to believe about this country. Therein lies the exceptional treatment of Black people as not simply a racial "other" but an existential threat. The only way to deal with a threat is to subdue it, swiftly, with a knee to the neck . . . or slowly in the weathering wear and tear of everyday life.

The irony is that Trevor would eventually die, not only from liver damage but also from lethal policies that would deny him the care he needed. Tragically for him, the dogma of rugged individualism is mixed with contempt for interdependence in the form of a stronger social safety net, which is ultimately something that we'd all benefit from.

As it turns out, even if you earn the "wages of whiteness," your body may still be paying a price. A team of economists, Anne Case and Angus Deaton, call it the *quiet epidemic*—between 1999 and 2013, the mortality and morbidity among non-Hispanic white Americans across education levels increased due to drug and alcohol poisonings, suicide, chronic pain, and disease. The economists attributed this epidemic of death to growing despair caused by declining wages, job insecurity, and a weak social safety net over the long haul—a process they admit mirrors the plight of Black communities in the 1970s and '80s. Whiteness, we have been told, necessitates deference and comes with special privileges. But the stories told by the bodies of white people remind us that a frayed social contract eventually makes everyone sick.

White people's vulnerability to the weather and their role in creating this climate are two reasons why the language of "allyship" doesn't make any sense, as it implies dominant groups are doing something for oppressed ones but don't need saving themselves. We are not all affected by the weather in the same way, but it encircles and impacts all our lives. And given that, the weather is anti-Black, white people's lives depend on the dismantling of anti-Blackness, as it rips apart the social fabric that they themselves are barely hanging on to by a thread.

In *White Rage: The Unspoken Truth of Our Racial Divide*, historian Carol Anderson excavates the subtle dimensions of anti-Black racism, the bureaucratization of rage, we might call it, as it infects our courts, legislatures, and the policies governing everyday life. From housing and education to voting and healthcare, whenever and wherever Black people have demanded full citizenship and access to social goods, white Americans have responded with a backlash. The trigger? Black ambition, Black resilience, and Black resolve in the face of an unceasingly hostile climate.

If the only way to justify white dominance has been to concoct a mythology of Black inferiority, then witnessing Black intelligence, ingenuity, and perseverance elicits an ongoing cultural crisis, if not pathology, for those who invented and, therefore, at some level *need* the n*gger, in James Baldwin's words. Black prosperity, in short, shines a scorching light on the lie of white supremacy.

While the idiom of white "rage" evokes the fiery heat of a cross, exemplified by the Tulsa Massacre of 1921, when white people burned a thriving Black community to the ground, the vengeful assault on Black life is often expressed in the ice-cold language of law: redlining, gerrymandering, and stop-and-frisk.

Even the federal government's Paycheck Protection Program, a cornerstone of the stimulus bill meant to offer some relief during the COVID-19 pandemic, contained provisions that disadvantaged Black businesses. By putting commercial banks in charge of administering the loans, the program gave large, majority-white businesses that had prior relationships with these lending institutions the upper hand. No Whites Only signs required, just the fine print of policy.

Cuts to public education, healthcare, and social services are today's backlash politics and form part of a long tradition of refusal. Going back to 1866, when newly free Blacks set up hundreds of schools across the South out of an abiding belief that education could counter oppression, many poor whites refused to join the so-called n*gger programs. If there were any chance that a public good would benefit Black Americans, it seems that many whites would rather feast on imagined superiority as their stomachs growl empty. This is not simply backlash politics, but boomerang politics that comes back around to harm them too.

Take the support for pro-gun laws, another potent symbol of freedom, patriotism, and white rage. The increasing rate of white suicide, as Case and Deaton document, is linked to the easier accessibility of guns. Gun advertisers use language like "restore your manly privilege" as a direct appeal to the Rugged Individual whose fragile manliness must be constantly buttressed; guns become phallic prosthetics.

When it comes to gun ownership, it's not just masculinity that is at stake, but race and class too. In colonial America, one of the first things that the elite planter class did to divide poor, white indentured servants from enslaved Negroes was to give poor whites guns so that they could patrol runaways and put down uprisings. The ruling class, comprising the first settlers who established plantations, monopolized most of the fertile land. This monopoly earned them great fortunes, and they had no plans to share that wealth. Instead, formerly indentured white servants were paid a "psychological wage" by being armed to patrol Blackness.

The ongoing legacy of racialized policing continues to wear Black people down, one harassing encounter after another. That is no surprise. But the racial paranoia that policing fosters *and* feeds on erodes the social climate for everyone. Anti-Blackness leads to divestment from social goods like education, employment, and healthcare that would foster safety and well-being *for all*.

What's more, the same racial paranoia that drives policing also drives pro-gun laws. In April 2020, hundreds of protesters, including armed white militia, paraded around the Michigan State Capitol with semiautomatic weapons, chanting "Our House!" "Let us in!" and "Let us work!" They were protesting the governor's extension of a stay-at-home order due to COVID-19. On one level this looked like just another display of "white privilege"—white men, even when armed to the teeth in a government building, did not elicit an aggressive police response. But is it *only* privilege at work when, in the context of over twenty-three thousand gun suicides each year, the rate among white men in the U.S. far outpaces those of other groups? From cuts to the social safety net to lenient gun laws, whiteness shows reckless disregard for even white people's safety.

Admittedly, I bring my own baggage to any discussion of gun violence. In 2016, in Hesston, Kansas, my sister-in-law was killed in her workplace. Renee "Randy" Benjamin was thirty years old and had only been working at Excel Industries in Hesston for about six months. Hesston, located approximately thirty miles north of Wichita, has a population of fewer than four thousand, and the Excel plant is one of the two largest companies in the area. Excel is renowned for manufacturing world-class outdoor power equipment like utility vehicles and riding lawn mowers, and Randy was so excited about landing her new job. She'd get home after a long shift and talk all about who worked on the line with her.

Then, on February 25, 2016, an employee opened fire on the Excel Industries plant with a semiautomatic rifle, killing Randy and two other coworkers and wounding fourteen others. We would later learn that the shooter was high on meth and alcohol and angry about being served a restraining order by an ex-girlfriend.

When my husband, Shawn, called to tell me that Randy was killed, it was the morning of my talk at the Moscone Convention Center in San Francisco—the same conference where I had been annoyed the day before about how generational identities were being sold to educators. I was still in my hotel room, racing back and forth between the bathroom and bed. I turned the phone speaker on so I could talk and get ready, when Shawn's voice broke in anguish.

Millions of Americans from all racial backgrounds are traumatized by gun violence. Yet Kansas is one of many states that allow the open and concealed carrying of handguns. It also requires no background checks for private gun sales or obtaining permits. Even among white families who have lost loved ones to gun violence (usually by suicide), the vast majority continue to oppose gun control legislation because they need to protect themselves from "invaders."

They have a *possessive investment in whiteness*, to borrow an idea from sociologist George Lipsitz, because in their minds the invaders who most threaten their investment are usually dark and menacing. Speaking to the hostile assertiveness of those seeking to maintain their status, the phrase "possessive investment in whiteness" provides a more apt description of the dynamics going on here than, say, "white fragility" (i.e., white defensiveness). Sure, white bodies and psyches may be fragile, but white politics are aggressive and deadly.

Anthropologist Brandon Hunter-Pazzara reminds us that, in 2016, George Zimmerman auctioned the gun he used in 2012 to kill seventeen-year-old Trayvon Martin. If that wasn't depraved enough, the woman who purchased the weapon for $250,000 intended it as a present to her son.

Let's sit with this for a minute. What kind of "profound neurosis," to borrow Toni Morrison's portrayal of racism, could motivate this perverse expression of motherly love—venerating the very thing used to steal the life of someone else's child? "My feeling is that White people have a very, very serious problem," Morrison said in a PBS interview in 1993. "And they should start thinking about what they can do about it." For their *own* sakes, I would add.

The gun is a racial icon, yes, one that melds together police violence and the everyday terror of white vigilantes. Going back to the colonial era, white men have deputized themselves as keepers of the racial order, protecting the law-abiding public from *those in the streets*. But each year, almost double the number of Americans die by gun suicide that do by gun homicide, and *white males* account for seven out of ten suicides. The racial paranoia of impending invasion makes sense for a people living on stolen land. But the threat was never the man in the street or across the border. It was always the man in the mirror.

The stories of white supremacy and white bodies riddled with bullets or shot up with opioids are part of the same frayed social fabric. White gun suicide is only one way our corrupt system wreaks havoc on those who are supposedly the beneficiaries of whiteness. What if we all, ultimately, would benefit by transforming the racist climate that, yes, rains down much harder on some but wreaks havoc on all of us in different ways?

Once and for all, we must abandon the zero-sum calculus of white supremacy. It's bad math and an even worse moral vision. True justice, as the Jamaican philosopher Sylvia Wynter waxes lyrical, is not grim retribution but shared happiness. That is not to say the way forward is all flowers and sunshine. On the contrary, it's quite the opposite. It requires treasonous activity on the part of those for whom the existing racial arithmetic was designed.

Historian Noel Ignatiev is famous for insisting that "treason to whiteness is loyalty to humanity," because, for him, white identity is synonymous with social domination. In 1997 a *New York Times* reporter asked Ignatiev, "You're white. Do you hate your own hide?" He responded, "No, but I want to abolish the privileges of the white skin. The white race is like a private club based on one huge assumption: that all those who look white are, whatever their complaints or reservations, fundamentally loyal to the race. We want to dissolve the club, to explode it."

What does that look like in practice? For Ignatiev, it involved defying race-based expectations and standing up for justice. And it entailed long-term commitment in the everyday ways that white Americans can choose to break the code. There are examples of white people doing this—like abolitionist John Brown, who, in 1859, led a raid on a federal armory at Harpers Ferry, Virginia. Or like Anthony Huber and Joseph Rosenbaum, who, in 2020, were killed defending fellow Black Lives Matter protesters from gunman Kyle Rittenhouse in Kenosha, Wisconsin. But the first rule for abolishing the White Club is to admit that there is a White Club—one that is devastating to those excluded *and* that poisons those who enjoy privileged membership. In a heated public conversation with writer Chinua Achebe, James Baldwin had this to say:

> We are in trouble. But there are two ways to be in trouble. One of them is to know you're in trouble. If you know you're in trouble you may be able to figure out the road.

This country is in trouble. Everybody is in trouble—not only the people who apparently know they are in trouble, not only the people who know they are not white. The white people in this country . . . *think* they are white: because "white is a state of mind." I'm quoting my friend Malcolm X . . . white is a moral choice.

A choice between white and *what*, Baldwin does not say exactly, perhaps because it's an open question, one that fostering viral justice can begin to answer.

Beyond the most obvious bad actors, we also must reckon with the reality that many of the policies and structures that govern our lives work directly against the social good, pushing a corrosive individualism cloaked in the language of "freedom." After all, the people typically in charge of creating antisocial policies can afford private healthcare, private education, private property—even private environments (from locating hazardous waste near low-income areas to blocking access to hundreds of beaches "for residents only"). The very people who don't believe in a commons are the ones designing an antisocial system for the rest of us to inhabit.

We're living inside a deadly game, one that was set up to ensure there would be winners and losers. Within such a world, racism will always be necessary to justify why some people seem to be winning, some losing, and others losing *their lives*. But in this context, we shouldn't simply strive for "more winners." We need to stop playing the game. We need to build entirely new worlds and ways of being with one another that don't involve resting on the necks of losers.

Viral justice requires that we challenge the corrosive individualism that infects every area of our lives, and work against the revolting distortion of "freedom" that prioritizes a sick individualism over mutual obligations. As poet Adrienne Rich said, "In the vocabulary kidnapped from liberatory politics, no word has been so pimped as 'freedom.'" The deadly strain of freedom, a freedom from mutual obligation, breaks society, erodes mutuality, grinds down our ability to care for one another, and eats away at any notion of a collective good.

Until we reckon with the fact that racism is productive, we'll continue to be caught off guard by its persistence and reissuance. Productive not in the sense of being "good" but in the literal sense of being able to produce things of value to some, even as it wreaks havoc on others. These productions include everything from segregated neighborhoods in which white assets appreciate and Black assets depreciate to the carceral system that preys on Black communities while providing employment, lucrative contracts, and cheap labor, especially for rural America. Racism also produces an international division of labor and resource extraction whereby the U.S. and Europe export garbage recycling to rural workers in China and India, import fast fashion made by child labor in Sri Lanka and conflict minerals for our cell phones from the Congo, outsource obscene internet images that digital content moderators in the Philippines and Kenya must wade through and delete, while formerly colonized nations continue to provide cheap workers to rich countries like the U.S.

We are taught to think of racism as a surprise storm surge, an aberration, a glitch, an isolated incident, a bad apple, in the back-woods, as outdated, rather than as a centuries-long climate, business as usual, the entire operating system, an attached incident, the entire orchard, in the halls of power, innovative, even viral. In sociology we often say, "Race is socially constructed," as in it is not natural or biologically determined. But we often fail to state the corollary, that racism *constructs*—sometimes literally, in the case of segregated neighborhoods and prisons, but also, more subtly, in the production of racialized threats.

This production can be seen, for example, in the portrayal of eighteen-year-old Michael Brown by the officer who killed him in 2014. To his friends, Brown was a "gentle giant" with a wicked sense of humor. To Officer Darren Wilson, he "had the most aggressive face. That's the only way I can describe it, it looks like a demon, that's how angry he looked." Racist vision produced a demon where someone's friend once stood. Anti-Black weather enveloped residents of Ferguson well before that friend lay dead in the scorching-hot sun.

Before her untimely death, Erica Garner-Snipes was working might-ily to make justice viral. So, too, are many family members who have lost loved ones to police violence, including Erica's grandmother, Gwen Carr. She is part of the Mothers of the Movement, a group of Black women whose children have been killed by police or gun violence. They've joined forces to educate the public about police brutality and support others dealing with the same trauma.

In 2015 Carr retired from her job as a train operator for New York City's Metropolitan Transportation Authority, and she now devotes her time to civil rights. After the murder of George Floyd in 2020, she was one of the first people to call and console the Floyd family. "Don't forget. You cannot let this go," she insisted.

But Carr admits that, at first, she was reluctant to get involved. In her memoir, dedicated to the memory of Erica, Carr describes her reluctance: "I don't think I am particularly brave or strong . . . I suppose I could just sit back and live off my pension and have a decent life and move to Florida and soak up the sunshine . . . but that was not how I wanted to spend my life."

Now in her early seventies, she's an active participant in the Movement for Black Lives—speaking at protests, helping to pass New York State's antichokehold bill, meeting with lawmakers in DC to advocate for the George Floyd Justice in Policing Act, working against the return of stop-and-frisk in New York City. Indeed, Carr is a testament to the fact this isn't only young people's work. We *each* have a choice to make, whether or not we've had our children swept away by the deadly storm of state violence or whether we've experienced racism's toxic weather in other forms. Viral justice requires that we direct energy not only outward but also inward at the layers of grief, rage, even shame that threaten to break open our hearts.

Recall the three types of work that organizer and founder of the mutual aid resource website Big Door Brigade, Dean Spade, outlines: dismantling harmful systems, providing for the immediate needs of people targeted by those systems, and creating alternatives to the harmful status quo. These are all essential elements for transmuting hostile environments. Organizations like Project NIA, founded by Mariame Kaba, offer hands-on tools and curricula for individuals and communities to use in transforming a culture designed to stifle Black life. "And if you think that this work is like programming a microwave," Kaba remarked, "where an input leads to immediate output, that's capitalism speaking."

Instead, growing the world we want is like the slow tending of a garden, transforming the plants by fostering relationships, trust, skills, community accountability, and healing. It requires cultivating new habits *internally*, seeding restorative ways of being together *interpersonally*, uprooting practices of inequality *institutionally*, and planting alternative possibilities *structurally*. If we only concentrate on our internal work while ignoring the fires burning all around us, we'll eventually be consumed. But if we only concentrate on putting out the blaze, we'll eventually burn out.

When it comes to collective healing as a foundation for social transformation, my friends Claudia Pena and Beth Ribet have taught me so much. Building on their work as community organizers and legal scholars, they started a Los Angeles–based organization called Repair that addresses a wide range of issues, from human trafficking and white nationalism to disability law and policy. Beth is a survivor of child sex trafficking, and her experience deeply informs the organization's approach to trauma and healing by moving beyond diagnosis to prescribing practical tools. These include the Healing Circles Project, which aims to build peer-led mental health supports; Tea Parties, which are community workshops on food justice and plant medicine; and Transformation, a series of lectures, conversations, and storytelling sessions about healing and social action. The one I attended focused on trust. One of my friends, Naimeh, noted how the feeling of intimacy and the courage of the speakers made her want to be more vulnerable and open. "It's kinda contagious," she said.

The point is, we can't wait for top-down change to engender alternatives. Rather, grassroots efforts are an essential part of worldbuilding. Not to mention, "grassroots" can literally mean working in the grass! Ron Finley, aka the "gangsta gardener," is a longtime resident of South Central Los Angeles, "home to the drive-thru and drive-by," as he puts it. But Finley is changing the earth one plot at a time. In 2010 he grew frustrated with how residential segregation had made it hard to purchase affordable fresh vegetables in his neighborhood. So he decided to plant food in his front yard. Well, not exactly his front yard—in the stretch of grass called the "parkway" between the sidewalk and the street:

> Funny thing is, the drive-thrus are killing more people than the drive-bys. People are dying from curable diseases in South Central Los Angeles . . . I got tired of seeing this happening . . . I see dialysis centers pop up like Starbucks. And I figured, this has to stop. So I figured that the problem is the solution. Food is the problem and food is the solution . . . So what I did, I planted a food forest in front of my house.

Pumpkins, peppers, sunflowers, kale, and corn. At first, the city cited him and threatened to issue a warrant for his arrest, but the idea caught on. Eventually, Finley and supporters got the city to change the law that prevented people from growing edible landscapes on parkways. Now he and his team at Green Grounds have planted over twenty urban gardens around LA. They also created a teaching garden to spread knowledge about organic farming with the aim of also creating jobs for local residents. "Growing your own food is like printing your own money," Finley likes to say.

For Finley, it was never simply about the food, though. He gets emotional talking about food-insecure neighbors who were shocked when they realized they could take whatever they wanted from his yard for free. His philosophy is to give a person a vegetable but also teach them how to farm, so they have skin in the game: "The air is better . . . you're changing the ecosystem when you put in a garden. We are part of the ecosystem, so that garden is changing us. And then that *beauty* factor! You get to walk out your door and experience nature every day. That's going to change you. I don't care how jaded you are."

Beauty is not frivolity, a luxury, nor should it be an afterthought. Even under the harshest conditions, we hunger not only for food but also for beauty and meaning . . . which is why art, aesthetics, and imagination are vital to world-building.

In the end, there is weather and there is *weather*. As long as there are skies above, there'll be storms that rain down on us below. Such is life. And sometimes the rain is even refreshing, putting out fires and washing away the stuff that weighs us down. But whether we drown in the water or find refuge together is another matter entirely.

We all know our parents will eventually die and, although we brace ourselves for that reality, we are rarely prepared when it happens. But there's no reason we should watch our fathers be suffocated to death by agents of the state, as Erica Garner-Snipes did, or have our mothers suffer two heart attacks (literally heart *aches*) by the age of twenty-seven, as Erica's children did. Many of us are forced to brace for some version of swift or slow death, a death we know is not inevitable but rather the result of a hostile racial climate and all the small, everyday ways that it leaves people deserted.

Recall how Michael Brown was not only shot down by Officer Darren Wilson in Ferguson, Missouri. Black folks being shot and killed by police is an all-too-common occurrence, but that his body lay outside in the middle of the street for hours in the sweltering summer heat brings to mind the title of an article in the *Atlantic* by journalist Adam Serwer: "The Cruelty Is the Point." Residents in surrounding apartments peered out their windows in disbelief at Brown's lifeless body—a horrific symbol of how so many communities are left out to dry. This shameful postmortem showed weathering—how even *in death* Black people are left exposed. *This* is what galvanized the movement for Black lives.

What, then, is the opposite of social abandonment? Not grand announcements, posturing, and virtue signaling, but caring complicity even when there's no audience to bear witness. In the Minneapolis neighborhood surrounding the site of George Floyd's murder, you'll see the usual signs—"Black lives matter" and "Abolish the police"—in people's yards and windows. But there's one in particular, leaning up against a tree, that speaks to an even deeper longing: "Take care of each other."

Here is a call for complicity that is not about what we need to change *out there* but rather about how we need to treat one another in our more intimate interactions that'll never make the headlines. Conspiring to care for one another is how we change the weather. It's what Minneapolis-based organizations Black Visions Collective and Reclaim the Block have been engaged in since 2017 and 2018: hosting popular education sessions, building trust with community members, hosting monthly Black Joy Sundays that encourage neighbors to connect and network, and crucially, prioritizing the physical well-being of organizers by hosting health justice workshops focused on the somatic impacts of racism.

In the aftermath of Floyd's murder, these local organizations swiftly mobilized local residents—calling city council members every night, sending them research, and even littering politicians' yards with handmade gravestones bearing Floyd's image—until, eventually, nine of the thirteen council members walked on stage at a rally led by Black Visions in Powderhorn Park, the neighborhood where Floyd was murdered. It was just thirteen days after Floyd's murder that the council members publicly pledged to dismantle the police. Making history, it turns out, is the result of years of planting and uprooting, tending and pruning—one community gathering, one direct action, one Black Joy Sunday at a time. This is how we all transform the weather. But the struggle continues.

As the first step in dismantling the police, Minneapolis education officials announced plans to sever ties between law enforcement and the public schools, a feat that my friend Marika Pfefferkorn and other local activists had been working on for several years. But then the school district set out to hire "public safety support specialists," and according to leaked résumés, of the twenty-four finalists, a majority were police officers, private security guards, and corrections officers. The job description, after all, stated a preference for applicants with "degrees and experience in criminal justice." You see, *right there*, in the fine print, a deadly status quo was seeded: a closed-door meeting to decide qualifications, the mindless typing up of a job description, the routine posting on a human resources page. This is where the school-to-prison pipeline begins.

So let's not be fooled. Politicians can stand up in front of thousands to proclaim their commitment to grand policy changes, as we witnessed in Powderhorn Park. Governments can give in to public pressure and rework city budgets so resources are invested where we think they should be. But as Marika, the executive director of the Midwest Center for School Transformation, points out, "If you don't actually change the culture of the system, you just replace who's doing it." She's right. It isn't possible to change a social structure without changing its culture, and we can't change culture without changing ourselves.

In December 2014, the night that New York City grand jury decided not to charge Officer Pantaleo in the chokehold death of her father, Erica Garner-Snipes sat in the back seat of a taxicab, stunned and reeling with anguish. Vexed by the traffic, the driver cursed under his breath at the crowds making their way across the Brooklyn Bridge. It didn't click at first, until Erica looked out the window and saw waves of people, bundled up with hats and gloves, of all ages and backgrounds, carrying cardboard coffins, staging die-ins in the middle of the street, holding signs—"I can't breathe"—and chanting her father's name. Suddenly, her pain was *our* pain, her anger *our* anger. Leaning out the window, she cried, "Thank you! *I'm* Eric Garner's daughter." A large throng surrounded the cab, calling back to Erica, "We love you, we're doing this for you guys!" That simple exchange parted the clouds: "It felt like, *wow.*"

It turns out, transforming the weather doesn't require magical powers. It just requires that we begin to plot—emboldening one another, strengthening our relationships, watering the alternatives we want to grow, and shouting love in all we do. Whether your plot is organizing protests, making art, or sabotaging the White Club, whether it's interrupting racist school practices, advocating for fair work conditions, or parenting the next generation of tillers, love is always there, just beneath the surface, nourishing all our efforts.

TWO

Hunted

Riding in the back seat of Grandma White's gold Chrysler always felt luxurious. Compared with Dad's dusty hatchback, it was a cruise ship sailing down Crenshaw Boulevard. At seven years old, I was already good at directions to and from our usual outings, Crenshaw Mall, the Los Angeles Bahá'í Center, or Baldwin Hills Park. The route was pretty much the same, heading down MLK Boulevard, past Louisiana Famous Fried Chicken, gliding by the green Audubon sign—Dad's old middle school—then a few more blocks before turning right on Fourth Avenue. If we got lucky, Grandma caught the green light at the corner of Fourth and Forty-Eighth Street. Otherwise, it felt like eons waiting there, my legs sticking to the leather seat, as passing cars zipped by us, bass thumping through the windows.

Although I usually tuned out the street scene as I chatted away to Grandma, on this day, my view sharpened as I caught sight of some boys from school. Time slowed as I witnessed them lined up against the fence not too far from Angeles Mesa. Their backs were turned to the street and their arms raised high. The officers patted them up and down, forcefully, desperate to find guilt.

I hadn't yet learned the word for shame, but I knew, from the burning in my eyes, that this public display of humiliation was not *only* for the boys. It was also my first clue that my friends, neighbors, and loved ones, were caught in a deadly game of cat and mouse—a twisted one in which the cat makes up all the rules and mouse is trapped repeatedly.

That moment on the street corner sizzles in my memory even now, every time I drive past a cop car or pass an officer in the street. I can't help but think, *They are out to get us.* Is it paranoia or premonition? You decide. But my seven-year-old intuitions about the rigged game were confirmed in a viral (and disputed) essay I read many years later, "Confessions of a Former Bastard Cop," in which a retired Officer A. Cab (short for "All cops are bastards") offers evidence from his real-life experiences on a metropolitan California police force. He readily admits to the vile machinations of the hunt: "We used to have informal contests for who could cite or arrest someone for the weirdest law. DUI on a bicycle, non-regulation number of brooms on your tow truck . . . shit like that. For me, police work was a logic puzzle for arresting people, regardless of their actual threat to the community. As ashamed as I am to admit it, it needs to be said: stripping people of their freedom felt like a game to me for many years."

This deplorable game is not limited to a few police departments or jurisdictions. It is endemic to policing itself. From the hundreds of people who were tortured under the direction of Chicago police commander Jon Burge between the 1970s and early '90s—electrocuted, suffocated, beaten into false confessions and given prison time—to the infamous ongoing abuses of police power cloaked in the popular rhetoric of professional heroism and sacrifice, I wonder whether future generations will look back at us, astonished at how we could justify such a wretched and wasteful system. Between 2015 and 2020, Los Angeles County spent $238.3 million, Chicago spent $252.8 million, and New York City spent a staggering $1.1 billion to settle police misconduct claims. It's hard to imagine the U.S. public footing a bill in the billions of dollars for any other municipal service the way it does for the police. If slavery was the "peculiar institution," modern-day policing is its ignoble offspring.

In this chapter, we will scrutinize policing and punishment from the perspective of not only those caught in its crosshairs but also all those who have been touched by the carceral system indirectly.

We will focus on the machinations of not only those who have been deputized by the state, donning uniforms and badges, but also those who have been deputized by our carceral culture to police Black life in public spaces. Likewise, we will question the easy distinction between those who we are told deserve mercy and those whose actions justify state-sanctioned brutality.

"Justice" in this context is not about police reform. Instead, it refers to the gradual abolition of an institution born of slave patrols and kept alive by the myths of virtuosity and necessity. Viral justice can be found in the small print of city, state, and federal budgets. In those documents, we find the redistribution of resources and reinvestment in social goods like housing, education, work, and community, which we need to sustain us. Viral justice is also about creating communities of care—articulating the kind of world we want *out there* in our relationships and interactions with strangers and friends *right here*. Throughout, we will ask, with educator and abolitionist Mariame Kaba, "*What else can we grow instead of punishment and suffering?*"

My younger brother, Jamal, and I grew up the same. Same home, same parents, same neighborhoods. But the police have been chasing him all our lives. "Chasing" is the wrong word. Hunting . . . he is hunted. Tender meat feeding a rapacious quota system—another deer head an officer can mount on his wall.

In his late teens, Jamal began showing signs of mental illness—schizophrenia, bipolar disorder, paranoia—we weren't sure yet. Things came to a head after he had gone missing and we found him collapsed, dehydrated and emaciated, after hearing voices that told him not to eat. My brother is over six feet tall, and when we located him, he weighed less than one hundred pounds.

A few years went by; then, during one of his episodes, Jamal grabbed a woman sitting next to him on the bus and held her for a few seconds in a bear hug. The woman screamed, the bus driver stopped the bus, and cops boarded and arrested my brother for attempted kidnapping.

With nearly twenty thousand employees, including more than ten thousand sworn deputies, the Los Angeles County Sheriff's Department is the largest sheriff's department in the world, and its jail, the Twin Towers Correctional Facility, is where those cops took Jamal. The jail's website boasts that it's "the nation's largest mental health facility." But after being caged in the Twin Towers, Jamal was so traumatized that he couldn't stand trial.

The Twin Towers, where approximately fifteen thousand people await trial, yet to be convicted of any crime, is part of what has become known as the "Abu Ghraib of Los Angeles." In a 2011 report titled *Cruel and Unusual Punishment: How a Savage Gang of Deputies Controls LA County Jails*, the ACLU's National Prison Project spells out a "pattern of brutal abuse . . . which at times crossed the line into torture." The report includes eyewitness testimony of Los Angeles County Sheriff deputies humiliating prisoners with sexual and racial epithets, and punching, kicking, and beating nonresisting inmates to the point of their needing surgery and hospitalization. It is a level of inhumanity that observers say exceeds even that of maximum-security prisons.

After reviewing testimony by inmates, former inmates, chaplains, and civilians, as well as reports, correspondence, media articles, and legal filings, even Thomas Parker, a former FBI agent who worked in the bureau's Los Angeles Field Office, came to a damning conclusion: "Of all the jails I have had the occasion to visit, tour, or conduct investigations within, domestically and internationally, I have never experienced any facility exhibiting the volume and repetitive patterns of violence." Now imagine your own loved one trapped inside this den of brutality.

Jamal was held in Twin Towers for several weeks before he was sent to Patton State Hospital in San Bernardino County for three months to be medicated so that he could take the stand. He was brought back to the Twin Towers, and it was several more weeks before he was brought before a judge, who eventually ruled that it wasn't a criminal case that needed to go to trial.

At the hearing, when the judge asked the woman on the bus whether Jamal had hurt her in any way, she said no, that he had held her for a few seconds. In that moment, she seemed remorseful that it had come to this. The judge, in turn, ordered that my brother be admitted into a mental health facility for one year followed by several more years of court-mandated psychiatric treatment. In exchange for an unwanted hug, our punishing institutions squeezed their tentacles around Jamal tighter and tighter.

The day my brother's criminal record was eventually expunged felt bittersweet. It came after years of harassment, profiling, jail, imprisonment, shame, trauma, and so much more that typing these words reignites a burning rage. Is it possible to wipe off a brand? How else can I describe the "mark of a criminal record," as the sociologist Devah Pager calls it, but as a modern-day brand? Rub . . . rub . . . rub . . . as much as you can, the scar left behind refuses to disappear.

Each time the carceral system brands a loved one, an entire family is marked. We feel the iron of a vicious system whose appetite seems limitless. When the beast decided it had had enough, it spit my brother back out. *Record expunged.* But not before forcing him to sit for years in its repulsive belly, corroding his spirit and consuming his mind. The stench of that beast snakes around us, tightening and releasing, squeezing and pulsing in what clinicians term posttraumatic stress, anxiety, and depression.

In an essay titled "Collateral Damage," sociologist Alyasah Sewell and public health researcher Kevin Jefferson explain, "People do not have to be inside the criminal justice system to feel the effects of the criminal justice system. In fact, the surveillance policies of the criminal justice system reach so far as to shape the health of people who have not yet entered into its gates." Is it any wonder that the health of entire communities is adversely affected by being criminalized? Higher blood pressure, higher rates of asthma, diabetes, and more—health conditions born of a ritualized pattern of terror and trauma. Even when we are not the prey, we feel hunted.

There's more. This is a social, not just an individual-level, trauma. Researchers who study animals tell us that those who are hunted, whether they are caught or escape, experience muscle damage, damage to red blood cells, and cortisol concentration. This is the weather engulfing those who are hunted—a downpour of psychological terror. The targeted animal continues to experience high levels of stress even after the chase, which disrupts their social structures "if they are a species that live in a group." And dread extends to other animals who are not the primary target, forcing the latter to live in an "ecology of fear," avoiding places where they might be more visible. How much more so in human populations, given what we know about the deeply social way humans live and construct their identities? Individuals may be the ones hunted, but families, neighbors, and communities also experience terror.

In January 2015, when Sergeant Valerie Deant arrived at a gun practice range in North Miami Beach, Florida, with other soldiers in her Florida National Guard unit, she was shocked to see a bullet-riddled photo of her brother, Woody, discarded in the trash. Pictures of other young Black men were in the garbage alongside his photo, also with bullet holes in their heads.

"I was like, why is my brother being used for target practice?" Deant told a reporter with NBC South Florida.

Just before Deant and her group arrived that day, police snipers with the North Miami Beach Police Department had been using the range, and they had chosen a lineup that included her brother's photo to practice shooting. According to the police chief, nothing about the officers' actions violated the department's rules. Not only did the police routinely use images of real people, but snipers also intentionally chose people who all appeared to share the same racial demographic for "face recognition drills."

Sure, the chief said, they could have used "better judgment" and not practiced with photos of people who had been arrested by the department and who might be on the streets of North Miami Beach, but no rules were broken, and no one would be reprimanded. Still, he offered, the sniper program would be suspended until they could create a larger inventory of faces. *Equal opportunity violence.* This is what happens when "diversity, equity, and inclusion" is turned into flowery wallpaper for a haunted house.

Despite the police department's attempt to play down this incident, public outrage ensued. Local residents called for the city to apologize and for the police chief to resign. Among the many responses, a group in the Miami area decided to post photos of themselves with the hashtag #UseMeInstead—a kind of viral justice that used social media to express antiracist solidarity. The idea sprouted in a closed Facebook group of Lutheran clergy, then quickly spread as people all over the country and of different faiths joined in. Together they shined a light on the violence of a system that trains armed agents of the state to target citizens.

"It's such a desensitization thing, that if you start aiming at young black men, and told to put a bullet in them, you become desensitized," Reverend Joy M. Gonnerman said. Although the posts predominantly circulated online, Gonnerman printed a stack of sixty-six eight-by-ten photos to mail to the department. "Essentially," she explained, "we're saying: We're watching, we're paying attention to this." Then, following a heated meeting at North Miami Beach City Hall, which included nearly two hours of public comment, the city council passed a law to permanently ban the practice of using mug shots for target practice. Good riddance.

And yet, as the North Miami Beach Police Department mug shot story went viral, a few things bothered me about how the offense was framed. At its best, #UseMeInstead is a powerful gesture of solidarity that encourages more people to question why Black people serve as the targets of policing practices and shooting drills. But how does replacing one target with another upend policing as a social structure? Do we really want equal opportunity profiling by the police, or do we want to abolish policing and all the harm it causes? Should we be trying to make it so all lives serve equally as targets? Or no lives?

Something else bothered me about the responses to the mug shot story. Expressing shock at seeing his forehead and eyes riddled with bullets, Woody Deant protested about the way he had been represented. "I'm not even living that life according to how they portrayed me as," Deant said. "I'm a father. I'm a husband. I'm a career man. I work nine to five." Fifteen years earlier he had been involved in a drag race in which two people died, so he spent four years in prison. But now he is, by all middle-class metrics, an "upstanding citizen" and "contributing member of society" who doesn't deserve such debasing treatment. But . . . who does?

Too often, when it comes to the criminal justice system, the defense of those deemed innocent is justified by the invention of a boogie man—the thug, the gangster, the troublemaker, the castaway, the *real* criminal who is a perfectly appropriate target for shooting practice. If we are not careful, our cries of outrage could inadvertently reinforce the border between those who we say deserve to be treated with dignity and those who we say can be hunted with impunity. This cultural boundary ricochets through our language and law, for example, in decarceration policies—such as getting rid of cash bail that penalizes the poor—that only apply to "nonviolent offenders." The nonviolent offenders are deemed to be a lower risk to society. The distinction between the "good" and "bad" immigrant is another symbolic boundary we use to justify who should be hunted down, torn from their families, caged, and deported. In President Barack Obama's words, immigration reforms should target "felons, not families. Criminals, not children. Gang members, not a mom who's working hard to provide for her kids."

As political geographer Ruth Wilson Gilmore notes, rhetoric like that from Obama insists "on foregrounding the relatively innocent: the third-striker in for stealing pizza or people in prison on drug possession convictions." But as Gilmore underscores,

the danger of this approach should be clear: by campaigning for the relatively innocent, advocates reinforce the assumption that others are relatively or absolutely guilty and do not deserve political or policy intervention . . . Such advocacy adds to the legitimation of mass incarceration and ignores how police and district attorneys *produce* serious or violent felony charges, indictments, and convictions. It helps to obscure the fact that categories such as "serious" or "violent" felonies are not natural or self-evident, and more important, that their use is part of a racial apparatus for determining "dangerousness."

For those of us whose family members have been labeled felons, criminals, and gang members, the line between those who are irredeemably dangerous and those deserving of policy intervention is not as bright as we are led to believe. This hit home for me again when, in 2019, I sat on a panel with "inmate #86G0206," as Donna Hylton sometimes calls herself, because she spent nearly twenty-seven years in the Bedford Hills Correctional Facility for Women, located about forty miles north of New York City.

When Donna was twenty years old, she was convicted of second-degree murder and two counts of kidnapping for her role in the death of Long Island, New York, real estate broker Thomas Vigliarolo. In her defense, Donna's lawyer pleaded "duress" and "coercion" because the leader of what turned into a murderous scheme threatened the life of Donna's four-year-old daughter to ensure Donna's participation.

Even so, Donna has never claimed to be an innocent bystander, and every day in prison she forced herself to "say his name," sobbing at the thought of "Mr. V," apologizing for not helping him in that desperate situation. But as someone who was herself tortured, trafficked, and sexually assaulted as a child, and repeatedly raped and abused as a teen (including by a police officer whom she had turned to for help), living in "a state of perpetual terror, confusion, and powerfulness" made Donna especially vulnerable to coercion and threat. Yet many of us are taught to simply write off the Donnas of the world, view them as dangerous felons, and lock them away. But as abolitionists remind us, *each of us is more than the worst thing we've ever done.*

Our public discourse and policy reforms continue to draw a bright line between "violent" and "nonviolent" offenses as if people charged with the former are not also the victims of violence and as if the people patrolling the streets and running the jails and prisons are not often vicious. Loosening the carceral hold on those deemed worthy of our investment too often means tightening the noose around others, including the many of us who love those criminalized as felons. One thing we can all do *yesterday* is question the simplistic boundary between good and bad sold to us by the powers that be.

The next time someone trots out "crime data" to justify continued investment in policing, remember that, as the author of *Usual Cruelty*, Alec Karakatsanis, explains, "what constitutes a 'crime' is determined by people in power." The stats usually don't include tax evasion, wage theft by employers, or the illegal seizures of property by police.

When Karakatsanis was at the public defender's office in Washington, DC, his very poor clients reported how DC police would routinely "stop them, search them at gunpoint, tell them to open their wallets, and take all the cash they had." Then his clients would get a letter saying that "if they wanted to challenge the police taking their cash, they would need to pay either $250 or 10% of the amount taken, whichever was more!"

Crime data doesn't include the violent crimes committed by police or jail guards—several million physical and sexual assaults occur each year, according to Karakatsanis. A 2021 RAND Corporation report is just the latest analysis of the alleged activities of gangs of sheriff's deputies operating within the Los Angeles County Sheriff's Department. As the report details, these gangs come complete with initiation rites: "So you have a kid who wants to be accepted, they would ask are you ready to get your ink? And that meant you had to get into a use of force and send an inmate to the hospital, sometimes by breaking the orbital bone. Some supervisors didn't even write the use of force, or some of the uses of force 'disappeared.'"

Author of *Invisible No More*, Andrea J. Ritchie, has spent over a decade documenting police violence against women of color, in which "cops fondled prisoners, made false traffic stops of attractive women, traded sexual favors for freedom, had sex with teenagers and raped children." Transgender women, sex workers, and those who use drugs and alcohol are also targeted because police know they won't be believed if they report an assault. Ritchie cites former Seattle police chief Norm Stamper, who said, "Sexual predation by police officers happens far more often than people in the business are willing to admit." Is it any wonder, then, that most survivors don't turn to police for help?

What makes victims distrust those who are sworn to serve and protect? Officer A. Cab sums it up succinctly: "I knew cops that pulled women over to flirt with them. I knew cops who would pepper spray sleeping bags so that homeless people would have to throw them away. I knew cops that intentionally provoked anger in suspects so they could claim they were assaulted. I was particularly good at winding people up verbally until they lashed out so I could fight them. Nobody spoke out. Nobody stood up. Nobody betrayed the code."

Implicit bias training, tougher laws, and community policing programs are no match for this licensed terror. Instead of minor tweaks, Officer A. Cab and a growing abolitionist movement led by incarcerated and formerly incarcerated organizers insists we should work toward stripping the power of police and prisons by ending qualified immunity, a legal doctrine that protects government officials from being held personally responsible for violations of the U.S. Constitution. Terminating civil asset forfeiture (which currently allows police to seize, then keep or sell, "any property they allege is involved in a crime"), breaking the power of police unions, requiring malpractice insurance, and defunding, demilitarizing, and disarming cops are also essential. These policy changes require cultural change, which each of us can contribute to by rejecting the myths that a few bad apples cause the problem and society would descend into chaos without the police out there to rescue us.

Viral justice is not limited to the public expression of solidarity. It also involves reckoning privately with how we create distinctions between those who have "earned" our respect and sympathy, and those we feel justified to dismiss and deride because they have been cast out of the category "human" (or were never admitted to it in the first place). As Gilmore reminds us, "Where life is precious, life is precious."

Gilmore, who has been active in the prison abolitionist movement for decades and is one of the cofounders of the organization Critical Resistance, was my professor at the University of California, Berkeley. I was enrolled in her seminar Political Geography of Race and Gender during my second year of graduate school when I gave birth to my younger son, Khalil.

The way she graciously welcomed his presence around the seminar table was itself a lesson in how to buck rules and create a caring environment. Amid the soundtrack of newborn gurgles and whimpers on the fifth floor of McCone Hall, we discussed everything from Italian philosopher Giorgio Agamben's book *Means without End* to the ongoing student protests on Sproul Plaza. At the time, I didn't fully appreciate how influential Gilmore's scholarship and activism were for a growing movement focused on imagining a world without police and prisons, nor how formative the class would be for my own teaching and scholarship.

During the same fall quarter when she welcomed a one-week-old pupil to the table, Gilmore had published an essay, "Fatal Couplings of Power and Difference: Notes on Racism and Geography," which we discussed as a class. Her writing style, not weighted down by the feigned academic neutrality I was growing accustomed to, made plain her political and moral commitments to social liberation. It spoke directly of viral justice by countering the idea that politics is limited to the level of the state. Instead, she illuminated the politics of women whose children had been imprisoned and argued that their work also produces urgent questions and insights for the social sciences. Knowledge is not just (and not even *mainly*) born in the hallowed halls of universities, but around kitchen tables, in community centers, in prison waiting rooms, and at protests.

For that reason, much of Gilmore's work is in conversation with community activists, those with "triple workdays—job, home, justice," who have an intimate knowledge of the carceral system. Organizations like Los Angeles–based Mothers Reclaiming Our Children (Mothers ROC), founded in 1992 by Barbara Meredith and Francie Arbol, have mobilized around the "symbolic power of motherhood" to challenge the system that locks away their children. In its early days, Mothers ROC organized support and strategy sessions in the community room of a public housing project. Members learned to organize on behalf of relatives who had been arrested and incarcerated on false or exaggerated charges.

Members of the group, who provided us with a model of viral justice, soon began to extend their reach. They organized a gang truce so family and community members could safely navigate their neighborhoods and participated in a public funeral procession for a young man killed by police. In the weeks to follow, they organized rallies and protests, and developed a sustained effort that gives family members tools to demand justice for children who are hunted by a ravenous carceral system. Don't forget, Gilmore writes. "All prisoners are somebody's children, and children are not alienable."

Although Mothers ROC centered the fight against anti-Black racism, it welcomed Latinx and white mothers of the incarcerated into its ranks. According to Gilmore, activists who engage in "social mothering" in this way present us with a "glimpse of utopia's work" by mobilizing across the many boundaries created by oppressive carceral geographies: "They come forward, in the first instance, because they will not let their children go. They stay forward, in the spaces created by intensified imprisonment of their loved ones, because they encounter many mothers and others in the same locations eager to join in the reclamation project . . . In other words, techniques developed over generations, on behalf of Black children and families within terror-demarcated, racially defined enclaves, provide contemporary means to choreograph interracial political solidarity among all kinds of 'mothers' losing their loved ones into the prison system."

This "choreography" of solidarity in the midst of terror does not only take shape in relation to the carceral state, but also among activists organizing in education, healthcare, work, and all the many places that have been starved so as to feed the rapacious appetite of the punishment beast.

I can't help but wonder how different my mom's experience would have been—trekking back and forth to the Los Angeles County Jail, then navigating the seventy-mile journey to Patton State Hospital in

San Bernardino County on public transportation, then visiting my brother at a court-mandated mental health facility in LA—if she had been buttressed by a community of women who intimately knew her plight. As Gilmore writes, "If it takes a village to raise a child, then it certainly takes a movement to undo [a police] occupation."

Just over one year into the COVID-19 pandemic, over 660,000 incarcerated people and staff had been infected in U.S. jails, prisons, and other federal facilities. Almost 3,000 had died. And like much pandemic data, this is probably an undercount. In many ways, prisons, like nursing homes, were designed to harbor illness. Grant Muldrow, a twenty-six-year-old inmate at the California Institute for Men, said that he "pressed a correctional officer about the lack of concern that her staff showed toward inmate health at a public meeting at the prison. 'I'm not a lifer nor am I sentenced to death,' Muldrow recalled saying, 'So are you telling me, with only a few months left [before release], that me and everyone else here just has to sit here and wait to die?' The officer's reply, according to Muldrow: 'Pretty much.'"

Public health, like public safety, has long been used to justify rounding up and isolating unwanted populations from the larger body politic. From ports of entry like Angel Island in the western U.S. and Ellis Island in the East (both also detention centers!), to the U.S.-Mexico border in the South, racialized bodies are routinely cast as a contagious menace to the white American population. In 1918, for example, as the Spanish flu swept through cities around the world, U.S. police harassed residents of Black communities. The Black newspaper the *Chicago Defender* urged the police commissioner to address prison overcrowding and said police stations were "doing more to breed disease than any other agency supposed to be working for good." In 2020 racial justice advocates made the very same appeal as jails and prisons, along with nursing homes, became coronavirus hotspots. This is at least one reason why, as public health policy expert Kenyon Farrow puts it, "public health activists who are truly interested in social and racial justice should in fact be calling for the abolition of the prison industrial complex as part of a strategy to reduce the possibility of current and future epidemics."

The COVID-19 pandemic exposed yet again how the field of public health offers a smokescreen for policing racialized people. In May 2020, as temperatures began rising and more people began agitating against shelter-in-place policies, law enforcement in various cities began enforcing social distancing rules *selectively*. In New York City, for example, the Brooklyn District Attorney released arrest rates showing that thirty-five of the forty people arrested for social distancing violations were Black: "The arrests of black and Hispanic residents, several of them filmed and posted online, occurred on the same balmy days that other photographs circulated showing police officers handing out masks to mostly white visitors at parks . . . More than a third of the arrests were made in the predominantly black neighborhood of Brownsville. No arrests were made in the more white Brooklyn neighborhood of Park Slope."

Other early reports showed that 68 percent of those arrested city-wide were Black, 24 percent were Hispanic, and only 7 percent were white. Meanwhile, the first person in Britain to be arrested under the Coronavirus Act of 2020 was a Black woman, Marie Dinou. She was detained and fined for failing to "provide identity or reasons for travel to police, and failing to comply with requirements," which authorities later admitted were bogus charges.

Similarly, Armen Henderson, a Black doctor who worked at the University of Miami and had been testing homeless people for COVID-19, was arrested while he was loading bags and boxes into his van outside his home. The reason he ended up in handcuffs? Because the officer suspected him of illegally dumping trash in the neighborhood. In the video of this arrest, we can see Henderson is wearing a mask, but the officer, who is yelling and pointing in the doctor's face, is not wearing one. He exposes Henderson not just to everyday racism but possibly the virus itself.

Indeed, the vast public health surveillance structures rolled out during the pandemic relied on predictable forms of containment and punishment that already target racialized people. They included technology such as contact tracing apps, disease detection via drones, and electronic monitoring. These things may appear harmless or even beneficial, but they often hide the types of racial profiling that are usually in our faces.

Technology can be used to police without (flesh-and-blood) police by employing technologically mediated forms of containment, which I have described in previous work as "New Jim Code." The point is, if we are not careful, the demand to defund the police could lead to a reinvestment in surveillance systems that penetrate every area of our lives under the guise of progress. In the wake of protests after George Floyd's murder, venture capital investors were primed to swoop in, promising to "democratize" public safety "by giving anyone with a smartphone the ability to document their side of the story, surveil the neighborhood, summon help, and feel connected." Instead of questioning the efficacy of policing, they decided to put the tools of policing into more hands.

When most of us hear the word "surveillance," we think of government spies, phone taps, covert CIA operations, and redacted FBI files. Some of us who are steeped in the Black radical tradition think of COINTELPRO, the U.S. government's counterintelligence program, which targeted activists, artists, scholars, and more—Malcolm and Martin, of course, but also Lorraine Hansberry, Huey Newton, Paul Robeson, W.E.B. Du Bois, and Audre Lorde. Nowadays, the word "surveillance" conjures up images of Big Tech, digital data, and electronic tracking enabled by the little computers in our pockets. Almost every time I give a talk on the subject, I make a point to focus not only on top-down surveillance, à la Big Government and Big Tech, but also on the many different forms of horizontal, interpersonal surveillance carried out by individuals as we go about our daily lives: employers stalking applicants' social media, neighbors posting information in apps about anyone they deem suspicious, and teachers using proprietary software to monitor students' body language for signs of cheating. As with viral injustice more broadly, *each of us* is enrolled—nay, *deputized*—to uphold a soul-sucking system that infects us with fear and paranoia.

George Orwell's Big Brother has spawned an army of, shall we say, Lil' Brothers. "Always the eyes watching you and the voice enveloping you. Asleep or awake, working or eating, indoors or out of doors, in the bath or in bed—no escape. Nothing was your own except the few cubic centimeters in your skull." We are constantly encouraged to monitor and report our suspicions, whether in neighborhood Facebook groups, by installing Amazon Ring doorbells on our front doors, or by downloading apps like Nextdoor, Sketch Factor, and Ghetto Tracker. It's no mystery that geographic segregation makes discrimination easier, allowing app users to brand entire neighborhoods and the people residing in them as dangerous and potentially criminal.

The Citizen app, created in New York City in 2017, is part of this genre of Lil' Brother solutions. It sends you real-time crime alerts based on a curated selection of 911 calls and provides users a way to report, live stream, and comment on purported crimes. It shows you incidents as red dots on a map, so you can avoid purportedly "dangerous" areas. *What could possibly go wrong*, right? In an age when Barbeque Beckys call the police on Black people who are cooking, walking, breathing, or bird-watching out of place, we have now invented an app to streamline racial profiling and harassment.

Citizen was originally given the less innocuous name Vigilante, a term that elicited criticism online. In its rebranding, it also moved away from encouraging people to stop crime, according to some reports. Now it simply tells them to avoid it. But the new moniker is also telling: from the legal codes embedded in our nation's founding documents that limited U.S. citizenship to "free white persons," to the computer codes that fail to accurately detect the images of people with dark skin in the digital world, race and citizenship are wedded together. At last count, Citizen had over seven million users, and it saw a spike in use during the 2020 racial justice protests. This led one observer to comment, "Citizen, and apps like it, owe some of their popularity to the fear of Black protest." Even though many of the reports on Citizen are unconfirmed or later refuted, it is often one of the top five most popular apps in the Apple App Store's news section.

During the pandemic, Citizen partnered with the Los Angeles Police Department to create an app, SafePass, for contact tracing. It has raised more than $133 million in investments, including by Peter Thiel, founder of the infamous data-mining company Palantir, whose software has been used in targeting and arresting parents and families of children detained by U.S. Immigration and Customs Enforcement, along with other surveillance operations directed at migrants, refugees, and asylum seekers.

But contact tracing is not Citizen's main priority. Rather, it has upped the ante by introducing a for-hire private security detail that app users can call if they are in distress. Behind the scenes, we are told, "sources close to Citizen have called it 'an anxiety sweatshop,' where employees are expected to produce frequent reports [of incidents transcribed from police scanners and other sources] to drive users to pay for products that include a 'digital bodyguard service' called Protect."

One observer describes the app as the *gamification of vigilantism*, profit derived from mass paranoia under the guise of buzzwords like "transparency," "empowerment," and "democratizing" public safety. These Lil' Brother apps reflect a deep-seated American obsession with vigilantism and law and order. We can see this obsession in the immense popularity of police dramas like *Law & Order* and reality shows like *Cops*. But the problem isn't just that media and technology companies manufacture our obsession from on high; it is also the mass participation of viewers and users like you and me.

On May 15, 2021, the CEO of Citizen, Andrew Frame, began furiously texting employees in the company Slack channel after getting reports of a wildfire in the Pacific Palisades area of Los Angeles County. Tips came in that the fire had been started by an arsonist, so Citizen began soliciting information from users, offering rewards for any tip that led to an arrest. It just so happened that Citizen's new live-streaming service, OnAir, had recently been launched, so the broadcast was sent to 860,000 users and was viewed by over one million people: "Citizen is OnAir: Arsonist Pursuit Continues. We are now offering a $30,000 reward for any information directly leading to his arrest tonight. Tap to join the live search." Frame saw this fire as the perfect opportunity to promote Citizen and was intent on turning the heat up on his employees: "First name? What is it?! publish ALL info," he told them as the fires inched closer to his Bel-Air home. In leaked texts, he continued:

FIND THIS FUCK. LETS GET THIS GUY before MIDNIGHT HES GOING DOWN.

BREAKING news. this guy is the devil. get him by midnight!@#! we hate this guy. get him.

Close in on him. 30k Let's get him. No escape. Let's increase. 30k. Notify all of la. Blast to all of la.

The more courage we have, the more signups we will have. go after bad guys, signups will skyrocket. period. we should catch a new bad guy EVERY DAY.

What one observer described as "a citywide, app-fueled manhunt" went on for over seven hours under the command of Citizen's CEO and led to the wrongful detention of an unhoused man. Good guys against bad, citizen against criminal. The entire spectacle was meant to provide a live proof of concept—"a risk, a test, an experiment"— that could drive up user numbers. Later that night, the Los Angeles Police Department made an arrest, but the person arrested was not the same individual identified in Citizen's hunt. Keep in mind, the city had already decided to join forces with the company on the SafePass contact tracing app—a decision that appears even more foolhardy after this debacle. So far, city officials have not announced plans to cancel the contract.

Watching the Malibu manhunt unfold, I couldn't help but think of the *Black Mirror* episode I ask my students to screen for a class on race, technology, and justice. From season two, "White Bear" follows a Black woman, Victoria Skillane, as she awakes, confused, in an empty house. As she sets out to discover where and *who* she is, Victoria is "pursued by masked hunters while speechless onlookers, seemingly in a trance, refuse to intervene." Most of the voyeurs, in turn, film Victoria on their phones as she runs and pleads for their help.

Only at the very end of the episode do we find out that the entire setup is staged. The hunters are professional actors, the phone-wielding bystanders are enjoying the thrill of the hunt after purchasing their tickets to a "justice park." A large audience glee-fully watches a video of the entire chase as they sit in the comfort of a theater auditorium. Victoria is the only one in the dark, until the last few minutes of the show when she (and the viewer at home) learns that she is caught up in this deadly game of cat and mouse because she was the accomplice in a child's abduction and murder and is now being punished.

With this revelation, the audience goes wild, delighting in her punishment. The question then becomes whether *we*, viewing Vic-toria through our own screens, ought to celebrate this poetic justice. What about after we learn that this is not a one-time punishment, because Victoria's memory is wiped clean so she can relive this tor-turous day again and again? Perhaps the most troubling aspect of Victoria's plight is that all of this goes down in the White Bear Justice Park, where the general public can purchase tickets to witness and participate in a spectacle of justice.

Sound familiar? Like the Citizen app, the hunt is gamified, and we can all play. As *Black Mirror* producer Annabel Jones remarked, this story is about "how we bring people to justice and what out-rages we can do if we feel morally justified." In short, this episode of *Black Mirror* is about us: "The torch-lit mob throwing blood-filled sponges at Victoria make one thing clear: If punishment is to be enjoyed, it's best enjoyed as a spectacle. There's something socially cohesive about it."

If retribution is riveting, a pathological source of unity, then we have to ask whether it is possible to foster social cohesion without an outcast and enemy. Does human bonding rely on someone else's bondage?

When it comes to racist practices of all kinds, especially the vio-lent escapades of police and vigilante mobs, we fool ourselves into thinking they represent accidental encounters turned deadly. In some cases, *perhaps*. But we must reckon with the fact that there is also a drive, a volition, and a pleasure that animates these violent encounters.

Recall the Snapchat video of a twenty-year-old white woman, Tabitha "Tabbie" Duncan, that went viral in June 2018. Tabbie is in a pickup truck, beer in hand, riding down a dark country road (in Missouri of all places). Along for the ride are two white men, one of whom can be heard off-camera asking, "Are we going n*gger hunting today or what?" To which Tabbie replies, "You get them n*ggers," as she takes a sip of beer and smiles toward the camera.

After Tabbie's (former) friend Brionna Haas posted the video, Tabbie lost her waitressing job at Social Bar and Grill and was booted from the U.S. Air Force Reserves, in which she had recently enrolled. Right on cue, Tabbie offered a flurry of familiar excuses:

I was intoxicated. Check.
I have Black friends. Check.
I have Black people in my family. Check.
I didn't mean it. Check.
I didn't know that I was being videoed. Checkmate.

In her book *Nice White Ladies*, sociologist Jessie Daniels argues that the Tabbies of the world are not just along for the ride but are some of the most dangerous drivers of white supremacy. White women (those in Volvos as much as pickup trucks) routinely weaponize their faux vulnerability, or "fauxnerability," to endanger others. Let's take, for example, Sarah Braasch, a white Yale philosophy PhD student, who called the police on a fellow Black grad student asleep in a common area; Jennifer Schulte, aka #BBQBecky, who called 911 on a Black family cookout at Lake Merritt in Oakland; or Allison Ettel, aka #PermitPatty, who reported an eight-year-old Black girl selling water in San Francisco.

"The list is alarmingly long," writes surveillance scholar Justin Louis Mann. In his essay "What's Your Emergency? White Women and the Policing of Public Space," Mann notes that "from California to New York, from gyms to parks, from department stores to universities, it feels like it is open season on black people." *Open season*, indeed.

The state-sanctioned hunt by police is bolstered by citizen policing in which white women loom large as deputies of the law. The phenomenon has become so routine, the script so predictable, that pop culture has anointed white women who take on this role as "Karen"—a meme for women who exhibit this and other types of entitled behavior. Of course, Karens disavow any racist motives behind their decisions to call the police. They claim to be acting for the public good and hide behind "a colorblind veil of rule following." As Mann explains, their actions are about white claims to public space—claims that have escalated with the "white return" to urban centers (following "white flight" from cities decades earlier): "Becky and Patty purport to act in the public's best interest, ensuring the preservation of a pristine, and implicitly white, public order predicated on the oppression of black people."

We may laugh at the circulation of Karen memes, but when white women weaponize their fauxnerability, they are building on a long tradition in which the public lynching of Black people falsely accused of wrongdoing has been carried out in defense of white femininity. It's only that now, the uniformed defenders are an easy phone call or click of an app away.

"Each time one of these incidents makes the news," Daniels reflects, "I think about the way we are connected, these Karens and me. We are the descendants of white women who instigated, encouraged, and benefited from white supremacy, shoulder-to-shoulder with white men. Yet I, like her, want the power to dial 911 and summon protection. But there's a tradeoff in this. My desire for protection and power to summon help from 911 means that I'm activating the launch codes for my body to become a missile that destroys lives and whole communities." And in the end, this anti-Black racism makes us all unsafe.

In the case of Amy Cooper, we watched a white woman activate the launch codes when Christian Cooper, a Black bird watcher, reminded her that her dog needed to be on a leash in the section of Central Park called the Ramble. Christian's recording shows Amy turning on her fauxnerability like a switch: "I'm calling the cops . . . I'm gonna tell them there's an African American man threatening my life," she says. Then, when connected, she tells the 911 operator, "There is an African American man—I am in Central Park—he is recording me and threatening myself and my dog. Please send the cops immediately!" By the time the police arrived, both Coopers had left the scene.

I don't know if you'd call it poetic injustice, but on the same day as the Central Park incident, one thousand miles west, Derek Chauvin murdered George Floyd in broad daylight after a shopkeeper called the police on him.

Since the creation of 911, "police officers have become the weaponized embodiment of social and racial bias, dispatched at the behest of semi-anonymous callers who (knowingly or not) may release devastating police violence." According to a 2020 study by the Vera Institute of Justice, most of the 240 million annual calls to 911 relate to *nonemergencies* like noise complaints, parking issues, and complaints about unhoused people. The universal emergency number is easy and convenient, yes, but we should critically assess it to see how it started and whom it ultimately benefits.

Although the adoption of an emergency number in the United States was a direct reaction to civil rights uprisings in the 1960s, it was originally rolled out by the U.S. government as a counterinsurgency tool in Caracas, Venezuela, helping authorities surveil militant groups. There had been previous attempts to introduce an emergency line, but only when the Kerner Commission proposed the number to suppress civil rights protests did the federal government decide to take swift action. So 911 got its start as a tool for anti-Black social repression. But it's not as if the Karens need to understand this history to know that "they are readily believed and that," in Daniels's words, "they face few consequences for words that can and do end lives."

After Amy Cooper's Oscar-worthy performance of white lady victimhood went viral with over forty million views, she was charged with falsely reporting an incident—a misdemeanor punishable by up to one year in jail. The charges were eventually dropped after she "completed five therapy sessions that focused on not using racial identities to harm ourselves or others." The sociologist in me is skeptical about the idea of antiracism therapy, a quick fix that seems more like an Olivia Pope publicity stunt than a long-term commitment to examining how our individual actions prop up deadly systems (a process better engaged in community with others). Even Christian Cooper has repeatedly tried to redirect media attention from the single encounter in Central Park to the broader context of racial profiling by refusing to cooperate with the Manhattan District Attorney's Office in their case against Amy: "It's not about her. What she did was tap into a deep vein of racial bias. And it is that deep vein of racial bias that keeps cropping up that led to much more serious events and much more serious repercussions than my little dust-up with Amy Cooper."

Some people have described Christian's stance as an instance of chivalrous behavior toward white women that lets her off easy. But we could also see it as reflecting part of an abolitionist ethos that insists that a criminal legal system that grinds down people's bodies and spirits on a daily basis can never be the source of real justice. I don't know if he identifies as an abolitionist, but Christian's decision not to cooperate with the district attorney contributes to an anticarceral future in which we expose the rotten roots that underpin our corrosive legal system. Simply throwing out the bad apples—the Amys, Tabbies, Beckys, Pattys, and Karens of the world—leads to a false resolution.

Instead, we need to retool everyday responses to distress and harm. So long as 911 is our only way to call on help in emergency situations, it will be used to police public space, control those deemed undesirable, and respond to a long list of situations that are often aggravated by the presence of police. We must seed alternatives that do not summon those ravenous hunters because, no matter what the situation, they are likely to find their prey.

"I'm horrified by the amount of sheer luck needed to stay alive," Haben Girma, a Deafblind Black woman living in the San Francisco Bay Area, told NBC News. For many disability justice advocates like Girma, the first Deafblind person to graduate from Harvard Law

School, law enforcement poses a significant threat because police fail to recognize disabilities in those they interact with. Even when they do, few officers are trained to effectively communicate and offer modifications that meet people's needs (despite its being required since 1990 by the Americans with Disabilities Act).

"Police can't see I'm Deafblind," Girma said. "They might see my involuntary eye movements and assume criminality."

Indeed, the list of Black, disabled people who have been assaulted and killed by police in recent memory—Freddie Gray, Laquan Mac-Donald, Tamir Rice, Eric Garner, Sandra Bland, Korryn Gaines, Natasha McKenna—is too long to name them all. In the United States, 50 percent of people killed by law enforcement are disabled. And among Black folks, more than half of disabled people have been arrested by the time they turn twenty-eight (including my brother). This is double the rate of their white disabled counterparts.

Krip Hop artist, scholar, and longtime disability justice organizer Leroy Moore reminds us, "If you look at recent cases of police brutality you will see that people with all types of disabilities—from autism to deafness to my disability, cerebral palsy—are being abused by police." But, he explains, "many times the disability is played down or not mentioned because parents are ashamed of it or the investigator has a lack of knowledge of disability factors in cases of police brutality."

A few months after we moved to Princeton, my mom and brother were planning an extended visit, and at first I was excited. Coming from Los Angeles, I knew my mom would love a month free from driving since everything she needed would be within walking distance of our home. And my brother, I hoped, would enjoy the chill pace, hanging out with his nephews, and getting around easily.

But as the day drew closer, I grew increasingly anxious thinking about how people would react to seeing a tall Black man with a "hidden disability" walking around town. How would they react to Jamal saying or doing things out of the ordinary that could easily be misconstrued as strange or menacing: singing or talking loudly to himself, walking up to strangers and carrying on a one-way conversation, dressing in ways that would make him stand out?

Scrolling through my Twitter feed one day, I saw a post saying that the Princeton Police Department would be hosting a meet and greet at the Panera Bread on Nassau Street. And so I had the bright idea to go and let them know that they might get some calls about my brother, and they should not overreact.

When the day came, I sat in a booth picking at a piece of bread and stirring a tomato soup, going back and forth about what exactly I would say. Maybe they would be better equipped if they had a photo of my brother in their database, noting his mental health status and the sorts of behaviors people might report. *No, no,* that was wishful thinking. *When has being included in a police database ever helped anyone?* It would more likely just put a target on his back.

I finally worked up the nerve, scooting out of the booth and walking to the back of the restaurant, where two officers had set up, one already in a chummy conversation with an elderly white patron. I had barely introduced myself to the officer who was free, an amiable white woman who put out her hand for a shake, when tears slowly started rolling down my face, surprising even me. I don't exactly recall what I blathered as I tried explaining my concerns, imploring them not to overreact to inevitable calls and complaints, not to misconstrue strange behavior for threatening, and mostly, *not* to hurt my brother.

To those officers, surely accustomed to thinking of themselves as the good guys, I must have looked bizarre. I faintly recall the female officer's slightly bewildered expression and her efforts to reassure me. I'm sure she believed, as many do, that the kind of police violence we had witnessed a few months earlier in Ferguson, Missouri, with the killing of Michael Brown could not happen in a place "like Princeton," with its gothic architecture wrapped in ivy, boutique shops, and five-dollar cups of artisanal ice cream with flavors like beet basil and lavender mascarpone. Police do not assault Black disabled people in places with vegetable- and herb-flavored dessert.

Just before I joined the faculty, the Center for African American Studies hosted an intergenerational gathering of activists from the Black Youth Project 100—racial justice organization based in Chicago—and the Student Nonviolent Coordinating Committee

Legacy Project, the main organization for students who had been engaged in direct action during the civil rights movement. No sooner had a group of Black Youth Project 100 members left campus on the first night of the convention to drive back to their hotel, than a (Black) police officer pulled them over. They allegedly had a broken taillight—which, on closer inspection, turned out to be in fine working condition. What ensued was a spirited conversation, caught on camera, between the youths and the officer about racial profiling, criminalization, and the ease with which white students take up space on campus and in town—a conversation that went viral because it was so rare.

And so I stood tearfully in the back of Panera attempting to explain to a perplexed-looking cop why she should not hurt my brother. The irony is that several years later, in that same spot, officers would shoot and kill a suicidal white man in his fifties. Scott Mielentz pleaded, "Just kill me. Just do it for me, guys." And *they did*. Suicide by cop in the heart of Princeton.

Thankfully, during his monthlong visit, my brother was not harassed or arrested. However, I noticed that almost every time he left the house, he wore a Princeton University T-shirt—a force field, bat signal, sartorial supplication: *Don't hurt me, treat me with respect, I'm not threatening.* Even though *he's* the one under threat! We never discussed it or made it plain—*I'm wearing this so they know I belong*—if only because it was so obvious. Indeed, wearing university apparel is one of *many* strategies, like whistling Vivaldi, that Black people are forced to deploy to put white folks at ease so they don't weaponize distress or act on their disdain.

Later, when Jamal and my mother came to live with us in Princeton, the police came to know my brother by name. Residents or shop workers would call the cops to report that he was walking through town with only one shoe on, or had taken off his shirt and was singing in a doorway, or was standing too long in one place and talking too loudly for their comfort. In response, an officer would talk to him calmly, or call my mom, or otherwise handle the situation without incident. While some might see this as "proof" that the police can be reformed for good, it doesn't address the reality that police officers are incentivized to make arrests, not help. And none of this can erase the trauma Jamal lives with daily due to his earlier arrest and frequent harassment before and after.

What mattered was not that Princeton police were especially "nice," but that Princeton residents are overwhelmingly white. It turns out that municipalities with a large white population are much less likely to deputize police to generate revenue for the city by using fines, forfeiture, and fees levied against residents. On the flip side, cities with large Black populations make up for budget shortfalls by aggressively enforcing parking tickets, traffic violations, and other minor infractions, and enforcement rests largely on the discretion of officers. After examining over 20,000 municipalities, data scientist Dan Kopf concluded, "The best indicator that a government will levy an excessive amount of fines is if its citizens are Black," aggravating an already tense relationship between police departments and communities.

When the U.S. Department of Justice issued its report on Ferguson, Missouri, after officer Darren Wilson killed Michael Brown, they highlighted the "suffering caused by the police treating people as 'potential offenders and *sources of revenue'* rather than as citizens to protect." This economic harassment is viral *in*justice at work, one vexing encounter with authorities after another, adding up to white noise against which more visible forms of police brutality periodically erupts.

After years of believing it was possible to tame the police, to make them less hunter, more helper, I now know that the solution is not better training. Instead, we must come to grips with the facts. The police cannot provide solutions to the long list of issues they are tasked with managing: economic precarity, mental health crises, homelessness, substance abuse, and more.

Before the murder of George Floyd, the Minneapolis Police Department was held up by many as a model of progressive police reform. It offered implicit bias, de-escalation, and even mindfulness training to officers. It embraced "community policing" and "procedural justice," buzzwords in the progressive reform agenda. The department even received training in mental health crisis intervention and purported to practice "reconciliation efforts" in communities of color. It checked all the boxes. And *still* police murdered Floyd.

This tells us that we are not going to diversify, implicit bias train, or tech-fix our way out of the racist status quo. Rather, viral justice requires each of us to demand that the money normally invested in policing be reinvested in what we actually need to sustain us: mental health services, better education, better healthcare, homes. The arrests and convictions of "bad cops" may offer some satisfaction. For those like Samaria Rice, the mother of Tamir Rice—the twelve-year-old who was playing with a toy gun in a Cleveland park when a cop shot him down within seconds of arriving on the scene—a conviction would offer some peace of mind. But even she admits we need radical transformation: "The whole thing needs to be dismantled," Rice says.

As attorney and author of *Becoming Abolitionists*, Derecka Purnell, tweeted the day before the jury came back with the decision to convict Derek Chauvin, the police officer who murdered Floyd, "Convictions won't save lives and we have to ask ourselves . . . do we want convictions or want to live? Do we want tired reforms or do we want freedom? Do we want to keep putting out hope in the systems that destroy our families? communities?"

As if to mock whatever faith we have left in carceral solutions to police violence, minutes before the jury in Minnesota's Fourth Judicial District Court found Chauvin guilty of second-degree unintentional murder, third-degree murder, and second-degree manslaughter, 750 miles east in Columbus, Ohio, another police officer shot a Black teenager, sixteen-year-old Ma'Khia Bryant, in broad daylight. April 20, 2021, at 4:45 p.m. local time. And that's just the murder that was caught on video that went viral. How many other violent encounters took place in that very moment when the jury foreman called out "guilty" for one officer's murderous actions?

But, but—apologists for police violence flood the comments section—*but Ma'Khia was wielding a knife.* She was in a fight with another girl in front of the foster home where she had lived for the previous few months. In the days that followed Ma'Khia's murder, a stream of responses from educators, social workers, and others who work with young people reminded us that unarmed professionals in other areas de-escalate fights among young people *all the time* without resorting to violence—much less murder.

"You want to stay connected and compassionate and verbalize that compassion to help whoever's going through the crisis realize that you're on their side and that you understand them and their emotions, even if they're holding a knife," said Kay Wilson, who works with teens in a youth leadership organization in Columbus, Ohio. "It's important to show empathy at all times," she insisted. But even if police officers could be trained to model this kind of response starting today, why should you ever believe an officer is now "on your side" in a moment of crisis when every previous encounter you've had with them involved some form of harassment, profiling, and disrespect, if not outright assault. Truly magical thinking, and yet somehow abolitionism is cast as far-fetched and fanciful.

A core element of viral justice, empathy goes hand in hand with abolitionist experiments in creating a world without police. Organizations like Creative Interventions, which was founded in 2004 by Mimi Kim, operationalize empathy by advocating for community-based harm response systems. Creative Interventions hosts conversations in cities around the country about how everyday people can avoid 911 calls and choose community-based alternatives.

In 2012 it released a toolkit that models this type of response, and in 2021 it launched the Storytelling and Organizing Project with collaborators in Chicago and New York City. On its website, you can listen to story clips that share examples of how people put justice into action—like the one about how a group of friends responded to hearing that their Black friend was surrounded and verbally assaulted on a crowded street by a group of white men. The friends organized local businesses on the same street to take a stand against racism.

You can also read story transcripts like one about a community mediator who facilitated a family meeting in which a mother confronted her son about his violent outbursts. Listening to and reading these stories shows us that community-based responses are possible, and that everyday people are seeding alternatives to the police with courage and creativity.

The Oakland Power Projects is another initiative, launched in 2015, to build community power that can resist the everyday violence of policing. It was developed by Critical Resistance (CR), an abolitionist organization founded in 1997 by Angela Y. Davis, Rose Braz, and Ruth Wilson Gilmore. It follows a simple three-step process: interviewing residents, listening and finding, and launching a project. In the interviews, CR members ask questions that we can all ask ourselves:

Where do you like to spend time?
Do you feel safe there?
Where do you feel most safe?
Have you ever called the cops?
What made you feel like that was the best option?
What happened as a result of the call?
Can you think of something else that might have solved the
    problem?
What do you wish would have happened?

Then CR members collectively listen to Oaklanders' interview responses and catalog what they hear—drawing out themes, needs, and desires. Finally, once they have identified a theme, they work with the people affected and those with particular skills and knowledge to design and implement a "power project." For example, when residents expressed concerns that seeking healthcare routinely led to police contact, CR recruited a range of health experts to create an Anti-policing Health Toolkit and "Know Your Options" workshops that empower residents to de-escalate emergencies and reduce engagement with cops when seeking healthcare.

Abolitionist organizing, after all, is not simply about getting rid of the police, but about imagining and investing in a "million experiments" with care and accountability: a Community Activation Bus that serves as a mobile educational, healing, and resource center in Minneapolis, Minnesota; a Community Love Fund that distributes recurring cash relief to formerly incarcerated women in Roxbury, Massachusetts; and Community HEAL Circles that create space for those most affected by violence in King County, Washington, to join small groups in a restorative justice process where they have access to childcare, meals, and other resources to support their participation. These "experiments" are led by survivors of violence for people who have lost loved ones to gun violence, and for those with incarcerated loved ones. They create circles of community, healing, and love for formerly incarcerated persons that allow them to explore topics such as trauma, shame, accountability, structural and generational violence, and their impacts on our bodies.

In the 1990s we saw another model of viral justice in a Brooklyn-based community group called Sister to Sister, which formed because mostly immigrant, working-class women of color were dealing with high rates of domestic violence. At first, they would call the police to intervene, but they found that the officers would often harass and arrest people for violating immigration rules, "and they wouldn't solve the problem."

According to historian Robin D. G. Kelly, Sister to Sister decided, "We need to keep the police out and we need to figure out a way to deal with domestic violence on our own. So they develop[ed] workshops, street theater, vigilance committees, trainings, so that men, women, kids in the community, understood how to deal with domestic violence, how to reduce it and recognize that . . . And as a result of their work, they were able to reduce the number of calls to police and reduce domestic violence significantly."

Although Sister to Sister may no longer exist, other organizations—like the Audre Lorde Project, which was founded in 1994—continue to be centers for community organizing in the New York City area. The Audre Lorde Project hosts several different initiatives, including Safe OUTSide the System—an antiviolence program led by Lesbian, Gay, Bisexual, Two Spirit, Trans and Gender Non-Conforming People of Color.

One of the resources it developed is the Safe Party Toolkit, which provides strategies for party throwers and goers to create a space in which safety and self-determination are a priority and where people can intervene in and prevent violence from happening—whether verbal harassment, physical abuse, or sexual assault. The toolkit develops community members' capacity to support survivors of violence as part of what the Audre Lorde Project calls "healing justice."

While the Audre Lorde Project strengthens relationships so community members do not have to rely on police, Solitary Gardens focuses on deepening the connection between people in prison and those on the outside. I first learned about Solitary Gardens from educator and abolitionist Mariame Kaba when we sat on a panel at the Free Minds, Free People conference in Minneapolis. Kaba described the work of artist-activist Jackie Sumell, who created what she called "solitary gardens"—garden beds that are the size of prison cells. They're made of mulch from the ground-up remains of cotton, sugarcane, tobacco, and indigo.

By using the main crops of chattel slavery, Solitary Gardens is "exposing the illusion that slavery was abolished in the United States." These cells are "gardened" by incarcerated people who send instructions to volunteers on the outside on what to seed the beds with and how. Over time, "the prison architecture is overpowered by plant life, proving that nature—like hope, love, and imagination—will ultimately triumph over the harm humans impose on ourselves and on the planet." Solitary Gardens is one answer to Kaba's question, "What else can we grow instead of punishment and suffering?"

Like many other examples of viral justice, Solitary Gardens started off in one place, New Orleans, but solidarity is contagious. Now there are gardens around the country, as part of a much broader social reckoning with the violence of incarceration. If policing and prisons sever social ties, then, little by little, initiatives like Solitary Gardens seed anticarceral social connections in the soil of our imaginations . . . a necessary step in growing alternatives to punishment.

Nowhere is the need for abolitionist alternatives more glaring than when it comes to child imprisonment. On any given day, seventy thousand children are incarcerated in the United States, more than five hundred of whom are younger than twelve years old. We spend between $100,000 and $300,000 each year to incarcerate a single child, though this varies by state. In California, for instance, the Oakland Unified School District spent $17,084 per pupil in 2019–20, and the same county spent $490,200 per youth on juvenile incarceration.

This grotesque "investment" signals not only a failure of government and society but a failure of imagination. Think about it: only a perverse racial arithmetic could justify pouring millions of dollars into caging children rather than investing in the very things that would allow them to thrive.

In his book *Juvenile in Justice*, photographer Richard Ross takes us beyond the statistics and gives us a glimpse into the intimate spaces of youth punishment and isolation. Produced over a dozen years, the book features photographs and profiles of over one thousand incarcerated children at three hundred sites in thirty-five states. These are kids, Ross reminds us, who "all live under the umbrella of trauma, poverty, abuse, neglect."

The cover of the book is a window into the brutality of juvenile detention. It shows a twelve-year-old Black boy in a windowless cell in Biloxi, Mississippi. He wears a yellow shirt with "Harrison County Juvenile Detention Resident" printed in all caps on the back and yellow pants. *Resident*, one of many euphemisms. In front of him, we see a tiny bunk bed with thin plastic mattresses on the bottom and top, no sheets, only coarse gray blankets sprawled across the surfaces.

The child's back is turned toward the camera to protect his identity, and he faces a dirty white wall covered with drawings and writing—the most visible of which is an image of a UFO taking off next to the phrase "North or Nothing." Ross implores us to ask ourselves, "What would you do if this was your kid?" That shouldn't be a rhetorical question. We should follow the lead of community organizers who do not buy into the demonization of people, young or old, who are criminalized.

Take Project Nia, an organization founded and directed by Kaba that tackles the devastating reality of juvenile arrest and incarceration. Headquartered first in Chicago and now based in New

York City, Project Nia hosts programs such as Liberation Library, which provides books to young people in detention centers and prisons, and organizes campaigns—such as one to close youth prisons in Illinois. Across more than a decade, the organization has offered over two hundred community workshops and published dozens of educational curricula on conflict resolution and transformative justice designed for each of us to adopt in our own locale. In this way, it provides a hub of resources and tools to advance viral justice.

Similar to Project Nia, the Bay Area Transformative Justice Collective is cultivating an abolitionist approach to harm and violence. By hosting "labs" for anyone who signs up on topics as fundamental as "How to Give a Good Apology" and "How to Use 'the Talk' to End Child Sexual Abuse," as well as study groups and potluck meals, the collective develops ways for people to intervene in immediate crises while building long-term spaces and strategies for healing and accountability. *Easier said than done*, for sure. One member of this Oakland, California–based collective, Layel Camargo, an Indigenous descendant of the Yaqui and Mayo tribes from the Sonoran Desert, expressed the doubts that many of us feel despite our conviction that the current system is untenable:

> I've begun to wonder whether Transformative Justice is even possible, if we can really respond to instances of violence or even harm, for that matter without calling the police. This week alone, I have attempted to deescalate a confrontation outside of my house, shown up to a vigil down the street from my house because of a shooting that led to a fatality, and had a mini conflict with my upstairs neighbors about doing some weed work while they were on vacation. It has left me feeling like if this is the kind of harm and violence I should be wanting to respond to I don't even know if I would have time to go work at my job for 8 hours because I would be in community accountability processes for days.
>
> Does anyone else feel like this? Does anyone else feel like we can't escape the easy fix feeling that can come from calling 911?

I certainly do at times. I think we all feel at some point that we're trapped in the world we've inherited and that creating alternatives to the status quo can be exhausting. So quick fixes can totally feel like a relief in the moment. But if those quick fixes prevent us from getting to the root of what is wearing us down to begin with, then perhaps the investment of time and energy in lasting change is worth it.

As it stands, those organizing alternatives to policing may spend five to ten hours a week, or more, on transformative justice work. But most of us just don't have the time or energy to respond directly to *all* the incidents of harm and violence in our lives. But as Camargo reflected, we can still "find small and big ways to practice core values. Values that foster interdependence, compassion and humanity and this week, especially, this week the most I can do is practice that for myself."

Indeed, we are all called on to practice what we dream possible, and that practice requires treating ourselves with the same grace that we try to exercise with others. *Little by little, day by day* is the refrain that keeps me going. I've learned viral justice is not only what we do "out there," but how we sustain ourselves "in here." We sustain ourselves, in part, through collective care.

Consider the immense financial costs of incarceration for those with loved ones locked up: the phone calls, prison visits, commissary bills, and legal fees add up quickly. But for the one in four women and one out of every two Black women who have a family member in prison, incarceration doesn't just take a toll on their bank accounts. State-sanctioned separation from a loved one is emotionally traumatic and stigmatizing, causing family members to experience grief, shame, and isolation. Gina Clayton-Johnson experienced these financial and emotional tolls when someone she loved was incarcerated while she was in law school. So in 2014 she launched the Essie Justice Group.

The Essie Justice Group, an Oakland-based organization that supports and advocates for women who have loved ones locked up— including Black and Latinx women, formerly and currently incarcerated women, and trans and gender-nonconforming members—is one such model of this.

Essie's Healing to Advocacy Model is a nine-week program that aims to break isolation and build organizing power by working with cohorts of twelve to fifteen women. They participate in three-hour weekly sessions, with transportation, childcare, and meals included. Together they move through "individually held pain to begin journeys of collective healing" so that, ultimately, participants gain the confidence to advocate for change. This is solidarity, not charity, in that the people most harmed by our current systems are the catalyst for viral justice.

The seemingly small interactions between neighbors and strangers are where we can begin living beyond a carceral culture and seeding communities of care. Every year, I return to the Los Angeles neighborhood I grew up in. Although my mom no longer lives there, my husband, Shawn; our two sons, Malachi and Khalil; and I all have close friends in the city, including some who bought the White House a few years after my dad passed. It remains the center of gravity for my family, the place that feels most like home.

On one of our LA trips, the boys were intent on training for fall sports, so they came with me a couple of nights a week to Rancho Cienega Sports Complex, a neighborhood recreation center that's been around since I was a kid. The complex includes Jackie Robinson Stadium—a running track that circles a football field where the Dorsey High School team plays, and which is open to the public at other times. With huge floodlights brightening up the stadium, it draws people of all ages who enjoy working out in the cool summer evenings.

Walking through the entrance, I saw a flock of tweens in the same purple T-shirt choreographing dance moves on the south side of the field, while several people finished stretching on the north. A couple of diehard runners ran up and down on the bleachers behind me, and the rest—sprinters, joggers, and shufflers—circled the track. The range of ages, activities, and abilities is what makes me love this particular sports complex. The woman pushing a stroller as she gets in her steps belongs there just as much as the Olympic hopeful pant-ing and nodding while her coach barks feedback at her, stopwatch in hand.

But before Malachi, Khalil, and I could take our places on the track, an older Black man walked up to us from out of nowhere.

"Good evening, family!" he called out to us, as I strained to recall whether we knew him from somewhere.

"Good evening," we each responded. He wasn't drenched in sweat, so perhaps he'd just finished a brisk walk. The boys tried moving out of his way, but he continued.

"Enjoying your summer?" To which they politely nodded yes. "Working out is great, but don't forget to exercise that precious mind of yours. What's your favorite subject?"

"History," Malachi replied. "Math," said Khalil.

"Those fancy phones might cost a lot, but this right here," he said, tapping his temples, "is priceless." The boys smiled awkwardly and nodded again.

"And be sure you listen to your mama!" he said. "She knows what she's talking about," he said, smiling in my direction.

The boys looked over at me with a smirk, as if asking, *Did you pay him to say that?* After another minute or so of counsel, with the elder encouraging the boys to live their best lives, he slipped out of the gate and into the night.

Malachi and Khalil whisked over to me, confused. *Did you know him?!* I laughed and reminded them where we were, Leimert Park Village, underscore *village*, where people of a certain generation, hailing from places like Arkansas and Texas, treat everyone like kin. I explained how common it was for me growing up to be *patted up* in the way they just were. This also explains why I've always felt like, no matter where I go, no matter what I do, there's a chorus of Black elders cheering me on, starting with Grandma White and extending to her circle of friends—to folks I've never even met before who act as if our fates are linked. Together they conjured a force field around me so that I could navigate the treacherous weather.

Mind you, this exchange at Rancho Cienega took place just min-utes away from the place I took that fateful ride thirty years earlier in the back seat of Grandma's gold Chrysler. Instead of Black kids pushed up against a fence and patted down by police, my boys were corralled and patted up by fictive kin. Instead of humiliation, contempt, and suspicion, they became the targets of esteem, ardor, and high expectations. Instead of police hunting them like prey, neighbors watched them like they were precious. As they circled the field that night, perhaps they felt the same cheer I have always known, lap after lap, panting, breathless, and alive.

THREE

Lies

The night before my first day of middle school, I tossed and turned. Staring at the pastel green paper on which my schedule was printed, I could not fathom how I would get from English in the main building to math class in the trailer at the very back of the school in just ten minutes. But the next day, racing down the crowded, covered walkway, I made it just in time.

Panting as I pulled open the heavy door, I found the name tent with "Ruha White" sitting on a desk in the back row of the long and narrow room. *Strike one*, I thought. I didn't like sitting in the back. I heard the teacher, let's call her Ms. Wylie, saying to no one in particular that we were seated alphabetically and that we should find our places. Then, after getting some first-day niceties out of the way, we got down to business. Ms. Wylie had already written a dozen problems on the board, and she proceeded to ask for volunteers. "Who would like to . . . ?" Before she could even finish, my hand shot into the air like a rocket.

But despite my mile-high arm, Ms. Wylie continued to scan the room, looking for volunteers. I looked around, confused, trying to catch the eye of anyone who was seeing what I was seeing. But there was no silent commiseration to be had. I was Patrick Swayze in the movie *Ghost* trying desperately to get Demi Moore's attention, but

Ms. Wylie was too dense to see me. I was in the back row, sure, but in this sardine can of a room, that was no excuse. In this sea of white students assigned to honors math, there was no way Ms. Wylie missed my colorful '90s knit top, asymmetrical mushroom hairdo, Dwayne Wayne–style flip up glasses, and five fingers stretched out in all directions. She was working hard to see through me.

Eventually, the bell rang. I packed up my book bag and staggered out onto the bustling walkway with the stink of Ms. Wylie's rejection still wafting over me. Again, the next day and the next, I tried mightily to get called up to the board, my hand shooting up straighter, higher, more frustrated each time. By Friday, I was propped up, my knee resting on the chair. I waved my arm as if reporting an emergency. Ms. Wylie was unfazed.

I had no idea yet who Ralph Ellison was, but I already felt the bitter taste of his lament: "I am an invisible man . . . I am a man of substance, of flesh and bone, fiber and liquids—and I might even be said to possess a mind. I am invisible, understand, simply because people refuse to see me." I eventually found my own words to talk to my parents about what was happening, and the rest, as they say, is history.

That is how it is with memory. The hurt looms like a shadowy figure crawling up the walls of the mind, while the resolution fades like a specter. But the resolution is precisely what we must magnify! How did my parents intervene, whom did they approach, what did they say? I will never know. I *do* know that while many people are forced to bite their tongues and swallow their hurt, others confront injustice and heal injuries every day, but without shining a light on that process, we lose out on the lessons learned, the wisdom won— all of which we need to pass on.

A few years earlier my parents had packed our belongings into a bright yellow Ryder truck parked in the driveway of the White House. They threw a small mattress and boombox into the back seat, squeezing them between boxes of clothes and books. Mom beckoned us to wave goodbye to Grandma White one last time, who had earlier slipped Jamal and me each a crisp ten-dollar bill as we ate pancakes and watched episodes of *He-Man* and *She-Ra*.

Now Grandma stood composed but teary-eyed on the porch. She stood there watching as we pulled out of the driveway and drove away. With the four of us packed in tight, there was nothing left for me to do but put my favorite cassette into the boombox and croon along to Whitney Houston with the earnestness of an almost ten-year-old:

> I believe that children are our future
> Teach them well and let them lead the way
> Show them all the beauty they possess inside
> Give them a sense of pride, to make it easier.

Six days and nights we drove, stopping at motels every night until finally we reached Conway, South Carolina, where dad would begin a new job as program director at Radio Bahá'í WLGI in nearby Hemingway.

For the next twenty-five years, I got used to moving every two to six years. First for my parents' work, then for my schooling, and then eventually for my work. Traveling lightly and planting roots quickly became second nature to me. My mom still teases that, in my teens, even for short motel stays, I would put up my favorite black, red, and green "Rasta Baby" wall hanging to cover whatever art hung over the bed. I was always determined to feel at home and to insist that my surroundings (however fleetingly) reflect something of me. In Conway, like in LA, we soon found a place to live that was a short walk from my new school. But unlike in LA, where I recall not one white student in any of my classes, the "integrated" schools of South Carolina left me exposed to the everyday racism of those whose job it was to nurture my potential.

At first, I was baffled as to why Ms. Wylie refused to call on me. But then I recalled an experience a few years earlier at a Bahá'í event in Hemingway. I overheard an elderly Black man from the nearby town of Kingstree recount how whites routinely called him "boy," even as an adult. Sitting on a bench outside the main hall where the discussion about "eradicating prejudices of all kinds" was being held, I told my dad what I had overheard, burning-hot tears streaming down my face. I was as much confused by my reaction as I was enraged by the original indignity. *Why did the old man's story feel so personal?*

Even though I didn't yet have the academic training, I already sensed that racism was about much more than one person's ill-treatment of another. It was an entire system of meaning that materializes through the complicity of individuals trying to keep one Black man (as a symbol of *all* Black people) in his place. "Hey boy" was also "Hey *girl* . . . you don't belong in honors math." This is when I first put two and two together.

"Education is the great equalizer," the lie goes. In this chapter, we will put the myth of meritocracy to rest and abandon once and for all the fairy tale that individual ability and hard work (or lack thereof) dictate our lot in life.

Schools in the United States and throughout much of the world reproduce existing social hierarchies. They are often engines of inequality, not opportunity. As educator and political activist Grace Lee Boggs diagnosed it, "At the core of the problem is an obsolete factory model of schooling that sorts, tracks, tests, and rejects or certifies working-class children as if they were products on an assembly line."

It's not just schooling as an institution but IQ, as a scientific concept, that we need to put under the microscope. The very notion of innate intelligence, with its roots in eugenic thinking, continues to quietly infect many aspects of our lives. The success of eugenics as a scientific and political worldview can be seen in its spread throughout our schools, workplaces, families—and even our own thinking. Indeed, the complicity of a wide range of individuals and organizations, rather than simply a top-down philosophy, makes the long afterlife of eugenics an example of viral *in*justice at work. If we are serious about seeding a solidaristic worldview, undoing hierarchies, and cultivating interdependence, then perhaps there is something yet to learn from our eugenics forebears—not in *what* they believed but in *how* they enrolled people, from humble farmers to exalted statesmen, in their world-embracing project.

Friedrich Nietzsche was right: "Unspeakably more depends on what things are *called,* than on what they *are.*" And what we are called usually says a lot about what we are *not* called. To be labeled as gifted is to be deemed not "at risk," which is another label the education system hands out to children. Victor Rios, former gang member turned sociologist, rejects the term "at-risk," insisting that the label pathologizes young people. Instead, the idea of *at-promise* youths calls into being the potential that every single person has but that only a precious few are given space and time to express.

After Amanda Gorman delivered her rousing poem at Joe Biden's inauguration, professor of education, Brittany Williams tweeted what many of us felt but hadn't put into words yet: "There's an Amanda Gorman at every HS you call underperforming, inner city, and/or the G word. Honor. Black Students. Art." There are legions of them—poets, scholars, orators, musicians, mathematicians. Some of their gifts are never cultivated, while others go unaccounted for by asinine aptitude tests.

Of the hundreds and hundreds of hours I have spent as a student—nineteen years total—my memories consist almost exclusively of the handful of times I was given the time and space to think and do things I really cared about: singing and dancing in a "gifted and talented" program, writing about Malcolm X in tenth-grade history, researching a paper on Black women poets in my International Baccalaureate program, creating a transcript of a fictional conversation between Karl Marx, Max Weber, and Émile Durkheim in my social theory PhD course. The countless late nights working on assignments that did not spark my imagination are a blur . . . forgotten.

But I also remember many of those long hours spent with my mom by my side. A social studies project in fifth grade required that I create a fifty-page "book"—a page for each state in the union—with state flags, state birds, and other trivia, all traced, colored, and annotated. Was it cheating or collaboration that my mom helped me piece together this tome? Whatever the case, I was also "gifted" with parents who showered me with support at every turn—from helping me with busywork in elementary school to sending funds to cover the bills in grad school. Not everyone has that. Too many people of all backgrounds experience abuse, neglect, and betrayal by family members. But in my case, I wasn't surprised to find a teacher's note buried in my old school records stating, "Parents are very supportive," right after "Needs to develop patience dealing with peers."

Humans are creatures of categorization, so cognitive scientists tell us. To survive as hunters and gatherers, we had to be very adept at knowing the difference between poisonous and edible plants, for example. So distinguishing between things is hardwired in our DNA, they say. But according to the philosopher of science Ian Hacking, our categories don't just name what already exists, they also bring things into being.

Ms. Wylie did not have a reference for "Black math whiz," so she refused to see one sitting right in front of her. Labels like "gifted and talented" do not simply identify specialness. They *create* it, and even weaponize it. This is why I call bullshit on any attempt to naturalize and scientize the kind of routine denigration Ms. Wylie perpetrated. Instead, we should call it what it was—*attempted* spirit murder. Although I didn't know what to call it, my spirit knew. And that bit of knowing lit a fire that still rages today.

"Spirit murder" is a term invoked by law professor Patricia J. Williams to remind us that racism has never simply enacted physical harm but also continuously robs people of dignity and self-worth, wounding us emotionally, "psychically." Racism is injurious not only in the immediate moment but also in the *aftermath*, when people are forced to "prove that they did not distort the circumstances, misunderstand the intent, or even enjoy it." Building on Williams's original formulation, abolitionist educator Bettina Love argues that, in schools, spirit murder entails a "loss of protection, safety, nurturance, and acceptance—all things children need to be educated." And children's other identities—gender, citizenship, religion, class, language, and sexuality—also make them vulnerable to the spirit murdering endemic in many schools.

Love describes how, as a freshman basketball player in college, she was labeled an "inner-city kid" and placed on the jock track (less academically rigorous for athletes). She looked around at her classes and noticed they were full of men's basketball team members. These students took semester-long courses like Indoor Recreation, Outdoor Recreation, and First Aid, while the other women's basketball players took regular general education classes in subjects like biology. When Love confronted the staff in the advising office about her schedule, they explained that because she went to an inner-city school and was an inner-city kid, this was her placement.

"And at that moment, I was so pissed off," Love said. "I'm 19 years old. I've done everything they told me to do to be successful. I've done my best. I've got good grades. I got a basketball scholarship. And here I am without the ability to decide what I want to be in life after everything that I've done to get here . . . And I was pissed off because it wasn't just one person telling me I couldn't be what I wanted to be. It was a structure in place. And nobody would let me around. Nobody would see that I was more than that. Nobody could see that I was more than an athlete."

Love transferred to a school where she would be seen and treated like a student-athlete with an open future. What if we all found ways to advocate for open futures? But not only that. What if we opened them up ourselves in the way we acknowledge the preciousness and potential of every single child we encounter: "I see you," is what educator and author Joy DeGruy urges us to say. I see *you*, not a distorted, deficient, stereotypical idea designed to control you.

Ours is an apartheid-like system in the United States, organizing children and their opportunities by race and class. Major cities segregate children across schools, and most districts segregate students using class tracking (honors, regular, and remedial classes in which students are classified by ability). In many places, there is even a glaring rhetorical distinction between the *education* of white and Asian American students from middle class backgrounds (whether in public or private schools) and the so-called *schooling* of everyone else.

Majority-white school districts receive $23 billion more in funding than school districts that serve students of color because they draw much more revenue from local property taxes due to historical redlining practices. Twenty-three *billion* dollars! In New Jersey, where I live, that translates to about $3,400 more per white student on average, and the gap is dramatically wider when comparing the richest and poorest schools. State educational budgets, which are supposed to fill in the gap between rich and poor districts, are not meeting this obligation. In places like Arizona, which allows parents to send their children to schools outside their home district, and where the schools receive state funding based on how many students are enrolled, "white flight" is depleting resources even further. As a teacher in Chicago's Bronzeville neighborhood told sociologist Eve L. Ewing, "People will take everything you have, then blame you for having nothing."

Schools should be incubators for growing empathy and solidarity. According to Boggs: "Children need to be given a sense of the 'unique capacity of human beings to shape and create reality in accordance with conscious purposes and plans.'" But, of course, the last thing those who seek to maintain their power and control over society really want is for every single person to have a genuine say in shaping reality. Thus, schools are places where future generations either come alive with possibility or are crushed by the weight of odds stacked against them. And in most places, these two processes coexist: children live in parallel realities where a handful are made to feel exceptional in specialized programs that awaken their potential, while everyone else is are anasthetized and taught to follow directions *or else*. These alternate universes can even reside within the same building.

School curricula, in turn, helps to justify the racial hierarchies found in school tracking. Our educational system is a propaganda machine for producing a whitewashed version of history. Chinua Achebe, the great Nigerian novelist and essayist, said in a 1994 interview with the *Paris Review*, "There is that great proverb—that until the lions have their own historians, the history of the hunt will always glorify the hunter." So it is with white lies masquerading as standard curricula that restrict the teaching of ethnic studies and critical race studies—distancing students from their history, from one another, from their potential to flourish in the world.

As writer Liz Dwyer reminds us, although people often think of "censorship in say, Nazi Germany or in the Taliban-ruled Afghanistan, let's not forget that in our modern American democracy, school districts across the country still try to keep kids away from texts they feel are too controversial." Listening in on white school board members decrying ethnic studies in Tucson, and considering the higher rates of graduation and college admission for Latinx students that resulted from the now-defunct Mexican American Studies program, one senses that the fight isn't just about curricula. The parents of many of the LatinX students excelling in their classes work for white-owned businesses and white families as "the help"—cleaning their homes, taking care of their children, landscaping their property. Latinx excellence, like Black excellence, upsets the social order.

But even more fundamentally, adults who advocate for a white-washed version of history are engaged in a kind of theft—intellectual and spiritual—robbing the next generation of an essential understanding of how we got here, how it could have been otherwise, and how they can be protagonists of a different kind of future that does not repeat the failures of the past.

Consider the 1921 brutal aerial bombing, killing, and looting that took place in the Tulsa, Oklahoma, neighborhood of Greenwood. A thirty-five-block thriving, prosperous community of ten thousand, Greenwood was so financially well-off, it was dubbed the "Black Wall Street" by Booker T. Washington. And then white resentment and mob violence showed up. In less than twenty-four hours, the entire structure of a city was transformed, not only traumatizing those who survived but also destroying the hard-won economic prosperity Black families had built up over generations and displacing the numerous Black people who lived and worked there.

Even today, we can witness the regular eruption of white rage directed at racialized groups who dare to step out of their assigned place. But we also see more people of all backgrounds willing to confront the vicious lies on which our social order is built, and they're demanding an honest curriculum. After the airing of an episode of the popular HBO series *Watchmen* that dramatized the carnage in Tulsa, social media filled with people expressing dismay that they had never heard of Black Wall Street or the race massacre of 1921. Even white residents who spent their entire lives in the city were shocked, questioning why they were not taught about the massacre in local schools.

Fortunately, it is never too late to reckon with the truth. To quote Septima Clark, pioneer of grassroots adult education programs that

propelled much of the civil rights movement, "I believe uncondi-
tionally in the ability of people to respond when they are told the
truth. We need to be taught to study rather than believe, to inquire
rather than to affirm."

Viral justice encompasses everything from how resources are
allocated, and educators are valued and trained to how curricula
are designed, students are empowered, parents are engaged, and
communities are mobilized. "We try to stimulate and enhance and
set in motion a yeasty, self-multiplying process," said Myles Horton,
founder of the Highlander Research and Education Center, formerly
the Highlander Folk School, one of the only fully integrated schools
in the 1950s and a training ground for many civil rights activists.

Stimulating a process of growth and transformation requires us
to rethink who we consider to be "educators" and where we think
education happens—not simply within the four walls of a classroom
but throughout every aspect of our lives. In addition, viral justice
requires that we reckon with the truth that our educational system
traffics in lies. Reckoning with this institutionalized hypocrisy is the
first step in incubating a better world in the minds and hearts of
young people.

Well before the COVID-19 pandemic, European colonists unleashed
smallpox on the Indigenous people of North America, demonstrating the genocidal effects of infectious disease. Intertwined with
this long history of settler colonialism and native genocide is the
transformation of human beings into property, or chattel, in law and
custom. Enslaved Africans were not simply exploited to enrich the
plantocracy—they themselves *were* the riches. Human beings were
bought and sold. They were reduced to capital, assets, goods, *things*.
They were *insured* and used as collateral, underwriting white credit.
The "New World," in short, was founded on white accumulation,
native dispossession, and forced labor, including the reproductive
labor of enslaved women whose childbearing capacity slaveowners
violently exploited to "naturally increase" the enslaved population.

Yet our textbooks tell a different story: peaceful pilgrims, Manifest Destiny, the White Man's Burden, and millions of "workers" brought from Africa to labor on agricultural plantations, as one McGraw-Hill Education textbook used in Texas in 2015 described those forced to endure the hell of slavery. The very place we go to for knowledge—school—reproduces lie after lie.

Ours is a eugenically structured society designed for the fittest to flourish and the vulnerable to die off. Ideas of fitness and chosenness provide the background buzz of our schools and workplaces, used to justify why some people rise to the top while others remain trapped in place. The open futures of some rest on the barbed-wired present of others. When people hear the word "eugenics," Nazi death camps and Hitler's dream of an Aryan nation come to mind. It's easier to imagine evil Nazi soldiers than the white-coated doctors who also managed the day-to-day evil of extermination.

In 2015 I visited Berlin and spoke to students from across Europe at a conference called "Imagining the Future of Medicine." The day after my talk, I spent some time at the Memorial to the Murdered Jews of Europe, and I decided to revisit the history of medicine in Germany, walking less than a kilometer to the Memorial and Information Centre for the Victims of the Nazi Euthanasia Programme.

Although the actual facility is no longer standing, there is an outdoor memorial of Aktion T4—an abbreviation for the Berlin address where about five hundred Germans were directly involved in the organization and operation of a campaign of involuntary mass euthanasia from 1939 to 1945. With cars buzzing by, patrons pouring out of the nearby Berliner Philharmonie concert hall, I was struck by the *banality of evil*, as Hannah Arendt put it. One of the plaques read,

> "The judiciary covered up the murder campaign. Many doctors were involved out of careerism, out of conviction or due to their blind acceptance of authority. In their view, healing and annihilation belonged together. As experts, they selected the victims, in the killing centres, they turned on the gas tap, in the psychiatric institutions, they murdered patients with drugs or let the inhabitants starve. They conducted experiments on patients or research

on the brains of the victims. Nursing staff helped the doctors with Aktion T4."

They selected, they turned on, they murdered. That's one thing I appreciate about the German approach to memorialization: no passive voice, no euphemisms. Yet revisiting this history with the sounds of children laughing in the background, rolling by on scooters as parents lie on the grass nearby enjoying the beautiful fall day, what struck me most was how mass genocide relies on the complicity of the masses.

Focusing on one evildoer overshadows the cumulative effects of many small decisions—"a bureaucracy of evil" that counts on people clocking in and out, conducting business as usual. These individuals weren't immortalized, and yet the machinations of a deadly regime wouldn't have been possible without their willingness to act or not act. In other words, *it takes a village to commit genocide*. But if eugenic world-building counts on many small actions, so too does *just* world-building.

It's easy to forget that German doctors modeled their work after that of doctors in the United States, though "forget" is the wrong word because our schools never teach this fact to us in the first place. Elite universities like Harvard, Princeton, Stanford, and Yale provided the eugenics movement with its scientific legitimacy, and leading foundations like Carnegie and Rockefeller sustained the movement materially. The Rockefeller Foundation funded the work of physician Josef Mengele before he became the "Angel of Death" at Auschwitz.

Although Nazi officials like Heinrich Krieger, who studied at the University of Arkansas from 1933 to 1934, based German legislation on U.S. race law, this deadly philosophy didn't sprout, as we might imagine, from the American South. It was not Little Rock or Birmingham, but Pasadena, California, that was the home of the Human Betterment Foundation, a leading eugenics association founded in 1928 whose board of trustees included bankers, physicians, philanthropists, justices, pastors, attorneys, university chancellors, and professors.

In short, this was *not* fringe science. Rather, eugenics was galvanized by scientific breakthroughs in heredity, which held out the possibility for "improvement" (according to racist, classist, and ableist metrics), and so it was taken up by many "progressives" of the time.

As historian of science Ayah Nuriddin documents, even some leading Black thinkers embraced eugenics as a means of racial improvement. The German eugenics program was not only inspired by U.S. anti-miscegenation and sterilization laws, but Nazi doctors pored over American scientific publications to find ideas. Hitler gushed with envy about the United States in *Mein Kampf*, and Nazis standing trial at Nuremberg quoted Supreme Court Justice Oliver Wendell Holmes in their own defense: "It is better for all the world, if instead of waiting to execute degenerate offspring for crime, or to let them starve for their imbecility, society can prevent those who are manifestly unfit from continuing their kind . . . Three generations of imbeciles are enough."

Californian eugenicists, in particular, fabricated the ideal of the blond-haired, blue-eyed master race. It's no surprise, then, that the Golden State was the epicenter of this deadly philosophy and program. In their quest for ethnic cleansing, eugenicists passed the first compulsory sterilization law in Indiana (1907), followed by the U.S. Supreme Court decision in *Buck v. Bell* (1927), which upheld a state's right to force sterilization on those deemed unfit to procreate. By the 1980s most states had repealed their laws, though it took West Virginia until 2013. Eugenicists also barred the marriage of thousands of people. They forcibly segregated thousands more in state facilities and eventually sterilized approximately seventy thousand Americans during the twentieth century, many with Spanish surnames. Data analysis has shown that in California, "Latino men were 23 percent more likely to be sterilized than non-Latino men. The difference was even greater among women, with Latinas sterilized at 59 percent higher rates than non-Latinas."

Again, all this happened in the light of day, carried out in government facilities, overseen by people with fancy titles, lauded in publications that traveled the world inspiring others—all in the name of human betterment. Eugenics, in other words, was not "pseudoscience." Calling it that is a way of distancing ourselves, obscuring how mainstream ideologies and norms, such as meritocracy and cutthroat competition, continue to perpetuate eugenic world-building practices in which only the fittest are allowed to survive.

Amid the 2020 racial justice uprisings, universities across the nation began removing the names of eugenics supporters from their buildings and honors—Caltech, the University of Southern California, Stanford, and Pomona College, among others. My alma mater, the University of California, Berkeley, disclosed that it had discovered a $2.4 million eugenics research fund, and that it had frozen its use and launched a review into how the university could have accepted such a gift in 1975. In addition to institutional reckoning, individuals have a role to play. Viral justice begins with each of us recalling and reclaiming this history and its ongoing legacy, asking ourselves the Toni Cade Bambara question again: "What are we pretending not to know today?"

After all, eugenic practices continued well past their heyday in the 1920s and '30s. Between 2006 and 2010, nearly 150 women were forcibly sterilized in California prisons. When I was an undergraduate at Spelman in the late 1990s, as part of my thesis research on the politics of childbirth, I interviewed a classmate who had delivered a baby via C-section. She recalled lying on the operating table and overhearing the doctor casually ask her mother, "So, while we have her open, should we go ahead and tie her up?" The doctor was referring to a process called tubal ligation, whereby fallopian tubes are cut, tied, or blocked so that eggs cannot pass from the ovaries to the uterus. My classmate's mother consented, and her daughter became one more casualty in a long line of Black girls and women deemed unfit and unable to make their own choices about their bodies and lives. This is an ignominious tradition that includes the experience of the famed civil rights activist Fannie Lou Hamer, who, in 1961, checked in to Sunflower County Hospital to have a uterine tumor removed, and walked out with what was called a Mississippi appendectomy—"an unwanted, unrequested and unwarranted hysterectomy routinely given to poor and unsuspecting Black women," usually postpartum, like my Spelman classmate.

In the archives of one of the most infamous facilities that carried out mass sterilization, the Pacific Colony, we find an intake form dated January 6, 1941, that recommends the sterilization of Andrea Garcia, described as *nineteen years old*, single, female, no children,

Catholic. In ableist language, her clinical history reads, "Mentally deficient girl, sex delinquent girl, unfit home." Her so-called affliction? A checked box tells us she is "feeble-minded" and includes the description "high imbecile grade" with an "I.Q. of 46."

The medical staff recommended her for sterilization, and the director of the facility approved her surgery. Garcia's file does not include the date of operation, so it is unclear whether it was ever completed. But we know "her mother sued the state of California and lost," and that "Garcia died in 2008, without having had any children." Here we witness how large-scale, horrific historical processes take shape right out in the open—under beaming fluorescent lights, amid the bureaucratic shuffling and signing of papers, in between casual office banter, and authorized by people with fancy titles—eugenic practices were carried out by individuals just doing their jobs.

Viral justice also entails redress and reparations. In 1978 ten Latinx women who underwent coercive sterilization at the University of Southern California Medical Center in the 1970s filed a lawsuit, *Madrigal v. Quilligan.* Although many of them only read and spoke Spanish, they had signed consent forms in English, which were often presented to them while in the middle of labor. This is not a story of a few villainous doctors. Rather, as Renee Tajima-Peña, the director of the film *No Más Bebés*, put it, several factors conspired to create a "perfect storm" of eugenicist action: anti-immigrant sentiment, fear that poor women were having too many babies, and anxieties about overpopulation, all of which produced a favorable "environment for abuse."

In the end, Judge Jesse Curtis sided with the doctor and hospital officials. However, the case incited greater awareness about and organizing around Chicana reproductive rights and led to critical changes to informed consent, including the inclusion of forms in multiple languages, seventy-two hours to think about the choice for patients under twenty-one years of age, and no threat of the cancellation of welfare benefits if patients decline sterilization.

Besides techniques like forced sterilization and infanticide, which would be considered negative eugenics, the eugenics movement also focused on propagating people with "good" genes through human betterment societies and other popular education initiatives. This "positive" eugenics was focused on *producing* rather than eliminating certain types of people. Like world-building projects more broadly, eugenics had to enroll the participation of individuals, families, and communities that could be counted on to internalize and perpetuate the logic of racial fitness.

In the 1910s Better Baby Contests became popular and acted as a precursor to the 1920s Fitter Families Contests, often held at county fairs as a form of popular education. They taught people how to judge themselves and others through a eugenic lens, creating rankings based on physical, mental, and moral health. While many characteristics were thought to be inherited and immutable, with nonwhites excluded completely, others could be shaped by improvements to one's habits and the environment . . . they could be influenced by the *weather*. In particular, when it came to baby betterment, the contests encouraged "better hygiene, adequate nutrition, and routine medical evaluations" alongside "good mothering strategies."

Ultimately, "human betterment" as a eugenic ideology rests on the denigration and rejection of those deemed irredeemably unfit: the racialized, the poor, and the disabled. As a worldview that still shapes social judgments, norms, and institutional practices, eugenics is alive and kicking, if not always in official state policy, certainly in the fine print of everyday life.

This must be what motivated high school students to petition the California Board of Education in 2013 to fully incorporate the history of sterilization and eugenics into the curriculum. After all, the omission of these practices in their curriculum is directly related to the persistence of eugenics in contemporary contexts. Although the students were not successful in making their case at the time, they are nevertheless an example for us to start right where we are, making the institutions in which we are most embedded the ground zero for advancing justice.

We've talked about how eugenics takes shape in schools, but it also infects hospitals, employment, and, of course, policing. And despite ongoing denigration, Black people have intrinsic value that should be reflected in all these contexts. As political philosopher

Joy James reminds us, "Black lives matter because we make them matter." A commitment to this basic principle connects the movement for Black Lives to the California students agitating within the educational system, to the plaintiffs in *Madrigal v. Quilligan*, and to *all* of us who choose to push back against eugenic worldviews that render life so cheap that deputies of the state can snatch it away in broad daylight.

Likewise, if the call to "reopen America" in the midst of the pandemic was a eugenicist siren, which relies on the idea that only the fittest deserve to survive, then the simple acts of wearing a mask, practicing social distancing, and sheltering at home *if you could* were an antieugenics commitment. But why can't we seem to bury everyday eugenics once and for all?

It is tempting to tell a story of the Great COVID Pandemic going back just a few years, in which the U.S. federal government made a series of monstrous decisions, from disbanding the pandemic response team in 2018 to slowly and ineffectively adopting public health measures. But the story goes back centuries, rooting our deeply stratified social order in genocide, slavery, and exploitation, and the way that Indigenous, Black, Asian, Latinx lives have long been rendered disposable in countless ways.

As with weathering, structural violence and preventable harms are often carried out by "legitimate institutions" and meted out while people perform routine activities. The question for us is, what job are *we* doing? Are we uprooting what ails us, seeding what helps us thrive? Are we creating a different historical trajectory in the fine print of our lives, promoting rather than violently restricting people's ability to flourish?

A few years into my job as an assistant professor at Princeton, I was asked to join a Princeton Preview faculty panel for admitted students and their parents. It was a crisp April day, and as I walked over to the Richardson Auditorium, I saw excited families pouring into Alexander Hall—the most iconic building at the heart of campus. Built in 1894 in the High Victorian Gothic style, its acoustics have been compared to those at Carnegie Hall, and on that day, every whisper and shuffle could be heard as parents and prospective students found their seats. A steep gabled roof loomed over us, and against the back wall of the stage, where the panelists sat, an elaborate mosaic showed scenes from Homer's *Iliad* and *Odyssey*. It was a space that somehow oozed majesty and whimsy at once.

So it must have taken many by surprise when my fellow panelist, sociologist Miguel Centeno, burst the bubble of distinction in which we were all floating when he remarked, "Yes, you are worthy. But you are also very lucky."

Lucky. Not a word one hears often enough in elite spaces. Being lucky doesn't mean you are not qualified. It just means many others could have been in your shoes but they were not chosen, and there are many more besides who might have qualified if given the same opportunities. Luckiness does not negate worthiness. It negates entitlement. Luck is the kryptonite of elitist delusions of specialness. And even then, the language of luck doesn't do justice to the sheer organization of selectivity—a key dimension of elite spaces—as a process.

For example, in reflecting on his experience at an elite boarding school, sociologist Shamus Khan recalls, "When less than a stellar student in middle school, tutors were hired. When wits weren't enough, I could fall back on my comfort within elite institutions—comfort purchased through a pricey education. These processes are more often than not obscured; elites, in embodying their costly experiences, simply seem to have what it takes." Khan went on to study his elite alma mater, St. Paul's School in Concord, New Hampshire, for the dissertation that would become his first book, *Privilege*: "If we think of other ethnographic studies of schools—and for many, their experience of school—the presence of rules, constraints, and punishments is paramount. These things, however, are almost completely absent from our story of St. Paul's. On campus, the world is present as a kind of blank canvas, ready for students to seize. Thinking of the world as a space of possibility is consistent with a meritocratic frame: the world is yours; all that is required is hard work and talent."

The illusion of self-made success, where everything is doable and constraints are largely absent, is only possible because the world has been cleared of obstacles in advance. This prior clearing allows the myth of meritocracy to thrive. It also allows students to have their learning associated with a sense of freedom—to think, question, and dream, as well as to physically move and claim space that is theirs. *Meanwhile, in a parallel universe* . . . If schools that cater to the privileged clear a path for young people to "be all they can be," what happens in the rest?

Many students are forced to navigate schools laid with booby traps designed to catch and contain them for small infractions of the rules. In *Progressive Dystopia*, anthropologist Savannah Shange illustrates how a school can uphold antiracist values while also administering racist disciplinary practices. The hallways of Robeson Justice Academy in San Francisco are decorated with images of Black artists and intellectuals like Audre Lorde and Frantz Fanon. Yet the school, which was born of the multiracial struggle in San Francisco, has the city's highest rates of suspension for Black students.

Zero-tolerance policies popularized under the Reagan administration to curb drugs and gun violence in schools also mandate predetermined and often severe consequences for minor infractions of school rules, such as talking back to teachers or wearing a uniform incorrectly. The consequences for Black and Latinx students are especially devastating: "When you deny kids learning time they fall behind academically because they're not in school," said Pedro A. Noguera, dean of the University of Southern California's Rossier School of Education. "Many times there's no provision to make up work you missed because you were in trouble. But, secondly, the longer you've been put out the more discouraged you become."

According to researchers Dorothy Hines and Jennifer Wilmot, Black girls, in particular, are "chastised and criminalized for meritless infractions including having 'too much attitude,' chewing gum too loudly, and talking 'unladylike.'" For every 20 Black girls in school, 2 will be suspended, compared with 1 out of every 167 white female students.

In 2014 the federal government warned that school districts that continue to suspend students of color at a higher rate than white students risked federal civil rights action. And in 2015 Randi Weingarten, the president of the American Federation of Teachers, the union representing public school teachers from kindergarten to high school and college, finally admitted that zero-tolerance policies were a failure both in terms of their stated intention to make schools safer and because they perpetuated racial inequities.

At a time when some people think the way to end school shootings is to arm educators, perhaps there are other ways to aid young people who are lashing out in distress. I'm reminded of the example of Keanon Lowe, the former football coach at Parkrose High School in Portland, Oregon. In 2019 Lowe disarmed a suicidal student, after which the student stood sobbing in the coach's arms. It's an example of extreme courage—I'm not sure what I would do if faced with a student with a gun—but Lowe's actions provide a powerful example of what can happen when our young people encounter adults who are calm and loving.

Some schools are taking it a step further, not only relying on the composure and care of individual adults but also adopting policies that express those qualities. They are replacing an impatient and callous zero-tolerance approach with *restorative practices*—rather than removing students from the classroom, schools work with students to address the harm done. This might involve holding conferences with students, parents, and teachers, or asking students to sit with a group of their peers to address any harm they have caused. It may involve bringing in educators like Calvin Terrell, whose work as a nationally sought-after mediator was instigated when he lost three people close to him to racist and gendered violence.

Based in Phoenix, Terrell is called into schools all over the country after police or gang shootings, suicides, student protests, or any kind of "blow up." Once on campus, he works one-on-one, in small groups, and with the entire school community to de-escalate, facilitate honest communication, and foster long-term healing in ways that, in his words, "do not 'sugarcoat' or 'pacify' the situation." With an understanding that what happens in schools is connected to what is happening in the larger environment, Terrell's team also "sets up in parking lots, backyards, gyms, parks, or any space available to build and better community." In all these venues he is guided by the Indigenous Nahuatl phrase "In Lak Ech," or "You are my other me"—what he calls "a healing tool for evolving relations."

This approach aims to strengthen relationships, rather than fracturing them as disciplinary practices do. "The aim is to reach a resolution at the end . . . restoring a trust, addressing a harm, making amends," said Thalia Gonzalez, a professor at Occidental College who studies restorative practices in schools. In many instances, viral justice is not about "restoring" but *creating* trusting relationships in the first place. It involves redefining how our relationships are structured and operate, so they express ethical mutuality rather than competition, zero-sum logics, and abuse of power.

A few years after the Princeton Preview faculty panel, in early 2020, I found myself addressing a warehouse full of employees at Virgin Orbit in Long Beach, California. Founded by billionaire Richard Branson, the company builds and operates small satellites for commercial and government use. I'd been invited to speak about the relationship between inequity and the kind of innovation they were up to under that roof. During the Q&A, someone sitting about ten rows from the stage asked how the STEM pipeline could best attract people from underrepresented groups. The question has started to irk me over the years. *It's not rocket science*, I thought, looking across the giant warehouse where literal rockets were being built.

"Attract" assumes Black, Latinx, and Indigenous students are not already attracted and ignores how, at every turn, they are undermined, underestimated, underresourced, and pushed out of STEM fields. "Attract" reinforces "the myth of Black disingenuity," to borrow a phrase from historian Bruce Sinclair, as if Black people have not been among the more prolific innovators, of everything from traffic lights to caller ID, despite the many obstacles in their way. The challenge is not how to attract underrepresented groups to STEM but how to stop repelling them! Alas, this dynamic of repulsion starts very early in a person's life.

In *Inequality in the Promised Land: Race, Resources, and Suburban Schooling*, sociologist R. L'Heureux Lewis-McCoy moves beyond the commonplace focus on an "achievement gap" between suburban and urban schools and instead zooms in on the often-overlooked racial inequities that persist *within* suburban school districts. How is it that even in resource-rich school districts, which many families consider to be the "promised land" of educational excellence, nonwhite families continue to be marginalized and underserved by administrators, teachers, and social networks?

With an in-depth qualitative approach to the question, Lewis-McCoy analyzes interactions in classrooms, schools, and communities to show how the educational goals of Black students and families are systematically undermined in ways that are not captured by macro-level analyses. He gives us a close-up look at how white families engage in *opportunity hoarding*—pressuring the school to change their children's teachers or move them into more desirable classes—even as they advocate for colorblind policies that ignore inequities. Lewis-McCoy explains, "The district's decision to listen to a vocal minority of affluent white residents shaped the policies that were prescribed and ultimately implemented, thus allowing the white families to hoard the best education-related resources."

The issue is not just that students are repelled from fields like STEM, but that they are repelled from school, *period*. In 2014 civil rights groups in my current state of New Jersey filed a complaint with the U.S. Department of Education charging the South Orange–Maplewood School District with racial segregation. The complaint noted that the district's disciplinary and tracking practices (i.e., assigning students to different class levels based on standardized tests and other metrics) disproportionately confined "students of color to lower-level classes" and also punished "students of color and students with disabilities to a greater degree." While white students formed less than 50 percent of the student body, they were over 70 percent of those enrolled in advanced-level courses. Meanwhile, over 70 percent of students in lower-level classes were Black.

Sociologist Whitney Pirtle explains how school tracking creates "schools within a school." In district after district, a disproportionately small number of the students in gifted and talented programs are Black—5.5 percent in Sacramento, California, where they made up over 16.3 percent of eligible students in the 2010–11 school year; and 3 percent that same school year in San Diego, a district that's 8 percent Black overall. On the other end of the tracking hierarchy, Black students are overwhelmingly relegated to remedial classes. As a highly educated Black parent, Pirtle could no doubt have had her son take the gifted and talented test so he might be assigned to a higher track of learning. Instead, she used her social capital to advocate for changes that affected *all* students. She did this by serving on school and district committees, discussing school assessment measures and budgets with teachers and administrators, and volunteering in her son's classroom. This is viral justice at work. Yes, Pirtle's relative job security and flexibility as a tenure-track college professor allowed her the time to do this. But she could just as well have chosen to do what so many others do by pouring her energies into making sure her son had an advantage over others.

It goes beyond the question of how to save one individual from discrimination and pushes instead for a reorganized system. Yet the accumulation of individual actions also matters. As award-winning journalist Nikole Hannah-Jones attested, after wrestling with the decision to enroll her daughter, Najya, in one of Brooklyn's highly segregated public schools or opt for private school, "One family, or even a few families, cannot transform a segregated school, but if none of us were willing to go into them, nothing would change."

When, in 2018, the New York City Department of Education proposed a pilot plan to desegregate some of the whitest campuses by reserving a quarter of the seats in sixteen middle schools for students with low scores on math and English exams, vocal white parents vehemently opposed it. Although nearly all principals and parents supported the plan, an angry confrontation at one Upper West Side school's parent meeting made headlines.

"I think there's a norm in white America right now to be really fixated on what you're losing, without questioning your own privilege to begin with, and I say that as a white woman," said Amy Wells, professor of sociology and education at Columbia Teachers College. "But then I think we cover it in the media in a very superficial way, that fuels this anger and frustration and doesn't really get to the core of the problem, which is that test scores are really not the best way to measure kids' ability and intelligence to begin with, and they're highly correlated with race and class." Do these parents not realize that their children will live less angst-filled lives in a society where test scores are not weighted so heavily? Or, do they believe suffering is the price we must all pay for success? What if they realized that antieugenics policies and practices can ultimately help white families breathe easier too?

Fortunately, there has been a growing movement to rid our education system of the stranglehold placed on it by the multibillion-dollar standardized testing industry, which opponents remind us has its origins in the eugenics movement. The racial justice reckoning during the pandemic accelerated that shift, with three-fourths of U.S. colleges suspending testing for fall 2021 admission and more than 60 percent of undergraduate institutions in the United States making tests optional for fall 2022. More heartening still, the University of California Board of Regents announced they were eliminating SAT and ACT scores for good. Though tracking may prove harder to upend, a detracking movement is also gaining momentum. The spread of viral justice in education has also shown us that eliminating what we don't need—testing and tracking—must go hand in hand with growing what we do.

In one of the most notable responses to the 2020 protests, the Los Angeles Unified School District decided to cut the police budget by $25 million and invest $36.5 million in a Black Student Achievement Plan. By December 2021 the district was already noticing the effects—lower suspension rates, higher proficiency levels in English and math, and more students taking college preparatory courses. Besides that, two other things struck me about the preliminary reports. The first was that the district had deliberately worked to implement a plan that was "fun," so that students would "want to come, they'll want to participate, they'll want to go to class, they'll engage in class." Again, not rocket science when we think back to our own childhood memories of when we actually enjoyed learning, when suffering wasn't the price to pay for success.

The other thing about the Black Student Achievement Plan, which I found baffling, was that, according to Los Angeles Unified School District senior director Jared DuPress, "this is the first time, historically, where we've actually allocated funds in a targeted manner to support the achievement of Black students in a concentrated manner across the district to really address those historic gaps in a really concerted effort." *The first time* . . . in 2021 . . . that funds were specifically allocated to support Black student achievement?

This is why, when people trot out racist tropes about cultural or genetic differences to explain the "racial achievement gap," exclaiming that "we've already tried investing in other solutions that don't work," I wonder *what parallel universe they live in* where targeted investment in Black students has ever been a priority. Indeed, it was only after residents demanded that city officials make Black lives matter in the fine print of municipal budgets that we began to witness what has always been possible. But let's not make the mistake of imagining that one, two, or even twelve budget cycles will be enough to counteract centuries of racist divestment. We are still in the early days of laying a new foundation on which to construct a new world of possibility.

The day I completed my PhD was anticlimactic. I picked up two bound copies of my dissertation, "Culturing Consent: Bodies & Rights on the Stem Cell Frontier," from Copy Central and dropped them off at a nondescript office in Sproul Hall, the administrative center of UC Berkeley's campus. My dad was with me, as I recall. He had to write a check for something, perhaps the cost of submitting my dissertation. I handed over the manuscript and check.

In exchange for a document that contained the results of four years of courses, two years of field work, and hours of writing, and rewriting, I was handed a commemorative chocolate lollipop with the coveted "PhinisheD!" label, which I devoured while Dad and I walked over to a Thai food spot on Durant Avenue for lunch. It was a gorgeous Bay Area day, and the sun washed over us as we ate on the restaurant patio, chatting about where a carload of relatives driving up from Los Angeles and one flying in from Australia (where most of my maternal side now resides) would stay during graduation.

Afterward we headed back to my apartment in UC Village, a sprawling complex where hundreds of student families juggled school-job-kids and tried to make it all work. After you hand in a dissertation, the academic gods allow you an afternoon of rest, so I sprawled out in front of the TV before Malachi and Khalil, arrived home from school.

As I clicked through channels, I was still in a haze, not really watching what was on the screen. But then I heard the theme song from *A Different World*, "I know my parents loved me, stand behind me come what may," sung by the inimitable Aretha Franklin. There it was, the long-awaited exhale, as my favorite childhood show about the travails of students at the fictional historically Black college, Hillman, began.

The episode was none other than "Radio Free Hillman," which includes a brief cameo from my favorite character, Dean Hughes (portrayed by actor Rosalind Cash), a Black woman who strides across the screen in a fabulous tan poncho that always looked like a cape to me. She wore an African choker necklace, big brass earrings, and long locs pulled up in a bright blue hair tie to match her blouse and belt. Watching her at that moment, I had a flashback to watching the episode when I was eleven—the same year Ms. Wylie refused to see me as I eagerly waved my hand in her math class and up to that point I had had no Black teachers. There, right in front of me, was not only a Black teacher but a *dean*. Then, like now, I was not sure what a dean actually does, but it took less than a minute of

seeing Dean Hughes on the screen—her style and mannerisms giving absolutely no f*cks while beaming boo koos of Black love—for
me to decide, "Someday I will be Dean Hughes." And then I went
on my merry way.

Funnily enough, in "Radio Free Hillman," the drama revolves
around charismatic and quirky student Dwayne Wayne's radio program called *The Time Machine*. It felt like a bit of poetry, then,
stumbling upon the earliest inspiration for my academic pursuits
on the very day of their completion. Dean Hughes strutted through
a time machine to give me a glimpse of a future that, until then, I
didn't know could exist. And although she was a relatively minor
character, she had an outsize impact on my life. Of course, if it
had not been for a long list of nonfictional people who invested in
me over the years, it is doubtful that the seed planted by the Dean
Hughes character could have borne fruit. But it is also true that
the *particular* fruit borne by my academic pursuits came from that
fleeting encounter with an eccentric and powerful Black woman
who planted herself in my imagination and stayed there for nearly
twenty years.

Winnie the Pooh was right: "Sometimes the smallest things take
up the most room in your heart." This is why I am a proponent of
seemingly small investments in the world, viral justice, because it
is the quality, not the quantity or size, of each contribution that
matters. This is the inspiration that Rosalind Cash offered me by
playing the role of Dean Hughes. In an interview with Pearl Sharp
in 1981 for BET's *Lead In* series, Cash noted that one of the reasons
we didn't see her name in the credits of that many TV and film productions is that she was very selective about the kinds of stories and
characters she was willing to depict: "I've always felt a responsibility
in doing film. That's why you might not see me a lot. There's a lot of
film I won't do. But whenever I'm doing a film, I'm trying to show
that power that we have."

Cash's choice to stand in her power and not lend her talents to
degrading portrayals of Blackness has rippled across my life, com-
pelling me also to try and choose wisely with an eye to quality over
quantity or popularity.

"That's the *whitest* word I've ever heard!" exclaimed a white class-mate after my older son, Malachi, used the word "heinous" in conversation as they sat together during a club meeting at Princeton High School. Every parent of a Black child is ready for the day their child is called the N-word or some other racial slur. But I had apparently been bracing for the wrong insult in 2017, in the liberal-ish town of Princeton, where white teens may fetishize Black pop culture but still expect little of actual Black people. A heinous mix of desire and disdain, so it seemed.

"Heinous," from the Old French *hainos*, means "inconvenient, awkward, hateful, unpleasant; odious." Perhaps it *is* the whitest word, if by that we mean to describe the inconvenient, awkward, hateful, unpleasant, and odious ways in which whiteness saturates our media landscape and infects our educational system, training people to see one another through the distorted lens of racism.

But if "heinous" is the whitest word, what is the *Blackest*? Or rather, is it possible to see one another beyond the color-coded lingua of white supremacy, and through the lens of justice and mutuality? I know it feels impossible at times, but look again . . .

One of the most pervasive lies in popular culture is that African American culture is hostile toward education. From the pages of the *New York Times*, to the speeches of Barack Obama, to the dozens of articles, books, and pundits pedaling this falsehood, we are repeatedly confronted with the idea that "low-achieving" Black students are to blame for ridiculing their "high-achieving" counterparts for "acting white."

If only Black folks could overcome their lack of educational ambition, their "oppositional cultural frame of reference"—a term articulated in 1986 by anthropologists Signithia Fordham and John Ogbu—then surely, we would join the ranks of other model minorities. While this denigration of Black peer dynamics often refers back to Fordham's two-year study of a Washington, DC, high school in the 1980s, it distorts the original account in several ways.

First and foremost, the popular uptake fails to place front and center the white institutional norms and practices that demand adherence if students have any chance of reaping the "economic and social rewards of academic success." Even in my initial draft of this section, I mistakenly referred to the popularized idea of "acting white," rather than what Fordham emphasizes as the "*burden* of acting white"—the original concept—with attention to *who* and *what* in the dominant culture produces the burden. For Fordham, high- and low-achieving Black students are all trying to navigate an oppressive environment as best they can: "Some resisted by refusing to comply with assignments, whereas others resisted by defying their teachers' low expectations and becoming academically successful."

The next time you hear anything approximating, "These kids just want to sit there and do nothing," and "These kids today don't want anything out of life," which are just two of the comments that led sociologist Angel Harris to write *Kids Don't Want to Fail*, I urge you to challenge this deficit language by pointing to all the land mines that might make *sitting there and doing nothing* a perfectly rational strategy for survival.

Having limbs is not the problem, but the many explosives planted in the minefield of curricula, neighborhoods, and more *are*. But even more vital, we can point to all the ways that Black youths, perceiving the landmines as they do, nevertheless conjure ways to fly. As sociologist Carla Shedd reminds us in *Unequal City: Race, Schools, and Perceptions of Injustice*, "Youth are highly attuned to the distribution of opportunity and the presence of social inequality." She quotes a teenager from a Chicago public school who, for the first time, sees what her suburban counterparts have at their disposal—"I feel like I've been cheated," she says. And one need only spend five minutes on TikTok to witness all the critical and creative ways Black youths refute "imperialist white supremacist capitalist patriarchy," as bell hooks described it, and how they channel their righteous anger by distilling complex histories and experiences of oppression into digestible clips, schooling their peers with science and satire, often causing viewers to LOL at the absurdity of the otherwise soul-sucking status quo.

A few years before the "heinous" incident, the principal of the local middle school in my town called me in to discuss an issue. I had been working with a local racial justice organization, Not in Our Town Princeton, to offer a community education series at the public library when one of the middle school teachers found writing scrawled on the wall of the girls' bathroom: *Welcome to America, where abortion is seen as murder, but a police officer killing a black kid isn't.* This was right after the murder of Michael Brown in Ferguson, Missouri, and like in the vast majority of schools, students did not have an outlet through which to process their anger, confusion, and grief.

I would later learn through the grapevine that the bathroom graffiti was written by a white student—a friend of my son's as it turned out—who had pierced through the color-coded hypocrisy of white supremacy with her bright pink marker. Her small act of defiance got the attention of school administrators and teachers, and along with other student agitators, she helped create outlets—other than the bathroom walls—for students to express their frustrations and organize against the racist status quo.

At Princeton High School, students pushed for the Racial Literacy and Justice course that has been cotaught for several years by two phenomenal educators: Dr. Joy Barnes-Johnson, who also taught earth science, chemistry, and STEM in the Twenty-First Century and was one of the only Black educators in the building; and Ms. Patricia Manhart, who taught high school history to both my sons and who embodied that John Brown—*your fight is my fight*—spirit and swagger. With both, I felt an instant kinship. In every interaction the subtext is always *I see you.* For Black parents, school is a battleground where we expect to go to war for our children. So in the rare instances when we can trust the adults in the building to care for their minds *and* hearts, there is no greater relief.

As she observed pandemic pods take shape, Clara Totenberg Green, a social and emotional learning specialist who works at a public school in the heart of Atlanta, grew concerned because, as she describes it, her school is "bordered by half-a-million-dollar homes on one side, and low-income apartments on the other, where a large portion of our Black students live." Although Green's school is diverse, it is not integrated, and Green found that white families continue to socialize primarily with one another. Moreover, their children are overrepresented in the gifted and talented track, and the parents dominate school committees.

Given that 75 percent of white Americans report "entirely white social networks, without any minority presence," Green predicted learning pods would reflect the existing racial segregation of people's lives. Not to mention, given the higher rate of COVID-19 exposure and infection among Black and Latinx families because of work and housing conditions, affluent white families had a public health rationale for keeping "higher-risk" children out of their pods. So what was an alternative to the pandemic pods?

Green wrote that she wants parents to "understand that every choice they make in their child's education, even the seemingly benign ones, have the potential to perpetuate racial inequities rooted in white supremacy." *Sound familiar?* Every choice is a potential poison or balm. "The history of public schooling in this country," she reminded us, "is one in which white parents have repeatedly abandoned public schools, or resisted integration efforts at every turn. As a result, schools are more segregated today than during the late 1960s."

You read that right. Schools are *more* segregated today than during the late 1960s. Racial progress is a story we comfort ourselves with, which obscures how racism shapeshifts. The Whites Only school sign comes down and the gifted and talented program goes up. *Brown v. Board of Education* formally desegregates public schools and "school choice" becomes the rallying cry, as families demand the freedom to opt out of their neighborhood school for more desirable alternatives. Segregation by other means.

As Green put it, "We can either take this moment to continue that pattern [of white flight] by retreating into the comfort of our own advantages, or we can act to dismantle racist educational policies, fight for equitable distribution of school funding and build authentic community with one another. Now is the time to reimagine our beliefs, our lives and what we're willing to do to create a future that works for all children."

This is what one Maryland school district did when it created "equity hubs," learning pods that catered to low-income families across forty-five schools during the COVID-19 pandemic. There are over two hundred thousand Black households without internet access in Maryland, representing 40 percent of all those without broadband service in the state. In this program, however, parents enrolled their children at local schools for supervised online learning and socially distanced interaction. The cost? No more than $50 a month (compared with the typical $1,300 a month per child for childcare). "This is an effort for equity for people who can't afford to hire a teacher or do the things that other parts of the county can do," noted Byron Johns, one of the advocates for the program.

Like pandemic pods, equity hubs simulated the experience of school while adhering to public health guidelines. But unlike in pods, the average income of families enrolled in equity hubs was under $30,000, with over one thousand families participating so far. Funding for equity hubs came from public and private sources, including a $3.6 million grant from the county government and school district. The aim was to tackle some of the difficulties that arose following the abrupt shift to remote learning during the pandemic—especially among children who were being cared for by grandparents who might not be able to assist with their laptops and Zoom sessions.

As Johns put it, "We're spending all of this money on virtual learning, and it does not work without the right kind of support structure for kids. For all the good-faith efforts that have been made for virtual classrooms, it doesn't work without support for vulnerable families." Technology, in short, can exacerbate inequities if the corresponding social infrastructure is not in place. But by centering the experiences of those who are too often ignored by those in charge, each and every one of us can contribute to building more supportive environments, even if we are not parents, so that every community becomes a hub of equity.

Dr. Barnes-Johnson and Ms. Manhart teach like their lives depend on it, planting seeds of love and solidarity in the way they show up every day. When I think of viral justice and power—the small and concerted decisions we each must make about how to move in the world, how to treat people and embed our values in our work and relationships—I think of them. And although the district was generally supportive, there is still a long way to go before Princeton public schools foster racial literacy and justice for all students. Whatever happens next will happen because students, staff, teachers, and parents decided to put in the work. The labor of spreading viral justice must be shared, not placed squarely on the shoulders of a few people.

More than likely, it will be students who lead the way. It was current and former PHS students—my neighbors Valeria and Kyara Torres-Olivares and mentees Priya Vulchi and Winona Guo—who organized their friends to shut down the main streets in town for a mass rally following the murders of Ahmaud Arbery, Breonna Taylor, and George Floyd. They expected five hundred people to join them and arrived early to mark the sidewalks with chalk to allow for social distancing. But over one thousand residents showed up at the intersection of Nassau and Witherspoon Streets, standing shoulder to shoulder with masks on and fists pumped. They chanted "Black lives matter" and "Defund the police," even as Princeton officers walked through the mostly white crowd with head-to-toe riot gear on, eliciting "boos." At least on that particular day, it didn't feel as if we were in the same America that turns away from the killing of a Black kid.

But what happens when racism and educational inequity meet a global pandemic? "The Latest in School Segregation: Private Pandemic 'Pods,'" announced a July 2020 headline in the *New York Times*. As it became clear that schools would not reopen that fall, people grew increasingly attracted to the idea of gathering small groups of students in different families' homes for their school's online instruction. Parents with means hired private teachers to oversee their children's learning, and they themselves rotated to help supervise.

In the end, education is not just about what happens inside the four walls of a classroom but rather about how that classroom engages the world, and about all the ways that our surroundings school us. As my own adolescent anger against injustice was being kindled in the late 1980s and 1990s, I found refuge in the boom bap of '90s hip hop: Poor Righteous Teachers' *Holy Intellect*; Brand Nubian's *All for One*; X Clan's *To the East, Blackwards*; Boogie Down Productions' *Edutainment*; Public Enemy's *Fear of a Black Planet*; Queen Latifah's *Black Reign*; De La Soul's *Stakes Is High*—these were my after-school tutors for all things related to Black power and creativity.

My first lessons came in the form of cassette tapes, but when I discovered *Yo! MTV Raps* (a weekend TV program showcasing the latest rap videos), I graduated to the next level. Not only was I memorizing lyrics, but I was also taking mental notes on hip hop aesthetics. Throughout middle school, I rocked colorful sweaters, oversized t-shirts, dungarees or acid wash jeans, black and white shell-toe Adidas, hoop earrings, and the requisite African medallion around my neck, mirroring many of the artists who were tutoring me via the TV screen. For every textbook that omitted Black contributions to history, math, science, and literature, there was a hip hop anthem correcting the script. And for every classroom with yet another white teacher at the front, I could find a music video for examples of intelligence and creativity that looked like me.

When the antiviolence anthem "Self-Destruction" dropped in 1988, with verses from a veritable Who's Who of conscious rap royalty, I took on the persona of MC Lyte, changing the lyrics to "MC White's on the microphone." Reciting the words of a gifted lyricist was an essential part of my education, and a precursor for finding my own words later. Nineties hip hop schooled me in a way that school never could. History, sociology, antiracism, art appreciation, and abolitionist lessons to a thumping beat. But by the time I hit seventh grade, I was ready for more.

I noticed that a number of artists included the letter *X* in their names, like Malcolm X: Sadat X, Mia X, X Clan. On the cover of the album *By All Means Necessary* (a riff on Malcolm X's refrain "by any means necessary"), the rapper KRS-One posed in the same iconic position as Malcolm, holding up a gun and looking out a window. Then the music video for "Self-Destruction" started with Malcolm's voice, a sampling of one of his speeches: "We all agreed tonight, all of the speakers have agreed, that America has a very serious problem." With echoes of Malcolm in so many of the songs I was listening to, at twelve years old I got ahold of a copy of *The Autobiography of Malcolm X*.

By the time I started reading the book, I had already heard Malcolm's fiery voice and was enamored by his love for Black people. But I quickly realized that it was a hard-won, *militant* type of love, if only because the world had wanted so badly for him to hate himself and, by extension, his people. In just the first few pages of the autobiography, Malcolm diagnoses something that had been troubling me but that I couldn't yet articulate.

"I was the lightest child in our family," he writes. "Out in the world later on, in Boston and New York, I was among the millions of Negros who were insane enough to feel that it was some kind of status symbol to be light complexioned—that one was actually fortunate to be born thus." Though I didn't know the word "colorism" yet, which describes intraracial hierarchies and discrimination based on skin tone, Malcolm's biography held a light up to a reality I saw all around me—including in the way my friend Mary became the target of bullying for her dark complexion.

Beyond ridicule from peers, the treatment of lighter-skinned Black children and youths by teachers and administrators contributes to intraracial opportunity gaps. Sociologist Margaret Hunter has shown how colorism among African American and Latinx communities affects housing, employment, criminal justice sentencing, depression, and, yes, education. In particular, lighter-skinned Black and Latinx students complete more years of schooling on average than their darker-skinned counterparts, and Hunter suggests that different mechanisms such as the "halo effect" are at play in this.

The halo effect is a propensity to allow a positive evaluation of one trait, such as physical attractiveness (due to racist beauty standards), to influence one's judgment about other attributes such as intelligence, integrity, and likability: "If the lighter-skinned students of color are more likely to be seen as the good kids in the class, then they are more likely to perform at higher levels because of strong teacher expectations. Those students may also be perceived to have fewer behavioral problems as the positive evaluation of their appearance bleeds over to the positive assessment of other characteristics." I am sure that the halo effect and related dynamics born of colorism played a significant part in how I was treated and performed academically. Not just in school but in innumerable exchanges—from strangers who stopped to offer me a compliment or encouragement as a child, to the bus drivers who let me board when I was short on change as a teen—the web of support I have felt most of my life was surely deeply interwoven with colorism. Not all Black children receive the same embrace.

I know this because of my husband Shawn's experience growing up as an impoverished kid with a single mom and six siblings in Frederiksted, St. Croix—one of the U.S. Virgin Islands. The population of St. Croix is roughly three-fourths Black, but Shawn experienced cold, callous, and unforgiving teachers; rude social workers; and hostile adults who all sound like would-be spirit murderers to me. *Not all skinfolk are kinfolk*, goes the saying, as a mix of colorism, classism, and straight-up cruelty slashes at an already tattered web. A single cut-eye, suck-teeth, or prickly tongue is all it takes sometimes.

Even now, light skin is fraudulent currency in the supposedly cerebral world of higher education, where, as in many other workplaces, attractiveness and aptitude are conflated in the way individuals are favored, evaluated, *celebrated.*

Sociologist Tressie McMillan Cottom, author of *Thick*, has written extensively about beauty, power, and Blackness. In one of the essays in *Thick*, she shares how a "senior scholar of great standing in [her] profession" told her "that being a dark black woman would prove a problem for [her] in academia."

She also surfaced this issue of colorism in response to a March 2021 Twitter thread about what folks weren't prepared for when entering academia. "I've said it before and will say it always: I was prepared for racism and sexism before academia but I was wholly unprepared for classism (and the Black academic variant of colorism). Deeply unprepared," she tweeted. "I had never had being dark matter so much to my life, in ways that I could see and touch, until I became an academic. Whew."

Even children who go to predominantly Black schools experience colorism because it operates across many different social institutions. Colorism, like racism, does not depend on the actions of overt racists to persist, nor on white people's presence and orchestration. Riffing on French sociologist Pierre Bourdieu, the most powerful systems are orchestrated without any need for a conductor.

So, then, how do we combat colorism in schools? Hiring more richly hued Black teachers and administrators, yes. But since colorism is internalized by everyone, a diverse staff won't by itself ensure that darker-skinned students thrive. Ongoing self-reflection on the ways in which colorism shapes everyday school dynamics should be a part of staff development and training because we can't change something that we don't name and discuss.

Hunter suggests that one place to start is with encouraging school leaders to apply a critical lens to already existing conversations about racism—such as asking students why so many of the leaders celebrated during Black History Month are light-skinned. Likewise, the racial equity audits that are growing more popular should pay attention to and evaluate colorism. We should be asking, Are darker-skinned students less likely to be placed in Advanced Placement courses? More likely to be formally disciplined? Less likely to be elected to student government positions? Proximity to whiteness creates intraracial hierarchies that we must confront because they dramatically shape people's lives and life chances.

In middle school, my love of '90s hip hop brought me to Malcolm, and Malcolm brought me to the Black intellectual tradition. This is why I love the work of professor of education Christopher Emdin, and his use of hip hop to teach science. Emdin cofounded the Science Genius initiative with hip hop legend GZA of the Wu-Tang Clan to introduce science curricula that utilize the power of hip hop music and culture throughout New York City. Researchers have found that program participants not only have increased attendance and test scores, but more importantly they express greater enthusiasm for science-related content.

"In my science class now, I pay more attention because I'm looking to add it to my music," said Jaiyer Millington, who was a rising senior at Brooklyn Preparatory High School at the time.

"It kind of tricks me into studying. I just passed my physics exam on accident," remarked fellow senior Peter Simms. In a spin-off program, students serve as ambassadors, collaborating with teachers on the Science Genius curriculum. And what started in New York City is now in schools in Houston, Toronto, Calgary, Jamaica, and more.

Emdin builds on the work of educational anthropologist Gloria Ladson-Billings, who inspired the shift toward *culturally sustaining pedagogy*. In her words, "Instead of asking what was wrong with African American learners, I dared to ask what was right with these students and what happened in the classrooms of teachers who seemed to experience pedagogical success with them."

Educators who, like Emdin, follow in the tradition of Ladson-Billings meet students on their cultural turf rather than forcing them to turn what they value off when they enter the classroom. They are valued as whole people—for who they are inside *and outside* school.

As Emdin writes in *For White Folks Who Teach in the Hood . . . and the Rest of Y'all Too: Reality Pedagogy and Urban Education*, "The way that a teacher teaches can be traced directly back to the way that the teacher has been taught. The time will always come when teachers must ask themselves if they will follow the mold or blaze a new trail. There are serious risks that come with this decision. It essentially boils down to whether one chooses to do damage to the system or to the student."

If spirit murder stifles, then Emdin and other educators in the #HipHopEd movement are enlivening the spirits and intellects of young people who feel seen, heard, and respected by them. In their essay "From Spirit-Murdering to Spirit-Healing: Addressing Anti-Black Aggressions and the Inhumane Discipline of Black Children," academics Dorothy Hines and Jennifer Wilmot focus on the specific racial and gendered assault on Black girls in school settings, arguing that spirit healing requires that we acknowledge the injuries that have resulted from anti-Blackness in our schools, end the disciplinary policies that deepen spirit injuries, and foster the educational imagination of Black children. This is an imagination that runs deep, despite the lie that Black folks are culturally opposed to academic achievement.

In *Cultivating Genius: An Equity Framework for Culturally and Historically Responsive Literacy*, education scholar Gholdy Muhammad reminds us that we need to root the future of education in its past. Her work shines a light on the nineteenth-century Black literary societies that provide a generative model for cultivating literacy in all schools, but especially for Black and Brown students. She develops a historically responsive literacy framework that includes identity development, skill development, intellectual development, and criticality—all of which rests on a deep appreciation for the genius that already exists in Black children. Like Emdin, Muhammad starts with the teacher: "To teach geniuses . . . charges teachers to cultivate their own genius that lies within them."

To teach genius, so to speak, also means we need to critically address that which restricts imagination, creativity, and critique, including our measures of "intelligence." For example, what if we read humor as involving intelligence instead of, as it is too often read, as unseriousness? In Tucson, Arizona, an English teacher, David Low, did just that.

Low recounted how his class, which was required to take yet another test "predicting" how well they would do, expressed their opposition: "In the test's margins, they doodled, wrote tiny editorials to the testing administrators and tried to force a dialogue." What some might see as students goofing off, Low understood as students' investment in their education by providing, through humor, critiques of the curriculum: "Taken as a whole, many of my students used humor as a deliberate act of critical thinking, imagination and social consciousness, which were exactly the qualities the predictive test was not evaluating."

While the predictive tests were eventually discontinued, Low's students took a risk in talking back through humor. Indeed, he noted, "teens are often branded as troublemakers and effectively criminalized." In this case, viral justice also required educators and school administrators to expand their imaginations. As Low concluded, "I say that humor is a radical means for reading and deconstructing the world and for writing a better, more equitable one."

Fortunately, many educators are already spearheading necessary changes, including the Free People, Free Minds community. When I attended the 2019 Free People, Free Minds conference in Minneapolis, I was introduced to the Black Lives Matter at School Movement, a national coalition started in 2016 to put forth four demands.

As you reflect on these demands, consider how you can support them by finding out the status of disciplinary policies, budgets, hiring, staff retention, and curricular development in your own schools. And for those of you outside the U.S., consider how you can intervene in the kinds of educational inequities that exist in your specific locale.

First, instead of administering suspensions, expulsions, and zero-tolerance policies, schools will invest in mediation and restorative justice processes that cultivate the "voice and vision" of students, faculty, and staff. Second, noting the rapid decline in Black educators across several locales, schools will prioritize the recruitment and retention of teachers of colors because studies show that "students excel academically when they are taught from someone in their own racial group." Third, all K–12 schools will integrate Black history and ethnic studies in the curriculum and all teachers will receive the training they need before incorporating these subjects into their curriculum. Finally, instead of having cops walk the halls, schools will invest in more counselors to address the racial trauma and everyday emotional well-being of young people.

It may be tempting to think these educational demands apply only in a U.S. context, where anti-Black racism garners the most worldwide attention. But schooling is the engine of social inequality around the globe, even in supposedly homogeneous societies. In Japan, where my husband's older sister resides, racial-ethnic minorities face every kind of discrimination imaginable—in housing, healthcare, employment, policing, *and* the educational system.

Zainichi Koreans, Burakumin, Okinawans, and the Ainu (Indigenous people), along with people of African descent and *hafu* (mixed race), face daily insults, humiliation, and hate crimes, sometimes simply for having a darker than average complexion. They are called *kitanai* (dirty), *makkuro* (black and dirty), *baikin* (microbe), *unchi* (poo), *kimo-chiwarui* (disgusting), and *kurokoge* (blackburn). But dark skin is not even a requirement of mistreatment.

Those who appear physically and ethnically indistinguishable from the dominant group but who are descendants of lower-caste Japanese like the Burakumin, or whose ancestors were colonized by Japan, like Koreans, also face nonstop forms of interpersonal and institutionalized racism. In a society where even the word "Korean" is a slur, and where racialized groups are considered intellectually inferior, it should come as no surprise that children who experience discrimination on a daily basis perform worse on aptitude tests and have high dropout rates. Compare that with the U.S., where Asian Americans are considered intellectually *superior* to their classmates, and where their performance often matches this expectation—a phenomenon termed "stereotype lift."

My point, one that I want to scream from the mountaintops, is that "intelligence" is not a genetic trait inherent to certain groups. Instead, it is socially manufactured—produced by the resources and attention one gets at home and the opportunities and "gifts" one experiences at school.

And just as Black people have founded Afrocentric schools sprinkled throughout the United States, Koreans in Japan have founded their own schools to celebrate Korean heritage and teach their language and history. But these schools, approximately sixty in all, are often denied accreditation and government subsidies (including school lunches and healthcare for students), and their students, numbering over twenty-five thousand, are ineligible for tuition assistance and, in some cases, even disqualified from admission to mainstream Japanese schools. As a report issued by the Human Rights Association for Korean Residents in Japan explains, they cannot even wear their ethnic Korean school uniforms in public places without eliciting harassment and violence.

For those like author Joel Assogba's three children, who were harassed by their peers at school for having mixed African and Japanese heritage, there is no passing or hiding. After the school principal and other parents refused to take the situation seriously, Assogba took action: "Many people look to politicians, or social activists to eliminate racism and discrimination. They certainly can make great contributions toward a just society," he explained. "But we, parents and teachers, also have a vitally important contribution to make." Plus, one can be a parent, teacher, *and* social activist, these are not mutually exclusive roles.

Assogba, who has published children's books about diversity and ostracization, encourages parents and teachers in Japan to talk openly with children about racism and discrimination—ask questions and listen to them. And to do that, adults must educate themselves. Assogba has developed antiracist curricula and workshops for teachers and parents to use throughout the country so they are better equipped to have these conversations. It makes sense that if schools are the engines of inequality, then education is also ground zero for social transformation.

Of course, Assogba is not naive enough to think that centuries of socialization and opportunity hoarding based on eugenic ideas of racial purity will change in one lifetime, much less in one workshop. But just because this is a long-term struggle does not mean we throw up our hands in resignation or defeat. When your own children's well-being is hanging in the balance, turning the other cheek is not an option.

Even those who seem to be the victors in the Academic Hunger Games are still trapped inside a world of someone else's design. Will we continue to conflate winning with freedom? Or will we build on a long tradition of people like William Luke, an Irish-born white man who moved from Ontario, Canada, in 1869 to teach at the newly built Talladega College in Alabama? The school is Alabama's oldest private historically Black college, and when Luke, who was also one of the founders, began teaching there, it was the only institution in the area willing to educate Black students.

Despite repeated warnings from the Ku Klux Klan to cease his activities, Luke refused. In 1870 he and seven Black men were lynched by the KKK for educating Black children—and, in Luke's case, for also paying Black workers the same as his white laborers. Luke's audacity is part of a broader struggle led by Black educators like Carter G. Woodson, who also emphasized that it is not just *whom* we teach but *what* we teach that distinguishes schooling from liberatory education. Historian of education Jarvis R. Givens describes the latter as "fugitive pedagogy" because the knowledge and values that Black communities have passed down over generations have, out of necessity, been transmitted in a covert manner, and yet they continue to shape Black educational practices today.

The truth is that creating learning environments that foster the potential and well-being of all children *is not rocket science*. It is much more demanding and consequential. Transformative education is a process of trial and error. As Septima Clark put it, "Don't ever think that everything went right. It didn't. Many times there were failures. But mull over those failures and work until we could get them ironed out." Viral justice requires confronting many of the foundational lies—such as the myth of meritocracy—on which our societies have been erected and laying a different foundation, brick by brick, in the hearts and minds of young people whose trust we can only begin to earn by telling the truth.

FOUR

Grind

My first real job was hostessing at the House of Blues in Myrtle Beach, South Carolina. It was one of those jobs where the eclectic, feel-good vibe was supposed to make up for the fact I was only being paid $7.25 an hour. At the time, I was living rent-free with a family friend, waiting to hear back from the one college I applied to, which means I didn't have much in the way of living expenses.

I walked to work, and, from a distance, I could see the colorful corrugated metal structure of the restaurant and bar and hear the music pouring out of the speakers surrounding the building. Warehouse chic is what they were going for. The design choices that make hipster enclaves look run-down—exposed nails, rusty panels, and crooked art frames—gave the building a distressed artsy aesthetic. It was an achievement.

As you walked to the main entrance, there was a long row of rickety rocking chairs with green cushions in front of a wall of American folk art. A painting of two Black women clad in bright yellow dresses stuffing pinkish meat through a contraption that spit out long rolls of sausage used to always catch my eye. "Those that respect the law and love sausage should watch neither being made," said Mark Twain. I'd soon learn that working in the service industry was mostly about hiding the work of sausage-making.

Donning a Janet Jackson–style headset, I looked like a backup singer in the "Control" video, strutting up and down the aisles, seating guests. If it was an evening shift, the lights on the hostess dashboard would be lit up with bright red circles showing where people had been seated. Given the seriousness with which I studied the board, making sure I'd filled all the servers' sections equally, you'd think I was steering the Starship *Enterprise*.

Some weekends I worked the World-Famous Sunday Brunch in the adjacent concert hall, setting up rows of tables and chairs where roused fans usually stood. The hall could hold over two thousand people, but only a few hundred could fit after converting the space into a restaurant on Sundays. My job was to keep the buffet looking clean and appetizing, and refill coffee and juice as gospel choirs electrified the room with foot-stomping, soul-stirring sets.

When brunch was over, and before we broke down the tables and swept the hall, I and the other servers and hosts would hurriedly fill to-go boxes of buffet leftovers—one of the only perks in all the restaurant jobs I'd have over the years. Of course, the best thing about the House of Blues gig was that I got discounted tickets for evening bands, including my favorite artist at the time, Erykah Badu, whose song "On & On" was number one that year. The free Badu concert, if nothing else, made House of Blues feel like a dream first job.

When I moved to Atlanta for college that summer, a succession of restaurant jobs followed: the cutely named Lettuce Souprise You; Café Sunflower, the fancy vegan place where Andre 3000 from the hip hop duo Outkast would get his takeout; the falafel spot whose name I wiped from my memory because the owner and I fell out after, God forbid, I requested time off for my son Malachi's first birthday.

The paltry paychecks meant I was always on the hunt for free or discounted food in whichever place had employed me. My most luxurious post in Atlanta was cashiering at Whole Foods Market, aka "whole paycheck," the health-food chain that started in Austin, Texas, in 1980 and has since become synonymous with pricey, organic groceries. At the location on Briarcliff Road, I was making

$8.25 an hour, and with the 25 percent "team member" discount, I could almost qualify as Black and Bougie. *Almost.*

Not to brag, but I was an *excellent* team member. If the number 48 bus was running on time, I'd get to work a little early and grab a coffee and two chocolate chip cookies to help me power through the shift. Because I had the PLU codes memorized, I checked out items with a swiftness: 4131 for Fuji apples, 4135 for Gala, 4069 for green cabbage, and 4554 for red, inspiring customers to switch to my aisle. And despite having already developed some introvertish tendencies, I was pretty skilled when it came to making small talk. I even learned the right amount of familiarity to show store regulars so they felt special.

Today, a cashier in an Atlanta-based Whole Foods makes between $13 and $15 an hour, according to GlassDoor. That's only $5 more than I made over twenty years ago. Meanwhile, the cost of living in Atlanta and most major cities has skyrocketed and, in 2017, Amazon bought Whole Foods for $13.7 billion in cash, reminding us exactly "where the money resides, where the money resides," to quote the internet meme popularized by car salesman Durell Smylie. But I digress. We will return to Amazon with greater fury in just a bit.

In this chapter, I will cast a critical light on labor, livelihood, and how people make ends meet in a society shaped by racial capitalism. And together, we will trace the paradox—nay, *hypocrisy*—that underlies the idea of *essential workers*, one of those prophylactic phrases that oozes from the lips of politicians and pundits as they try to conceal the many ways in which people are made disposable. Especially during the COVID-19 pandemic: essential to praise, essential to exploit, essential to gaslight. Against this rhetoric, we must insist that those who do the thankless work that keeps society afloat, those who make the sausage, are essential to care about, essential to listen to, essential to lead, essential to fucking *pay.*

When it comes to capitalism, even those who recognize its harms have a hard time imagining any other way of organizing society, and so our only option is to make capitalism more "compassionate." But wouldn't it be a good idea to start reimagining material and social values—centering both on shared prosperity and well-being, rather than private accumulation and institutionalized greed? This entails demanding concrete policies through collective action, policies like Universal Basic Income, a federal job guarantee, baby bonds, canceling student debt, a four-day workweek, paid vacation, guaranteed sick leave, and disability accommodations. It also means we must demand reparations for those whose ancestors were enslaved.

Reimagining the place of work in our lives also means understanding that *rest*, like healthy foods, clean water, and fresh air, is essential. Rest, in other words, is not an extravagance we must earn, or a getaway we must save up for. The popular call for more "self-care" is enticing, but what if our everyday lives didn't require escape? Can you imagine?

If the struggle to make ends meet is one of the principal causes of weathering, then viral justice is about creating social relations that are vivifying instead of exhausting. And, as in other contexts, viral justice means each of us doing our part to shift norms and patterns of expectation when it comes to labor, productivity, and rest.

When I moved across the country for grad school, it was the first time I wasn't paying the bills by seating customers, busing tables, ringing people up, bagging groceries, or cleaning up other people's messes. Over six years at Berkeley, I had a string of part-time gigs as a research or teaching assistant, usually two or three jobs at a time on different parts of campus working for different professors and departments. I worked these jobs on top of my fellowship that was supposed to be enough to cover my living expenses.

With two kids and a husband in school studying ancient Semitic history and languages, the fellowship stipend, about $2,000 a month (the cost of rent in family student housing), didn't cut it. On top of a full load of classes, Shawn also worked several different construction jobs off and on over the years, from wiring low-voltage cables to remodeling commercial retail spaces. Each year, our rent in family student housing increased but fellowship stipends remained the same—a pattern that mirrors the relationship between rent hikes and stagnant wages in the broader economy, and that students routinely protest, demanding a rent freeze.

At least once a semester, I'd find myself applying for yet another short-term emergency loan offered by the university for students in a bind, though it would be more apt to call it the ongoing insecurity loan. It never ceased to impress me that if I showed up to University Hall first thing in the morning and submitted the paperwork, there'd be a $1,200 check waiting for me by the end of the day. Bureaucratic efficiency at its finest. But, I wondered, does it still count as an "emergency" if the financial crisis occurred at such reliable intervals?

Still, I had no idea how little academic research labor is compensated relative to the time we spend getting credentialed, until I was trying to rent an apartment as a postdoctoral fellow in Los Angeles. When Min, my soon-to-be Pakistani landlord, looked over the rental application, he was flabbergasted that the University of California, Los Angeles, was paying someone with a PhD only $40,000 a year: "That's too little! You should really talk to them," he said. But, of course, there was no one to talk to. The academic pay scale for the University of California is set by some mysterious committee somewhere, and I had neither the heart, nor the courage, nor the time to go searching for the Wizard.

The only reason I didn't give up on grad school to pursue less precarious employment was that my mom and dad kept sewing up the holes in the tattered safety net that was keeping my young family afloat. It wasn't easy for them. It meant that in sending us funds on a regular basis, they were always behind on their own bills. But they were determined to see me through because, I imagine, they knew that what awaited me outside the ivory tower would not be much better. Plus, my mom, who had a bachelor's in chemistry, *nearly* finished a master's degree in education at the University of Massachusetts, and my dad had *almost* completed his doctoral dissertation in education at UCLA, so they were determined that I should break the pattern and get that damn degree.

Like many immigrants to this country, my Indian mother's teaching credentials and experience didn't mean much to U.S. employers. Throughout the years, she worked a string of jobs—secretary, elderly care, domestic work, and more—that had nothing to do with what she studied. There was a stretch in the early '90s when she worked at a local nursing home in Conway, South Carolina, but was quickly shocked by the conditions residents there endured. When she tried to intervene, coworkers deemed her a menace for "making them look bad," and so she left after only three weeks.

Not until we left South Carolina to live in the Marshall Islands was she able to work in education again. My mom's experience fits into a broader pattern in which "essential workers" who are Black or immigrants of color are left to perform the most degrading types of work in our society. And as a rule, it seems, our society places the least value on anything deemed to be care work. We witnessed how *carelessness* was institutionalized and amplified during the COVID-19 pandemic, when the very people holding society together were not held up in return. They were called essential workers, yes, but they were also *devalued*.

In 2020 forty million Americans lost their jobs. At the same time, the nation's billionaires saw a 10 percent *increase* in wealth—$282 billion added to their net worth (totaling $3.229 trillion) compared with 2019. Many observers have pointed to the way that, before he was murdered, George Floyd was laid off from his job and reported by a shopkeeper for spending a counterfeit twenty-dollar bill. Meanwhile, over the course of a single day in the first few months of the pandemic, the eight richest men in America saw their wealth "increase by a combined $6.2 billion, for a total of $653.8 billion." During this period, there was a wave of gig workers organizing both in solidarity with Black Lives Matter *and* to protest their own mistreatment as independent contractors at tech companies like Instacart, Amazon, Google, Uber, Lyft, and Postmates. They called attention to issues that long preceded the COVID-19 pandemic but that took on more urgent, life-and-death stakes due to the virus.

Flexibility! Freedom! Autonomy! These are some of the endless buzzwords and promises churned out by the marketing gurus employed by gig economy businesses. Dog walkers, caterers, house cleaners, babysitters—all these jobs involve discrete, short-term, or freelance tasks with no guarantee of future employment. As it has become harder to get more stable employment, in part due to the "disruption" created by tech companies, more people are entering this segment of the workforce, and even more are asking whether these jobs are really "flexible," or just precarious. Does their labor engender "freedom" or risk? Are the workers really "independent" or disposable?

For many years, into her sixties, my mom provided elderly care as part of the informal economy. Employers paid her off the books with no formal contracts, benefits, or sick leave. She had a lot of experience caring for Grandma White in her later years, and when she died, my mom started working for a close family friend, a family acquaintance, then my aunt and uncle until they, too, passed away. This was all before there was "an app for that." The devaluation of care work, in other words, existed long before tech bros came on the scene, though their designs often hide, speed up, and spread existing forms of inequity, making it harder to discern and harder still to change the oppressive status quo.

It's not just Uber and Lyft, or Airbnb for home-sharing, but a growing list of platforms that form the so-called gig economy. There is also Handy and TaskRabbit for cleaning services; Insta-cart, GrubHub, and DoorDash for grocery and food delivery; Care .com and SitterCity for child and senior care; Upwork, Fiverr, and Amazon Mechanical Turk for people to carry out short-term tasks; and Nomad Health, which matches health professionals to freelance clinical work. *Get Paid to Play, All. Summer. Long.* That's how one ad for Care.com puts it, as if work were leisure, not labor.

But despite promises to "disrupt" business as usual, these digital labor platforms are embedded in and reinforce long-standing forms of racial, gender, and class inequity. Domestic work, for example, long associated with the free and cheap labor of women, especially Black and immigrant women, continues to be undervalued and risky despite the introduction of digital tools to match workers with employers. "The management mechanisms used by care-work companies today are shaped by centuries of suspicion about the mostly Black and brown women who perform essential reproductive labor in the United States," explains University of Pennsylvania communications professor Julia Ticona. White women are the majority of nannies, which is basically a form of domestic work, but they are higher paid and usually held in higher esteem.

Not surprisingly, the bulk of ride-hailing drivers are men, the majority of domestic workers are women of color, and within these sectors, other forms of stratification come into play.

The authors of a report entitled *Beyond Disruption: How Tech Shapes Labor across Domestic Work and Ridehailing* insist that the gig economy is not a sector unto itself but is shaped by the history and inequities of different types of work. It's true, some features of these apps offer care workers an added layer of security and accountability—for example, by archiving correspondence with employers in an app's messaging function. But the adage holds: what *we* have access to has access to *us*. Platforms and other businesses employ opaque management software to surveil and scrutinize workers' every movement, communication, and productivity, creating the feeling that we are "constantly watched."

As with other forms of surveillance that now encompass large swaths of people across different races and class groups, racism underpins all worker surveillance. Ticona points to lantern laws in the eighteenth century that required Black, mixed-race, and Indigenous people to carry lanterns when they walked the streets of New York City without the company of a white person. Those laws, she said, remind us that surveillance is nothing new: "Though some of the technology used today might be novel," she said, essentially, "asking workers to make themselves visible to prove their trustworthiness is an old practice of social control."

And precisely because of their precarious status as independent contractors, it is hard to know exactly how many people are engaged in gig work: in 2017 the U.S. Bureau of Labor Statistics reported that 55 million people, or 34 percent of the American workforce, were gig workers, including 1.6 million people paid by tech platforms. Some of these people performed freelance work in addition to holding a main job. Others worked across three, four, even five platforms, piecing together a livable income by cleaning homes, delivering groceries, and driving.

Then the pandemic hit. According to one survey, 52 percent of respondents who worked in the global gig economy lost their jobs and another 26 percent had fewer hours. But the impact was uneven: the number of active Lyft riders fell by 60 percent, to 8.69 million, and the number at Uber fell by 75 percent (though Uber Eats food delivery was at an all-time high). At the same time, Instacart announced three hundred thousand new "shoppers" as more people opted not to go to the grocery store themselves. Though it was an occasional convenience before the pandemic, food and grocery delivery became essential to those who could afford it during COVID-19.

While there are important differences across these platforms—ride-hailing is considered "on-demand" work, Care.com is an example of a digital marketplace, and TaskRabbit is a hybrid of both—they all share features that tend to disempower workers. For instance, digital platforms measure workers' performance using ratings and reviews, and penalize them for low scores through "time outs" and deactivation.

Since they are not technically employees of a company, they can be terminated without recourse. Plus, they are not eligible for benefits such as health insurance or sick pay if, let's say, a global pandemic hits (Instacart, for its part, *did* offer paid leave if shoppers could show a positive COVID-19 test result, which wasn't always easy to produce in the early days of testing shortages). And during the pandemic, Instacart workers (who shop at grocery stores and deliver food to people's homes) reported that a flood of new customers were falsely reporting that their orders had missing or incorrect items, which reduces workers' ratings and makes them ineligible for larger orders, ultimately affecting how much money they make. Through the technological innovation of a rating system, deceptive customers can create a problem for the Instacart worker and play a role in determining how much they will be able to work in the future. And this is just the tip of the iceberg when it comes to the travails of gig workers. So what recourse do they have?

Well, gig workers find creative ways to share tips for navigating the often "opaque platform policies" and protocols designed to benefit companies and their clients first and foremost. Care workers use Twitter hashtags like #nannyproblems and Facebook groups, some with thousands of members, to share tips for finding jobs and navigating problems that arise with employers, as well as to commiserate. Drivers, in turn, use social media and chat apps like WhatsApp as hubs for information and community: "Ridehail drivers use forums to crowdsource intelligence on new pricing schemes, to dissect companies' policies, to commiserate over bad passengers, to compare wages and ratings, and even identify incidents of potential wage theft."

When Uber and Lyft started experimenting with a new pricing scheme in which they charged customers a higher fare than they were paying drivers, drivers learned about it by comparing screenshots of passenger receipts with their wages. A rider could pay ninety dollars, and a driver might only earn thirty dollars. Journalists learn about these issues on worker forums, and media stories about gig labor conditions help validate what workers have been experiencing by creating a "feedback loop." The authors of *Beyond Disruption* describe how many workers become "interdependent, seeking each other out to cultivate community, find information, and solve collective problems."

Such efforts by gig workers exemplify viral justice. Indeed, growing interdependence through everyday forms of connection and resource sharing is the foundation for social and political organizing that can demand legal protections for gig workers. In 2019 eleven women working for Instacart in different states, from Florida to Ohio to California, who had never met, formed the Gig Worker Collective to build power and advocate for fair pay and safe work conditions.

It grew out of a Facebook group, which now has more than fifteen thousand members, where delivery workers expressed frustration over companies' changing pricing schemes—adding customer "service fees" that did not go to shoppers, stealing tips from drivers, removing a three-dollar "quality bonus" for shoppers who earned a five-star rating, and more. In response, the Collective has organized several nationwide strikes that have garnered widespread media attention and customer support—with many deleting the app in solidarity. And although Instacart has not publicly acknowledged the group, the company offered ten thousand kits of personal protective equipment following one of the strikes demanding better COVID-19 safety measures, among other things.

Along with the higher profits that can be earned by classifying workers as independent contractors, companies also hope to manage possible resistance to poor working conditions and nefarious company practices. Under the U.S. National Labor Relations Act, employees have "the right to form or join unions; engage in protected, concerted activities to address or improve working conditions." The problem is this federal law does *not* apply to independent contractors. In California in January 2020, legislators passed AB5 (popularly known as the "gig worker bill"), making it harder for businesses to classify workers as independent contractors. This would have required companies to start paying hundreds of millions of dollars in payroll taxes and worker compensation.

Market competitors Uber, Lyft, and DoorDash joined forces to defeat the bill. Together they spent more than $200 million to overturn the law, funding a massive voter campaign in favor of a November 2020 ballot proposition, "Yes on 22," making it the most expensive ballot measure in the history of the United States.

Prop 22, in a nutshell, officially mandates the designation of ride-hailing and delivery drivers as contract workers. The companies vigilantly fought labor protections to supposedly "protect" drivers' flexibility, freedom, and autonomy. Every time drivers logged on to the app to start work, they got messages telling them to vote yes on the measure. Companies also ran ads warning that if they were forced to accept drivers as employees, their prices would go up, the number of drivers would be cut, and they might even be forced to stop doing business in California.

Meanwhile, in early 2021 the U.K. Supreme Court ruled that Uber drivers are indeed "workers" eligible for employment protections and benefits. The decision was based largely on the level of control the company exercises over drivers—setting their fare, punishing drivers when they do not comply with the terms of employment, and even prescribing what drivers can discuss with riders. Doesn't sound very "independent," does it?

As one observer put, the U.K. ruling "has the potential to upend a fundamentally exploitative business model." And it is catching on. The European Union's twenty-five member states have followed suit. They are shifting the burden of proof to companies to justify employment status, affecting an estimated 5.5 million workers who are misclassified as self-employed. These significant shifts are the direct result of widespread organizing on the part of workers, including a flurry of court cases contesting misclassification.

It remains to be seen whether the U.S. will continue perpetuating the lie that gig work is "entrepreneurship," or whether we will finally introduce a national framework like the one created by a coalition of organizations led by the National Employment Law Project, which protects platform workers' basic legal rights.

A key feature of viral justice is looking at the conditions right under our own noses so that each of us can confront exploitation and injustice in our own backyard. My backyard, of course, is academia.

Academia, it turns out, is kept afloat by gig workers—adjunct professors, contingent faculty, part-time lecturers, and contract workers—who form 75 percent of the 1.8 million faculty members in the U.S., with increasing percentages in Canada too. These are college instructors who work on short-term, temporary contracts, typically teaching many more classes than their permanently employed counterparts, but with less job security than most other college employees, such as dining hall staff and campus safety officers. My fictional heroine, Dean Hughes from *A Different World*, would be incensed to see that deans like her have job security, but adjuncts—even if they have more teaching experience than their tenured and tenure-track colleagues—do not.

The proportion of adjunct faculty has grown since the 1980s, when cuts in public funding for higher education encouraged administrators to replace expensive tenured faculty with part-time lecturers as they also invested in flashier amenities to lure students—a new athletic complex or fancy STEM building. After all, adjuncts, the majority of whom are women and people of color, cost a fraction of what those on the tenure track do—*no benefits, no sick leave, no pension*. In many places, they do not even receive an office of their own or administrative support to carry out their work. Underscoring their second-class status, at most colleges and universities, adjuncts are not invited to take part in faculty governance conversations, meaning they cannot even weigh in on the decisions colleagues and administrators make about the conditions of their employment.

If academia still carries the hierarchical legacies of the medieval world in which it was born, then contingent faculty are among its serfs: "Both the feudal state and the modern university share the basic characteristics of being hierarchies held together by power structures, flows of resources and the fealty of the lower orders to those above them," is how one observer put it. The university president is king. Boards of trustees are bishops who court the king and check his power. Deans and other top-level administrators are dukes and earls. Each department is a fiefdom overseen by a baron, or department chair: tenured faculty are the knights who help the barons keep order in their fiefdoms. The peasants are not, as one might think, the undergraduate students but rather the adjunct faculty and graduate student workers who toil day in and day out in the intellectual fields, with little power or pay. And these distinctions are further stratified by race, gender, class, sexuality, disability, first-generation, and citizenship status, among other things.

Most undergraduate students don't realize the vast gulf between precarious and, at least in theory, permanent professors until, perhaps, the shit hits the fan, and contingent faculty make their grievances public through labor strikes and other measures. I didn't really *get it* until I was a postdoc at UCLA and was offered a part-time lectureship by another department—not the one I was affiliated with for the postdoc. They needed someone to teach a new course on stem cell research ethics to students majoring in biology.

When I asked my adviser about the pros and cons of accepting the position, he cautioned that, although the short-term benefits may seem good—added teaching experience and a little more money than I was making—it could derail me from ultimately getting a tenure-track position after the postdoc. ("Tenure," by the way, is a lifetime appointment, but faculty members can be terminated for financial reasons or ethical violations. It was designed to protect academic freedom so professors could not be fired for addressing controversial issues in their work. Tenure *track* is the period usually lasting six or seven years in which newly appointed professors are working to meet their institutions' research, teaching, and service requirements for tenure.) The time I would pour into prepping a brand-new course would take away from the stuff I would be evaluated on when I hit the job market: research and publications. He'd seen people get inadvertently "trapped" in a teaching track—language that belies the devaluation of teaching by institutions supposedly dedicated to it.

Without my postdoc adviser's caution, I would have likely accepted the job—in part because after being a grad student for so damn long, it felt more "grown up" than the postdoc. Plus, there was something subversive, I felt, about teaching STEM students to think carefully and critically about their research. But I'd have plenty of time for that *after* I secured a position, was the message I received . . . *security*, that elusive coin that academia hoards and rations.

What my adviser spoke to was the divide in higher education between the prioritization and valuation of research and teaching in terms of salaries, prestige, and what get lauded as significant contributions to our disciplines. Although many tenured and tenure-track faculty are also overworked, especially women of color, who take on a much higher proportion of the "invisible labor" on which universities depend, some of us working at schools with lighter teaching loads may take for granted the "army of temps" that make this lighter load possible.

In spring 2021, the *New York Times Magazine* columnist and MacArthur Genius award recipient Nikole Hannah-Jones was denied tenure at her alma mater, the University of North Carolina–Chapel Hill, despite her record of scholarship and the strong support for her promotion by department faculty who had just recruited her for the prestigious Knight Chair in Race and Investigative Journalism. Every other Knight Chair—all the white men who had previously been named to the position—had been given tenure. Due to right-wing political backlash against the 1619 Project, a public education initiative she had created with the *New York Times* to commemorate the four hundredth anniversary of the beginning of slavery, powerful people behind the scenes were intent on obstructing her appointment.

The 1619 Project reframes American history by centering the reported arrival of the first enslaved Africans in 1619 and illuminating the innumerable contributions of Black Americans to this nation. Following criticism by conservative groups, and public statements made by Arkansas newspaper publisher Walter Hussman, the university's board of trustees overturned the faculty's decision to grant Hannah-Jones tenure. They instead offered her a five-year contract, which is the gold standard in academic gig work.

Given Hannah-Jones's prominent profile, public uproar ensued, with a stream of news articles, social media posts, and in-person protests shaming the university, rebuking the board of trustees, and bemoaning the plight of Black women faculty "to be twice as good to get half as far." Eventually, the board of trustees reversed its decision. But it was too late. Less than a week later, Hannah-Jones announced that she had accepted a position as the Inaugural Knight Chair in Race and Journalism at Howard University, a tenured position in the Cathy Hughes School of Communication, where she would create a Center for Journalism and Democracy: "I've spent my entire life proving that I belong in elite white spaces that were not built for Black people," Hannah-Jones explained to CBS News. "I decided I didn't want to do that anymore. That Black professionals should feel free, and actually perhaps an obligation, to go to our own institutions and bring our talents and resources to our own institutions and help to build them up as well."

Supporters on social media, in turn, were giddy: *Go where you are valued, not where you are tolerated!* was the refrain tweeted again and again, with the implication that at historically Black colleges and universities like Howard and my own alma mater, Spelman, faculty are, by definition, valued. But the story on the ground is not that simple.

After the social media festivities subdued, a Howard University lecturer, Imani Light, published an open letter to Hannah-Jones on Medium. In it she detailed the insecurity, indignity, and abuse experienced by a growing cadre of contingent faculty at Howard, herself included. For starters, their meager salaries—$48,000 annually—are lower than what a first-time public kindergarten teacher in Washington, DC, earns.

Notwithstanding that those kindergarten teachers deserve higher salaries, $48,000 a year is extremely low for a college faculty worker given the educational credentials and work experience held by many of them. Adding insult to injury, Howard lecturers must reapply for their positions each year, not knowing whether they will have a job the following fall; then, after seven years of teaching and service to the university, they are unceremoniously discharged, ineligible for reappointment. "Regardless of the strength of your courses, the demonstration of your dedication to the University and your students, or even the strength of your student evaluations, at the end of Year 7, Howard waves goodbye," explains Light.

It's about respect, yes, but also about handing over that cold, hard cash. Like Rihanna insisted, *B*tch betta have my money*.

Howard adjuncts had had enough, and in 2018 they voted to form a union, calling for an end to annual applications and to the seven-year limit, as well as substantial salary increases, among other demands . . . all very reasonable. But the administration has not agreed to any of them. In her open letter, Light declared that "Howard University has rivaled the likes of Amazon and Wal-Mart in their efforts to first block and then break the Union of non-tenure-track faculty. The Administration waged a propaganda campaign to undo organizing efforts. And after that failed to interrupt our creation, they side-stepped in-house attorneys to hire external legal counsel with experience thwarting Union organizing and collective bargaining."

Light called on Hannah-Jones, and by extension other "star" professors, to support a fair and equitable contract and stand with the majority of faculty, the "workhorses" of the university, as another observer put it, *who work where they are not valued, only where they're tolerated*, and who do not have the luxury to walk away from a tenured job with multiple offers on the table. (Hannah-Jones responded by expressing public support for her colleagues.) At the same time that Howard's administration ignores adjunct faculty's demands, it touts a new, $3 million golf program funded by celebrity donors and likely affecting only the tiny fraction of students who want to be the next Tiger Woods, rather than the many who would benefit from professors with more time for their questions.

Awful policies and vanity investments are not unique to Howard but are symptomatic of the broader corporatization of colleges and universities, which has been on the rise since the 1980s. Each year, the richest schools proudly publicize their ballooning endowments—$53.2 billion for Harvard, $42.3 billion for Yale, $37.7 billion for Princeton in 2021—and yet graduate student workers at many of these same institutions must go on strike to demand a fair contract and livable wage.

Each year, too, the news stories of adjuncts living out of cars, relying on the university's food bank for meals, and even selling plasma elicit a new wave of shock and awe. *How could highly educated academics in the hallowed halls of higher education be forced to scrape together enough to live on?* Marx would answer, "The bourgeoisie has stripped of its halo every occupation hitherto honored and looked up to with reverent awe. It has converted the physician, the lawyer, the priest, the poet, the man of science, into its paid wage laborers." So at a certain point, shock at the debasing working conditions of adjunct academic labor, however sympathetic, becomes just another barrier to acting on what we all know to be the case—that the whole damn system is guilty as hell.

"They're kind of like the Uber drivers," said Gary Rhoades, who studies higher education at the University of Arizona. "COVID just heightens and surfaces the already existing inequities."

"Second-class citizens," "aliens," "disposable," and "serfs"—these are just some of the terms that contingent faculty use to describe their experience in the documentary *In Search of Professor Precarious*, which follows the labor struggles of "sessionals," the term used most frequently for temporary academic staff in Canada. But adjunct faculty are not taking this academic exploitation without a fight. Labor strikes, unionizing, and popular education are just some of the actions sessionals are taking in Canada. And in some places, such as Quebec, strong and organized unions have successfully won protections and pay equity: part-time lecturers, for example, earn the prorated equivalent of their full-time counterparts throughout Quebec, plus benefits and paid leave, reducing the incentive for universities to "cut costs" by hiring more adjuncts. And little by little, these demands for justice are going viral.

In the U.S., where a full 75 percent of college faculty are not on the tenure track, forming "the new majority" of college instructors, collective bargaining has resulted in 25 percent higher overall salaries, regular raises, pay protections, better benefits, and professional development funds. In 2015 roughly 750 Boston University adjuncts voted to unionize, joining a nationwide movement that includes over 50,000 faculty on more than sixty campuses spearheaded by Faculty Forward and the Services Employees International Union. When my former Boston University colleague contacted me to sign a petition to support unionization, she had to do so covertly, using a nonuniversity email address because the administration was actively opposing her efforts and could monitor her correspondence if they chose, putting her already tenuous position in jeopardy. Surely those of us with more secure employment have an obligation to speak out and stand with those who are taking such risks. But the inequities endemic to academia go far beyond those between tenured, tenure-track, and adjunct faculty.

The exploitation or justice that one group experiences, adjunct academics in this case, has ripple effects for everyone. Solidarity, it bears repeating, is not charity. It is born out of the recognition that our fates are linked. For families and students, it means recalling the connection made by former U.S. Assistant Secretary of Education Diane Ravitch: "teachers' working conditions are children's *learning* conditions." It means following the example of students in the U.K. who stood shoulder to shoulder with faculty and staff at over seventy universities during nationwide strikes in early 2020—this despite threats of punishment from their institutions and despite disappointment with how the strikes disrupted learning in the short run: "You will see us on the picket line, holding sit-ins in university buildings and campaigning for better working conditions . . . We know that this is not just a fight for improved pay, workload and pensions: this is a fight for our education," wrote the National Union of Students in the *Guardian*.

For tenured faculty, it means confronting the fact that, despite the idea that "it's a job for life," our employment is not fully secure. Indeed, some colleges and universities are dismissing tenured faculty and hiring part-time lecturers to replace them. In the state of Wisconsin, the situation is "worse than your garden-variety corporatization" because, in 2015, not only did then-governor Scott Walker slash $250 million from the higher education budget, but he also made it relatively easy for any professor in the state system—tenured or not—to be laid off by the governing body that oversees public education "using maddeningly vague criteria." It is no coincidence, of course, that the people dismantling tenure are the same people who believe professors are indoctrinating "our kids" with left-wing lies and that academia is swarming with "social justice warriors," as if the latter is a bad thing. These are the same people leading the charge against anything and everything dubbed "critical race theory"—meaning *this* book would be banned in public schools in states that have passed legislation barring instruction on how racism is endemic to this nation.

Meanwhile, those of us with positions of relative power and privilege, no matter the profession, should not look away from the weak labor protections, exploitation, and neglect of workers around us. One way we can support the cause is by participating in organizations like Tenure for the Common Good, which brings together tenured faculty to act both on their own campuses and nationally because the "exploitation of contingent faculty degrades us all." Among the group's many initiatives, they are advocating for a Safe Labor Seal that confirms that an institution is adhering to "basic standards of good labor practices in hiring and employment."

At most places without huge endowments, the issue is not so much that the university is hoarding wealth but that it is being deprived of resources. On these campuses, faculty can organize as a union, a faculty senate, or simply a group to demand more funding for higher education from state and federal governments. They can also demand a greater role in governance decisions, especially about jobs, and work toward more stable tenure-track positions.

But casting our sights even further, now is the time for a collective reckoning at institutions that tout their commitment to the "public good" but too often put their private interests first. Those billion-dollar endowments I mentioned earlier—they are tax exempt, along with the real estate that universities sit on. This same real estate often houses for-profit research in biotech and related fields, wherein the university collects income from patent royalties, copyright and trademark licensing programs, and other ventures, so that higher education is now "a lucrative 'shelter' economy."

We're supposed to accept that amid all this profit seeking, there is a net positive impact on the public. But given the constancy of "town-gown" tensions, which sometimes erupt into full-blown legal battles, it would seem "the public" does not quite buy the feel-good platitudes. In many locales, universities are the most powerful land-lord, buying up properties and displacing residents. Urban studies scholar Davarian Baldwin dubs them "UniverCities" and notes that they may indeed bring desired amenities (for some), but this infu-sion of capital is often costly, especially for the Black and Latinx communities who live in the "shadow of the Ivory Tower." So what would it look like for university faculty to link arms with those in overshadowed neighborhoods who are demanding that the univer-sity's policies and its purse get in line with its platitudes?

After spending five years fighting in court, in 2016, my employer, Princeton University, was finally compelled to pay more than $18 million to settle a lawsuit disputing its property-tax exemption. The suit, brought by residents of Jackson-Witherspoon, a historically Black neighborhood in downtown Princeton, argued that the uni-versity was making money from commercial ventures run out of tax-exempt buildings, particularly in the biotech sector.

Like many nonprofit schools and medical centers, Princeton offers a voluntary payment in lieu of taxes (PILOT), which is a fraction of the assessed value of its real estate holdings—about 170 buildings that rely on the town's water, sewer, and fire services. More municipalities across the nation are also questioning whether they can afford to "allow wealthy Ivy League schools or big nonprofit hospitals to remain off tax rolls while they scramble for money" to provide government services. Princeton residents argued that "while local property taxes increased, the university still received tax exemption for buildings where research had generated millions of dollars in commercial royalties." One resident called the university a "hedge fund that conducts classes," arguing that despite the "nonprofit" designation, Princeton is a profit-making entity.

Then there are institutions like the University of Pennsylvania that refuse to even pay PILOTs. As part of the 2020 racial justice uprisings, over five hundred faculty and staff joined forces with a local advocacy group, Philadelphia Jobs with Justice, to petition the university to "address the root causes of racial inequality, which include systems of public finance that enrich wealthy, private, majority-white institutions" while underfunding public institutions. They urged the university to invest a fraction of what it would pay in taxes in the city's public schools. So far, the administration has not budged on the demand for a permanent commitment to pay PILOTs, opting instead to contribute a one-time gift of $100 million over ten years to remediate lead and asbestos contamination in Philadelphia schools.

Obviously, there is a huge gulf separating the small number of elite institutions and the vast majority of schools that are not cushioned by billion-dollar endowments, a gulf mirrored in the resources and respect showered on a small cadre of elite professors and withheld from the majority of instructors, adjuncts, and graduate workers alike. But we mustn't lose sight of the fact that these disparities are the by-product of broader forms of economic extraction that we must also work to undo. The point of pulling back the curtain is so that we can set our sights higher, not only demanding just treatment of everyone working on campus but also organizing with those living and working around it. As Baldwin's work shows, *another university is possible*, one that "helps meet the local desires for affordable housing, sustainable food systems, cooperatively owned workplaces, and a shared right to the city."

Ultimately, we witness how the gig work that holds together higher education in the United States, United Kingdom, Canada, and beyond finds its counterpart in the widespread precarity experienced by people in other industries worldwide. Still, we have seen how it is possible to challenge the exploitative status quo by linking arms, speaking up, and organizing around the principles of shared prosperity and collective well-being.

From academia to tech giant Amazon, the engine of progress is dragging many people along the tracks. In pursuit of "frictionless" user experiences, we must ask ourselves, who are the imagined users for which all this ease is manufactured? Is technologically mediated convenience only possible if those powering our platforms suffer? And how is suffering veiled by the slick design of apps that apparently place the world at our fingertips? As Princeton graduate student Aliya Ram asked after reading a draft of this chapter, "What is it that we're saving all this time for? If we make life totally frictionless then, what, will we just slide to the grave in an Uber?"

One, two, three clicks and I can have a steaming-hot bowl of noodles outside my door within the hour via Postmates, get emergency tampons delivered late into the evening via Instacart, or even take a swim in a stranger's pool if I sign up for the relatively new app Swimply—all without interacting directly with another human being. But the "frictionless" design of our favorite apps helps to hide and perpetuate the violent frictions of our world. Drawing upon Kyle Chayka's book *The Longing for Less*, graphic designer Iordanis Passas explains, "Minimalism always obscures complexity: The minimalist interface you use to order your takeout sits above a complex network of gig workers that make sure your ramen is still warm when it arrives. Go ahead, open your Amazon app. The simple presentation hides the complicated system just below the surface, whether that is the infrastructure for data collection or the multi-conglomerate corporation." And, I would add, it hides the labor violations on which so much frictionless digital convenience rests. *Less* friction for some means *more* friction for others.

With a global workforce of over six hundred thousand plus an army of one hundred thousand temps during the holiday season, Amazon is the despotic face of racial capitalism.

In 2021 legislators finally introduced the U.S. Platform Monopolies Act to try to rein in some of the worst excesses of Amazon and other tech giants. They noted that when a company controls the platform or marketplace on which its own products are sold, that leads to a fundamental conflict of interest in which the big companies act as gatekeepers and unfair competitors to smaller businesses. But in addition to what happens on the platform, Amazon's reputation has taken a hit because of how the company mistreats workers on the warehouse floor.

One of the most shocking examples to date came after historic tornadoes swept through the Midwest in December 2021. Even more than the images of a collapsed Amazon warehouse in Edwardsville, Illinois, where winds brought down the roof and toppled the facility's thick concrete walls, screenshots of text messages between a delivery driver and her boss show us in real time what it looks like to be exposed to hostile weather:

DRIVER: Tornado alarms are going off over here.

DISPATCH: Just keep delivering for now. We have to wait for word from Amazon. If we need to bring people back, the decision will ultimately be up to them. I will let you know if the situation changes at all. I'm talking with them now about it . . .

DRIVER: How about for my own personal safety, I'm going to head back. Having alarms going off next to me and nothing but locked building around me isn't sheltering in place. That's wanting to turn this van into a casket. Hour left of delivery time. And if you look at the radar, the worst of the storm is going to be right on top of me in 30 minutes.

DISPATCH: If you decided to come back, that choice is yours. But I can tell you it won't be viewed as for your own safety. The safest practice is to stay exactly where you are. If you decide to return with your packages, it will be viewed as you refusing your route, which will ultimately end with you not having a job come tomorrow morning. The sirens are just a warning.

This exchange began eighty minutes before a tornado struck the Edwardsville warehouse, killing six employees. Later, an Amazon spokesperson admitted that the dispatcher should have immediately instructed the driver to seek shelter, rather than threaten her employment if she stopped deliveries.

On a more routine basis, we also hear the stories of Amazon "pickers" expected to pick up four hundred items an hour in their fulfillment centers and drivers who have had to "piss in bottles and shit in bags" in order to meet their delivery quotas. Frances Wallace, a Black Amazon worker in Bessemer, Alabama, described working ten-hour shifts with a thirty-minute lunch and two fifteen-minute breaks: "From the first day that I worked there, I was ready to quit by the end of the day. It was very high pressure. We didn't get much training . . . Me being a diabetic, I don't even have time to really check my sugar and make sure I can get something to snack on in that amount of time."

The more these horrid conditions come to light, and workers take to the streets, the more the company has been desperate to give itself a pro-Black facelift. At the very same time that Amazon was working hard to crush the unionization of mostly Black and Latinx workers in its Bessemer warehouse, it aired what would end up being the most popular Super Bowl ad of 2021.

In it, a Black woman is shopping for an Alexa product, admiring the new design: "It's flawless, isn't it? I mean I literally could not imagine a more beautiful vessel for Alexa to be . . . inside." Her voice drifts off as she peers out the store window and sees a bus glide by showing an ad for a new movie on Amazon Prime starring Michael B. Jordan. He, it turns out, is an even more beautiful vessel to embody

Alexa. The scene switches to the same woman in her kitchen, cooking as she asks sexy "Alexa," now embodied by Jordan, the kinds of questions that are frequently asked of digital assistants: "Alexa, how many tablespoons in a cup?" Then she commands him, "Alexa, dim the lights." A room full of her friends gawk as the handsome assistant, shown with blue eyes so the viewer knows he is a robot, slowly pulls off his shirt.

All this is happening as the woman's husband nervously tries to interrupt: "Alexa, lights on!" And in the closing scene, the woman lies in a bubble bath surrounded by candles with Jordan, who reads her an audio book while they soak to the tunes of slow jams, as her husband presses desperately against the door, "Honey, other people have to use the bathroom around here, too."

On its own, the ad is marketing genius—sexy, savvy, and funny as hell. Tech consumption, after all, is never simply about convenience, but about *desire* . . . and the commercial is brimming with it. On the heels of a Big Tech backlash—dubbed by some "tech lash"—which has included more public scrutiny of racist tech platforms and systems, Sexy Black Alexa offers a much-needed facelift. Instead of seemingly clueless white tech bros like Mark Zuckerberg or villainous moguls like Jeff Bezos, Amazon wants us to associate its products with steamy Hollywood hunks like Jordan.

But is that *really* what most Black women, as depicted in the commercial, are dreaming about? Instead of helpful digital assistants waiting to answer every question and satisfy every need, Black women working in Amazon fulfillment centers must contend with algorithmic overseers whose automated wishes the workers must fulfill at breakneck speed. There we find employees shuffling up and down warehouse ladders, picking items from the shelves as fast as humanly possible to meet daily quotas, rushing back from restrooms looking nervously at their TOT (Time Off Task) points, which can be used to justify termination: "It'll notice if you took too much time, it'll notice that immediately," said Frances Wallace. "It" being her algorithmic overlord.

Rather than Sexy Black Alexa, Wallace, who was a supporter of the Bessemer unionization drive and is a Black Lives Matter activist, said she dreams of a society in which people are "not being worked like dogs all the time" and where they "don't have to work to the bone just to be able to provide . . . Every human being should have the right to food, to water, to shelter, and to be comfortable in life."

It turns out that the buff and chiseled torsos of digital assistants don't make people forget about their own throbbing legs and aching arms following a ten-hour shift. The cosmetic facelifts of corporate marketing campaigns are a poor substitute for a deeper transformation of grinding work conditions.

A few months after Amazon successfully fought off the union vote in Bessemer by messaging employees via the company's internal app, holding captive audience meetings (wherein bosses discourage employees from voting for a union), and using other manipulative tactics, the company tried something new: AmaZen, coffin-size meditation booths installed in the middle of warehouses where employees can choose from a library of guided meditations, chant positive affirmations, and be serenaded by "calming scenes and sounds" as plants surround them, tinted blue skylights hover above, and cooling fans circulate the air. AmaZen was designed to help workers "recharge the internal battery."

The company, it seems, got the wrong message when, a few years prior, the predominantly East African workers in the Saint Paul, Minnesota, warehouse staged a Prime Day strike, holding aloft signs that exclaimed, "We are humans, not robots." As I wrote in *Race after Technology*, the origin of the word "robot" comes from the Czech *robota*, which means "forced labor" or "servitude."

It's not that workers need to recharge their batteries; companies must stop treating workers like automata. One observer wondered "when, exactly, its overworked staff is supposed to use the AmaZen booth. Is it during their notoriously short breaks? Should they break off five minutes of their lunch to stare at another Amazon computer screen?"

The AmaZen booths are part of the company's WorkingWell program, which was kicked off in May 2021 with the goal of using "scientifically proven physical and mental activities, wellness exercises, and healthy eating habits to help recharge and reenergize the body, and ultimately reduce the risk of injury for operations employees."

Here, we see the ultimate corporatized version of self-care: we'll work you to exhaustion and pay you abysmally but encourage you to feel Zen about it. Just like the universities and colleges sending their overworked staff and faculty messages about taking care of their mental health, AmaZen wants you to forget that the same people claiming to care about your well-being are the ones enforcing the working conditions that make you unwell. Amazon wants a facelift, but workers are demanding an exorcism because, otherwise, coffin-size wellness booths can only prefigure the premature death that awaits them.

Although the Bessemer union drive did not result in a union, *yet*, Amazon workers are not staying quiet. Sure, the company continues to throw its workers lavender-scented bones as Jeff Bezos circles in space—a four-minute, $5.5 billion trip on a Blue Origin lunar lander. "I also want to thank every Amazon employee and every Amazon customer because you guys paid for all of this," Bezos said. Meanwhile, workers are continuing to demand higher pay and humane work conditions:

Boss made a dollar
I made a dime
That was a poem
From a simpler time.

Now Boss makes a thousand
And gives us a cent
While he's got employees
Who can't pay the rent.

So when boss makes a million
And the workers make jack
Then that's when we riot
And take our lives back

#WorkingClassSolidarity

In poetry and music, we find the heartbeat of an alternative reality, inviting us to tune in to the seemingly small insurrections happening right under our noses . . . or behind our screens.

Take an initiative by workers employed as independent contractors on the Amazon Mechanical Turk (AMT) platform. AMT allows businesses and individuals (i.e., "requesters") to outsource simple and repetitive tasks to the over one hundred thousand crowdworkers, or "Turkers," based in over one hundred countries, with a majority residing in the U.S. Turkers typically get paid cents per task and are compensated only for those tasks that requesters "approve." Requesters, in turn, don't have to explain why they reject a task that has been completed.

AMT is described variously as a crowdsourcing platform, a microlabor marketplace, "*artificial* artificial intelligence" in that it offers human computation as a service, and "a meeting place for requesters with large volumes of microtasks and workers who want to do those tasks." These tasks include writing product descriptions, identifying content found in photos or videos, annotating data, and answering questions (including many social science surveys). Workers, in turn, set their own hours and decide which tasks they want to accept. "Freedom!" "Flexibility!" "Autonomy!" Or is it?

Once again, for many workers, buzzwords translate to the white noise of an exploitative workplace, including the "low pay, slow pay, poor communication, and arbitrary rejections" experienced by many on the platform. One study of 2,767 Turkers who had completed 3.8 million tasks found that "workers earned a median hourly wage of only ~$2 an hour." What makes this human computation so effective is that workers are treated like mere "software components" hidden behind a screen. So if invisibility is part of the problem, then viral justice would entail shining a light on this hidden labor.

Enter: Turkopticon. This website and browser extension "allows workers to publicize and evaluate their relationships with employers," and it was developed by critical informatics researchers Lilly Irani and Six Silberman in 2008 in collaboration with Turkers. Its tagline: "We help the people in the 'crowd' of crowdsourcing watch out for each other—because nobody else seems to be." So now, when

Turkers are browsing available tasks, they can see a button shows community-generated reviews of requesters, and they can report and avoid "shady" behavior like late payments or unexplained task rejections.

As Irani and Silberman put it, Turkopticon developed as an "ethically-motivated response to workers' invisibility in the design of AMT," allowing Turkers to rate and evaluate requesters' level of communicativeness. Rather than submitting to surveillance, atomization, and extraction, Turkers can foster accountability, transparency, and community. A 2014 study found that "effective wages among requesters with 'good' reputations on Turkopticon were about 40% higher than effective wages among requesters with 'neutral' or 'bad.'"

But like all efforts, great and small, to *take our lives back,* just because we can doesn't mean we will. Like other online forums, Turkopticon is not free of harassment and abuse. Indeed, the technical maintenance and repair to keep it going is the easy part; fostering trust, dealing with conflict, and maintaining relationships—*that's* the never-ending challenge. Turkopticon offers mutual aid and connection among Turkers by, for example, hosting virtual meetups to address issues people are having on the platform. In working to foster community and build worker power, Turkers remind us that *people* make up "the system," and that it's not simply oppressive forces *out there* but corrupting dynamics inside our organizations and initiatives that can foil efforts to spread viral justice.

On May 5, 2020, New Orleans–based sanitation worker Rahaman Brooks joined his coworkers, all Black men, on the picket line at the trash collection headquarters in the Ninth Ward of the city. Brooks held aloft a sign that read, "I am a man," the same phrase popularized by civil rights protesters in the 1968 sanitation workers strike, during which Martin Luther King Jr. delivered his "I've Been to the Mountaintop" speech the night before his murder. The "hoppers," as Brooks and his coworkers are called because they have to hop on and off the trucks, picketed from four to eleven in the morning, a full day's shift, to show that they "are ready and willing to work," but not for poverty wages, and not in deference to the trash company's cavalier attitude toward personal protective equipment, paid sick leave, and other safety measures.

Metro Service Group, the company that employs hoppers in New Orleans, gets away with all of this by not hiring the workers directly as full-time employees. Instead, it works through a temp agency called PeopleReady and thereby avoids providing healthcare, sick days, pensions, and vacation pay. Like many companies that employ gig workers, Metro does not pay payroll taxes on what the hoppers earn. As Brooks explained, "At the end of the day, them people get rich off our backbreaking. They sit in the office and collect the funds and we be outside going home sore, barely walking, unable to play with our kids."

When Brooks and other hoppers went on strike, Metro initially contracted with another company, Lock5, to hire incarcerated people to work as hoppers through a work release program, though Lock5 pulled out of the agreement once it found out there was a labor dispute. Prison labor, undocumented labor, immigrant labor, gendered and racialized labor . . . all code for *exploitable* labor.

One of the barriers to building power and solidarity among workers is that most Americans believe they are middle class, assuming that only blue-collar professions count as part of the working class. But according to Marxist analysis, your class is not determined simply by how much money you make. A Wal-Mart store manager may earn less than a New York City train operator, but the manager has the power to fire all the employees in the store. Class is, foremost, a relationship of power. And "the working class" isn't composed simply of those who may identify as such. At one level, workers include *everyone who needs to work to live*, even if they are not working at the moment.

When Dan Price, the CEO of Seattle-based Gravity Payments, found out that one of his employees was working a second job at

McDonalds to make ends meet, he took a drastic step. He cut his own salary from $1.1 million to $70,000 and, in 2015, raised the minimum wage of all 120 staff members at his financial services company to $70,000 a year.

For doing so, he was called the "lunatic of all lunatics" by a presenter on Fox Business. Among the five hundred million interactions about his "wage bomb" on social media, right-wing radio personality Rush Limbaugh summed up the capitalist anxiety the best: "This is pure unadulterated socialism, which has never worked, that's why I hope this company is a case study in MBA programs on how socialism does not work, because it's going to fail."

Well, Gravity is indeed studied in MBA programs, including Harvard Business School's, but not because Price's experiment failed. Over the next six years, the company's revenue tripled and staff numbers grew by 70 percent. Employees have also been able to pay down debt, purchase homes (a tenfold increase), and save for retirement. The company's customer base has doubled, and customer retention rose from 91 percent (already high) to 95 percent.

It's not just money that staff were given, but also what some consider the most precious currency of all: *time*. Price instituted unlimited time off for everyone at the company and has become a vociferous critic of income inequality, calling out the hypocrisy, greed, and illogic of a capitalist system in which, although economic productivity has increased precipitously since 1971, earnings have remained stagnant.

Price takes no prisoners when it comes to other CEOs and the excuses they make for upholding the status quo. When Jeff Bezos stepped down as CEO of Amazon, Price noted that Bezos "got $8.44 billion richer in his first day of retirement. So he got more money for not working one day than 270,000 Amazon warehouse workers make in an entire year. And Bezos pays a lower tax rate than any of them. Still think the system is fair?" It's Price's juxtapositions that really hit home: the day billionaire Richard Branson went on his much-touted space jaunt, Price tweeted, "Call me strange but if you can afford to start your own rocket company and send yourself to space you can afford to pay more than $0 in taxes."

It's not just about money and time but also about *power*, which Price is disrupting by advocating policies that fly in the face of the top-down decision-making processes used in most workplaces. For example, as vaccination rates increased, and many company leaders were making unliteral decisions about whether to bring employees back to the office, Price asked his staff what *they* wanted to do and then shared the results on social media:

> 7% want back in the office full time
> 31% want office-remote hybrid
> 62% want to work from home full time
> I told them: Do whatever you want. Employees know how to do their jobs better than any CEO.

Like viral justice in other arenas, the changes at Gravity were contagious from the start: the company was flooded with "stories from ecstatic workers elsewhere who suddenly got raises from converted bosses . . . even, in one case, at an apparel factory in Vietnam." Besides that, résumés poured into the company—4,500 the week after the salary increase was first announced—and new customer inquiries jumped from thirty a month to two thousand in the two weeks after Price dropped the "wage bomb." Tammi Kroll, a fifty-two-year-old former executive at Yahoo, even took an 85 percent pay cut to work at Gravity, choosing a more meaningful and joyful work environment after years of chasing bigger and bigger paychecks.

We learn about the concept of scarcity in Economics 101, but societal scarcity is intentional and manufactured. As a society, we have the means to guarantee everyone a well-paying job, healthcare, education, and housing. But the way forward requires a substantial redistribution of global wealth. Not only that, but true justice also entails guaranteeing that workers' rights and dignity are codified in law and upheld by institutions and workplaces.

Price demonstrated that it's not that difficult for people in power to change how they understand the relationship between work and compensation. But also, one's ability to do paid work should not be the measure of one's value or the price of full social and economic inclusion, as the disability justice movement reminds us. Somewhat paradoxically, we must buy in to the idea that we are bound together in something called a "society" to create the guarantees that make us one.

Viral justice, then, requires that we reimagine work and redistribute wealth as an essential part of ensuring that everyone has "broadly equal access to the social and material conditions necessary for living a flourishing life." Kali Akuno is one of the founders of Cooperation Jackson, a Jackson, Mississippi–based grassroots initiative that is creating a "solidarity economy" based on democratic and cooperative principles. The group's long-term goal is to create a federation of local worker cooperatives—such as an incubator that supports the development of new cooperatives, an education and training center, and a cooperative financial institution.

At the heart of all Cooperation Jackson's work is the idea that organizing and empowering the working class, especially Black and Latinx communities, will catalyze "the democratization of our economy and society overall." Although Mississippi is technically the poorest state in the nation—a direct result of its reliance on the human property and free labor it lost with Emancipation—this initiative focuses on drawing on the wealth of skills and creativity in Black Jackson. "If there's one thing, in a general sense you can say about the experience of people of African descent in the Western Hemisphere is how we've been able to take a little bit of nothing and turn it into some beautiful things," reflected Akuno.

Learning by doing is a key feature of viral justice in general, and of worker-owned enterprises in particular. As Akuno puts it, "We are trying to learn how to be democratic. We don't know how to do that. I've never lived in a democratic society. I really don't know what that looks like." And the only way we can learn is by doing—trying out different ways of organizing work, budgeting for what people need, and even producing food.

One of the first enterprises of Cooperation Jackson was Freedom Farms, which grows organic vegetables that are distributed to co-op members and sold at the local farmer's market. The project engenders relationships between people, between people and their work, and between people and the land. Even the "dirtiest" job, such as turning over soil on a farm, is recognized as meaningful because it is connected to a larger set of relationships. As the founder of Soul Fire Farm in upstate New York and author of *Farming While Black*, Leah Penniman reminds us, "Our Black ancestors were forced, tricked, and scared off the land until 6.5 million of them migrated North in the largest migration in US history. This was no accident . . . To farm while Black is an act of defiance against white supremacy and a means to honor the agricultural ingenuity of our ancestors."

When I visited Jackson in fall 2018 to give a talk at the Mississippi Civil Rights Museum, I also learned about residents who had created a café and catering business, lawn care cooperative, Community Production Center (tech education, makerspace, and fabrication lab), and Green Team focused on waste management, recycling, and composting. They had plans to focus on solar insulation, auto repair, healthcare, and childcare. More recently, the cooperative has announced plans to expand its community land trust and build affordable housing that can be purchased with "sweat equity and time-banking" (currency that involves the giving and receiving of service hours).

Like viral justice more broadly, Cooperation Jackson is reimagining our relationship to work by working differently and prioritizing mutual care and cooperation over cutthroat competition and manufactured scarcity. How might we each apply these insights to our own place of work? In my case, it looked like my graduate school cohort at Berkeley deciding to work together on assignments and applying for extramural funding together, even though we were supposed to be competing against each other. It looked like us also taking time outside class to organize in pursuit of a more hospitable environment in the Sociology Department and university overall, even though in many cases we would not be around to directly benefit from the changes. *Cooperation Berkeley* we might call it. So what do the principles of cooperation look like in your locale?

As with abolitionist organizing, which seeks to redirect public funds from death-making institutions to life-affirming ones, budget justice involves redirection *and* imagination in which we ask, *What if?* *What if* every single year, local and state governments poured billions of tax dollars into economic development? *What if* they "provided cooperatives with the same kind of technical assistance, zoning allowances, procurement preferences, tax incentives, and other benefits they currently give away to for-profit firms and wasteful mega-developments . . . ?" It's not about whether we can afford to invest in social programs and collective well-being. As historian Daniel Wortel-London reminds us, *the money is there*: "Seeing money as a centralized public utility, rather than a private and finite resource, clears the path for one of the most venerable of progressive demands: a job guarantee."

It's not just *where* the money goes, but *how* it goes. Participatory budgeting, which canvasses community opinion on where to invest public funds, offers a model for democratizing public investment processes so that community members have a say in spending. Participatory budgeting started in Porto Allegro, Brazil, in 1989 as an antipoverty initiative that sought to invest in clinics and sewage systems in villages, and it managed to lower child mortality by nearly 20 percent in cities that adopted it for over eight years. The model has since spread to over seven thousand cities around the world. People have used participatory budgeting to allocate funds in "states, counties, cities, housing authorities, schools, and other institutions" from towns of twenty thousand in Germany to regions of fourteen million people in China.

With offices in Brooklyn and Oakland, the Participatory Budget Project has partnered with over a dozen U.S. cities from Greensboro, North Carolina, to Seattle, Washington, often starting with neighborhood assemblies in which delegates are elected or volunteer to craft in-depth proposals on the ideas that are generated. Community members reconvene to learn more about different projects and eventually vote on which to fund. To date, they have facilitated $300 million in public funding for over 1,600 community-generated projects involving 402,000 participants. Participatory budgeting is also being taken up in the workplace, with employees brainstorming, consulting, and deciding how best to invest a portion of company funds.

There's another kind of economic labor we haven't talked about yet—that on social media, which merges labor and leisure, profit, and play, and maybe even transforms what counts as "work." In addition to independent contractors like Uber drivers and platform entrepreneurs like Care.com nannies, Instagram and TikTok content creators are also part of a new "hustle economy."

But as sociologist Tressie McMillan Cottom explained, this entrepreneurial activity is not often thought of as work. Not only *is* it work, hustling is also a "pressure valve for the formal economy," which Cottom noted reproduces racial inequality by shifting more and more economic risk to individuals and communities. Hustling may seem empowering and inclusive, but Cottom implored us to pull back the curtain on the "theater of the hustle" to see who's really running the show.

As vaccine rates increased and travel restrictions eased in 2021, my family and I headed to Los Angeles to visit friends and relatives over the summer. We ended up renting a place across the street from a "TikTok house," which hosts a group of young people who produce content for the social media app TikTok.

Residents are often sponsored to live in such houses, otherwise known as "content houses" or "collab houses," by a talent manager or entertainment agency that represents the group. Some of them are self-organized by one of the influencers. Either way, their job is to produce dances, skits, and other content that earns clicks, likes, sponsorships, and profit on social media apps. And while these TikTok houses are often depicted as huge mansions with pools and movie theaters that rent for tens of thousands of dollars a month, others, like the four-story New York brownstone with twenty-something "entrepreneurs" camped out in closets, are more ragtag upstarts.

Just around the time we moved in across the street from one of these houses, I also started fielding journalists' requests to comment on a labor strike by Black TikTok users who were fed up with people stealing their content and not giving them credit. "This app would be nothing without Black people," is how Erik Louis, a Black TikTok user and one of the strike organizers, put it.

For Louis and other Black creators, it was important to show how essential Black creativity is to the platform, so they staged a digital walkout. They wouldn't leave altogether but instead decided to post videos that expressed their frustration and anger over the appropriation of their work for others' gain.

The way it works online is that popularity—as evidenced by the number of followers you have, the number of people engaging your content, and the number of videos you've produced (among other factors)—translates into TikTok currency. This is generated in several ways: other users can donate virtual currency, or coins, directly to their favorite accounts, which is called *gifting*; influencers can design and sell their own products, called *merchandising*; popular personalities can be invited by companies to events as special guests, or *brand partnerships*; and influencers can promote products using their own unique style and receive payment from companies, or *marketing*. Record labels and music promotors are among the biggest sponsors of TikTok content, as they attempt to make songs go viral.

TikTok also started a Creator Fund to pay users who have at least ten thousand followers and who receive at least one hundred thousand video views in a thirty-day period, among other criteria. Those who are eligible can cash out once they earn fifty dollars, but so far, most TikTokkers are reporting a much smaller payout than they'd hoped, and fewer video views after signing up for the fund.

Amid all this creative commerce, Black creators have produced wildly popular dances that often go viral once white influencers copy them without recognition or credit: "Anyone that uses TikTok will tell you young black creators choreograph the vast majority, if not all, of the dances that go viral," said regular TikTok user Rachel McKenzie, who is white and supported the strike.

Although the issue of appropriation is a long-standing one across social media platforms—and society as a whole—things got really heated in March 2021. *The Tonight Show* host Jimmy Fallon invited TikTok star Addison Rae Easterling, who is white, to perform some of the most popular TikTok dances on his show. She had not created any of the dances she performed, including one of the most well known, a dance called "Renegade."

"Renegade" was originally choreographed by Jalaiah Harmon, a fourteen-year-old Black TikTok creator from the greater Atlanta area. Only after a significant social media backlash did Fallon invite Harmon and the other original dance choreographers onto the show. *Who really cares?* some might ask rhetorically. *This isn't serious business, unlike, say, the dehumanizing experience of Amazon workers.*

"Since the founding of this country, Black art forms, Black dance forms, have been appropriated, watered down, repackaged and used to make money by white folks," explained University of Pennsylvania professor of communications Sarah J. Jackson. "And so, if you put it in that context of that longer history of basically stolen labor and stolen creativity, then you start to see why it matters to people and why it's important to people to be credited for the origins of these things."

By staging a cultural labor strike using the very platform on which their work is stolen—all while raising awareness of that theft and organizing themselves around specific demands for credit and compensation—Black content creators showed us how to make justice go viral, digitally.

I still remember how I felt the first time I saw the *Agency Job* by British street artist Banksy. Banksy's painting riffs on a famous oil painting created in 1857 by French artist Jean-François Millet, the first major European artist to portray working-class subjects. Millet's painting *The Gleaners* shows three peasant women leaning over in a wheat field, collecting leftover crops after a successful harvest. "Gleaners" were those who "scoured the fields at sunset and picked up, one by one, the stalks of wheat missed by the harvesters." It was repetitive, back-breaking work carried out by the poorest of the poor.

Millet's piece, which the French bourgeoisie saw as glorifying the poor, provoked their anxiety and anger, not least because they had just survived the French Revolution of 1848 and the socialist movement was spreading. Millet, for his part, was desperate to sell his work and had to reduce his original price to 3,000 francs, even though now *The Gleaners* resides in the Musée d'Orsay in Paris and has been referenced countless times by artists and social critics who take up its implicit critique of class oppression.

Back to Banksy's interpretation, which depicts one of the laborers, originally on the far right holding sheaves of corn, as a Black woman who is literally cut out of the original scene. Now she is shown seated on the frame of the painting, legs crossed, looking away from the day's toil as she smokes a cigarette. Here a smoke break becomes refusal and respite amid the drudgery of the work. I love *The Agency Job* because it reminds me that we are fighting not only to transform the conditions of work—so we are all paid well and treated well—but also for the right to rest. Banksy reframes the horizon of possibility by having a Black woman sit on the frame.

For Nap Ministry founder Tricia Hershey, rest is a form of resistance and reparation because "it disrupts and pushes back against capitalism and white supremacy." In grind culture, rest is only condoned because it makes us more productive. It is a reward for hard work, a *to-do* item on our never-ending checklist, an obligation so that we can hustle harder the next day. But rest does not require justification. It is not a luxury. We do not need to *earn* rest. It is not an indulgence, or a means to an end. The point of rest is not to "recharge our battery," as Amazon's wellness program would have us believe, but simply to be. "You are not a machine, stop grinding," implored Hershey.

The Nap Ministry invites us to reflect on how we have internalized and perpetuated grind culture by what we value, how we fetishize work, idolize side hustles, and denounce "laziness"—a racist trope selectively weaponized against those who are Black and poor. Again, rest is not an indulgence reserved for those who are rich and white. Rather, as one observer put it, "To be Black in America is to live through a continuous cycle of exhaustion—from slavery to civil rights to Black men and women being killed at the hands of police and even the plague of grind culture fueled by Western values."

Thus, many movements, from racial justice to disability justice, have grown more vocal about centering rest as an essential part of our existence. Black Power Naps, founded by artists Navild Acosta and Fannie Sosa, for example, creates installations and performances that explore the racial gap between who gets quality sleep and who gets to revel in the right to rest just for the sake of it.

Every industry is fueled by a variant of grind culture. In academia, it is summed up by the warning *Publish or perish*, though the threat applies well beyond publishing, to the nagging pressure to be *always* working on something to prove one's value. This realization hit me as a tenure-track professor when one of my colleagues, the only other woman of color in the department at the time, was promoted from associate to full professor, which I mistakenly believed to be the top of the proverbial ladder. *She made it! Let's celebrate!* I foolishly thought. Nope. The water cooler conversation quickly turned to, *Now that she's a full professor, what prestigious fellowship will she win, what endowed position will she get?* It dawned on me, this *never* ends. A hatch opened in the ceiling when I thought she had reached the top, and she was expected to keep climbing.

Like most workplaces, academia is fueled by anxiety and competition. The grind can be even more insidious in professions where workers are thought to have a "calling." Who needs to pay rent *and* car insurance when you can sustain yourself with a love for teaching? If passion is believed to be your fuel, the bosses will likely take you for a ride.

Rather than stashing half a dozen books in my suitcase "to catch up on the literature" during family trips, responding to work emails late at night ("It'll just take a second"), or scheduling calls with students on the weekends because my office hours filled up during the week, I now give myself permission to exhale. I also welcome talking about nonwork stuff whenever I can. Even as a grad student, it annoyed me that people seemed to bring up work when we were "off the clock," so to speak. Can we normalize other interests, please?

Now I make room in class and my research lab for students to share aspects of their lives that don't involve being students—movie recommendations, favorite recipes, and other things they enjoy doing outside the frame of academia. Like Banksy's painting, I try to carve out the space for those I work with to put down their loads, take some deep breaths, and inhale the fact that *they are enough*. You don't have to prove your worth or perform your value for me. These are small things, for sure, but isn't that part of how norms change? By questioning what we value, by shifting how we treat one another?

There's no doubt that my undisciplined disposition toward the academic grind is much less risky now that I am a tenured professor who has already "proved herself" than it is for those with more precarious positions—whether grad students, untenured, or contingent faculty. It is no secret that at absurdly wealthy universities, like the one I work at, faculty are drenched with support—sabbaticals for writing, research budgets to hire assistants, grad students to help with grading, highly skilled staff for assistance with everything else. What looks on the surface like one person's prolific output is actually the result of an entire institution conspiring to ensure one's productivity. All that support gives me more time to work *and* more time to rest, if I so choose.

Even so, the most senior Black women continue to be judged by harsher standards and second-guessed by students and colleagues, so refusing to perform hypercompetence or fetishize overwork can still be hazardous to our reputations. Institutionalized inequality currently makes rest a luxury, though we must insist otherwise. Viral justice, in the end, requires us not only to value people's labor, concretely, but also to profess our intrinsic value beyond what we produce, and to conspire together to transform the terms on which we work and rest.

FIVE

Exposed

Early September 2000: I clocked out of Whole Foods and raced across the street to catch the number 48 bus just as it began pulling away from the curb. Grocery bags crashing into each other, I banged hard on the back door, hoping the driver would stop.

"You got lucky today, young lady. I'm in a generous mood," the driver quipped as he opened the doors. I pushed my way into the mass of commuters pressed against one another, angling myself between armpit and pole for the thirty-minute ride, until I caught a glimpse of the bright awning at Green's Beverages, my signal to press the bell.

Once the back door creaked open, I braced for the Atlanta heat, as thick as car exhaust. Passing the foul dumpsters outside Dugan's bar, I tried breathing through my mouth, picking up my pace as I rounded the corner on Somerset Terrace and reached the black iron gate surrounding my apartment building. There was the building manager watering the small, lush courtyard out front, and in his usual dry manner, he barely nodded in my direction. After two years, I still wasn't used to his northern aloofness, which felt all the more jarring after a day of pleasantries exchanged between strangers. There was no time to take his curtness personally; today, I had much more pressing matters to attend to.

Inside, I put the groceries on the counter and rushed into the cramped bathroom of our apartment. A minute later, heart racing, palms sweaty, I called Shawn in to join me. We stood together, staring at the pregnancy test strip. My cycle usually ran like clockwork, so deep down, I already knew. But I still held my breath, waiting for the second pink line to appear.

I had just celebrated my twenty-third birthday and had spent the summer cashiering at Whole Foods. Senior year at Spelman was about to start, and I had already started stress-planning my schedule around Atlanta's sparse public transportation. Getting from my apartment in Midtown to campus in the Southwest, and then to work in the Northeast—on time—was going to be like *The Amazing Race* meets *Groundhog Day*. But all that residual worry melted away once the pink confirmation of the test strip declared, Now *you* are someone's mode of transportation.

Weeks later, Shawn and I were on the southbound train leaving North Avenue Station headed to West End, which was Spelman's stop. On this particular day, the rocking motion and morning sickness didn't mix. A bitter taste washed over my tongue, turning my stomach inside out. I had been feeling queasy for the last twenty minutes, but when we passed Five Points, the train lurched before we got to the next station, and I couldn't hold it down. The doors opened, and just as commuters rushed in to find seats, I turned wide-eyed to Shawn, who opened his backpack just in time for me to retch.

The next minute was the longest, most awkward moment of my life as I tried not to look at the commuters sitting and standing around me, and they tried not to look completely disgusted. When we finally arrived at the next stop, Shawn quickly slipped out to catch a train in the opposite direction so he could go back home and clean out his bag. I continued to campus and went to class, trying to erase the public embarrassment from my memory. It was the first and last time I felt nauseous while pregnant, and I vowed never again to take a multivitamin on an empty stomach. Until that day, the meaning of the bright pink line hadn't quite hit me, that here was a creature who could push my insides out for all to see. I felt mortified and exposed, but also lighter, nervous and eager to show the world my insides.

I only had two cravings: bags of crisp nectarines from Kroger, and scoops of apple crumble pie with vanilla ice cream from Soul Veg on

North Highland, which I could inhale in one sitting. Shawn definitely won the award for Best Supporting Partner in the Production of a Baby. Every night he'd rub almond oil on my belly, as much to soothe his own nerves as mine, I felt. Nevertheless, it was reassuring to have someone else witness those little limbs, like in the movie *Alien*, floating across the inside of my abdomen.

Over winter break, Shawn and I would head over to Lenox Mall for dinner and a movie, and one night, while we were window shopping, we happened upon the cutest dark green, knitted sweater—our first baby purchase. Never mind that it was from Gap. It could easily have been a beloved hand-me-down that one of our grandmothers had sewn. So we took it home and placed it in a drawer until Malachi was big enough to wear it.

Over the next few months, *Ruha's Amazing Race* continued. Crossing Ponce de Leon Avenue each morning, waiting for the number 2 bus, I could see into the floor-to-ceiling windows of the Ford Factory Lofts, once an automobile assembly plant, now offering "amenity rich, contemporary living"—for those who could afford it. To my right was the sprawling secondhand shop Paris on Ponce, where we purchased a funky plaid tweed loveseat for the apartment.

The Poncey-Highland neighborhood in Atlanta was a hodgepodge, known not only for being the home of the Jimmy Carter Presidential Library and the huge city park Freedom Parkway but also for "Murder Kroger," the grocery store directly across from the number 2 bus stop. The store got its name from the 1991 murder of a twenty-five-year-old woman who was fatally shot in the parking lot. Since then, three other incidents—a dead man found in his car in 2002, a college student murdered in the Lofts next door in 2012, and a construction worker fatally shot in the chest in the parking lot in 2015—have helped the store's nickname endure. Without knowing all the gruesome details at the time, this was my view waiting for the bus each morning.

As my pregnancy advanced, the daily commutes felt longer and longer. Getting on the bus each morning, already crowded with commuters, I greeted the driver and paid my dollar and some change. Passing the seats for the disabled and elderly, already occupied, I would squeeze past people holding the bars and seatbacks to stay upright. Then, once the bus began to rock side to side, I would look around, not too desperately, hoping that maybe today I would catch the eye of someone, *anyone*, who thought I deserved a seat.

In this chapter, we'll consider the many ways that people are left standing, not just those with swollen ankles and bellies but all those exposed to social judgment, cruel treatment, and callous indifference. The thing about being exposed is that you are watched but never seen. You are singled out and also lumped together. You are critically examined but poorly treated, not only in everyday interactions but also within institutions that purport to serve you. The very medical professionals whose learning and expertise we must rely on when we are most vulnerable routinely traffic in gross falsehoods and stereotypes disguised as "tailored" medicine, such as the false belief that Black patients have thicker skin and feel less pain. Yet at times, some of us may also play the part, feigning strength when we feel weak, in order to buttress ill-treatment.

This is no way to live. Vulnerability is a fundamental part of the human condition, not a weakness. It's not something we have to hide or overcome. What is it going to take to create a world where we can be vulnerable but not exposed?

Rather than each of us having to grow thick skin, develop "grit," and feign superhuman strength, imagine if we could unclench our jaws, let our shoulders melt, and shed the layers of armor that life requires. What if we could make real James Baldwin's insight that "love takes off the masks that we fear we cannot live without, but know we cannot live within"?

I admit, there have been many times in my life when I have masked up (and not in the good public-healthy way). I wore a mask of my own design, embellished with fancy jewels that dangled, disguising my sadness, distracting me from my insecurity. I not only feigned strength when I felt weak, but there was a stretch in grad school when I even claimed (and sorta believed) that needing love was for the weak. I turned callousness into a virtue because I felt exposed. That blinged-out mask was the only thing separating my fragile insides from the hostile weather.

But over time, I have encountered many individuals and groups—some of which you'll meet in the pages ahead—who are heeding Baldwin's counsel, taking off the masks and weaving connection, care, and love. As he conjured it, love, "not merely in the personal sense but as a state of being, or a state of grace—not in the infantile American sense of being made happy but in the tough and universal sense of quest and daring and growth." And as Toni Morrison cautioned in *Paradise,* love is not that "silly word you believe is about whether you like somebody or whether somebody likes you or whether you can put up with somebody in order to get something or someplace you want . . . Love is none of that." Instead, love accepts that we are all "human and therefore educable, and therefore capable of learning how to learn." Love, I now believe, is the brick, mortar, foundation, *and* pillar of the world we're trying to build where we can be vulnerable but not exposed.

I was twenty-three when I found out I was pregnant, so not a teenager. But I was still much younger than most college-educated women who decide to become mothers. Keep in mind, too, this was during the early 2000s, a time when the inflamed rhetoric of "babies having babies" was heavy in the air.

A few years before, sociologist Kristin Luker had written *Dubious Conceptions: The Politics of Teenage Pregnancy,* offering a powerful refutation of the "epidemic of early childbearing" that politicians and pundits were clamoring about. The book employed statistics and stories to pick apart the stereotypes about teenage motherhood. Luker demonstrated that, contrary to racist depictions focused on Black girls, most teenage mothers were actually white and, at eighteen and nineteen years old, were legal adults.

Luker debunked the hysteria around this particular "epidemic" by noting that early childbearing had been just as common in the 1900s. She also presented data that suggested early childbearing was a *measure* (i.e., a by-product) rather than a *cause* of poverty and social ills. According to Luker, parenting young was a perfectly logical choice for those who had limited opportunities in life. In sum, social circumstances, not individual deviance, were at play. Not only that, according to Arline Geronimus's early research, Black women were more likely to have healthier pregnancies in their late teens than midtwenties because they were less weathered. Those fueling hysteria about teenage pregnancy did not want to hear about any of these facts.

At the time, as an undergraduate at Spelman, I didn't have all these statistics at hand, but I knew intuitively that I was not the problem. It was clear to me that the reproduction of those who are white, wealthy, and able-bodied is smiled upon, while color, lower-class status, and disability mean one's baby is seen as a burden. As life would have it, after leaving Atlanta for graduate school at the University of California, Berkeley, I would become a student of Professor Luker's, digesting the data after already having lived part of the story.

Back at Spelman, for my Contemporary Theory term paper during junior year, I was digging through archives when I came across a 1989 interview with Toni Morrison in *Time* magazine, in which she was questioned about "the crisis." The interviewer asked her whether teenage pregnancy shut down opportunity for young women. "You don't feel these girls will never know whether they could have been teachers, or whatever?"

> They can be teachers. They can be brain surgeons. We have to help them become brain surgeons. That's my job. I want to take them all in my arms and say, *Your baby is beautiful and so are you and, honey, you can do it. And when you do, call me—I will take care of your baby.* That's the attitude you have to have about human life . . . I don't think anybody cares about unwed mothers unless they're black—or poor. The question is not morality, the question is money. That's what we're upset about.

At Spelman, an institution known as a bastion of Black, middle-class respectability, I was somewhat of an oddity. Luckily, one of my best friends had recently had a baby, so I didn't feel so alone, and I would soon find a tribe of undercover mothers who shared resources—secondhand baby items, breastfeeding tips, and child-care recommendations among them. We bonded over our shared experience of not conforming to the ideal of the "Spelman woman."

Founded by white missionaries who sought to educate (i.e., civilize) Black women, the college had a major preoccupation with virtuousness. From the start, Spelman's dress codes were the perfect tool to enforce strict adherence to modesty. In the late 1800s, Victorian-style long skirts and high necklines were the norm. Through the 1960s, students were expected to dress "like ladies" while in classes, dining halls, and chapel. Shorts and jeans could only be worn on special occasions or in the privacy of a dormitory. For town visits, hats and white gloves were required—all with an eye to winning the respect of white society (and donors), which required carefully cultivating a virtuous image of Black womanhood.

In 1961 the writer Alice Walker was awarded a scholarship to attend Spelman, but the administration frowned upon her growing civil rights activism. After two years, she left for Sarah Lawrence College in New York, escaping what she found to be Spelman's "puritanical atmosphere." By the time I got there in 1997, Spelman's first Black woman president, Dr. Johnnetta B. Cole, had just finished her term, so the emphasis on conservative respectability had relaxed somewhat. But the dominant image of a Spelman woman was still someone who could succeed in a white world, and now her armor was corporate chic. Those of us who didn't fit, or want to fit, the mold found one another quickly. Two of my closest friends, Abena and Iyabo, shared my eclectic style and long locs. We wore colorful prints and sandals as we sat together on the grass that we were, instead, supposed to walk around.

We weren't the only misfits. Sister Omelika, as she was called on campus and in the wider community, was a professor of dance whom I gravitated toward. Her African dance class my senior year gave me the only A minus I got in college, bringing down my GPA a few tenths of a percentage. That minus is one of many reasons I have an abiding respect for the arts—acing math exams was one thing; understanding the physics and geometry of the human body in motion, quite another.

Omelika wasn't quite as militant as Debbie Allen in *Fame*, but when she sat down in front of the class, djembe between her knees, hands hovering for a moment as she scanned the room with a slight smile, you knew this would be no easy A. Occasionally, I saw Omelika gliding across campus—stunning African garb, long locs and head tie, with drums hung over her shoulder. Just that fleeting sight reassured me that it was possible to move through the world differently, defiantly. She, I'm sure, was not privy to how her bold style, her comportment, and what and *how* she chose to teach affected me, like the butterfly effect, where small movements have larger consequences.

There were other faculty and staff whom I looked to—Jamila Canady, Opal Moore, Bahati Kuumba, Cynthia Spence, Donna Akiba Harper, Mona Phillips, Beverly Guy-Sheftall, and Barbara Carter— who cultivated a plot in their pedagogy that was equal parts caring and demanding, so that more of us felt fortified. But for others I encountered on campus, getting pregnant, *well*, that was pushing things a little too far from Spelman's brand of respectability.

Walking through the campus gates each morning, I wasn't just carrying a baby inside. The degrading narrative of what it meant to be young, pregnant, and Black accompanied me. According to that false tale, I was lazy, promiscuous, and irresponsible—stereotypical tropes that Spelman had been trying for over a century to distance itself from. I felt, in a word, exposed.

I will never forget the first time I stopped by the student health clinic to ask whether the health insurance plan covered pregnancy-related care. A Black woman behind the desk barely looked up when she noted with slight irritation that "yes, it was covered, like any other illness." Pregnancy, but especially Black pregnancy, was a disorder that required aggressive treatment.

In my feeble attempt to shed some of the stigmas, I would often find a way to slip in some mention of "my husband" when interacting with strangers and acquaintances as a way to wrap my unruly body in a veil of heterosexual respectability. I was trying mightily to distance myself from that creature stitched together by cultural tropes and political rhetoric—a waddling "mistake" in the eyes of some, swollen with Black life. But as the kids say nowadays, *respectability would not save me.*

Black women in the United States are 2.5 times more likely to deliver their babies preterm and three to four times more likely to die during pregnancy and childbirth than white women, the latter regardless of income and education. Black college-educated women have a higher infant mortality rate than white women who never graduate high school. Even tennis champion Serena Williams experienced near-fatal complications after the birth of her daughter. Had it not been for her insistence that *she knew her own body* in the face of medical staff who did not initially take her concerns seriously, she believes she would have died.

But the growing attention to Black maternal mortality may itself be a kind of debilitating exposure as Black women are rendered "spectacularly and dangerously visible," in the words of Jennifer C. Nash, professor of gender, sexuality, and feminist studies. Nash offers a biting critique of the way that politicians, journalists, activists, and even Black feminists depict Black mothers through the "frame of crisis," tethering their flesh to "disorder" and using their plight as "a distinct form of Left political currency" that has become a "synonym for pain."

Whereas in an earlier era Black motherhood represented deviance and pathology, now it is a symbol of "tragic heroism" because of the "proximity to death"—that of children slain at the hands of police or death due to obstetric violence. But according to Nash, this political attention and media exposure rarely extends beyond symbolic support. This is a sobering caution, no matter our particular cause, that while the language of "crisis" may seem like the best way to garner attention in the short term, in our rush to raise awareness, we may end up reproducing the very same racial tropes we were trying to oppose.

The good news is that there is a deep well of Black, Indigenous, and immigrant know-how about supporting the well-being of birthing people and babies. It includes broad access to midwives, doulas, and a caring community not just before, during, and after childbirth but also through miscarriage, abortion, infertility, and menopause.

Serena Williams herself reflected on this after her near-tragic ordeal: "What if we lived in a world where there were enough birth attendants? Where there was no shortage of access to health facilities nearby? Where lifesaving drugs and clean water were easily available to all? Where midwives could help and advise mothers after birth? What if we lived in a world where every mother and newborn could receive affordable health care and thrive in life?"

As with so many other problems, obstetric violence is linked to a wide range of social issues. SisterSong—the largest multiethnic reproductive justice coalition in the U.S.—insists, "all oppressions impact our reproductive lives . . . [and] we can only win freedom by addressing how they impact one another." While that certainly feels daunting, this interconnection is an invitation for us to start right where we are, joining with others to seed justice in our backyards.

It turns out that maternal and infant health is the most sensitive indicator of the overall health of any society. It's no wonder, then, that during the COVID-19 pandemic, researchers found that Black and Latinx pregnant people were five times more likely to be exposed to the virus than others. But even before that, racism in various forms has required oppressed communities to develop ways to resist and reimagine how they engage healthcare. These other approaches—defiant and life-affirming—offer insights that are essential to viral justice more broadly.

But a profit-driven healthcare system that incentivizes high-tech interventions—and prioritizes convenience for doctors over low-tech forms of social support and traditional expertise like midwifery— has stood in the way of public investment in what is known to work. Cesarean sections, for example, take about forty-five minutes to perform, whereas a vaginal birth usually takes hours or even days. A 2013 study of seventy-two hospitals across sixteen states found that C-section rates go up during times of the day that correspond to meals and shift changes: the doctor's schedule takes priority.

If that wasn't bad enough, hospitals and doctors generally earn more money for cesareans than they do for vaginal births because the former is considered major surgery. This means they are incentivized to take advantage of clinical gray areas like "abnormal labor progress" and so end up performing the higher-risk procedure when it's not necessarily warranted.

It's no wonder that the U.S. has one of the highest rates of C-sections in the world—almost double the rate of France, Sweden, and Finland, which have publicly funded healthcare systems. When you have a scalpel, every labor groan sounds like a mother in distress. Although cesareans can be lifesaving if a mother or baby is in immediate distress, they are performed routinely in many hospitals even though they entail serious risks like hemorrhaging, blood clots, and more. But the paradox of Americans paying more for worse healthcare extends well beyond maternal and infant health.

Compared with the other eleven Organization for Economic Cooperation and Development nations, the U.S. has the highest rate of chronic diseases, lowest life expectancy, highest suicide rate, fewest physician visits, and highest rate of avoidable death even though our country spends *the most* per capita on healthcare. The money goes to expensive technologies and specialized procedures, and as a result, we end up with one of the highest rates of hospitalization for preventable causes.

Research on physician-induced demand—the hypothesis that doctors can influence their patient's treatment to suit the physician's self-interest—is growing. In 2009 researchers in Minnesota found that when financial incentives were removed, the number of C-sections went down. In 2016 economists tracked a large number of births in California and Texas and found that patients who are *also* physicians receive 10 percent fewer C-sections than the average patient, even when doctors have a financial incentive to elect surgery. "So obstetricians appear to be treating their physician patients differently than their non-physician patients," said healthcare economist Erin Johnson.

Black women, in turn, are the demographic with the highest rate of C-sections in the U.S. Watch out if you're in labor nearing a shift change in a hospital that pays doctors more for surgery *and* you are Black. Serena Williams's near-fatal experience occurred right after a C-section. So what the hell is going on?

Some observers try to attribute the higher rate of maternal mortality and preterm birth among Black women to higher rates of obesity, diabetes, and other risk factors. But researchers note that these preexisting conditions don't account for much. Elliot Maine, a clinical professor of obstetrics and gynecology at Stanford, said we should focus on the way hospital staff treat Black women differently from white women: "Are they treated with dignity and respect?" "Are they listened to? Are they included as part of the team?" Or are Black women exposed to the whims of medical professionals who routinely discount their concerns, downplay their needs, and harbor disdain for those they regard as unfit mothers?

Many people still assume that genetics are the driving factor of health disparities. But in a classic study comparing African American women, African-born Black women, and white women, researchers explain that "African immigrants to the U.S. and white women born in the U.S. had similar pregnancy outcomes. So if there is any genetic pre-disposition for low birth weight babies, it's doubtful that it falls along what we call racial lines. It turns out that when African women immigrate to the US, *it takes only one generation* before their daughters are at risk of having premature babies at a significantly higher rate and with poorer birth outcomes." As neonatologist Richard David put it, "There's something about growing up as a Black female in the United States that is not good for your child-bearing health. I don't know how else to summarize it." But even this misattributes the source of harm—the problem is not growing up Black and female, but growing up in a racist and sexist society.

Why do our social diagnoses tiptoe around the source of harm? *There's something about having legs and walking through this minefield that may blow you to bits.* Is the issue our having legs, or people deciding to plant fucking explosives in our path? For those who really care about health equity, the first step is to stop producing fuzzy X-rays of reality. *Racism*, not race, is a risk factor. White supremacy, not Blackness, is bad for our health. Cis-hetero-patriarchy, not femaleness or queerness or transness, is killing us.

In 2000, when I became pregnant, I didn't yet have this language or these studies at my fingertips. I just knew that at every turn—on the bus, on my college campus, in the media—to be young, pregnant, and Black felt like a problem. And the weight of a growing baby and the cultural baggage of Black pathology was getting too heavy. I had to lighten my load.

I reached out to my friend Abena, who had recently delivered her daughter with a local Black midwife, Sarahn Henderson, or "Mama Sarahn," as she was affectionately known throughout the community. In our first meeting with her, Sarahn picked Shawn and me up from the train station closest to her house. The first thing I noticed was her waist-length locs braided into two long plaits that flowed over her shoulders. She couldn't have been more than five foot tall and some change, so the plaits gave her a playful and easygoing aura.

When we arrived at her ranch-style home, we made our way into the den, sitting on pillows on the floor with the familiar smell of essential oils and incense in the air. That first meeting was mostly about us—*What are you excited for? What are you nervous about?* It wasn't that she spoke slowly, but that she seemed to turn each word over at least once, making sure it was carefully, gently delivered.

At some point, Sarahn asked whether I had any concerns about the shape of my body changing after giving birth. Her question made me realize how little time I had spent imagining myself that far into the future. I wasn't simply a vessel, but a person whose worries, small and large, were important. The space she held for me to stretch and grow into a new identity as a mother mirrored the process my own body was undergoing. And although I must have stammered out a response, at no point did I feel anxious or incapable. Instead, her questions drew out reflections on things I hadn't even begun to consider. And at that moment, my trust in her was born.

By the time we met her, Sarahn had been "catching babies" in the greater Atlanta area for over two decades, even though midwifery was effectively illegal in Georgia (and still is). She had even delivered one of my college classmates, which tells you how long she had been in business. Though "business" is not quite right, because her Birth in the Tradition practice offered a sliding scale of prices and, for broke college students, she charged a whopping $1,200, payable in monthly installments. By comparison, the average cost for hospital births in the U.S. is over $10,000, though it can rise to as much as $30,000, depending on complications and the length of stay. Sarahn's fee also covered monthly, then biweekly and weekly, prenatal visits, as well as labor support for however long it took, and two to three postnatal visits as needed. This inventory does not even begin to speak to the *quality* of care and education we received, which was priceless.

Given that pregnancy was my major preoccupation that year, I decided to make the politics of childbirth the focus of my senior honors thesis. On May 8, 2001, I had just put the finishing touches on the paper, entitled "A Moment of Conception: Racism, Capitalism, and Patriarchy Converge in the Uterus," a qualitative study comparing obstetrics and midwifery. The work of legal scholar Dorothy Roberts had been a huge influence on me. Her groundbreaking work *Killing the Black Body*, published in 1997, documents how the medical and scientific establishments have used Black women's bodies as a continuous site of experimentation and criminalization.

Reaching as far back as chattel slavery, when the "father" of modern gynecology, J. Marion Sims, performed surgeries on unanesthetized enslaved women—and examining everything from the harsh treatment of drug-addicted pregnant women by the criminal legal system, to the mandatory application of long-term birth control to Black teenagers—Roberts reframed "reproductive rights" as being about not simply individual freedom but social justice. Now a dear friend, Dorothy and I have joined forces on dozens of events over the years.

Like the book in your hand now, my thesis wasn't only concerned with diagnosing a problem but also with how Black women have tackled the problem and resisted racist medical coercion to foster their own approach to health. I dove into the history and ongoing work of Black community-based midwives in Georgia who delivered babies at home regardless of the law. And given that I was pregnant at the time, the stakes could not have been higher, nor the timing better, as the ink was literally drying on the page when my first contraction hit.

With a skip in my step, relieved to be done, I planned to stop by Kinkos to have the manuscript bound before dropping it off in the Sociology Department in Giles Hall. But as I reached over the counter to hand the stack of pages to the young cashier, I felt a light needling across my lower back. When he told me the bound manuscript would be ready in twenty-four hours, I explained that I didn't have that long. I was in labor and needed it bound ASAP. Oh, how I *wished* it was ASAP.

After two long days with Sarahn, her apprentice, my mother, and Shawn circling around one another in our cozy apartment off Ponce, I pushed out an obdurate 7.5-pound creature with a cone-shaped head that everyone promised would round out with time. This was a week before my college graduation, and it turned out that the A minus in African dance notwithstanding, I was the valedictorian.

Months earlier, as part of a group project for my Medical Anthropology class, my group decided to act out a birthing scene using Professor Daryl White's large wooden desk as a prop. As he and our classmates looked on with amusement, we performed a frenzied spectacle involving a patient (yours truly) huffing and puffing in the throes of childbirth as a nurse and doctor continuously checked several devices. The patient was confined to her bed and never consulted directly. The two medical professionals kept looking at the clock on the wall, first noting that the patient was taking too long, then hurrying her up because it was the end of their shift, and finally rushing her into surgery. End scene.

We then contrasted the obstetrical approach with the unhurried technique of the midwife. The midwife was unbothered by the laboring woman moving freely around the room, deciding what positions felt best—and the midwife conferred with her before suggesting ways to ease the pain. Finally, we led a discussion that connected the skit to the anthropology of childbirth literature. (I don't recall strong-arming my groupmates into choosing this topic, but it's not out of the question.)

One of the books we discussed was a beautifully illustrated tome, written by an anthropologist, depicting how people give birth worldwide. It was one of many texts that made me feel less strange and afraid, as I observed women around my age pushing out babies without high-tech monitoring or medical intervention. Early twenties, after all, is not "too young" to have a baby in most places on the planet. *Plus*, I thought to myself, *if someone could squat in a field and have a baby, surely I could push one out in my apartment.* This imagined kinship with "women for all time" helped ease my doubts about what I was capable of.

One of my other go-to books was *Birthing from Within*, by home-birth midwife Pam England and psychologist Rob Horowitz. From them, I learned that in 1927 a full 85 percent of people gave birth at home and that home births remained a majority even through the mid-1940s (55 percent). But by 1975, less than 1 percent of births took place at home with a midwife. So what happened?

One of the major developments was that the American Medical Association and the American College of Obstetricians and Gyne-cologists began a campaign to discredit midwives and home births to increase their own legitimacy and earning power. And since the majority of midwives were Black, it was easy for doctors to spread suspicions that they were "dark, dirty, ignorant, untrained, incompetent women" who used witchcraft and sorcery, and to cast white, male doctors as the safer bet. Later, even certified nurse midwives, the vast majority of them white, would join the effort to discredit and exclude Black "lay" midwives from their ranks.

But here's the thing: the anti-Blackness of obstetrics has turned out to be deadly, *not* just for Black people but for those of all backgrounds. Recall our discussion in chapter 1 about the surprising stories that "privileged" bodies tell. The medicalization of childbirth creates a "cascade of interventions" that increases the risk to everyone giving birth. If white Americans were a separate country, they would still rank twenty-third in the world for infant mortality, according to neonatologist Richard David. From the time they are born, white babies are also paying the price for anti-Black racism in medicine, albeit not as steeply as Black infants.

When my contractions first started, I sent a transcript of my graduation speech to one of my professors because I had no idea how I'd feel afterward and whether I'd want to be out in the world so soon after becoming a milk dispenser. It turned out that with Mama Sarahn's expert aftercare, which included a soothing sitz bath with a blend of traditional herbs, I felt energetic, alert, and ready to move about almost immediately.

Delivering a child on my terms reinforced an already stubborn orientation I had against convention. Although I learned a lot in the Atlanta University Center library stacks about how medicine sought to discipline birthing bodies, I didn't quite realize what that disciplining entailed until my own body was contracting, leaking, tearing, and howling. Knowledge about childbirth is undisciplined, embodied, experiential, and felt; "Sometimes a scream is better than a thesis," as Ralph Waldo Emerson put it. Yet medically managed reproduction sedates the screams of those whose knowledge about their own bodies is deemed a nuisance.

Echoing the words of sociologist Barbara Katz Rothman, who said, "Birth is not only about making babies, it is about making mothers—strong, capable mothers who trust themselves and know their inner strength," in the face of what she recently termed *biomedical imperialism*. Sarahn described the feeling she had after delivering the first of her five children at home: "I did it! Especially when you've been told you can't do it. It gives you this feeling that if I can do this, I can do anything. And I think this feeling helps you to conquer fears you might have in any other aspect of your life."

That was certainly the new-mom swagger that I felt—not only did I squeeze out a stubborn babe who was not at all motivated to leave the comfort of my body, but I also delivered *myself*.

The "baby blues," as Mama Sarahn calls postpartum depression, is not simply an individual illness but a predictable by-product of a frayed social fabric. This means that any and everything we do to stitch ourselves back together so that we feel less exposed can promote collective health and well-being. For example, Black birth workers draw on West African and other traditions in which the extended family and community do almost everything for new parents. All someone who has just given birth has to do is focus on recuperating and getting to know the baby. Sarahn's postpartum doula services, for example, include up to six weeks of breastfeeding support, running errands, preparing meals, cleaning the home, massages, and of course, herbal baths.

My mom and Shawn helped with cooking, rocking, and burping a colicky Malachi, dosing him periodically with Gripe water, and let me sleep and nurse intermittently. I felt vulnerable but not exposed. And a week after giving birth, I stood energized on the stage in Sister's Chapel at Spelman College, where, once upon a time, even wearing pants could draw the ire of administrators and students. There I delivered my valedictorian address to the class of 2001 with leaky breasts . . . not because I was exceptional, but because I was surrounded by people who seemed to take Toni Morrison's gospel to heart: "Your baby is beautiful and so are you and, honey, you can do it. And when you do, call me—I will take care of your baby."

Viral justice means that people can access and afford nonmedicalized approaches to childbirth. Sarahn has served those who are so-called high risk, including delivering twins and babies in the breech position, both of which would lead to C-sections in a hospital setting. While wealthy families and celebrities have started popularizing home births, for several decades Sarahn's business, Birth in the Tradition, has served families of all means with a sliding price scale based on what people can afford. Mama Sarahn remixes Marx with midwifery: *from each according to her ability, to each according to her need.*

We already know how to keep Black mothers and babies alive and well. Research now confirms that midwifery and doula support improve maternal and infant health. They lead to fewer complications and interventions; lower C-section rates; low rates of preterm birth; fewer low-birthweight infants and fewer neonatal deaths; higher rates of breastfeeding; reduced postpartum depression and anxiety; and increased positive birth outcomes—not to mention, they save money.

A 2013 study of over two hundred expectant mothers in Greensboro, North Carolina, in which half were doula-assisted births and the majority were low income and living in high-poverty neighborhoods, found that those who did not work with doulas were twice as likely to experience complications for the mother or baby, and four times as likely to have a low-birthweight baby. In a comprehensive review of twenty-seven clinical trials involving nearly sixteen thousand women across seventeen countries, people who had continuous support during childbirth experienced shorter labors and fewer C-sections, were less likely to report negative feelings about childbirth, and were less likely to develop depressive symptoms. But why is that?

The "harsh environment theory" proffers that as childbirth has been medicalized and moved outside the home, pregnant patients are exposed to "institutional routines, high intervention rates, staff who are strangers, lack of privacy, bright lighting, and needles"—which are stressors even when we're feeling our best. Doulas help to buffer this harsh environment and advocate on behalf of the birthing person. More interesting still, studies of birthing people's perceptions of pain during labor find that those who are accompanied by doulas report less pain, which in turn leads to fewer interventions that could turn risky.

This Doula Effect, wherein individuals who are trained to care for and accompany others can change a person's hormonal levels, offers a powerful testament to how we can each intervene in hostile climates to change the weather. In the case of childbirth, it's not simply about adopting a particular mind-set—either for or against pain medication, for example. Rather, the relationship between a doula and a birthing person, including frequent eye contact and soothing touch, can suppress stress hormones and create a spike in oxytocin and endorphins. In other words, we can literally be one another's pain relief through similar forms of care and accompaniment. How different would that be from the current practice of healthcare workers who underestimate Black pain and medical professionals who seem to cause *more* distress?

Yet doula and midwife support aren't options that our healthcare systems and insurance industry support, although this started to change as COVID-19 made hospital births increasingly risky. At the height of the pandemic, many hospitals were forced to implement policies that deepen the experience of medical alienation—such as only allowing one support person for the birthing person in the room during labor. And with reports of expectant mothers and midwives testing positive for the virus after delivering in hospitals, the number of individuals seeking home births surged.

Robina Khalid, a licensed midwife in New York City, described getting flooded with calls from women who no longer wanted to deliver in the hospital during the pandemic, most of whom she couldn't accommodate. The state, in turn, began trying to quickly authorize birthing centers as alternatives to hospitals—a long-overdue development. As Khalid noted, we should all be questioning whether "the average pregnant person needed to be cared for in a space that houses sick people to begin with." Not just *questioning* but refuting the idea that the safest place to have a child is where there is the highest concentration of pathogens that could infect and kill you, even before COVID-19.

Between April and June 2020, a team of researchers in Philadelphia examined nearly 1,300 blood samples of people who had given birth, looking for coronavirus antibodies. This included people who had been infected but may not have shown symptoms. They found that just over 6 percent of the individuals overall were carriers. But when they looked at the results by race, they were shocked to find that 10 percent of Black and Latinx individuals had been exposed, compared with 2 percent of white and 1 percent of Asians. "When I saw the data, I almost fell out of my chair," said Scott Hensley. But are the findings really that surprising when we consider the larger environment to which people are exposed?

We know from chapter 1 that many people are weathered by chronic stress borne out by decades of persistent racism, which is how Rachel Hardeman, a reproductive health equity researcher at the University of Minnesota, commented on the study just mentioned. Black and Latinx individuals are more likely to work in essential jobs, and many live in multigenerational households and use public transportation. That they are five times more likely to have been exposed to COVID-19 is overdetermined by multiple factors conspiring to put them in harm's way.

This is precisely why many midwives, both before and after the pandemic, also specialize in providing wraparound social support, or "gap management," as Jennie Joseph, a Black midwife in Florida, called it. This is where a team of birth workers supports expectant parents as they address things like mental health, food, housing security, and immigration status. Win-win-win, and yet so many people continue to lose out.

In March 2020, coinciding with the early days of the pandemic, the Black Maternal Health Caucus proposed federal legislation that would fund education and training for community-based birth workers (the Perinatal Workforce Act), address how social determinants affect maternal health (the Social Determinants for Moms Act), and fund community-based organizations for doulas and midwives (the Kira Johnson Act), all with a focus on tackling Black maternal mortality by integrating racial bias and discrimination training and accountability.

In 2016 Kira Johnson, whom one of the bills is named after, was a thirty-nine-year-old Black woman pregnant with her second child when the unthinkable happened. Now, keep in mind, Kira had all the right insurance and was in "perfect health." She spoke five languages, ran marathons, and had a pilot's license, among other signs of class privilege. When her obstetrician told Kira and her husband, Charles, that she would need to deliver by C-section, they were concerned but tried not to worry.

After coming out of surgery, however, Kira began feeling severe abdominal pain. She shook and grew pale, and for over ten hours, her family begged the medical staff to run tests. One of the nurses looked Charles right in the eyes and said, point-blank, "Sir, your wife just isn't a priority right now." Charles noticed blood in her catheter, which spurred the staff to order tests and a CT scan. But it was hours before she was taken into emergency surgery, where doctors found

3.5 liters of blood in her abdomen. During the C-section, it turns out, they had lacerated her bladder, and Kira died tragically on the operating table. Even more enraging than the original surgical mistake is the thought that she could have been saved had the medical staff not dismissed her and her family's concerns.

Probably the only reason we even know Kira's story is that her mother-in-law, Judge Glenda Hackett, is a well-known TV personality. But I've also kept tabs on the story because Kira died at Cedars-Sinai in Los Angeles, the same hospital where my father passed away two years earlier.

I wasn't there by his bedside to see staff rush in and try to jumpstart his heart, his torso bouncing violently in the air to no effect. I didn't have to be there to know that, like Kira's, my mom's concerns about his deteriorating condition were not taken seriously until it was too late.

Viral justice, I'm convinced, starts with acknowledging that the medical industry will continue to produce premature death so long as it remains an *industry*. No cultural competency trainings or antiracist trainings, however comprehensive, can redeem it. And if we are serious about growing an entirely different approach to healthcare, we need not only a different economic model but also relationships between patients and healthcare professionals that are grounded in mutual trust and respect.

Given that the doula and midwifery approach centers the whole person and prioritizes autonomy, trust, and collaboration, it is a model for our entire healthcare system and beyond. Viral justice draws on the example of community-based health workers as a template for birthing a fundamentally different approach to healing. And we don't have to start from scratch. Each of us can follow the example of doulas, caring for and accompanying people in our families, schools, workplaces, and neighborhoods as we confront a hostile climate together.

When Malachi was about one month old, I experienced my first public intervention as a young parent. I needed some groceries and

Shawn was still at work, so I bundled Malachi up in his oversize green knitted sweater on top of a light gray onesie that covered his legs and feet, complete with a matching beanie. I squeezed him into the baby carrier so his head was facing my chest. As I rounded the corner into the parking lot of Murder Kroger and made my way to the store entrance, an elderly Black woman who was loading her trunk walked over to me and began taking off his clothes. First his hat, then his sweater, and finally she loosened the first few buttons of his onesie, saying, "You gone give that chile a heatstroke."

Granted, it was mid-June on a sweltering day in Atlanta, and he was dressed for fall in New England. But to my mind, I was planning ahead. I was taking my baby into a store blasting air-conditioning, especially when we got to the produce section. Parenting, I would learn, involves walking a fine line between protection and suffocation. And in that moment, I perceived the difference between what could have been an embarrassing dressing-down, one that made me feel foolish and exposed, and what I experienced as a loving correction, one that seemed to whisper, "You don't have to know everything, chile, 'cause we got you covered." So, how else can we learn to fortify each other when folks are at their most vulnerable?

For some, it may entail supporting organizations like the Minnesota Prison Doula Project, which supports people locked up in women's prisons around the country. Through this program, doulas assist birthing people over the course of the entire pregnancy—accompanying them at the hospital for the labor and delivery; remaining present through the traumatic experience of separation from their child (including taking photos of the baby for the new parent, something that wouldn't happen otherwise); and supporting them through the post-separation grieving process with one-on-one counseling and by facilitating parent-child visitation sessions.

Started in 2008, the project has become a model for other states. Although no government agency keeps track, approximately twelve thousand people are estimated to be pregnant in U.S. jails and prisons each year. Some prisons allow doulas to be physically present during labor and birth, but even then, because most facilities don't have nurseries, people who are incarcerated typically only have twenty-four hours before they're separated from their newborns. Doulas in Tutwiler Prison in Alabama will record the mom's voice reading a book so the baby can listen later, and they help with mother-baby bonding through scent by exchanging hats and blankets with the babies.

Ancient Song Doula services in New York City is part of a growing #BeyondBirthwork movement dedicated to fighting for racial justice in maternal health, supporting communities of color to navigate social welfare and healthcare systems, and connecting these communities to a variety of supports. But to do that, they need all of us to demand recognition and fair compensation for their work on the part of public agencies. The New York State doula pilot program would allow Medicaid reimbursement for doula services. Proposed by former governor Andrew Cuomo, the pilot program is just one example of how to spread the Doula Effect to those who could most benefit. Even so, according to Jennifer Nash, there is an important debate under way among doulas about how "the entry of the state 'into the room' can quickly complicate the question of who a doula serves: her birthing client, or the state that reimburses her for her services."

Since 2016, Ancient Song has also been assisting those locked up at Rikers Island with one-on-one consults, prenatal support, childbirth education, meditation, art therapy, and pain management, though they aren't allowed to attend births. They also offer postpartum and lactation support in the jail's nursery, which is only available to select women who get into the nursery program.

The doula model of community care and activism is spreading in other ways. *Death doulas*, in particular, offer accompaniment to individuals and families on the other end of life. Death doula Alua Arthur, the founder of Going with Grace, has an infectious smile and vivacious personality, brightening whatever room she enters with her bright clothes and jingling bracelets and earrings—the exact opposite of the mood that typically surrounds death in mainstream U.S. culture. Alua, who is based in Los Angeles and is also an attorney, leads an end-of-life support team that offers training for those interested in joining the ranks of death doulas. And what could have been more crucial in the midst of the COVID-19 pandemic?

Elizabeth Perez initially worked as a birth professional serving over 250 families in New York City from 2014 to 2020. Now, when Black women are 243 percent more likely than white women to die during or shortly after childbirth, she has also taken up end-of-life services. "It is necessary for us to know how to proceed both in honoring the dead and creating space for grief," Perez said.

Not only has the pandemic forced people to think anew about giving birth in the potentially lethal environment of hospitals, but with death and dying thick in the air, it has also demanded new ways of breathing through life's transitions. The most heartbreaking experiences, for many, have involved an inability to be at the bedside of loved ones as they took their last breaths, or to be with family members in person for funerals, grieving and celebrating the lives of those who have passed. Similar to traditional doulas, death doulas support people before, during, and after death; much of their work is preparatory for the entire family. Alua is a member of the National End-of-Life Doula Alliance, whose mission is to create a cultural shift in American death practices.

As part of her training, Alua didn't just get a certificate in death midwifery. She also worked at a hospice, interned at a funeral home, learned all about life insurance and financial planning, and studied with estate planners and grief counselors. She said she wanted "to see all aspects of how we deal with death in our culture right now," so that she could holistically support people through the process.

As Alua reflected, "There are a lot of practical details that really should be dealt with before they die, because otherwise it becomes so much more of a nightmare to do afterward."

Death, like birth, is an industry. By 2023 the U.S. death care market is estimated to bring in revenues of $68 billion, with costs of a burial ranging from $7,000 to $12,000 on average. Put simply, many Americans cannot afford to die. My mother-in-law is buried in a potter's field outside Atlanta because she passed away when Shawn and I were still students and could barely afford rent, much less the exorbitant costs of a middle-class burial. And when my dad passed, I learned the hard way how expensive it is for families left holding the bill.

Although my mom and I managed to pay for a plot in Inglewood Park Cemetery, the casket, and the graveside funeral, there wasn't quite enough left to cover a headstone. Plus, we were exhausted by all the choices required by the death care market and the other mundane loose ends that come when someone dies suddenly: I had to pack up my dad's office at the real estate company where he worked, run down his outstanding debts and make sure those got paid, and organize his memorial—create the program and arrange for food, flowers, and music—amid the flood of calls, texts, and Facebook posts expressing condolences. I sometimes imagine how different the circumstances surrounding my dad's death would have felt had my family been accompanied by Going with Grace. The service is as much a balm to the family afterward as it is to the individual beforehand.

In the week between his death and the funeral, I awoke in the White House every morning with my face moistened from a wet pillow as I remembered again and again that he was gone. I let the sorrow spill into the pillowcase for a few minutes each morning, but then it was back to funeral planning. Maybe we could've pulled together the money for a headstone at the time, but considering its permanence, we wanted to get it right. So for four years, my dad's grave was unmarked, until finally a group of my closest friends in LA, who often visited his gravesite, got together and surprised my mom with the money needed for a headstone.

As COVID-19 cases spiked in New York, the issue of where to bury all the bodies in an already dense city became another source of fear and trauma for residents.

For over 150 years Hart Island, a 101-acre strip of land off the coast of the Bronx, has been the city's potter's field where the indigent and anonymous are laid to rest. During the pandemic, it became a site of mass, unmarked graves for the many unclaimed bodies. It's where an estimated one million people have been interred over the years, and where erosion has sometimes caused bones to surface on the beachfront. Apropos of the dominant approach to death, Hart Island is out of sight and out of mind—"a necropolis within the metropolis, cut off from the living population geographically and psychically," according to journalist Jody Rosen. But as with so many other grisly aspects of our world, COVID-19 is shining a light on what we have chosen to ignore—that, even in death, segregation has long been a hallmark of our deeply stratified society.

Drone footage of Hart Island makes plain the indignity of dispossession. Usually, it's the job of people imprisoned on Rikers Island to carry out the daily work of burial; they are paid one dollar an hour. Due to the surge in deaths and for safety reasons, the city hired contract workers, who could be viewed atop forklifts unloading plain wooden coffins into rows and pouring dirt on top, "with the unceremonious diligence of a street repair team scooping asphalt into a pothole," wrote Rosen. Look closer still, and we must reckon with the routine injustices, the many small deaths that those who are buried en masse have had to contend with all their lives.

In April 2020 fifty-seven-year-old Tami Treadwell got a call from her daughter in the middle of the night saying that Gregory Treadwell, Tami's ex-husband, with whom she shared children and grandchildren and whom she was still very close to, had died at home of suspected coronavirus. "The Seafood Queen of Harlem," as she is known throughout the city, is a popular food truck vendor, and Gregory was a produce delivery driver who continued to work until he came down with a fever. A doctor advised him not to go to the hospital, and soon after, his daughter found him nonresponsive in the apartment.

Tami rushed over and, following the coroner's instructions, put ice on Gregory's body to slow the decomposition. Still in shock and having just witnessed the paramedics manhandle her daughter, who was asking for an update, Tami stood on the sidewalk outside the building, weeping and screaming as she tried to make sense of what was happening—that she might have to keep icing the body for up to three days because of a shortage of funeral homes.

It took calls to over twenty funeral homes until finally one in Englewood, New Jersey, told Tami they could collect Gregory's body. Still, after all that, she was not defeated. Sitting on the beige couch in her apartment, she recalled that frightening night. Taking a deep breath, lump in her throat and tightness in her chest, Tami reminded us,

> We done been through worse shit than this . . . This is an opportunity for us to come back stronger, and greater, and better than ever before. That's what *I'm* gonna do, for myself, for my business, and for the people around me that I love. I wanna be better than I was before this Rona shit hit. I wanna be better than I've ever been before because we don't know what's gonna happen, or what's around the corner. And that just gives you a resilience and a determination to be the best you you can be while we have whatever time left we have here on this earth.

If Tami can come back from the icy depths of despair, the sorrow born of abandonment by a city that she has loved all her life, then you and I can wake up each day and be better than we were before this Rona shit hit, by supporting those around us through life's transitions, big and small. Rather than looking away from the pain, we can follow the example of doulas and embody an everyday practice of care and accompaniment. In *Earthseed: The Books of the Living*, Octavia Butler writes,

> We can,
> Each of us,
> Do the impossible
> As Long as we can convince ourselves
> That it has been done before.

So let us remind ourselves that we build on a long tradition of enacting social solidarities by caring for one another's well-being. For example, the People's Free Medical Clinics created by the Black Panther Party for Self-Defense (BPP) drew on the "ingenuity of the Panther rank and file and members' abilities to mobilize local resources" in opening over a dozen clinics in cities across the country between 1968 and 1973. The party worked in partnership with "both lay and *trusted-expert* volunteers—including nurses, doctors, and students in the health professions—to administer basic preventative care, diagnostic testing for lead poisoning and hypertension, and other conditions, and in some instances, ambulance services, dentistry, referrals to other facilities for more extensive treatment." Few Americans know that government-sponsored neighborhood health centers were developed in response to BPP activism.

Like Mama Sarahn and other midwives, those volunteering in the Panther clinics were not only concerned with people's physical health but also helped people navigate issues with housing, employment, and social welfare programs. According to BPP leader Fred Hampton, "First you have free breakfasts, then you have free medical care, then you have free bus rides, and soon you have FREEDOM!"

This is one of the reasons that the Panthers' "survival programs" were such a threat to the FBI, leading its director, J. Edgar Hoover, to state in 1969 that the BPP was "without question . . . the greatest threat to internal security of the country." This reminds us that the seemingly small things, such as providing free breakfast to kids and medical checkups to neighbors, may be more than meets the eye and can have exponential effects—exposing the failure of the Powers That Be and showing what is possible when we work together.

When Malachi was fourteen months old, Shawn and I packed up our Atlanta apartment on Somerset Terrace and moved across the country to Berkeley, California, so we could both start graduate school. Little did I know at the time that I would end up completing my dissertation fieldwork in a building that once housed a Panther free clinic in Oakland, an experience I'll return to in the next chapter.

Our new home in UC Village, an apartment complex housing hundreds of student families, was idyllic in many ways. Clusters of buildings were designed around courtyards where residents from all over the world left their backdoors open, and parents could keep an eye on kids while cooking dinner or completing a paper due the next day. It was common to see harried students catching the number 52 bus up to campus as grandparents pushed strollers around the neighborhood, trying to get babies to sleep, or running after toddlers on the community playground. It wasn't long after we moved in that I called my mom to ask whether she might be able to come for an extended stay to help us juggle all the balls.

I gave birth to Khalil during my second year of graduate school. After about a day of contractions and three howling pushes, he arrived much faster than anyone was prepared. Student health insurance didn't cover home births, and we couldn't find anyone who had a sliding scale like Sarahn did, so we had to get to the hospital in time for our nurse-midwife to catch him. When I was getting closer to "transition," that critical phase right before it's time to push, I crouched on all fours in the back of our blue Volvo wagon as Shawn wove in and out of afternoon traffic to Alta Bates Hospital.

"Code stork, code stork!" I heard the voice over the loudspeaker call as someone pushed me through the hallway in a wheelchair while Shawn parked the car. I was perched facing the back of the chair because there was no way I could sit normally as surges of pain flamed around my torso. A nurse must have helped me get onto the bed, where again I stayed on all fours, my fingers gripping the back of the bed and my unrepentant howls spilling out into the corridor.

The midwife would later tell me that "code stork" is the emergency broadcast to let people know there's a baby being born outside the labor and delivery ward, which we fortunately avoided. Shawn and the midwife almost missed the show, rushing in just moments before Khalil made his debut. My water didn't even have a chance to break, so Khalil arrived "en caul," fully wrapped in the amniotic sac that had held him for nine months.

I would eventually learn that en caul births are rare, especially for vaginal deliveries, affecting fewer than one in eighty thousand babies. Most doctors and midwives have never witnessed one. Perhaps as a consequence, many legends exist going back millennia about babies "born with a veil"—superstitions that said they couldn't drown, that they would be protected in battle, and that they were destined for greatness. Historical records depict people sewing cauls inside pouches to wear as protective amulets. Midwives were known to steal cauls to sell to lawyers who believed it would help them win their cases. One ad in a British newspaper in 1874 appealed specifically to sailors: "TO SEA CAPTAINS: For sale, a Child's Caul in perfect condition. £5."

Some believed "caulbearers" were clairvoyant, conversant with ghosts, or possessing special eloquence in general. Some records speak to the value people imbued in the caul itself—bequeathing it in their wills or turning it into powder for use in medical potions. Many cultures have simply regarded the caul as a sign of good luck.

Without subscribing to the lore surrounding caul births, I find something illuminating about this thin translucent tissue that protects all of us at some point while we grow into fleshy beings, in that cauls represent the types of tender fortification that we continue to need throughout life.

It turns out Khalil's birth was so swift, and my support system so supple, that I found myself back in classes the following week. Every Monday, Wednesday, and Friday, I dashed out the door of Barrows Hall, threw my tote bag into the milk crate basket on the back of my bike, and raced downhill through Ohlone Greenway, toward the Village.

As I rounded the corner on Gooding Way, breasts tightening with milk, I could hear the whining of a baby before I could see him. The only reason Khalil wasn't wailing yet was because his nana was rocking him vigorously, up and down, side to side on the back patio so she could see me coming. After I hastily dropped my bike and rushed through the gate, my mom handed over the bundle, his rolls of fat resembling those of the Pillsbury Doughboy, except this one was waiting impatiently for dinner. All around us, I witnessed this intergenerational tag-teaming, hundreds of families juggling school, work, and family. The feeling that *this has been done before* helped ease the stress, though there were still many nights with colicky Khalil (apparently, being born en caul doesn't make colic go away) when I understood deeply why sleep deprivation is an effective method of torture.

The idyllic village setting, which let us put down our guard, also posed a threat when we got a little too carefree. On a cool summer day when Malachi was about six and Khalil was four, we heard a high-pitched howl coming from the other side of the courtyard. Khalil was running in the direction of our back porch, tears streaming down his face and blood spraying from his chin and neck. Panicked, I raced out of the sliding door and scooped him up while Shawn grabbed a fistful of paper towels to stop the bleeding.

Through all the fluids, we were finally able to see the gash underneath his chin, almost to the bone and shaped like a smile. With Malachi's help, we pieced together the accident—they were riding their bikes in circles around the courtyard when Khalil lost control and fell headfirst into the edge of a curb. But with no insurance and making just enough between my campus jobs and Shawn's construction work to cover food and rent, we decided not to go to the ER for stitches. For over a week, we watched and waited, dressing and redressing the wound, hoping it would close on its own without getting infected.

Fortunately, Khalil turned out to be an "overhealer." Not only did the bloody smile close within days, but a thick keloid bubbled over it as reinforcement—"like watching a spell from Harry Potter," I joked to Shawn, making a virtue out of necessity. But my light-hearted humor concealed the anger and helplessness I felt in having to weigh my child's well-being against the cost of a hospital visit.

"Thick skin," it turns out, is one of many racist stereotypes that underwrite medical racism. Black patients are routinely undertreated, in part, because health professionals believe they feel less pain. In 2016 researchers at the University of Virginia found that half of the white medical students in their sample held a range of racist false beliefs: Black people age more slowly, their nerve endings are less sensitive, their blood coagulates more quickly, and their skin is thicker than whites'. Not surprisingly, the students who held these erroneous ideas underestimated the pain of Black patients in mock medical cases. Moreover, these ideas have been used to justify the gross asymmetry of medical provision in the U.S.

My colleague Keith Wailoo, author of *Pain: A Political History*, points to even earlier evidence of the pain gap, including a study from the 1990s in which white patients with long bone fractures received more pain medication than Black and Latinx people. He describes this as a "divided state of analgesia in America: overtreatment of millions of people that feeds painkiller abuse at the same time that, with far less public attention, millions of others are systematically undertreated." The privileged, as we discussed in chapter 1, may experience short-term reprieve, but the scourge of addiction has also left a trail of white bodies in its wake.

Ultimately, it boils down to whose pain is considered real and worthy of relief. Anti-Black racism justifies the rationing of empathy. But as the writer Kali Holloway observed, "This idea of black immunity to pain is purely magical thinking, rooted in longstanding, widely circulated and scientifically baseless beliefs that essentially cast black people as something other than human." *Magical*, like my own allusions to Harry Potter when it came to Khalil's quick healing. The idea of Black superhumanity, even if it's an expression of maternal love, is tied to subhuman treatment. My own magical thinking born out of economic precarity may seem harmless, but when the stereotype of Black stoicism in the face of pain is institutionalized and wielded by healthcare professionals, it ends up justifying the rationing of care on a massive scale.

There is one sure sign of how dreadful our current system is: although the U.S. spends $10,624 per capita on healthcare, Cuba performs better on most health indices, including infant mortality and life expectancy, while spending $987 on healthcare per capita. In Cuba, healthcare is a right under the constitution, not a commodity as it is in the U.S., and the overwhelming emphasis is on preventative care. For example, pregnant women see their local doctor seventeen times on average before delivery, and physicians, who all receive free education, are required to practice at least two years as a family doctor.

Since 2001, Cuba has even been training medical students from impoverished and oppressed communities—many of them Black and Latinx students from the U.S.—at no cost and encouraging them to work in neglected areas once they return. Nimeka Phillip, one of those doctors, said one of the biggest adjustments when she returned was spending less time with her patients. Enter: "land of the free," where we all pay the cost.

Cuba has also pioneered the development of numerous vaccines and new treatments for HIV, cancer, and now COVID-19, holding some 1,200 international patents and selling medicines to over fifty countries well before the pandemic, despite half a century of U.S. embargoes. In 2015 the World Health Organization confirmed that Cuba was the first country in the world to eliminate HIV and syphilis transmission between mother and child. And Cuba has also eliminated diseases like measles and mumps for which vaccines exist, unlike the U.S., where vaccine resistance led to nearly 1,300 people contracting measles in 2019, the greatest number of cases since 1992.

This is not to paint Cuba as paradise, or some kind of socialist utopia. There, too, there is a two-tiered system where foreigners and elites receive access to special facilities, and sending doctors on medical missions abroad has become Cuba's most lucrative export and diplomatic tool. Some of these physicians have decided not to return to Cuba for economic and other reasons.

And in summer 2021, uprisings led by Afro-Cubans shook the island. The largest in decades, the protests were triggered by multiple factors: the police shooting of yet another unarmed Black Cuban, anger and frustration over food and medical shortages, curbs on civil liberties in the wake of COVID-19, electricity outages, and economic struggles. And the uprisings were inspired, in part, by a revolutionary anthem created by Black artists, "Patria y Vida" (Homeland and life), that was blaring in the streets.

Economic precarity hits Afro-Cubans even more than their white counterparts because Black people are often kept out of jobs in the relatively lucrative tourism sector. Afro-Cubans also have far fewer family members living abroad, which means they have less access to remittances that are a major source of relief for many islanders. As University of Pennsylvania professor and Black Cuban American Amalia Dache said, "The colonial system of race did not end with the revolution . . . You don't hear from Black Cubans. They are invisible on the island. Their pain, their suffering is invisible. And we need to listen to Black Cubans, who are the ones largely that are in the prison systems."

Yet for much of the pandemic, the news out of Cuba was that it was doing a better job than the U.S. at containing the virus, crediting two new experimental drugs with keeping the death toll down. Cuba also sent over four thousand health professionals to thirty-seven countries to care for over three hundred thousand patients, including in Lombardy, Italy, which was the hardest-hit region in the world at the time of the medical brigades' arrival. While it was common for Cuban medics to travel to places like Indonesia, West Africa, and Haiti, this was the first time they had been invited to a country with a world-renowned medical system, but one that was unable to cope with the pandemic. In 2021 Cuba's Henry Reeve International Medical Brigade was nominated for a Nobel Peace Prize.

Some critics, including the Trump administration, described Cuba's medical brigade as a form of "modern slavery," accusing the Cuban government of "human trafficking." Meanwhile, medical professionals who work abroad in a "hardship" post earn up to ten times more than their counterparts who stay on the island—even after the Cuban government retains up to 95 percent of the payments by the host country or sponsoring international organizations. And there continue to be waiting lists for doctors who want to participate.

Nevertheless, the Trump administration forced allies to cut ties, leaving many vulnerable communities who rely on Cuban doctors without care during the pandemic. For John Kirk, a professor of Spanish and Latin American studies who has spent over a decade studying Cuban medical internationalism, "Cuban doctors represented the threat of a good example of what public health could be—and that's why they had to be stopped."

Indeed, life-sucking systems persist by donning the cloak of inevitability, as in, *There is no other way to administer healthcare but a for-profit structure. It is naive to think otherwise!* To survive, these life-sucking systems must go to war against alternatives. If the Cuban approach to healthcare wasn't such a threat, why would U.S. politicians take such pains to denigrate and dismiss it? These for-profit proponents do not want us asking that question or this one: What *could* a more expansive approach to public health be?

For starters, it is not simply about affordability and access, however important those are for advancing health justice. You can have free and easy access to something that kills you. Recall the easier access white Americans have to opioids and the devastation wrought by that "privilege." Viral justice, by contrast, focuses on how racism infects our healthcare system above and beyond the issues of access and cost.

Following the murder of George Floyd, a number of municipalities in at least seventeen states, from California and Michigan to Texas and Massachusetts, passed resolutions to declare racism itself a public health emergency. Since 2015, before the current wave of murders, a national organization formed by medical students, White Coats for Black Lives, has been demanding that medical schools address racial justice in the curriculum, in medical care, and in communities since the murder of Michael Brown at the hands of police in 2014.

From where I sit, there are at least two medical traditions that exist: one that enables and the other that opposes racism. The first, exemplified by Floyd's original autopsy, which blamed preexisting health conditions for his death, entails the historical and ongoing collusion of doctors and scientists with the powers that be. The experimentation from 1932 to 1972 on Black men in Tuskegee, Alabama, that was the U.S. Public Health Service Syphilis Study is a standout historical example of horrific collusion. But in this century, we've seen the torture of captives at Guantánamo, the sterilization of inmates in U.S. prisons and ICE detention centers, and the exposure of families to toxic lead paint to study the most cost-efficient methods of abatement. Not to mention the everyday neglect and mistreatment of Black, Indigenous, Latinx, disabled, femme, poor, trans, imprisoned, veteran, unhoused, undocumented, immigrant, and other vulnerable patients across the globe. This tradition, let us call it *Medicine as Objective Oppressor*, was also responsible for building the intellectual foundation of scientific racism and mobilizing foot soldiers for eugenic policies worldwide.

When it comes to this first tradition, the medical establishment doesn't only betray patients but also debases practitioners, those who are socialized into its noxious norms. The poor treatment that you and I may experience reflects the toxic culture of medical training. Those with less power in the institutional hierarchy are routinely hazed and harassed by higher-ups. A recent study of more than 27,500 medical students found that over 35 percent of students from underrepresented groups had experienced mistreatment by faculty members. The numbers are even higher for women and for students who are Black, Latinx, Indigenous, or queer. It is not a story of a few bad apples when the whole damn orchard is rotten. And yet we aren't helpless in the face of medical mistreatment.

There is also a tradition of seeing healthcare providers as not only healers but truth tellers, whistleblowers, conscientious objectors, witnesses, and community partners. We might call this other tradition *Medicine as a Moral Force*. It involves those who use their status and authority to challenge those with power—people like Mona Hanna-Attisha, a pediatrician and public health advocate.

Dr. Mona, as she is affectionately called, supported residents in Flint, Michigan, who raised the alarm about their children being exposed to dangerous levels of lead after state officials switched the city's water supply to the Flint River. She put her career at risk by encouraging Flint residents to stop drinking the water and announcing her urgent findings before they were vetted by other experts.

There are people like Uché Blackstock, who worked on the front lines of the pandemic in New York City, treating hundreds of patients with COVID-19 while publicly advocating for structural changes in the healthcare system. "As of August 4th, [2020,] about 18,000 Black, 6,000 Latino, 600 Indigenous, and 70 Pacific Islander Americans would still be alive, if they had died of COVID-19 at the same actual rate as white Americans. Sit with that," she tweeted.

This is what public health researchers call "excess death," or the number of people who would still be alive were it not for the persistence of social inequity. Among the foremost voices for health justice, Blackstock tellingly left a position in academic medicine due to the hostile climate to work in urgent care, and more and more people inside and outside the medical industry are organizing against abuse.

A growing network called the Health Justice Commons has created a Medical Abuse Hotline where we can make our voices heard. The network is a community-led service that gathers people's stories and data about harms they've experienced in order to guide ongoing health justice advocacy. Founded by activists in the San Francisco Bay Area, it is also a source of referrals and tools that individuals and groups can use in other locales.

They offer "Know Your Rights" workshops, trainings to help people understand data on air pollution and its role in creating disabling environments, and strategies for resisting the criminalization of abortion and treatments for gender nonconforming folks, among many other popular education courses. Most importantly, efforts like this remind us that we do not have to resign ourselves to Medicine as Objective Oppressor.

At the same time, medical schools need to dramatically increase the recruitment and support of Black, Latinx, and Indigenous medical students. Recent work shows that physician-patient race concordance leads to better clinical outcomes in a range of contexts, and yet only 5 percent of all doctors are Black. This turns out to have dramatic repercussions in the context of childbirth.

Researchers at George Mason University found that when Black infants are cared for by white physicians, they are three times more likely to die than white babies. The study, which was published in August 2020, examined 1.8 million hospital births between 1992 and 2015 in the state of Florida. Researchers found that the benefit of having a Black doctor was pronounced for challenging births and in hospitals where more Black babies are delivered. While the exact mechanisms producing these outcomes have yet to be identified, it's surely a lethal mix of institutional and interpersonal factors, which need to be urgently addressed in medical training and the healthcare industry more broadly.

But no matter their background, we need to ensure that all current and future healthcare practitioners are knowledgeable about the history and contemporary manifestations of racism in medicine, the principles of antiracism, and the strategies for dismantling structural racism. After all, it is possible to create a racially diverse faculty and student body, but the same underlying logic of medicine as social control can still persist.

Medical students and physicians of all backgrounds need to demand that academic medical centers meet the needs of local Black residents and other communities of color. "We need, in every community, a group of angelic troublemakers," is how civil rights activist Bayard Rustin put it after returning to the U.S. from India in 1948. This should be the standard of care that we all demand of healthcare professionals. As important as it is for them to take responsibility for countering medical racism, our health is affected by the larger climate of anti-Black racism, so we all have a part to play. In addition to pushing for a stronger public safety net, how else do we cultivate collective wellbeing?

In our everyday lives, we can engender viral justice by creating and fortifying connections with people for mutual support and accountability during times of stress and hardship. If growing "thick skin" is needed in a dangerous environment, then shedding the layers, getting to be *thin*-skinned for a change, is a feature of the world we want.

This is especially the case for Black women who are routinely told (and tell ourselves) that we must be "superwomen." It sounds like a compliment, but like all "positive" stereotypes, it has a punishing underside. In practice, it means that we are not granted space to feel the full range of human emotions—hopeless, sad, worried, exhausted, lonely, grieved, heartbroken, confused, compassionate, content, carefree, exuberant, and more.

Instead, Black women are cast as the emotional "help." We are expected to take care of others, including those with no shortage of #WhiteTears. The only emotion that mainstream white culture allows Black women is anger, but even then, not real anger . . . a shallow, caricatured, hip-shaking, eye-rolling shell of an emotion—all noise but no sound, ventriloquized, demonized, laughable, scripted by those who have no clue how it feels inside the shell. Superwomen, after all, are still not human.

Thick skin is what we grow to shield ourselves from hostile weather. But if we had more collective forms of support and protection, we could shed our individual layers and be vulnerable.

For nearly six years, I have been gathering regularly with a group of Black women, ranging in age from their late thirties to their mid-eighties. We're all in various stages of life, with different occupations and income levels, hailing from different religious traditions including agnostic, Bahá'í, Buddhist, Christian, Jewish, Muslim, and Yoruba. But what brought us together was a shared intention to engender justice in our work and relationships. After the COVID-19 pandemic hit, we met virtually, with about ten to fifteen people showing up on any given week.

The gathering usually starts with check-ins about the previous week before we deep-dive into a particular topic that relates to our shared commitment to the "spirit of justice," which is what we call the group. At many of the gatherings, we call out the names of friends or relatives who need healing prayers and invoke the names of those who have died. For all the Strong Black Women™ whose imagined invincibility has justified all manner of violation and superhuman expectation, it is a space to shed our thick skin and be vulnerable.

I was motivated to start the gathering with my friend Kaytura in 2017 when I realized that most of my closest friends lived in Los Angeles, and that I would be living in Princeton for the foreseeable future. Plus, I wanted to connect with people outside the rarified halls of the university with all its stuffiness and pretention. Even better, as one of the younger members, I get to pull off my professor hat and take notes from the elders in the group, whose life experiences are edifying.

Importantly, vulnerability does not come "naturally," nor is it an inevitable result of our shared background as Black women. There have been times when our discussions have grown uncomfortably tense, feelings have been hurt, and bonds have been strained. But such is the nature of friendship, that when we grow close enough to let our guards down and vulnerable enough to share our truths, there is a risk of injury.

"Tending" to our relationships, as I think of it, doesn't come easily to me. From the Old French *tendre*, "to stretch," the cultivation of tenderness calls on us to stretch beyond ourselves. Admittedly, I tend to be quite awkward when it comes to this, and I usually (perhaps unfairly) blame grad school for stunting my emotional intelligence. I love teasing my sista Naimeh for her frequent "microaffections," which is what I call her follow-up messages in a group chat where she makes sure a previous comment hasn't accidentally rubbed someone the wrong way. And though I tease her, I know that my own thoughtlessness over the years has created rifts in more than one friendship.

The point is, we must actively tend to our relationships in the way that we hold space for one another; communicate with care, especially when we disagree; and most of all, find ways to support one another in tangible ways.

At one point, our Spirit of Justice group decided to make material our mutual support by starting a *sou sou*, which is a West African word for a savings fund that everyone contributes to and receives a disbursement from on a rotating basis. The trust we have for each other provides a sharp contrast to the argumentative, frenemy portrayal of Black women on reality television, such as on various *Real Housewives* franchises and *Love & Hip Hop*. And true aficionados of hip hop know all too well that what Biggie advised in "The Ten Crack Commandments"—Number Three, *Never Trust Nobody*—is a warped view of the ancestrally derived love that has helped Black people thrive on these shores for centuries.

We've held space for one another during big crises from cancer to COVID-19 deaths, as well as during all the "little deaths," which is how one of our members put it after losing her job and apartment within the first few weeks of the pandemic. But mostly, we come together to accompany one another through all of life's contractions. We created this shelter from the hostile weather well before COVID-19 hit, and when everyone started sheltering in place, for many of us, the group became a lifeline.

I am convinced that we can all grow the kind of world that fortifies us rather than wears us down by tending to the seeds of that world—truthfulness, kindness, patience, forgiveness, joy, and more— starting with those closest to us. But it takes practice.

And, lest we be tempted to romanticize social support, not all forms of care and cooperation are oriented toward justice. I remember in graduate school when, in a gender studies course, professor

Raka Ray assigned Kathleen Blee's classic text, *Women of the Klan: Racism and Gender in the 1920s,* first published in 1991:

> Beneath this flag that waves above,
> This cross that lights the way,
> You'll always find a sister's love,
> In the heart of each TRI-k.

"Tri-k," otherwise known as the KKK. In reading about Klan women's motivations, I came to see that bubbling beneath the fiery hate associated with white supremacist groups, there is a toxic mix of affection, loyalty, sacrifice, idealism, and yes, even "love"—a contorted, constricted, rationing sort of love.

They hate others because they love white people; they love white people because they hate others—ardor and aversion sewn together like conjoined twins. Of course, today, the care and cooperation most white folks extend to one another is not accessorized with a fiery cross. But it can still help reproduce the racist status quo, so long as those who already have ready access to material and symbolic goods hoard resources and opportunities for those they deem worthy of their affection and investment.

In the end, the denigration of Black life is not only institutionalized in healthcare. It is also kept alive in our everyday interactions, as when passersby look on with mild disdain at a young pregnant Black woman or a doctor ignores the pain of a Black patient in distress. Like all forms of oppression, racism flourishes when its targets internalize disdain, accepting—to some degree—the terms of their subordination. Scholars call this "internalized oppression" or "symbolic violence." Activists sometimes call it "self-hate" or "false consciousness." The point is that the most powerful forms of social tyranny are in no need of ferocious tyrants.

When my boys were younger, I was hypervigilant about controlling their movement in public spaces—shushing them if they got too loud and reining them in if they were too rowdy. I was trying so hard to defy the stereotype of the Bad Black Mother that infects our cultural imagination, yet this toxic trope ended up infecting me. As when I bundled my newborn in layers upon layers in the middle of June, my protective instincts became suffocating.

The unruliness of my children, I believed, was a measure of my unworthiness as a parent. No one had ever sat me down and taught me this racial calculus. But I knew, in my bones, that even Black play was a menace. I knew it before twelve-year-old Tamir Rice was gunned down by police in a Cleveland park. I knew it before Tamir's family was sent a bill for the dead child's last ambulance ride. I knew it before the officer who shot Tamir said he thought the child was twenty years old. I knew it before reading studies about how white Americans, from police to college students, view Black children as older and less innocent than their white peers. I knew it before encountering the literature on "play deprivation" experienced by Black children who do not have ready access to safe outdoor space and equipment, whose play is often stifled or policed, and who suffer from the elimination of play time in school, among other factors. Without being explicitly told, I knew that my children needed to *sit still and be quiet*. I had to police them . . . before the police could.

The engine of white supremacy does not require a big bad boogie man in a white hood or in the White House, as long as enough of us continue to grease the wheels of anti-Blackness. Viral justice requires that we find a way, any chance we get, to throw a wrench in the system. What would it look like to create space for all children to play vigorously, weep loudly, groan deeply, and tussle with their friends without being judged menacing? I recall the warm smiles in checkout lines, or a stranger's kind word about my children, and feeling it was safe to exhale and loosen my grip. It will take everything, each of us sewing part of the social fabric, until finally no one is left exposed, until finally everyone is covered in a light layer of tenderness, akin to a caul, fortification that nevertheless allows us to breathe, stretch, and grow.

SIX

Trust

"What am I reading?!" I texted my colleague Keeanga in disbelief. Minutes earlier, she had sent a link to the news report, "Remains of Children Killed in MOVE Bombing Sat in a Box at Penn Museum for Decades." Scrolling down, I saw that it was not only Penn but our university, Princeton, that housed the children's remains for years. Twelve-year-old Delisha Africa and fourteen-year-old Katricia "Tree" Africa were killed on May 13, 1985, when the City of Philadelphia dropped a bomb on the row home of the Philadelphia political and religious organization MOVE, destroying over sixty homes in the largely Black neighborhood in the process. The five hundred police officers who had descended on the neighborhood had already fired over ten thousand rounds of ammunition in the house.

Members of MOVE, which was founded in the early 1970s and still exists today, all take the last name "Africa" and advocate for Black liberation, animal rights, and environmental justice. MOVE is not an acronym but a philosophy. "Everything that's alive moves. If it didn't, it would be stagnant, dead." By 1985, the organization had experienced years of criminalization and brutalization, with many members already politically imprisoned at the time of the bombing; they were incarcerated after a confrontation with the police that led to the death of an officer. Those incarcerated, despite their claims of innocence, included the mothers of Delisha and Tree. In all, the bombing killed founder John Africa, five other adults, and five children aged seven to thirteen.

About two months after the news broke about Delisha's and Tree's remains, Consuewella Dotson Africa died at the age of sixty-seven. The mother of Tree, as well as another child who had died in the bombing, twelve-year-old Zanetta, Consuewella had been exposed to COVID-19 but, as Janine Africa shared, "she had gotten over COVID, and the doctors were saying she started having lung problems, and they were saying it was because of stress."

Learning about the children's remains devastated Consuewella: "The situation just put so much on her that it tore her down." But in the months following the revelation of the remains, other secrets also surfaced, including testimony by ex-members who called MOVE "a cult." These survivors described their experience of "coercive sexual relationships, child marriages, death threats, financial crimes, and several forms of psychological control," and they said that with the light being shone on the remains of other MOVE children, "their own story is important to reveal."

It wasn't until I was an adult that I learned about the MOVE bombing. But most of my Philly friends recall that day with vivid detail—the smoke snaking upward into the sky, the crowds gathered on the street in disbelief. It remains one of the most traumatic chapters in a long saga of racist state violence. Rubbing salt on the wound, a grand jury cleared officials of criminal charges for any wrongdoing. And like so many previous chapters, new revelations would deepen the pain of that earlier violence.

On April 21, 2021, we learned that the Philadelphia Medical Examiner's Office sent the remains from the attack—pelvic and femur bones—to Professor Alan Mann to verify whom they belonged to. But even after the investigation was closed, the remains were unceremoniously stored in a cardboard box on a shelf, first in the Penn Museum, then in Mann's lab at Princeton when he accepted a position at the university's Department of Anthropology.

"It's like this never ends and no matter how much time passes, and you hope that things can get to a place where you can begin to heal some, it's right back up in your face. I haven't cried this many consecutive days since 1985," said a childhood friend of the victims, Mike Africa Jr. "They were bombed, and burned alive," he added. "And now you wanna keep their bones."

With each new revelation surrounding the MOVE remains, the banality of evil becomes more pronounced. People just doing their jobs, clocking in and out, shuffling boxes from one office to another, adhering to disciplinary norms, no Big Bad Boogie Man in sight. If this is how the horrors of injustice are produced, through everyday activity, then so too will this be how we produce the ameliorating practice of justice.

This chapter interrogates trust as the fragile fiber that holds together our social fabric. From the many creative conspiracy theories that arose during the early days of the pandemic to varied attempts to address "vaccine hesitancy" among nonwhite populations in the U.S., the U.K., and other countries with long histories of white supremacy, the problem is not simply a "lack of trust" on the part of the downtrodden but a lack of *trustworthiness* on the part of dominant institutions.

Racialized groups are too often valued as research subjects and *devalued* as patients. This institutionalized hypocrisy erodes trust. As we see in the case of the MOVE victims' remains, police violence and scientific violence often converge. The deadly practices of law enforcement and city government provide corpses that allow scientists to hone knowledge from which we all supposedly benefit. Trust, in short, is a tattered thread holding together many of our social interactions; no doubt strengthening this thread is a vital component of viral justice.

As we will see in this chapter, on the rare occasions when scientific and medical racism are acknowledged, the people and institutions responsible for them are hidden from view. So let's shine a light on them. To engender trustworthiness, as a first step, we have to tell the truth about past and ongoing harms. No sugarcoating, no euphemisms, no false equivalency or "both sides played a part" bullshit.

The revelations surrounding the MOVE remains seemed as if they came straight out of a Jordan Peele horror film: Black people once again trapped in a warped white imagination. Peele's *Get Out* takes white liberalism to task for its contradictions—in the movie, the very same people who proudly proclaim they would vote for Barack Obama for a third term buy and sell younger, healthier Black bodies to ensure their own longevity.

Peele's later film *Us* presents a dense allegory about the underside of the American dream, in which both the individual and society as a whole have monstrous doubles. The MOVE case reminds us that academia, too, is a haunted house of horrors. To think that, stuffed in a cardboard box at Princeton, there were the bones of children killed by their government. But the horrors don't end there.

The MOVE victims' remains were also used in an online course titled Real Bones: Adventures in Forensic Anthropology, taught by Mann's former student Janet Monge and streamed on the popular platform Coursera. The five-part class was still available for registration after the story broke. In one video, after holding up the bones to the camera,

> Monge describes the remains in vivid terms. They consist of two bones—a pelvis and femur—that belonged to a small girl probably in her teens that were discovered held together "because they were in a pair of jeans."
>
> The pelvis was cracked "where a beam of the house had actually fallen on this individual." The fragment showed signs of burnt tendons around the hip joint.
>
> "The bones are juicy, by which I mean you can tell they are the bones of a recently deceased individual," Monge continues. "If you smell it, it doesn't actually smell bad—it smells kind of greasy, like an older-style grease."

This, to me, is the most telling part of the entire saga: in the name of research and teaching, Black death becomes a tool, a resource, an *adventure* (à la the title of the course), something to savor and smell. More troublingly, initial responses from university spokespeople played down the controversy, *Nothing to see here . . . workaday science . . . business as usual . . . this is how it's always been done . . . how would any of these fields exist without racist and colonial violence?* I couldn't help thinking about the place I earned my PhD:

"UC Berkeley, through decades of systematic looting, has one of the largest collections of human remains in the country," reported the *Daily Cal*, the university's student-run newspaper. And since the collection includes hundreds of thousands of sacred objects and ancestral remains that are federally classified under the 1990 Native American Graves Protection and Repatriation Act, Indigenous activists have been fighting these institutional practices for decades. So far, only about 19 percent of the collection has been repatriated as required by federal law.

Those who like to pretend racism is a relic of some bygone era do so by adhering to a shadowy caricature of white supremacy. Meanwhile, each day brings a new reminder for Black folks that people in positions of power are disdainful or indifferent toward Black lives.

No need for the scowling bigot hurling racist epithets in our direction. We can simply point to a box in an Ivy League professor's office with the decaying bones of Black children inside while their mothers are locked away as Exhibit A. We can log in to an online class where the instructor holds up the bones of those same children while noting they smell greasy as Exhibit B. Containment and exposure are two sides of the same rancid coin: "Imagine our babies in some stagnant lab like that. Our children had life, they were not some specimen," lamented Consuewella Doston Africa, who learned about her daughter's remains through the media.

Just days before the MOVE case came to light, Penn Museum had agreed to repatriate remains in the Morton Crania Collection, which includes some 1,300 human skulls. Samuel G. Morton, dubbed the "Father of Scientific Racism," measured, compared, and displayed the skulls of different racial groups to provide scientific legitimacy for white supremacy. He relied on grave robbers to obtain skulls, including at least fourteen taken from a Philadelphia almshouse where African Americans had been buried and fifty skulls from an African burial ground in Cuba.

Lest talk of grave robbers and stolen corpses makes this sound like a hidden history, the Morton Crania Collection was not a secret. But after the protests following George Floyd's murder in 2020, many institutions were forced to reckon with their complicity in maintaining a deadly status quo. Returning the stolen remains in the Morton collection was one action Penn took.

After revelations of the MOVE remains emerged, Princeton's decision to try to track them down and, on July 2, 2021, return them to the Africa family was another. These are small steps to begin owning up to an injurious legacy. But what can individuals—those of us who work in these institutions—and groups, whether universities, hospitals, schools, banks, or other industries that have their own skeletons in the closet, do?

In the pages ahead, we will shine a light on everyday forms of mistreatment in scientific and medical institutions, from the mundane to the spectacular, thinking about the relationship between the two. We will also think about what is required to build trust and the concrete practices needed to engender trustworthiness amid the rubble of decaying systems. I'm not talking about trust-building projects that seek to maintain death-making institutions, like those called for by police reform, but rather the everyday people and institutions that help us relate to one another in life-affirming ways. In doing so, they redesign research and medicine to be less extractive and they aim to repair—as much as possible—a long history of harm.

When my Spelman sister, poet, and now professor Bettina Judd went off to graduate school, she had a medical ordeal. Following the onset of sudden, throbbing pain, she visited one hospital after another searching for relief. But doctors minimized her debilitating pain with diagnoses of menstrual cramps and bladder infection and demeaned her with repeated questions about her sexual history. Eventually, Bettina ended up at Johns Hopkins Hospital, where, for fifteen hours, she waited with her grandmother by her side as morphine dripped into her arm and her patience waned.

Finally, when the doctor said she would need yet another pelvic exam, the third one that day, she lost it. "Fine, do whatever you have to. Gynecology was built on the backs of Black women anyway!" she exclaimed.

We know the names of three of those Black women: Anarcha Westcott, Betsey Harris, and Lucy Zimmerman, who were enslaved in Alabama and whose unanesthetized bodies were used by J. Marion Sims from 1845 to 1849 to experiment with gynecological surgeries that "launched his career."

In 2018 the statue of Sims that stood tall in New York City's Central Park was finally brought down, and in late 2020, following nationwide protests for racial justice, a monument was erected in Montgomery, Alabama, where Sims conducted several of his experiments, to honor the "mothers of gynecology." As medical historian Deirdre Cooper Owens notes, enslaved Black women not only were Sims's surgical patients but also worked alongside him as surgical *nurses*, learning more about cutting-edge gynecological techniques than most American doctors in the mid-nineteenth century.

The artist spearheading the Montgomery installation, Michelle Browder, remarked at a press conference that "Anarcha changed the world. If you're a female and you had a pap smear, you know Anarcha. If you're a female and had any type of James Marion Sims retractor or spoon in your vaginal area, you know Lucy and Betsey and the others that were experimented on."

We have inherited not only the techniques honed on these women's bodies but memories of them and their unaccounted pain. In a book of poetry Bettina would later write, she penned a verse in the voice of Anarcha: "Sims invents the speculum, I invent the wincing."

That is how it is for many of us. Our ancestors rest just beyond the veil, whispering, scheming, cheering, and sometimes hollering at the absurdity of it all—that we still find ourselves wincing today as we are forced into our third pelvic exam. Perhaps they are loud in death because they could not scream out in life. As Bettina wrote, "An army of black women who knew too well the shenanigans of the medico-industrial complex crowded my bed." They looked on as Bettina was diagnosed with an ovarian torsion, which required immediate surgery to remove the dead organ. It was not lost on Bettina that *the same teaching hospital that harvested Henrietta Lacks's cells also owned her dead ovary.*

Lacks's death at Johns Hopkins generated an entire biomedical industry that continues to use her "immortal" cell line. As with any other cancer patient in that hospital ward, the tissue from Lacks's body was initially harvested by biologist George Otto Gey from a cervical biopsy. As anthropologist of science Hannah Landecker details in *Culturing Life: How Cells Became Technologies*, HeLa cells were like no others before them—growing and dividing so "luxuriantly" that they became not only a scientific object but an economic entity.

.But as literary and legal scholar Karla Holloway notes, "it was also an 'eternal life' that had not been officially revealed to her heirs and descendants." Not only was her family kept uninformed, but researchers actually collected blood from them for decades under false pretenses as they sought to understand what made HeLa cells so special.

Lacks's remarkably durable cells have been bought and sold innumerable times by labs, academic institutions, and companies around the world. They are the basis of well over sixty thousand scientific papers and were used by Jonas Salk to test the polio vaccine, among other medical breakthroughs. According to National Institutes of Health director Francis Collins, HeLa cells are the basis of over eleven thousand studies, including those that were focused on a COVID-19 vaccine.

The same cells that, in 1951, swiftly ravaged Lacks's body after she was prematurely discharged from the hospital would later come to sustain a multibillion-dollar biotechnology and research industry indefinitely. But as Lacks's son Lawrence put it years ago, "She's the most important person in the world and her family living in poverty. If our mother so important to science, why can't we get health insurance?" Perhaps this is why Lacks's story captured the popular imagination. Her story is a symbol of the duplicity of a nation in which American dreams rest on the nightmares of some. It is no wonder that, in 2010, Rebecca Skloot's book, *The Immortal Life of Henrietta Lacks*, flew off the bookshelves. Or that Johns Hopkins University was forced to publicly acknowledge its role in that epic scandal. That year, the university hosted the inaugural Henrietta Lacks Memorial Lecture and announced scholarships for local high school graduates, monetary awards to community organizations, and a talk by Skloot. Each fall thereafter, different students, organizations, and keynote speakers have participated in this ritual of institutional atonement.

Alas, in 2015, I stood in front of a buzzing auditorium at Hopkins, preparing to deliver the Sixth Annual Henrietta Lacks Memorial Lecture. Hundreds of people poured into the Turner Auditorium on the medical campus—clinicians, researchers, students, community organizers, and Baltimoreans of all ages. Standing at the podium, I double-checked that my slides were cued up, then kicked things off with a photo taken by the famed Baltimore photographer Devin Allen. The image shows a young Black boy holding a sign that says, "Less talk, more action," as he marches with others in the middle of the street. And so I told the audience, "Good sounding rhetoric masks inaction, and reforms too often work like a Band-Aid covering up a cancer. And so, although I was invited here today to talk, I feel accountable to this child to offer something more than lip service. Because the question that this child, and the larger Black Lives Matter movement, is raising, is really one that all of us have to address in our own way: How do we, how will we, operationalize justice in our lives, in our work, in every single context, including health and medicine?"

As I delivered my lecture, I noticed a group of teenagers at the top of the hall scanning the room for seats. Walking behind them was an elderly couple who seemed to know exactly where they were headed, like an annual pilgrimage. I continued,

Hippocrates reportedly said: "Wherever the art of medicine is loved, there is also a love of humanity." Because, ultimately, after we peel back all the various layers, titles, affiliations and fancy degrees in which folks come packaged, many people drawn to health-related fields are motivated by a desire to alleviate unnecessary suffering in the world and operationalize their love for humanity in tangible ways . . .

But I'm not talking about a kind of Valentine's Day sentimen-
tality, or a kind of charity model of "helping the underserved." I'm
talking about a much deeper sense that my well-being is bound
up with yours, that as long as we allow this Apartheid model of
health care, housing, education, and policing to persist, then even
the so-called "haves" will not be allowed to rest easy.

In the talk I described a recent trip to South Africa and noted that
Indigenous San leaders, whom geneticists were hoping to partner
with to create a database, knew the story of Lacks. "They and many
others are watching what's happening here in Baltimore to learn IF
and how institutions and communities can work together in the face
of historical trauma and systemic injustice. Is it possible to create
community-engaged research that interrupts oppressive systems
rather than simply reproduces them?"

Over the next hour I went on to connect my research on the
California stem cell initiative to insights from Sun Ra and science
fiction, and back to Lacks, before outlining five ways that we need
to expand our *bioethical imagination*: "I am continually amazed at
how much innovation and excitement there is around regenerating
the human body, but not the body politic. How is creating heart cells
that can beat in a petri dish considered less far-fetched than making
sure everyone has access to quality primary healthcare? This kind
of lop-sided imagination has got to go!"

As you can surmise, this was not your typical academic event,
as the mood was decidedly mixed. We were there honoring the
life of Lacks, celebrating the contribution of HeLa cells, but also
acknowledging the ongoing rift between the university and community, encapsulated by the way many locals refer to Johns Hopkins University as "the plantation." The story of Lacks was "already
embedded in Baltimore narratives about the *untrustworthiness* of
Johns Hopkins," according to Judd. And so spirits assembled in the
rafters that day, as they had crowded around Bettina's bed, while
the weight of recent injuries hung heavy in the air. The annual
lecture, along with named scholarships and a historical exhibit on

the medical campus, is part of how the institution tries to make amends—an acknowledgment of the past even while new scars are produced.

But what does it mean to make amends? Is it with highly visible annual events and commemorations? And how might these events serve to distract from, or at least gloss over, ongoing dispossession and extraction? As we gathered to honor Lacks that day in 2015, Johns Hopkins University was planning a "life-sciences hub" to be built in a historic neighborhood in East Baltimore known as Middle East. The construction process eventually tore down two thousand row houses and "relocated" about 740 mostly Black families. Like the biomedical breakthroughs born of Lacks's demise, a state-of-the-art medical campus has been erected on the ruins of Black Baltimore. As community health researcher and equity scientist Lawrence T. Brown described it, "When you're living here, it's like you're living on the plantation, because Hopkins wants to make sure it controls everything around it."

Cell by cell, brick by brick, medical breakthroughs seem to require that some of us be broken. What, then, can it mean to "trust science" when salt is rubbed in old wounds on a daily basis? This was the question nagging me as I stood behind the podium at Hopkins as the Q&A began after my lecture. It is a question born from the experience of those who have lived in America's nightmare . . . those looking up at the hubris of America's medical dream.

"Given everything we've heard today, what advice do you have for increasing Black participation in clinical trials?" an audience member asked in the final minutes of the symposium.

"Well," I paused, looking for the faces of the elderly Black couple whom I had observed at the start. Were they among the families displaced to make room for the Hopkins plantation? Did anyone care if they could access basic health services, or only that they sign up for clinical trials?

"Well, actually, I wouldn't encourage Black participation in clinical trials," I heard myself saying. *Blasphemy*, I thought to myself, standing in the belly of biomedical research.

"In fact, until Black folks have access to free and high-quality healthcare, I think we should withhold our participation," I said, looking around at the nervous reaction, half expecting my mic to be cut. And that's how I left it, advocating a clinical boycott at an event celebrating clinical research.

Ultimately, the effort to build trust between communities and researchers cannot focus solely on encouraging participation in clinical trials. We need to consider all the reasons why medical mistrust might exist. In doing this, we must account for and work to challenge the many ways in which Black and other vulnerable communities are violated by medical and research institutions—whether through the handling of MOVE children's remains, the harvesting of bodies to advance science, the pathologizing of patients who are not believed during visits to the doctor, or the displacement of hundreds of Black residents to expand a university. Without addressing the many forms of harm that Black people experience from these institutions, all the talk about trust and participation in scientific research falls flat.

In December 2020 Anthony Fauci, director of the National Institute of Allergy and Infectious Diseases and the most recognized government spokesperson during the COVID-19 pandemic, called on the Black community to trust the COVID-19 vaccine because one of its lead scientists is a Black woman, Kizzmekia Corbett: "So, the first thing you might want to say to my African American brothers and sisters," Fauci remarked at an event hosted by the National Urban League, "is that the vaccine that you're going to be taking was developed by an African American woman. And that is just a fact."

Social media, in turn, had a field day with Fauci's invocation of Corbett . . . a mix of humor, cynicism, and historic record straightening:

I don't care if she's made of vibranium . . . I'm still not taking the vaccine.

Did she have full control of developing the vaccine? Or she is a poster child?

That's nice . . . we still not taking that godforsaken poison but bless her heart

Ummm . . . SO WAS EUNICE RIVERS LAURIE . . . THE BLACK NURSE WHO COORDINATED THE TUSKEGEE SYPHILIS EXPERI-MENT!! (Ahem) for 40 YEARS!!! #fuckouttahere

"Vaccine hesitancy" is what some experts call it, though as trans-national feminist studies scholar Nicole Charles says, for people who have experienced a long history of medical coercion, it is bet-ter termed *suspicion*. Note, for instance, the inevitable reference to Tuskegee . . . we'll come back to that in a minute. Although in March 2021 there was little difference in reluctance to take the coro-navirus vaccine across racial groups in the U.S., according to early surveys, including those released by NPR, NAACP, and UnidosUS, only 14 percent of Black Americans trusted the safety of a vaccine, and 18 percent trusted its effectiveness.

It's not that Black folks necessarily have more distrust for science, or authority in general; it's that our distrust is pathologized. Is it any coincidence, then, that the first American to receive a COVID-19 vaccine was a Black woman, Sandra Lindsay, a New York City inten-sive care nurse who has been on the front lines of treating corona-virus patients? From where I sat, it seemed that making Black folks the face of the vaccine was an attempt to counter distrust through representation. "Healing is coming," Lindsay said, in front of dozens of flashing cameras. "I want to instill public confidence that the vac-cine is safe," she explained after receiving the inoculation at Long Island Jewish Medical Center in Queens.

There is no way of knowing whether making a Black woman the face of a vaccine rollout can help counteract centuries of racist ordeals with medicine. Just as my own cynicism toward the use of Corbett as a poster child began to peak, a friend chimed in to the Spirit of Justice group chat about the vaccine, "You know a Black woman helped create it!" Others replied with a mixture of pride and relief. So it seemed the medical marketing was working as planned, at least in some circles.

But truly transforming the relationship between the medical establishment and Black communities will take more than savvy racial representations. The first step, perhaps, in engendering justice is to acknowledge that the festering wounds are much more recent than the historical experiments that took place on J. Marion Sims's surgical table or the detached clinical notes about Tuskegee farmers. Institutions have to put these ongoing harms under the microscope and make genuine amends. Cosmetic representation is no substitute for substantive redress and real change in the values and priorities of knowledge production.

In the 1990s researchers at Johns Hopkins Kennedy Krieger Institute (KKI) knowingly exposed 108 newborns and children to lead paint in order to study the effectiveness of different lead abatement methods. Exposure to lead is toxic and often deadly. Specifically, it is "destructive for human development and growth. Even at low levels, toxic lead exposure causes damage to the executive reasoning area of the brain. It also causes behavioral difficulties, elevated levels of impulsivity and aggression, and increased odds for depression and panic disorder," according to Lawrence T. Brown, who spent many years as a Morgan State University professor and community advocate in Baltimore.

Ironically, in 1951, Baltimore became the first U.S. city to ban the use of lead paint in housing. But then, like other industrial cities, Baltimore experienced tremendous economic decline, massive job loss, and budget cuts, so it didn't enforce the new lead prevention program. Landlords, in turn, threatened to abandon their low-income properties because the cost of removing the toxic substance was far more than the buildings were worth. So KKI scientists teamed up with Baltimore landlords in the 1990s for a Repair and Maintenance Study that actively sought out families to take up residence in 107 apartments. The properties underwent different levels of abatement, or the permanent removal of lead paint, that cost $1,650, $3,000, or $7,000, all dramatically less than the full-scale abatement, which could be $20,000 or more.

Keep in mind, none of this was happening in secret, nor was it a side project carried out by a few people under the cloak of darkness. The research was led by professor of global health Mark Farfel and funded by the U.S. Environmental Protection Agency and the Department of Housing and Urban Development. And yes, the Johns Hopkins Institutional Review Board, which is responsible for ensuring that all research conducted on human beings is done according to established ethical guidelines, signed off on the study after some changes to bring it into compliance with governmental requirements.

To study the effectiveness of different abatement levels, researchers periodically measured lead levels in the home and tested the blood of younger children living there. But at no time did residents receive treatment when they presented with higher lead levels. And although parents signed consent forms, the contract did not clearly and fully disclose the housing conditions or study objectives.

In 2001 a Maryland court of appeals ruled that the KKI researchers knowingly exposed children to lead and compared the study to Tuskegee—the notorious forty-year study of untreated syphilis in Black farmers by the U.S. Public Health Service—because the Baltimore residents were not fully informed of the nature of the research.

"It can be argued that the researchers intended that the children be the canaries in the mines, but never told the parents," Judge Dale R. Cathell wrote. In their defense, KKI researchers noted that that the majority of children saw lead levels go down, and since landlords were not willing to pay the cost of full abatement, their study would offer options to reduce lead exposure in the long run.

This "better than nothing" logic is an enduring feature of institutional violence. In a choice between full and partial exposure to harm, the powers that be tell us that "partially" harming people is actually beneficial. Plus, once the study results are in, we will be able to help so many more people! Of course, if researchers were called on to put their own children's bodies on the line, no amount of lead would be tolerable. I am left wondering where Western science would be without social inequities that allow it to manufacture its double-edged magnanimity.

In 2011 the lead study participants brought a class action lawsuit against KKI. According to the formal complaint, "KKI used these children as guinea pigs . . . Nothing about the research was designed to treat the subject children for lead poisoning . . . As a direct and proximate consequence, these children, their siblings and other minors visiting these particularly abated homes ingested and suffered permanent brain damage and other damage." In 2017 a sibling of one of the study participants, who was too young to be enrolled in the study but who was exposed to the toxic environment nonetheless, sued the property owner in *Courtney Tomlin v. City Homes et al.* and was awarded $1.2 million in damages. Many other Baltimoreans have also sought reparations for lead poisoning, a "lead check," as they are commonly called.

In a twisted turn of events, two of those who filed suits were also high-profile victims of Baltimore police violence—Freddie Gray and Korryn Gaines. Gray's and Gaines's stories reveal how victims of environmental injustice and police violence are often one and the same.

Years before police threw twenty-five-year-old Gray into the back of a police van, exposing him to a "rough ride" that injured his spine and eventually killed him, Gray and his twin sister were exposed to lead as children in Baltimore public housing. The siblings, who had been treated for lead at KKI as children, were found to have dangerously high levels of lead exposure—almost double what the State of Maryland considers poisoning.

They won a settlement against the owner of 1459 N. Carey Street, where they had lived as children. In a 2008 deposition, Gray explained, "All the schools that I went to, I was in special education," which researchers show is often the first step toward the criminalization of disabilities, and one of the many ways in which young people are pushed into the crosshairs of the police. Gray never graduated from high school and was arrested more than a dozen times, eventually spending two years in jail.

Gaines had a similar experience. Four years before a SWAT team gunned her down in her apartment in 2016, the twenty-three-year-old filed a lawsuit claiming that a "sea of lead" paint had made her ill. Showing weapons on Instagram, she wrote, "They can try to come get it they gon leave with more Lead than they poisoned me wit."

The president and CEO of the Green & Healthy Homes Initiative, Ruth Ann Norton, calls lead poisoning Baltimore's "toxic legacy." In the early 1990s, she said the group found that thirteen thousand children in the city were poisoned with lead, though the number would have been thirty thousand if they were collecting at today's levels. Nationwide, the numbers are even more devastating, with reports indicating that thirty-seven million housing units in the U.S. have lead paint and more than three hundred thousand children are diagnosed with unsafe levels in their bodies each year.

Mona Hanna-Attisha, a physician whistleblower who exposed the poisoning of water with lead in Flint, Michigan, said in 2016, "If you are going to put something in a population to keep them down for generations, it would be lead."

In the aftermath of the police murders of Gray and Gaines, Lawrence Brown concluded, "Lead interrupts the stress reaction and so it distorts the way people view threats and so I think that's absolutely germane to both Freddie Gray and Korryn Gaines. If [lead poisoning] is in fact disturbing and exaggerating the threat then you can understand why Freddie Gray is running and why Korryn Gaines has a shotgun when the police are knocking on her door."

While Brown is highlighting relevant context not causation, I am uneasy about how connections drawn between lead poisoning, "neurocognitive impairment," and police violence can be interpreted. It is true: lead poisoning has long-term harmful effects on the brain. But this is not the same as saying that Gray's and Gaines's brains caused their deaths. The police did that. I cannot emphasize this enough: a focus on structural determinants of health, such as recognizing that exposure to lead poisoning can impact cognitive abilities, should in no way be used to imply that victims of police violence are bringing about their own deaths.

Too often, preexisting health conditions or disabilities are used to explain the murder of Black people by the police. Even more insidious is when the racism of research designs, such as the lead abatement study, is acknowledged as affecting physical or mental health, only to be used to deny the racism of police killings of Black people. For Black Baltimoreans, focus on poisoned bodies should not provide an excuse for trigger-happy police officers.

It is vital that, as medical ethicist Harriet A. Washington writes in her book *A Terrible Thing to Waste: Environmental Racism and Its Assault on the American Mind,* we underscore that disabilities are not a function of "innate inferiority." We must especially remember this because blaming the Black victim is an American pastime, part of a white supremacist cultural script that we are all taught to recite. As Washington explains, "When gross poisoning became impossible to ignore, the Lead Industry Association blamed 'ineducable black and Puerto Rican parents' for making lead poisoning a 'problem of the slums'; public-health workers 'taught' Baltimore homemakers to clean using Spic and Span; a public-health official accused Baltimore mothers of intentionally manufacturing their children's lead ingestion by placing lead fishing weights in their mouths." Black mothers, in particular, are frequently scapegoated not only for the poisoning of their children but also for higher Black incarceration rates, high school dropout rates, COVID-19 rates, you name it. The only way we can begin to seed justice is to tear up the script of Black cultural pathology.

How we name things matters. If you try to visit Wikipedia to read up on KKI's Lead-Based Paint Abatement and Repair and Maintenance Study, you'll find nothing, nada, zilch. Rather, the study is cataloged under the "Baltimore Lead Paint Study"—as if the residents of Baltimore themselves conceived and executed this scientific disregard for Black life. In the same way that people often talk about the "Tuskegee Syphilis Experiment" rather than the U.S. Public Health Service Syphilis Study, the beleaguered places, rather than the powerful people and institutions, are named, blamed, and remembered. These names, Baltimore and Tuskegee, become forever associated with the shameful episodes in America's history, while the white establishment evades stigma and responsibility.

This is the power—like a superpower—invested in whiteness, as well as corporate and state power, to remain invisible when needed and to occupy all the space desired when they have something to gain. How can we ever seek repair for past harms or prevent future ones if we fail to name the protagonists? Our racial grammar requires a use of active voice: we must name the people and institutions that enact harm and structural violence. Let me suggest that next time you hear someone talk about these clinical experiments, remind them to name the *U.S. Public Health Service* and *Kennedy Krieger Institute* as a first step in truth-telling. In this seemingly small way, we can each work against the pathologizing of Blackness, even as we shine a light on those who would rather remain in the shadows.

In 2013 German researchers published a scientific paper that included Henrietta Lacks's full genome sequence without the family's knowledge or permission. Of course, it wasn't simply *Lacks's* genetic information that was made public in that paper, but also the genetic information of all her biological relatives—including their potential risks of disease.

"That is private family information," said Jeri Lacks-Whye, Lacks's granddaughter. "It shouldn't have been published without our consent."

Those German scientists broke no laws, nor did they violate established ethics protocol. As Rebecca Skloot pointed out at the time, "The whole system allowed it. Everyone involved followed standard practices. They presented their research at conferences and in a peer-reviewed journal. No one raised questions about consent."

Yet these standards were put in place before it was possible to upload someone's genome sequence to a website and receive a detailed report of their medical predispositions, such as whether they might be diagnosed with Alzheimer's, alcoholism, or a mental illness. Now imagine someone posting that health information online for anyone to see.

As Francis Collins commented, "This latest HeLa situation really shows us that our policy is lagging years and maybe decades behind the science. It's time to catch up." In addition to upsetting the Lacks family, others in the scientific community lamented how this latest episode in the HeLa saga would further erode public trust in science.

The publication of the paper also led to new National Institutes of Health rules that give the researchers "controlled access" to the genome data of HeLa cells, requiring that researchers using National Institutes of Health funds to get their studies approved by a board that now gives Lacks's family members a literal seat at the table. This arrangement echoes the demand of a health justice activist I interviewed early on in my studies—we want to be *at the table, not on the table*, when it comes to biomedical research, he said.

In her book *Private Bodies, Public Texts: Race, Gender, and a Cultural Bioethics*, Karla Holloway illustrates how Black women are "particularly vulnerable to public unveiling." The publication of Lacks's genome was a second public unveiling that reignited the pain and controversy surrounding the initial appropriation of her tumor cells. While community representation in scientific decision-making does not, by itself, engender trust in research initiatives, the hope is that it could at least mitigate future harms.

In August 2020, in the midst of the COVID-19 pandemic, I was invited by Lacks's family to participate in a virtual "CELLebration" in honor of what would have been Henrietta's one hundredth birthday and to kick off a year of health justice initiatives in her memory. I was joined by National Institutes of Health director Francis Collins; Rebecca Skloot, the author of *The Immortal Life of Henrietta Lacks*; Helen Wilson-Roe, a Black British artist who had painted portraits of the Lacks family; and Lacks's grandchildren, David Lacks Jr. and Jeri Lacks-Whye.

As part of the event branding, all the panelists were asked to wear Lacks's favorite color, red. So I pulled out a bright red, cropped vintage blazer that I had recently purchased on Etsy. Despite the emphasis on celebration, it was jarring, I found, to speak about the dark underbelly of medical racism with all of us drenched in such bright attire. But perhaps that was the point?

Like the mixed mood at the Lacks memorial lecture five years before, the desire to celebrate Lacks's "gift" to humanity sat uneasily with the circumstances of her untimely death at age thirty-one. What does it mean to hail someone's contribution to medicine when it came without their knowledge or consent, and was premised on their suffering and death? And how can we honor Lacks's life if we don't also acknowledge that the mistreatment she experienced still characterizes healthcare today? Sure, there are no longer signs that point to the "Negro wing" of a hospital. But ongoing racial segregation of our towns and cities, our deeply stratified health insurance structure, and even new medical technologies continue to do the work those signs once did.

For instance, the pulse oximeter, or "pulse ox" for short, is a standard device in medical care that helps people detect the level of oxygen in our blood. The lower the number, the lower the oxygen level, and the more severe one's condition. If you've watched any medical drama on TV, then you've seen a pulse ox clipped onto a patient's finger as a routine part of hospital care. And during the COVID-19 pandemic, more and more people started using them at home to provide a sign for when to rush to the hospital. But as it turns out, the pulse ox does not work as well for people with darker skin.

Pulse oxes use infrared light to read the color of your blood, so when your blood contains more oxygen, the machines sense more light. But before the pulse ox can "see" your blood, light must pass through your skin. As anthropologist Amy Moran-Thomas observed, darker skin absorbs light, which means pulse ox readings may hide the true oxygen saturation level for darker-skinned individuals.

The readings may lead Black people to believe they are in the expected range when, in fact, their oxygen has sunk to a dangerously low level. It is possible, then, that individuals who are sicker than they appear may not know to rush to the hospital. Or, if they are already at the hospital, they may be sent home prematurely, like Lacks. Medical technologies can perpetuate medical racism under the guise of neutrality—it's what I call the New Jim Code.

Over the years, many members of the Lacks family have become ambassadors of her legacy, traveling the country and speaking to audiences near and far about how HeLa cells have advanced science and medicine across numerous fields. For many Black folks, her story resonates precisely because it is *not* simply a thing of the past.

In December 2020 a Black physician in Indiana, Susan Moore, died due to complications from COVID-19 just weeks after posting a video lamenting how her white doctor had dismissed her concerns: "I put forth and I maintain if I was White, I wouldn't have to go through that . . . He made me feel like I was a drug addict," she said in the video. "And he knew I was a physician." She added, "This is how Black people get killed, when you send them home."

The racist treatment Lacks faced—whether in the initial substandard care she received, or in the extractive treatment of her body, or in the withholding of information from her family—still haunts medical care today. Her story echoes in the insults and injuries our own loved ones continue to experience in emergency rooms, clinics, and nursing homes without nearly enough headlines and hashtags to shine a light on them.

When I was a graduate student at the University of California, Berkeley, conducting fieldwork in a Bay Area hospital that served a largely Black, Latinx, and Asian population, a Black sickle cell patient asked, "Why am I in such demand as a research subject, when no one wants me as a patient?"

Next door to the clinic was a research program that offered families an experimental treatment that entailed umbilical cord blood transplants for children with inherited blood disorders like thalassemia and sickle cell disease. Here I got a front-row view of how medical research and healthcare are often conflated. *At the table, not on the table.*

It was around this time that I was asked to speak publicly at a national conference about the benefits of an experimental stem cell treatment for sickle cell and other blood disorders. I was still a graduate student, and the director of the stem cell program asked if I could travel out of state, all expenses paid, to talk about the procedure. He coached me on talking points and supplied slides, and since he had granted me access to the program as a field site, I found it difficult to say no. Later, I worried how the visibilizing of Black spokespeople, like Kizzmekia Corbett and nurse Sandra Lindsay, colludes in keeping Black people and their allies in the room, but on the wrong terms.

The sickle cell patient's question—"Why am I in such demand as a research subject?"—not only echoes a long history of medical apartheid but foretells scientific racism in the midst of COVID-19.

In early April 2020 two French scientists suggested on live TV that a coronavirus vaccine should be tested on Africans: "If I could be provocative, should we not do this study in Africa where there are no masks, treatment or intensive care, a little bit like it's been done, by the way, for certain AIDS studies or with prostitutes? We try things because we know that they are highly exposed and they don't protect themselves?" said Jean-Paul Mira, head of the intensive care unit at the Cochin Hospital in Paris. He said this in conversation with Camille Locht, research director at the French National Institute of Health and Medical Research, who agreed with the idea of conducting clinical trials in Africa. Although later, Mira apologized.

What distinguishes this episode of scientific racism from the many that have preceded it and the many others that take place behind closed doors every day is how quickly it went viral. Social media enabled people all over the globe to respond to and refute this explicit denigration of Black people. For example, the former footballer from Cote d'Ivoire Didier Drogba tweeted, "It is totally inconceivable we keep on cautioning this. Africa isn't a testing lab. I would like to denounce these demeaning, false, and most of all deeply racists [sic] words."

Historically, this is exactly how Europe and the United States have treated the continent—as a testing laboratory. From sterilization in Namibia to forced Depo-Provera contraception in Nigeria to AZT drug trials offering thousands of HIV-positive women a placebo rather than a treatment known to be effective in preventing transmission of the virus from mother to child, medical colonialism always comes wrapped in a White Savior flag. Like KKI's lead abatement study, the experiments in Africa were justified because "we need to find simpler, more cost effective" alternatives. So whether we are talking about France's thirty-five-year medical campaign in Central Africa, in which people were "forcibly examined and injected with medications with severe, sometimes fatal, side effects," or the forty-year U.S. Public Health Service Study in Tuskegee, Black people have been treated as test subjects for much longer than many people realize. And whether people know the historical details or not, scientific harms ripple into the present.

Jacqueline Temple had been experiencing respiratory problems for months. But when the seventy-two-year-old resident of Leimert Park, the same Los Angeles neighborhood in which I grew up in the White House, took a COVID-19 test, her results came back negative. So when Temple received an invitation to participate in a COVID-19 antibody study, she expressed hope that maybe it would tell her she had been exposed to the virus and recovered. Then she had what she calls a "Tuskegee Moment": "Every time I think about 'experimental' or 'we want to study you' or 'there's no cure, but we can treat you' . . . Tuskegee is in the back of my mind," Temple said. When presented with Temple's story, it is easy to chalk up Black people's ambivalence toward science and medicine to "issues of trust." Like using the language of "preexisting conditions" to blame Black people for societal injustices, focusing on distrust places responsibility on those the scientific and medical establishment has harmed.

During the Q&A portion of a virtual talk I gave at Williams College in October 2020, a student calling in from Brazil asked whether Black Americans' distrust of research could be one of the reasons that pharmaceutical companies go overseas looking for diverse populations to test drugs on. "Are Black bodies in Brazil a proxy for Black bodies in the U.S.?"

I couldn't say for sure, but what came to mind was anthropologist Adriana Petryna's work *When Experiments Travel: Clinical Trials and the Global Search for Human Subjects*. Petryna explains, "While the National Institutes of Health have mandated diversity in clinical trials, it is less clear how the industry has interpreted this policy of inclusion and how it is taken up in offshore research."

It's true that, in 1998, the U.S. Food and Drug Administration started requiring clinical studies to keep track of race, gender, age, and other demographic data so that trial sponsors could analyze the safety of drugs in different subgroups. But on Petryna's broad tour of trials around the world, one quickly gets the sense that there is so much more going on behind the scenes in what sociologist of science Steven Epstein calls a "vexing and time-consuming body hunt." As one of Petryna's informants put it, "Companies can now pick and choose populations" in order to pass the standard safety tests.

The search for pharmaceutically "naïve" populations that are not taking multiple drugs at the same time, as the vast majority of people in the U.S. are, is an ongoing challenge for drug companies. The many ways that these companies manipulate data to produce favorable results on the safety and efficacy of drugs would make even a die-hard sciencephile think twice about the so-called objectivity of the scientific method.

Tens of thousands of people in Brazil, South Africa, Argentina, and Turkey participated in Pfizer's COVID-19 clinical trials, but these countries will have to wait years to receive enough of the vaccine to inoculate the population. According to one forecast, some may never get that far. "Vaccine apartheid" is what some observers call it when pharmaceutical companies use the bodies of people desperate for medical attention to hone scientific breakthroughs and then deny those same populations the fruits of the research.

Remember: predatory inclusion and perpetual exclusion are two sides of the same coin. So it behooves health justice advocates to demand an end to harmful experimentation *and* insist on medical inclusion for effective treatments. I, for one, signed up my family to receive the COVID-19 vaccine as soon as we were eligible.

Frankly, I think far too much ink has been spilled on Black distrust in science and medicine—and I include my own ruminations in this. Report after report documents how Black people lack confidence in physicians and hospitals and are less likely to seek care or to adhere to recommended treatment plans. We are training our attention on the wrong thing. The question is, What are scientific and medical institutions doing to *demonstrate their trustworthiness*—concretely, not symbolically? No more grand announcements. No more forming committees, subcommittees, and taskforces on diversity, equity, and inclusion. No more trotting out "Black faces in high places." If it wasn't obvious by now, the distrust is deserved.

A month after the CELLebrate symposium Shawn and the boys headed over to Trenton for their biweekly appointment at the Classic Razor Sharp barbershop. As usual, they were gone all afternoon as Star, their barber, always took his sweet time, asking questions about school, cracking jokes, hopping on and off phone calls, while working meticulously on Khalil's fade and Malachi's high top. When the initial shock of the COVID-19 pandemic had waned, and New Jersey shops were able to reopen, we discovered that not much had changed at Razor Sharp.

Sure, customers had to make appointments now, the sounds of children playing in the Boys & Girls Club next door had not yet returned, and everyone wore masks. But the usual ruckus of conversation inside the shop continued—disagreements about whether Donald Trump would win a second term as president, or whether defunding the police was a realistic goal. The place still smelled like frankincense and myrrh, though the aroma was harder to appreciate through masks. Child-friendly flicks like *Avatar* and *Mulan* played on the TV above customers' heads, visible through the mirrors that lined the opposite wall. And brothers from the Nation of Islam, decked out in pressed suits and bowties, continued to make their rounds, dropping off stacks of the *Final Call*, a copy of which Shawn grabbed that day on his way out because he knew I'd be interested in the cover story.

On the front page of the *Final Call*, the newspaper founded in 1979 by Minister Louis Farrakhan and published as the official paper of the Nation of Islam, a headline shouted, "Don't Take Their Vaccine!"

in bold red and black letters. In smaller print it read, "The history of medical abuses and deadly acts against Black people demand Blacks convene their own experts, seek alternative treatments from around [the] globe and the U.S. must drop its unjust embargo to allow Cuban doctors to help save lives." As I read on, I realized that this was no standard antivaxxer manifesto. It was a rejection of the white establishment's vaccine, specifically the Trump administration's rushed attempt to produce a vaccine before the November election.

The speed and callousness of vaccine production, the paper warned, poses a familiar danger: "Remember the Tuskegee Syphilis Experiment? Remember what they did to the Native Americans with smallpox in blankets . . . How can you trust them with a vaccine after you know what they have done and that they are capable of doing it again, on a bigger and broader level?" Similar suspicions circulate far beyond the pages of the *Final Call* and were present well before COVID-19. Think of it as a collective side-eye cast from Black Twitter and Black barbershops toward the medical establishment.

Given the level of activity in Razor Sharp, it is no wonder that in recent years public health researchers have taken note of barbershops and beauty salons as important community institutions for healthcare advocates. A 2008 pilot study including twenty-seven barbershops in Richmond, Virginia, found that 100 percent of surveyed proprietors were willing to allow their shops to be used for prostate cancer education. In Los Angeles, physician Bill Releford started the Black Barbershop Health Outreach Program in order to rebuild trust using "credible, existing, community infrastructures." This is part of a broader effort by health advocates and researchers to engage African Americans through churches, fairs, and other community-based organizations.

For example, in Michigan, the National Kidney Foundation of Michigan trained nearly seven hundred hair stylists to deliver health promotion messages in beauty salons to almost fourteen thousand clients of all genders, with 60 percent reporting that they took preventative health steps as a result. But the power of barbershops and salons goes beyond leveraging the trusted role of individual barbers and stylists. The institutions themselves are a space for frank dialogue and debate, which makes them an especially potent site for health promotion.

As one observer put it, "Unlike other community settings, the barbershop, by its very nature, invites men of varied backgrounds to let their hair down without judgment, prejudice or expectation. It is our 'country club.'" To date, the Black Barbershop Health Outreach Program has successfully reached over ten thousand men nation-wide through a grassroots, volunteer-driven effort, and the idea is catching on. One significant drawback is that these spaces are not often inclusive of Black queer and gender-nonconforming clients, though now there are more Black queer-owned shops advertising themselves as welcoming spaces.

In my old neighborhood in Los Angeles, nine barbershops teamed up with the Martin Luther King Jr. Community Hospital to launch Man Up!, a health education and outreach campaign. In 2019 dozens of barbers were trained to talk with their customers about the common health risks that Black and Latinx men face, especially prostate cancer, heart disease, and diabetes, and encourage them to get screened. On the first Saturday of every month, the barbershops hosted free blood sugar, blood pressure, and BMI screenings.

To top it off, James Pickens Jr., the actor who plays Dr. Richard Webber on the hit medical drama series *Grey's Anatomy*, made several appearances at two barbershops—Just Showin Off on El Segundo Boulevard in Willowbrook, an unincorporated neighborhood of Los Angeles County that borders Watts and Compton; and the Place to Be in nearby Carson—to encourage patrons to take advantage of the free services. He was motivated to do this in part because members of his family had died from prostate cancer.

This kind of community-based health advocacy can certainly contribute to viral justice. But even when science and medicine come wrapped in culturally relevant packaging—brought to us by Black representatives and endorsed by Black institutions—they do not guarantee trust. Some folks might find even more reason to question what's happening behind the scenes because the powers that be appear to be trying so hard to "sell us on something." It is not simply the message that matters, but the messenger, and whether genuinely caring relationships underwrite calls to participate in public health campaigns.

Those who want to tackle the disproportionate burden of COVID-19 on Black communities have turned to Black spokespeople to engender trust in a vaccine. Recall Kizzmekia Corbett? The viral immunologist is doing her part to address vaccine hesitancy. To her credit, she has been outspoken about concerns—"You've earned the right to ask the questions"—as well as about the role of systemic racism in the pandemic: "Trust, especially when it has been stripped from people, has to be rebuilt in a brick-by-brick fashion."

Corbett encourages other physicians and scientists to join in slowly building building relationships with people, perhaps taking a note from writer and doula adrienne maree brown's exhortation that we should "move at the speed of trust." This means taking time to genuinely listen to and address people's concerns, rather than try to sell them on something. And it means changing course if institutional priorities run counter to ethical and social values.

Rather than trot out Black spokespeople in front of the cameras for every new public health campaign, what if we invested in community-driven health initiatives all along? We would not only multiply the number of Black doctors and nurses working in Black neighborhoods, but we'd also pour resources into training legions of Black midwives, doulas, health justice advocates, guidance counselors, and mental health advocates—those who really, truly love Black children, who want to see single mamas win, who refuse to stigmatize the formerly incarcerated, who listen first and foremost to disabled folk, who embrace with open arms our queer kin, and who counteract the isolation of our elders.

And the thing is, these community health stewards don't necessarily need "medical training," narrowly construed, as long as they refuse to pathologize Blackness, and believe mightily in vibrant Black futures. That, I think, is completely worth it *and* feasible, especially when we start divesting from death-making industries, such as policing, prisons, and the military, and strengthening the social fabric that actually helps us thrive.

Take Panola, Alabama: In a state with one of the lowest COVID-19 vaccination rates in the country, 99% of adults in this rural town are fully vaccinated thanks to a few residents. Dorothy Oliver and friends went door to door, asking neighbors about their worries, laughing with them about their needle phobia, expressing sadness about loved ones who had been lost in the pandemic, and reminding each person how their decision could impact others. Then, on the day of the vaccine drive, Dorothy and her crew stood under a tent in the pouring rain with the visiting nurses they had scheduled to administer the vaccines, until everyone on their list drove up, one by one, to receive shots.

"I just felt like I had to do it because the government, *nobody* does enough in this area. This area here is majority Black, kinda put you on the back burner. I mean you don't have to put anything else with that. I don't have to elaborate on that one!" she said laughing, because the anti-Blackness was so self-evident. But so is her love and tenacity. Ever since losing her husband, a truck driver who was injured in an accident and was unable to get to the nearest hospital in time to save his life, Dorothy has been determined to bring life-saving medical interventions to those in her town. This is the lesson from Panola: we can pour billions and billions into vaccine development, but our public health is indebted to those weaving a strong social fabric—ensuring people feel seen and heard, acknowledging their fears and hopes, and refusing the "organized abandonment" of our social policies by insisting on access to critical goods and services. This is viral justice at work.

In the week leading up to Thanksgiving 2020, images circulated online showing crowds of travelers waiting in line at U.S. airports, even as public health experts cautioned Americans not to gather in large groups. Black physician and health justice advocate Uché Blackstock tweeted her concern that one patient after another came to the hospital seeking COVID-19 tests to clear themselves for family gatherings, which she did not advise them to attend: "The one phrase that I use with my patients to stress an important recommendation that I'm trying to make is, *If you were my family member, I would . . .* and I mean it with love." By invoking kinship in an environment typically characterized by clinical detachment, a context in which we are often made to feel like slabs of meat with varying temperatures and weights, to be seen not only as a person but as a *loved one*, well, this is perhaps one of the most powerful sowers of trust.

Among the many responses to Blackstock's tweet, two stand out: Joe Sparkman, a Black multiple sclerosis patient activist, responded, "I absolutely love when I hear my doctor say this. It automatically builds a level of trust and I feel like they care." Another responder, Karen Killian, tweeted, "This is so important. I had to make a difficult decision regarding a procedure as my Mom's caregiver. I appreciated the surgeon for speaking to me like family and not clinical and detached."

Proponents of Western science and medicine typically build their credibility on strategic detachment—remember the way that white male obstetricians discredited Black midwives by, in part, invoking their own clinical distance. When it comes to engendering trust, however, genuine interest, authentic feeling, and a sense of kinship may be exactly what the patient ordered. But paternalism is also an element of kinship, and whether one hears the preceding exhortations as caring or manipulative depends on the who, what, where, when, and why of it. In short, context matters.

Whether individually or institutionally, trustworthiness must entail telling the truth. What if those working in the healthcare industry blew all the whistles and trumpets when they witnessed patients being talked down to, ignored, labeled as noncompliant, and even criminalized? That would be viral justice at work. It is these seemingly small acts of care that can deprivatize integrity and publicly shift institutional culture.

In 2020 the American Public Health Association decided to tell the truth. Following up on an earlier declaration that called out police violence as a public health crisis, the association declared racism "an ongoing public health crisis that needs our attention now." Surely, this was an important statement in a society in which many white folks consider racism a figment of the Black imagination.

But in the end, it doesn't matter how much truth you tell if the economic underpinnings of biomedicine remain tied to a market logic in which profit overrides the well-being of people, and organized abandonment is the cost of doing business. In the U.S., most graduates choose fancy medical specialties over primary care, sometimes to make medical school debt—an average of $215,900—"worth it." This not only creates doctor shortages in many parts of the country, like Panola, but disincentivizes preventative care. Is it any wonder that the child mortality rate in Cuba is lower despite the fact that "per-capita healthcare spending in the U.S. is the highest in the world"? More time devoted to patients, authentic communication, and preventative care on the part of healthcare professionals have life-and-death consequences and should have been prioritized yesterday.

After a week of agony, my friend Bettina's dead ovary was finally cut out, and her uncle packed her into his car and drove from Hopkins to her grandparents' home in East Baltimore to recover. Once she was feeling strong enough, Bettina began to paint and write, remembering and telling different stories about her experience:

> In 2006 I had an ordeal with medicine and was found innocent or guilty. It feels the same because I live in a haunted house. A house can be a dynasty, a bloodline, a body.

> There was punishment. Like the way the body is murdered by its own weight when lynched. Not that I was wrong but that verdicts come in a bloodline.

> In 2006 I had an ordeal with medicine. To recover, I learn why ghosts come to me. The research question is:
> Why am I patient?

Although her poems seem to speak for the women whose violated flesh made possible the easing of her own pain, they are also taut with her own anger and sadness, born of her communion with their spirits.

Indeed, these spirits taught Bettina something she could not express in dry, disembodied academic prose full of methods, findings, and tidy conclusions: "As a researcher, I could do them little justice, as research had done them no justice." It turns out that knowledge born of anger requires a different vessel—poetry and poiesis, making room for spirits to do more than wince. Viral justice is about all of us making room for pain . . . past and present.

Bioethicist Derek Ayeh asks, "After forcing black people to suffer centuries of unethical medical experimentation, what does American medicine owe them? . . . Equality is not enough to repair the racist dysfunction of the medical system. Just as America owes a debt for decades of unpaid slave labor, the medical system must pay reparations for its failure to treat black bodies with care."

For Ayeh, tackling America's segregated medical infrastructure requires "investing in doctors' offices, hospitals, and outpatient resources located in the community and it means training doctors to focus on health issues prevalent in the community." But what about viral justice when it comes to scientific research? Inclusion is about not only accessing medical services but shaping medical knowledge.

Perhaps we should start with the disability justice refrain—"nothing about us without us."

It turns out that disability and environmental injustice are deeply connected. Insults from the water, air, and soil are imbibed, inhaled, and ingested, getting under people's skin, especially those already deemed disposable. No wonder that members of those communities have been at the forefront of environmental justice advocacy and a growing movement of "citizen scientists."

Even though they don't usually have formal training in the sciences, their experience of environmental harms is essential to asking better questions. But not only that. Citizen scientists also learn methods of scientific investigation to answer those questions themselves—for example, when city officials planned to construct yet another waste facility in a Black and Latinx neighborhood of Los Angeles, a local environmental justice group mobilized residents to map existing waste facilities, review the literature on the health effects of contaminants, take photos of the mishandling of toxic material, and more.

Perhaps one of the most well-known examples of citizen science takes us back to Flint, Michigan, and the problem of lead poisoning. There, residents took matters into their own hands when government officials lied about the dangers posed by the corroding pipes bringing poisonous water into their homes. In 2015 a group of residents began a collaboration with professors at Virginia Tech—the university provided the "technical plan, analytical support, and funding, while Flint residents donated their local knowledge, homes as test sites, and hard work." As in citizen science more broadly, so-called laypeople not only pick up research skills to investigate issues meaningful to them, but they also bring their unique expertise to the table.

Ultimately, Flint residents managed to collect an impressive city-wide sample of water lead covering 269 Flint homes. It was eventually determined that one in six homes had lead levels exceeding Environmental Protection Agency standards, with thousands of children exposed. "One of the worst environmental crimes in US history," is how Virginia Tech environmental engineer Marc Edwards described it.

The work of citizen scientists ultimately led the Michigan government to declare a state of emergency, followed by the declaration of a federal emergency by President Barack Obama, which mobilized the Federal Emergency Management Agency and the National Guard. Over the next several years, the city undertook a massive project to replace lead service pipes. In 2020 victims of the Flint water crisis were awarded a combined settlement of over $600 million.

It all started with one person, LeeAnne Walters (aka "Resident Zero"), who, in the summer of 2014, noticed unexplained rashes, hair loss, and other symptoms in her children. After numerous calls and emails, in February 2015, Walters finally convinced the city to test the brown water flowing from her tap. She also had her children's lead levels tested, and they came back alarmingly high.

By this point, Walters was reading and researching everything she could about water chemistry. She testified at city council meetings and began communicating with Environmental Protection Agency regulation manager Miguel Del Toral, who discovered that "Flint wasn't using federally-mandated corrosion controls that prevent lead from leaching off pipes into the water supply." But astonishingly, officials *still* continued to deny there was a problem. So Del Toral connected Walters with researchers at Virginia Tech who supported her in mobilizing neighbors to carry out their own citizen testing, and the results gained national attention.

As in other examples of viral justice we have witnessed, Flint residents not only took to the streets in protest, testified at city council meetings, and made their voices heard in the media, they also worked quietly, behind closed doors, in the intimacy of one another's homes—over kitchen sinks where the poisoned water flowed and around dinner tables where neighbors conspired to do something about it. To "conspire," as literary scholar Kimberly Bain reminds us, is to *breathe together*, and for those organizing in Flint, their shared vulnerability as mostly working-class women became a catalyst for organizing across racial differences.

As one observer put it, "They believed each other before anyone else would, and those desperate threads of trust end up holding them together through health scares and the protracted wait for help." When faced with the lies of untrustworthy institutions, they spun their own threads of trust in pursuit of the truth.

But the point is not to idolize the citizen scientists in Flint or romanticize any of the other examples of viral justice in this book. The reality is always messier on the ground, and the "wins" are often incomplete, as people far and wide are still fighting to have their environmental justice concerns taken seriously by state officials and corporate executives. One thing is for sure: scientific research in which communities are full partners—where those without fancy titles hold formal leadership roles, where they help formulate the goals of a study, and where those partnerships are designed to last over multiple years—has proved more effective in creating concrete change than research missing community participation.

With this in mind, University of Illinois Chicago researchers who wanted to understand vaccine hesitancy during the COVID-19 crisis reached out to community partners—grassroots organizations based in Black, Latinx, and Orthodox Jewish Chicago neighborhoods, plus one in a white rural county in Illinois. Their goal was to better understand the many different causes of vaccine hesitancy, so they invited members of each organization to enroll in the university's new citizen scientist certificate program so that they could help "shape research questions, collect and analyze data, and advise on how to disseminate the results." They would start with the study on vaccine hesitancy, and eventually branch out to address other health issues.

Sage Kim, associate professor of health policy and administration and principal investigator for this project, explained that before the pandemic, "there was a disconnect between research and community engagement. We have learned that we need the community to play a role in all aspects of research, or it would be impossible to handle this pandemic and other public health concerns." Indeed, although "disconnect" doesn't quite get at the deceit and indifference that have too often characterized the way that institutions have engaged with marginalized communities. As an Alaska Native saying goes, "Researchers are like mosquitoes; they suck your blood and leave."

Earlier we observed how activists are petitioning the University of California, Berkeley, to repatriate sacred objects and remains. But for Indigenous communities, *nothing about us without us* means not only objecting to exploitative scientific endeavors but integrating Indigenous and Western knowledge in initiatives of their own design. The Summer Internship for Indigenous Peoples in Genomics (SING) was cofounded by Kim TallBear, Canada Research Chair in Indigenous Peoples, Technoscience, and Environment and professor at the University of Alberta. SING engages the full spectrum of researchers from undergraduate students to public health professionals from across the globe.

In addition to creating a context in which participants do not have to code-switch, SING allows researchers to wrestle with the history and power associated with Western medicine and prioritize the research questions that matter most to their communities rather than the scientific establishment. Program participants have been instrumental in changing the ethical guidelines at major scientific publications like *Science* and *Nature Communications*, calling for more intense community engagement and more robust protocols for handling genetic samples and data.

SING is part of a broader movement to decolonize education and integrate Indigenous knowledge and scientific methods into academic and research institutions, which has been gaining momentum since the establishment of Canada's Truth and Reconciliation Commission. Amber Sandy, a member of Neyaashiinigmiing, the Chippewas of Nawash First Nation, and coordinator of Indigenous knowledge and science outreach at Ryerson University, explained that Indigenous researchers must be *at the table*: "You really have to be there, be hands-on to build those relationships and that trust."

Moreover, when news broke in 2021 that the unmarked graves of hundreds of children were found at the site of a residential school in Canada, and horrifying stories about the treatment of these Indigenous children at Catholic schools were shared widely, not many people probably knew about the long collaborative research process that led to the tragic discovery.

In May of that year, the Cowessess First Nation began to use ground-penetrating radar to locate unmarked graves. The project was a collaboration with the local Saskatchewan Polytechnic, where members of the surveying, engineering, and technology faculty have been working with the Cowessess First Nation since 2018 to use these tools in a way that addresses pressing issues. "We took technology and applied it to a community problem that needed to be solved," the head of Saskatchewan Polytechnic said.

As in other forms of viral justice, trustworthiness requires confronting power dynamics that privilege some forms of knowledge over others. It rests on the foundation of genuine connections with those most harmed by oppressive institutions, based on the right of these communities to wield scientific tools in ways they consider ethical and define the questions that matter most to them.

As a non-Indigenous researcher, Deborah Bolnick, remarks about the medical and scientific establishments, "You have to be willing to know that history and put in the labor to get beyond that. To do this work you have to be willing to not see yourself as the authority, but rather as somebody who is going to listen to other authorities."

Likewise, for TallBear, decolonizing science means a lifelong practice: "If you're going to work with Indigenous communities collaboratively on genetics, you have to be willing to make lifelong relations." Once again, decolonization is about the low-tech labor and relationships it takes to prefigure a world in which research is not extractive and where excluded and exploited communities are integral to the process. Viral justice is also about acknowledging and working to repair, however difficult it is to do this, past and ongoing harms.

So what might medical reparations look like? Following the racial justice uprisings of 2020, University of California, San Diego, professor of cellular and molecular medicine Samara Reck-Peterson began discussions with her lab about what they could do as scientists to "create actionable change against racism and injustice." After hours of conversation and in consultation with some members of the Lacks family, they decided to donate to the Henrietta Lacks Foundation—one hundred dollars for each new HeLa cell line they create in the future and for each one that they have created in the past—and they are encouraging other labs to do the same.

One of the key participants in those discussions was Alex Stevens, a graduate student in biology at UC San Diego. In the midst of the protests, he observed that "racism is everywhere," even in science. He had never heard of Lacks until he was an undergraduate student and one of his professors suggested he dig into the literature. "I remember having a sense of shock that the field I was trying to get into had a long history of exploitation of minorities," he said.

The Henrietta Lacks Foundation, which was founded by Rebecca Skloot and seeded with a portion of her book royalties, provides financial assistance to those who were "involved in historic research without their knowledge, consent, or benefit." It includes members of the Lacks family, descendants of men in the U.S. Public Health Service Syphilis Study, and others. Reck-Peterson acknowledged those who think that a complete moratorium on the use of HeLa cells is in order, saying, "We are moved by the pride that many Lacks family members have in HeLa cells, and their hope that they will continue to be used for positive advances in research. This is one small step towards justice we can take as scientists." Reck-Peterson's decision inspired the Howard Hughes Medical Institute leadership to make a six-figure gift to the foundation for the ongoing use of HeLa cells. "We felt it was right to acknowledge Henrietta for the use of HeLa cells and to acknowledge that the cells were gained inappropriately," said Erin O'Shea, president of the institute. "And to acknowledge that we have a long way to go before science and medicine are really equitable."

In this series of decisions, we observe the convergence of many different factors: a professor's decision to encourage reading outside the canon, a student's decision to bring those insights to bear at his university, a lab director's decision to act beyond the conventions of scientific norms, a medical institute's decision to put its money where its mission statements are—realizing lofty ideas about diversity and inclusion by reckoning with the history of racism in science and medicine.

All of these might seem like small steps, but together they are trying to shift how institutions operate. This by no means repairs the harm that has been done to the Lacks family or the ongoing fracturing of trust, of which HeLa is one of the most prominent symbols. But each of these decisions bucks the status quo, helps to seed different possibilities, and gives us an example of how change can unfold. Crucially, none of these were top-down phenomena where powerful institutions, like the Howard Hughes Medical Institute, simply decided to do the right thing. They entailed numerous smaller actions . . . viral justice.

In the end, I am convinced that "trust in science" is the wrong goal. Instead of chasing that mirage, let us turn our gaze underfoot. To recover from a centuries-long plague, we must first magnify its source, study its contours, and listen to its victims.

It took a couple of days to catch our breath after the revelation that remains of the victims of the 1985 MOVE bombing had been stored on Princeton's campus. Then, spearheaded by professor of religion Judith Weisenfeld, my colleagues and I published an op-ed in the *Daily Princetonian* that criticized the university's initial denial that the remains were still on campus. We called on the university to move instead toward repair and restitution.

What does that look like in practice? Our statement asked the university administration to apologize to the family for using the victims' remains without consent and to make public whether the remains were used in other courses or research, both of which Princeton University president Chris Eisgruber agreed to do. MOVE, in turn, called on Princeton, the University of Pennsylvania, and Coursera to not only apologize, shut down the course, and start an investigation with a MOVE-approved investigator but also track down and return the remains immediately. MOVE also asked that Janet Monge's employment be terminated and that a financial reparations grant be made to the MOVE family "for profits made by the use of our relatives as teaching tools and research objects."

Then, on May 15, 2021, at the annual rally commemorating the bombing, mothers of the victims went even further. Asked whether they would sue the city, which by this point had changed its story several times about whether it had cremated other remains from the bombing without families' consent, Janine Africa replied, "For us to sue and then for them to have to give us money lets the city off the hook. We're not going through that."

Instead, the mothers had one demand: free writer and activist Mumia Abu-Jamal from Mahanoy State Correctional Institution in Frackville, Pennsylvania. Abu-Jamal, who has maintained his innocence and long supported MOVE members, has been a political prisoner since 1982, after being convicted for the murder of Philadelphia police officer Daniel Faulkner. In this demand, they remind us how the violence of our carceral system is bound up with the harms caused by our scientific and medical institutions. Addressing one without the other ignores how racism plagues every part of our body politic. But also, the experiences of abuse reported by former

MOVE members forces us to consider how often, in opposing the violent status quo *out there*, our own organizations can perpetuate violence *in here*. How much deeper it cuts when the harm hails from those you thought you could trust.

What if, in remembering Henrietta Lacks, we also remembered Onesimus? Onesimus was an enslaved African in Boston who lived in the early 1700s and brought African medical knowledge about disease inoculation to the thirteen American colonies. He was owned by a well-known minister and one of the key architects of the Salem witch trials, Cotton Mather. When Mather asked Onesimus whether he had ever had smallpox, Onesimus responded, "Yes and No," going on to explain how he was inoculated: "People take Juice of Small-Pox; and Cutty-skin, and Putt in a Drop."

This practice, known as variolation, involves collecting infectious material (such as pus) from a smallpox patient and administering it to others in a controlled manner to build up immunity. It got its name from the scientific name for smallpox, variola. Of course, some people still suffered severe symptoms and even died, but at far lower rates than those who were infected naturally.

Mather soon learned that the practice was widespread among other Africans in the colony and that enslaved people with a scar on their arm—indicating they were immune to smallpox—fetched a higher price. Not only was variolation common among Africans, but it was also practiced throughout the Ottoman Empire, China, and India long before Europeans "discovered" it.

Teaming up with local apothecary Zabdiel Boylston, Mather—with Onesimus's methods in hand—set out to spread the practice of inoculation but was met with intense resistance . . . not unlike the antivaxxer sentiments that circulate today: "Their rage came from many sources; fear that inoculation might spread smallpox further; knowledge that the bubonic plague was on the rise in France; and a righteous fury that it was immoral to tamper with God's judgment in this way. There was a racial tone to their response as well, as they rebelled against an idea that was not only foreign, but African (one critic, an eminent doctor, attacked Mather for his 'Negroish' thinking)." After smallpox had ravaged Boston, the effectiveness of Onesimus's medical knowledge became difficult to refute. Half of Boston's population of eleven thousand was infected, with about one in seven people dying of the disease. By contrast, of those who were inoculated, only one in forty died. So it appears *Negroish thinking* was a lifesaver.

What would it mean if we were not only haunted by the memories of those who winced in pain, but also called on the spirits of those who were a source of healing? After all, Black people, past and present, are not simply victims of scientific mistreatment but inventors of medical knowledge. White people and institutions are not only the protagonists of harm—J. Marion Sims, U.S. Public Health Service, and KKI researchers—but also beneficiaries of African expertise and Black brilliance. This refutation of the White Savior myth and recasting of roles is vital in engendering viral justice. Our collective imagination about the past and present matters. And we all have the ability to recount a wider range of stories as part of imagining anew a science and medicine that are worthy of our trust.

SEVEN

La Casa Azul

Today the White House is blue. The house I grew up in is now the color of a boundless, teeming ocean. On a block of muted hues, it stands out. It's blue like a "blues-soaked America, a blues-soaked world, a planet where catastrophe and celebration—joy and pain—sit side by side," as Cornel West would put it.

When close family friends Rubi and Lucas bought the White House from my mom, one of the first things they did was paint the exterior—La Caza Azul, an homage to artist Frida Kahlo's blue house in Mexico City. It's an unapologetic blue that recalls the turbulent waters their African forebears were forced over in order to toil in Borinquén, the Indigenous Taino name for Puerto Rico. It reminds me, too, of the Caribbean Sea their parents crossed searching for an open future in North Philly, just as the Whites once had in moving to LA . . . great migrations filled with blues.

Although the appeal of the White House for Rubi, Lucas, and their two sons was its ample space, perfect for a growing family, by the time my mom handed over the keys, it was run *all* the way down, *weathered*, you could say. In multiple spots, the weary black-shingle roof was caving in, leaking after the rare rainfall. The linoleum-tiled floor was coming up in the den and kitchen, broken pieces exposing the unfinished wood and nails underneath.

An ancient gooseneck bathtub faucet gave away the age of the house, and earthquake-wrought cracks on the walls were inching wider and wider with each shimmy and shake. And the kitchen, *oh* the kitchen. It was a hot mess. The vents over the stove didn't work, so the upstairs bedrooms bore the uninvited smell of curry. The faded wooden cabinets, the color of stale toast, were on their last hinges. As for my poor mom, chef extraordinaire, stewing pots of lentils and potatoes and frying up baskets of purees on the rickety electric stove was like forcing Coltrane to make music on a recorder, the simple woodwind instrument kids play to torture their parents.

The White House, no doubt, had the blues.

And Rubi and Lucas took on the Herculean task of infusing it with joy and beauty, pulling out the many worn parts, restoring others, and fashioning a new home, piece by piece. So now, when you walk up the porch steps and through the giant yellow door, you're greeted with gleaming wooden floors that run the entire length of the first floor, not a broken tile in sight, and no walls separating the living room, den, and kitchen anymore. Their goal was to be able to squeeze the greatest number of bodies into the space for the greatest amount of fun.

Once you're in, turn to the left, and you'll see orange, blue, and white Moroccan tiles framing the fireplace. And on your right, plants of every size and shape line the front window that was once marred with a hole in the middle. Around the room, you'll spot a few pieces of Grandma White's old furniture—an oversize chair and couch once covered in plastic are now reupholstered in striking patterns.

Walk in a bit farther, and paintings by Afro-Latinx artists—Sheena Garcia, Samuel Lind, and Salvador González—will demand your attention as they hang on gleaming white walls. Philly graffiti artist Dan One's depiction of Frida Kahlo, her face the color purple, will catch your eye. So, too, will Gina Echeverry's blue lady expressing the melancholy of mothers waiting for husbands to come home from war. At every turn, this house of blues exudes a kind of stubborn beauty, a joy that refuses to kneel in defeat.

And it's not just the colors that beckon. It is the sense that you, too, are welcome under this roof. Just linger a while and you'll spy dozens of kids come and go, riding their bikes, skates, and skate-boards down the block, racing to open the side gate without asking, shooting hoops with Little Lucas in the yard, sprawling out on the huge front porch with markers and paints that Rubi has laid out for them to use.

If it's close to dinner time, a few kids will be on the back patio scarfing down bowls of one of Rubi's famous stews. If you happen to stop by on the weekend, you might get recruited for one of the neighborhood service projects—serving dinner at a downtown women's shelter, or prepping hot meals for a holiday food drive, or collecting book donations to set up a library in a friend's Kenyan hometown. Stay long enough, and you might even get to attend Soulful Friday, a monthly arts gathering in the living room where Lucas will kick things off with an original spoken-word piece:

This is a love poem
A hug you to death poem
A hermanos and sistas in protest poem
Not a division poem
A unity poem
A Herculean effort poem
I lift you up when ya down poem
This is a love poem
Amor por palabras poem

And it'll hit you, these are not just words to him. Stop by on Father's Day, you'll catch Lucas setting up tables and chairs in the backyard, and then little by little, it will fill up. First, the OGs, older dads, and grandpas will arrive, Mr. Martinez and John John from next door, then haggard new papas will stumble in, stealing a few precious hours away from their daddy duties. Soon the loving, raucous laughter will commence—with guests chowing down on whatever Lucas has on the grill, playing cards, and chopping it up.

Then, right on cue, one of the OGs who has lived across the street since he was a kid will recall a story about growing up across from my dad, and all the other guys will nod their heads slowly, taking it in as if for the first time. Dad's spirit, I'm sure, is smiling down on all the sweetness. Oh! And if you're extra lucky, and show up on a Bahá'í holy day, you're sure to hear music streaming from the yard, curated by DJ Lucas himself, as you elbow your way to the buffet table for some mouthwatering grub. First up, Rubi's lentils and sweet potato, spinach, and coconut stew. Maybe there is some chicken, and there's definitely a scoop of potatoes, carrots, and *arroz con gandules* waiting for you—the unmistakable smell of sofrito forcing you to take a bite before you find a seat.

Sure, it will feel weird at first, the way all these strangers greet you as if you're kin. But soon you'll get used to it. And then you'll wonder, why couldn't it always be like this?

A peace not war poem
A shut down ICE poem
A unit familias poem
A shatter the wall poem
A you and I make we poem
A we and us make a new world poem

Here in this little plot of LA, like so many other corners of our planet, folks aren't waiting for things to change magically from above. They are plotting—conspiring with their neighbors, rewriting social scripts, seeding new worlds in their own backyards. They have elected to sow beauty, service, and connection right where they are as a daily practice—until new patterns sprout and spread. They seem to have taken Angela Y. Davis's supplication to heart: "You have to act as if it were possible to radically transform the world. And you have to do it all the time."

We don't have to travel halfway around the planet to help "those less fortunate." We can start with the things right under our noses *or* on top of our heads. Over, under, in between, getting my hair braided as a girl was my first lesson in patternmaking. My cornrows felt like a spiritual helmet, and the noisy, unapologetic purple and pink beads in my hair announced that I'd arrived. My braids reminded me of who I was, where I came from, and that even if it took six godforsaken hours, my head held something like a map, in case I ever got lost.

So, too, with the new patterns we can each weave in our families, workplaces, schools, and neighborhoods, like La Casa Azul, reminding us who we are to one another. If, as James Baldwin put it, "hope is invented every day," then each of us has the potential to be an inventor, designing worlds and remaking structures, even those with decrepit roofs falling down and linoleum tile coming up. We can start building the kind of world we need amid the rubble of the one that we can't stand:

> This is not a public announcement poem
> Nor a clinch your purse when ya see me poem
> Not a shoot me poem
> But an embrace who I am poem . . .
> A let's change the world with love love poem
> A it takes a barrio poem

The kinship, love, and solidarity fostered at La Casa Azul, *inventing hope every day*, is viral justice at work. It entails transmuting the many forms of harm that plague our lives into an environment that is habitable, life affirming, and invigorating . . . refusing to wait for official sanction.

I think 2020 will go down in history as the Year of Public Announcements about Antiracism. Following the brutal killings of Ahmaud Arbery, Breonna Taylor, and George Floyd, people worldwide rushed into the streets demanding justice: from a group of workers at the McMurdo Station in Antarctica, to nearly two hundred people in Tunis, to one thousand protesters in Osaka.

Floyd, in particular, became a rallying point for protesting racism and repression far and wide. In a case that some called the "Czech George Floyd," the death of a Romany man, Stanislav Tomas, in Teplice, Czech Republic, at the hands of officers sparked nationwide protests over anti-Roma racism in Europe. The police, widely known for their brutality toward the country's approximately 250,000 Roma people, were filmed kneeling on Stanislav's neck and shoulders. The initial doctor's report even claimed Tomas's death was likely due to intoxication . . . peak gaslighting at work again.

To be sure, the global outpouring following Floyd's murder was not just about solidarity with the movement for Black lives, but an opportunity to shine a light on homegrown forms of oppression— whether of Roma in Europe or Papuans in Indonesia, the latter rallying around the hashtag #PapuanLivesMatter and likening Floyd's murder to that of a Papuan student, Obby Kogoya, whose head Indonesian police stepped on while he lay facedown on the ground. "I'm seeing more enthusiasm among Indonesians in educating themselves about racism and what's happening towards West Papuans," said Veronica Koman, an outspoken pro-Papuan human rights lawyer. This enthusiasm, in turn, has encouraged people to question one racist symbol, policy, and practice after another.

Statues and murals were removed, tagged with graffiti, and torn down, including Virginia's Jefferson Davis statue, which was toppled by protesters; a statue of Philadelphia's racist ex-mayor Frank Rizzo was removed from its place of honor across from city hall; and a statue of seventeenth-century slave trader Edward Colson, who was known for tossing the bodies of the ill or dead overboard to recoup insurance money, was unceremoniously torn down and thrown into the harbor in Bristol, England.

NASCAR announced it would prohibit the Confederate flag from all its events and properties, and the State of Mississippi finally decided to change its flag, which bears the familiar symbol of white supremacy . . . For those who have grown up terrorized by the everydayness of racist longings, this is *not* nothing. Nor is it *everything.*

In an incredible about-face, the NFL admitted it should have listened to Colin Kaepernick and other players who have been taking a knee and speaking up against police violence for years. The NFL, whose players are 72 percent Black, made plans to play "Lift Every Voice and Sing"—often called the Black National Anthem—during major games as part of its $250 million social justice initiative (this was met with considerable pushback by members of the NFL's predominantly white fan base, who call the decision "divisive" and "political").

After Donald Trump tweeted threats that he would deploy the military to quell the 2020 uprisings, U.S. Army officials told soldiers to disobey any orders to attack peaceful protesters. Likewise, Boston Metro Bus drivers said they would not transport police to protests or protesters to police, among other instances of conscientious objection.

Numerous organizations and companies announced forms of support for Black lives. For example, the cosmetic company Sephora decided to devote 15 percent of shelf space to products from Black-owned businesses. TV programming responded—the show *Cops* got canceled, HBO dropped *Gone with the Wind* from its lineup, and streaming sites like Hulu and Netflix highlighted Black programs and offered many of them for free download. Professional groups rallied, including scientists around the country who took action to "shut down STEM" by calling out how racism shapes their work, striking for Black lives, and committing to concrete changes.

Not to be outdone, the parody news outlet *The Onion* announced that Quaker Oats was changing the name of Aunt Jemima syrup to "Sheila"—replacing the historically racist mascot with "a Black female lawyer who enjoys pancakes sometimes." Parody turned prophecy when five days later Quaker Oats announced it was changing the image in an effort "to make progress toward racial equality."

Technology giants, for their part, released an impressive array of corporate solidarity statements—over sixty public-facing documents issued between May and June 2020: Instagram "ensuring Black Voices are heard," TikTok "standing with the Black community," Facebook "fighting systemic inequality in our world," and IBM, Amazon, and Microsoft announcing plans to end or pause their facial recognition programs with the police. The latter three knew about the bias and abuse associated with many of their products for years, but only in the wake of mass protests did they decide to act.

Perhaps most noteworthy of all, calls to defund and even abolish the police grew mainstream. The Minneapolis City Council announced plans to sever ties between the police department and public schools as part of a broader reinvestment in communities. Mayor Eric Garcetti of Los Angeles announced a $150 million cut from the police department budget to invest in "youth jobs, health initiatives and 'peace centers' to heal trauma," and New York State passed legislation repealing a law that has allowed law enforcement to shield police misconduct records from the public. Whereas activists had long been demanding these policy changes, only after mass public protest did we witness changes that seemed impossible just months earlier, announced one after another.

More symbolic efforts, such as Washington, DC's new "Black Lives Matter Plaza" spelled out in giant yellow letters in front of the Washington Monument or Texas realtors' announcement that they would stop using "master" to describe bedrooms and bathrooms due to its connotations with slavery, attracted more critical attention. The DC chapter of the Black Lives Matter Global Network called the DC mayor's grand gesture "a performative distraction from real policy changes" and a way "to appease white liberals while ignoring our demands." And critics on social media responded swiftly to the renaming of bedrooms:

> But you're still going to disproportionately deny black people housing and home ownership smh.
>
> Doing all this isht no one asked for them to do.
>
> Or, real estate agents can just treat all consumers of color fairly and equitably instead of racially steering them.
>
> This is not on the list of my concerns . . . at'all . . . redlining . . . yes . . . higher interest rates . . . yes . . . the difference in appraisals for black folks . . . yes . . . masters with en suites . . . not as much.
>
> Ohmigod just defund the police people.

It comes down to distinguishing between the superficial and substantive changes taking place amid the multiple assaults, from public health to police violence. At the same time, we mustn't mistake small with inconsequential actions or assume that all substantive change requires grand gestures. Too often, we can dismiss certain efforts as performative if they do not provide instant or obvious results. Nor can we always predict how what gets dismissed as performative might compel people to act, politically grow, and create community.

"I'm actually super bored with the concept of performativity," said abolitionist Mariame Kaba. "I think about sites of struggle as just constant learning . . . be super curious, come with what you know, be willing to learn, and be willing to be transformed in the service of the work."

On June 27, 2020, I took a writing break for lunch and opened my Princeton inbox. There was a message to the university community from President Christopher Eisgruber announcing that the board of trustees had "voted to change the names of both the School of Public and International Affairs and Wilson College," concluding that "Woodrow Wilson's racist thinking and policies make him an inappropriate namesake for a school or college whose scholars, students, and alumni must stand firmly against racism in all its forms." Just like that. With a single vote, the school founded in 1930 and named after Wilson in 1948 would no longer bear his name. Swift but also belated, I thought. The president's message ends by calling the steps taken by the board of trustees "extraordinary measures," while critics swiftly refuted that characterization.

Almost five years earlier, a Princeton student organization—the Black Justice League—had occupied the president's office for thirty-plus hours demanding several changes to the university, including renaming the school and college that bore Wilson's name. I served as the pizza delivery person for the protesters, collecting funds from colleagues and running the pies to them through a side entrance where no university guards were posted. I recall the students' clarity and bravery even as they were threatened with disciplinary action, insulted by peers, and made the target of violent threats that forced the core group to hunker down off campus in the immediate aftermath of the occupation.

At the time, the university made a number of concessions but decided not to remove Wilson's name. Fast-forward to June 2020, and what once seemed utterly far-fetched—that one of the oldest universities in the nation would defer to the demands of a band of protesters—happened seemingly overnight. Though not quite. Student activists planted the seeds, impressing on the university how vile it was that they should be forced to identify with an individual who, among other insults, did not see Black students as worthy of admission and even erased "the presence and accomplishments of Princeton's early African American students" in an effort to justify his own policy of exclusion. Yet when the Black Justice League made the demand to remove Wilson's name, they were clear that it was only one part of a much larger institutional reckoning.

"Instead of showing me your diversity statement, show me your hiring data, your discrimination claim stats, your salary tables, your retention numbers, your diversity policies, and your leaders' public actions against racism," implored professor of engineering education Monica Cox after yet another corporate statement of solidarity.

The trap is when symbolic change becomes a permanent placeholder for redistributing power and resources, when bringing down a memorial or changing the name of a building stands in for a repatterning of our social relations. As when, in the wake of the 2020 racial reckoning, journalistic institutions around the U.S. decided to finally start capitalizing the *b* in "Black" as they do with references to Asian, Latinx, and Indigenous people. But as one critic put it a year after the shift to uppercase, "They didn't bother with the harder, more impactful work of diversifying their coverage or their newsrooms, which are far whiter than the populations they cover in almost every market in the country."

Weary advocates of racial justice are by now used to lip service, PR stunts, and half-hearted reforms, and the public was inundated with statements expressing support for the protests that swept the world. But was this viral justice or viral publicity? Which of these announcements and about-faces would move us closer to a world in which Black life is truly valued, and which of them constituted a savvy veneer for business as usual? For many of us, the long list of pronouncements in support of Black lives felt a bit like "too much, too fast" *and* somehow "too little, too late."

Progress. One symbolic step forward, two violent steps backward—so is the history of white backlash in the United States. So long as competition and scarcity are the governing logics of our social order, what seems like advancement for subordinate groups will always be met with hostility from dominant ones. No matter how many Black Lives Matter lawn signs are printed, the game is still designed to have winners and losers.

Inside such a game, racism will always be necessary to justify why some people are winning and some losing, and still others losing their *lives*. The point is not simply to ensure there are more winners. We have to step outside the game to build an entirely new set of social relations that does not require losers. One that ensures everyone has "broadly equal access to the material and social means necessary to live a flourishing life." We can do this. But first we have to unshackle our collective imagination.

In this book, we connected the dots between various types of harm, from police violence to viruses, dissecting the stressors and oppressors that lead to premature death. We attuned ourselves to the soundtrack of anti-Black racism that rings through our homes and neighborhoods, our schools, our bodies, even our spirits. We must train ourselves to perceive differently. Renowned writer Octavia E. Butler called this a *radio imagination*, where the point is not simply to break the record but to compose new ways of relating to one another and organizing our world that are life affirming, sustaining, and soul stirring.

In March 2020, when most U.S. states began issuing stay-at-home orders, Shawn and I decided to collaborate with the Princeton Public Library and our local bookstore, Labyrinth, to offer daily "Stories from around the World"—virtual story times for younger children. Our two sons are grownish, so we were tickled to pull out all the old books we used to read to them. Parables, adventures, poetry, lyrical collections, and funny "tails" like *Walter, the Farting Dog*.

On the day we started it, the Zoom link was circulated far and wide on local listservs and social media, and about forty-five families logged on. About five minutes before we finished, just as I was finishing *Walter*, someone used the screen-sharing function on Zoom and projected a crude image of a chubby white man in a thong with his genitals bulging for all the children to see. As I scrambled to figure out whether I could stop the sharing or if I had to shut down the link, we heard a man's voice repeat the N-word over and over, letting us know this was not a youthful prank but targeted and racist harassment.

Ours was one of the first reported cases of "zoombombing" in the week that everyone was moving to remote work, school, and social interaction. Soon after, the cases seemed to sweep across all types of online events and meetings, and dozens of news outlets contacted me about our experience because I had tweeted about it. Initially, I was stunned by what happened, but I could not be completely surprised. I had let my guard down, thinking, *We're in the middle of a goddamn pandemic, and this is a children's event* . . . But I quickly shook off the shock because there is no quarantining racism.

This was mild harassment anyway, when compared with the routine calls, emails, and online attacks that my colleagues and I experience for telling the truth about this country. The chair of my department, Eddie Glaude, likes to quote James Baldwin—"To act is to be committed, and to be committed is to be in danger." The fact something so benign as stories for children from around the world warranted zoombombing reminds me about the seriousness of seemingly small things.

On second thought, it is not so insignificant—our effort to spread some joy and fun in the early days of a global pandemic in a way that embraces people from different cultural backgrounds. By giving voice to the possibility that this crisis could unite us, despite all evidence to the contrary, we posed a threat that elicited harassment.

A few weeks later, I was finishing up another event, hosted by Data for Black Lives, a social justice organization focused on grassroots approaches to technology. This meeting brought together activists, scholars, students, public health practitioners, and more to create a racial justice response to the inequities surfacing around COVID-19. Just as my Zoom breakout session was about to wrap up, a seventeen-year-old Black computer science prodigy, Josh, spoke up. "Excuse me, did you write this book!?" he asked, holding up a copy of my last book, *Race after Technology*. He continued, gushing about how important it was in his work addressing automated forms of racism, and I gushed right back, explaining how *he* was exactly the kind of reader I had in mind when I wrote that book. In a beautiful and spontaneous forty-five-second exchange, our excitement and mutual admiration were palpable. As a reader and a writer, we required each other. We were *interdependent*.

Later, I would learn that Josh recorded the exchange, and as it circulated on Twitter, I wondered, "What's the opposite of zoom-bombing?" Friends posted so many great candidate terms, but my favorite is "zoom*blooming*" (no surprise it was suggested by wordsmith extraordinaire Eve L. Ewing). It is closest in sound and spelling to the original, unwanted disruption, and it connotes a feeling of liveliness and growth that counteracts the gloomy sameness of life under quarantine where racism is still viral.

In such a world, zoomblooming, viral justice, viral joy, and more are balms. Plus, we owe it to ourselves to name the world we cannot live without, even as we diagnose the world we cannot live within. Let us excavate, name, and water all the forms of justice and solidarity blooming in the rubble of pandemics and policing.

You will recall that the first step in confronting all that white noise is for each of us to discover our plot: In what area of your life do you, or *could* you, question the roles and narratives you've inherited, and scheme with others to seed a different world? In the documentary *Mountains That Take Wing*, Yuri Kochiyama asks Angela Y. Davis about developing political consciousness: "Where do you think it has to begin?" and Davis replies, "Well, I think it begins wherever you are, right?" Right!

Keep in mind: this is not Lone Ranger work, nor will every meaningful act be joyful. Viral justice differs from the idea that individual (consumer) decisions are enough to address large systemic issues. We all need trusted friends and comrades at every step, and we must connect with collectives and movements to really shake things up.

After determining our plot, assessing harmful ways of thinking, and doing things—hailing our squad—it's time to start taking small but significant steps in changing established patterns of thought and action. These lines of action aren't a substitute for grander initiatives that work to overturn or institute macro changes in our laws and policies. Those remain vital. But macro changes go hand in hand with a transformation in our social relations. Legal statutes mirror and magnify what we choose to stand for every day.

If you'll let me geek out for a moment, civil rights activist Grace Lee Boggs appeals to quantum physics to explain the relationship between seemingly small actions and larger structures:

> Changes in small places also affect the global system, not through incrementalism, but because every small system participates in an unbroken wholeness. Activities in one part of the whole create effects that appear in distant places. Because of these unseen connections, there is potential value in working anywhere in the system. We never know how our small activities will affect others through the invisible fabric of our connectedness . . . the real engine of change is never 'critical mass'; dramatic and systemic change always begins with 'critical connections.'

Think of it like this: hanging a Whites Only sign in the front window of a store is a small thing *only* if we fail to consider how it reflects and reinforces broader ways of thinking, condoning, and institutionalizing racial injustice. So, then, what is the antiracist equivalent?

As a small-business owner, perhaps you'll start by hanging a neon sign that reads, "White supremacy won't die until white people see it as a white issue they need to solve rather than a Black issue they need to empathize with," as did Glory Hole Donuts on Gerrard Street in Toronto, or simply, "Resist white supremacy," as did Cox Farms, a 116-acre family-run farm known well before the current wave of protests for its antiracist road signs in northern Virginia.

What if we each became a sign—embodying a more just reality—one that welcomes everyone who passes by to enter into a more expansive imagination of what we can build together?

Viral justice is in all the fine print, the micro-ways that are easy to skip over. After all, it's possible to run a Whites Only business in practice with an antiracist sign on the door.

Beyond signage, that would mean looking at whom we hire and promote, whom we assign to the back versus the front of the store, and how we treat employees, customers, and those who cannot afford to be customers.

A powerful image circulating on social media shows a storefront where, in the left window, a sign proclaims, "We welcome all races, all religions, all countries of origin, all sexual orientations, all genders. We stand with you. You are safe here." In the adjacent window of the same store, a smaller sign reads, "Restrooms are for customer use only." The caption reads, "Almost all accommodations made by liberals based on identity do not include the poor."

In a racial capitalist society where citizenship is routinely conflated with consumerism and politicians encourage Americans to *buy, buy, buy* to express their patriotism, inclusion is always contingent, transactive, and conditional—even when we don't say the quiet part out loud. But this doesn't mean we shy away from the economic underpinnings of justice. Instead, as my former teacher Ruth Wilson Gilmore urged when it comes to money, "Really follow it—not pretend to follow it."

This is precisely what has been happening in Seattle, Washington, with the Solidarity Budget, a broad and powerful coalition of over two hundred local organizations that decided to band together in the wake of the 2020 protests. Together they are making a range of demands—including the defunding of the police, housing for all, Indigenous sovereignty, safe and affordable public transportation, childcare, education, food support, digital equity, disability justice, and a Green New Deal. They're "connecting what we *don't* need and what we *do* need."

Shrinking the number of police officers and shrinking the number of prosecutors as part of shrinking the criminal legal system leads to fewer people cycled through the King County Jail—most of whom are shuttled through the city's municipal court for misdemeanor offenses. The demand to stop police sweeps of homeless encampments is tied to the demand to invest in affordable housing throughout the city.

Rather than hand over more money to police for surveillance technologies, the Solidarity Budget invests in "tech for the people," in which digital stewards work with community members. It created a Guaranteed Income Pilot Program to cover childcare, food, and other basics, because too often people are forced to choose between these essential needs. Noting that the city spends twenty-six times more on policing than on climate, the Solidarity Budget also invests in climate resilience through spending that helps transition low-income households from oil heat to clean energy. That, in turn, lowers climate pollution *and* reduces residents' utility bills.

In short, Seattle Solidarity Budget organizers successfully shrank the police budget two years in a row while winning investments that center the city's most marginalized residents. By tearing down the silos across their many interests, coming together to consult, hosting public education meetings over Zoom, rallying at city hall, showing up to provide testimony at city council meetings, and more, they remind us that "a budget is more than a budget. It is a moral document that states *who* and *what* we value."

Even more, their work brings to life the fact that all our struggles are connected, that *we* are connected. In doing so, they are bringing to life Gilmore's assertion that "abolition requires that we change one thing, which is *everything.*" No small feat, for sure. But the only way we can change things is by changing things, one budget line item after another . . . wonderfully boring in practice yet bold in vision.

When we toured La Casa Azul at the start of this chapter, it probably sounded too good to be true. After all, I did not mention all the heartache that breezes quietly through the curtains, snakes slowly up the stairs, and hangs heavily from the ceiling. Sorrow and joy, consorting like two old lovers in that blues house.

There's the ancestral blues of the Whites going back generations, the grief surrounding my dad's untimely death, the anger wrought by a ravenous carceral system that tried to eat my brother alive, and the weariness of my immigrant mother making ends meet. This might be one reason why South African artist Nelson Makamo, whose series of stunning blue portraits explores the many blues of Black life, says, "Our genetic code is blue."

Not to mention the more recent struggles of Rubi and Lucas once they decided to turn the White House blue—barely piecing together a down payment (thanks largely to Rubi's dad, a lifelong factory worker in Philly who pulled money out of his 401K), living out of suitcases with Rubi's brother Juan and his family for months as the contractors kept changing the date and cost of renovations, and the list goes on. And there is also the ongoing, embodied blues of Rubi, who, like Frida before her, struggles with chronic debilitating pain. Yet amid all this, they have a vision—tearing down walls and laying a fresh foundation following a new blueprint.

"Don't ever think that everything went right," as Septima Clark put it in chapter 3. So it is when we build anything new, whether physical structures or the social fabric of a community. It can feel like we're drowning in an ocean of blues, but when the pain and anger rip into sound, a "blues-soaked world, a planet where catastrophe and celebration—joy and pain—sit side by side" . . . our individual blues can turn into music.

In the end, if inequity and injustice are woven into the very fabric of society, then each twist, coil, and code offers a chance for us to weave new patterns, practices, and politics . . . new blueprints. The vastness of the problems we face will be their undoing when we accept that we are patternmakers. Whether in seemingly simple exchanges or more elaborate forms of community organizing and world-building, this is a microvision of change.

"Nothing is too small. Nothing is too, quote-unquote, ordinary or insignificant," noted the poet Rita Dove. "Those are the things that make up the measure of our days, and they're the things that sustain us. And they're the things that certainly can become worthy of poetry." Perhaps they are already poetry:

This is the love poem
The wash all the hate in the world poem
A blessing disguised as a Black man poem
A el negrito wit talent from the hood poem

Living poetically, to me, is not about everything being precious, picture-perfect, or Insta-ready. It's about attuning to the seemingly trivial, the ordinary, and what's too often taken for granted. Fact is, every single one of us can weave new patterns of thinking and doing, whether internally, interpersonally, or institutionally. And these patterns must, of necessity, take many different forms, drawing on our varied skills, interests, and dispositions. We need the loud and ferocious world-builders as much as the quiet and studious ones. The last thing we need is for everyone to do or be the same thing! So whether you want to scream or whisper, write poetry or live it, *now* is the time.

ACKNOWLEDGMENTS

If you have made it this far, then you know that this entire book is, in a way, one long acknowledgment: family, friends, teachers, students, organizers, colleagues, artists, midwives, even strangers who over many years have cared for me without coddling, taught me without knowing, held me up without bowing down, challenged me without apology. I have tried my best to pour out onto these pages all that's flowed into me.

My ride or dies—Akia, Alisha, Claudia, Julie, Kamal, Laura, Liz, Naimeh, Razi, Rina, Rubi, Tatiana, and Zhaleh—your friendship continues to rearrange me. Kaytura and the entire Spirit of Justice crew, you all have taught me so much about intergenerational healing and truthfulness as the "foundation of all human virtues."

I am inspired every day by my colleagues in Princeton's Department of African American Studies. In previous books I have gushed on and on about the remarkable people whom I get to work with and whose kindness, vision, humor, and dedication to our collective mission have me convinced I won the Office Lottery. I'll just add to my previous testimonies that they prove to me day in and day out that it is possible to create a world *within* a world.

As for the collective labor that makes a lie out of that one name on the cover—journalists, scholars, poets, photographers, students, tweeters, four anonymous peer reviewers, and so many more—I am indebted to your insights, stories, questions, and suspicions.

My literary agent, Sarah Levitt, was the first to set the wheels of this project in motion: "I'm hungry to read anything you have," she DMed on Twitter in spring 2020. But for Sarah's generous appetite, I don't think I would have spent the first few months of the COVID-19 lockdown conceiving what would eventually become this book. I quickly realized that writing was exactly the daily therapy I needed—churning all those apocalyptic headlines and social media notifications into something that might, in the end, offer some nourishment.

I am deeply grateful to my editor, Meagan Levinson, and the entire Princeton University Press team, for caring as much about this project as I do. Meagan provided me the perfect amount of space and stimulation, asking questions that forced me to meet myself on the page in a way I have never done before. May every writer be so lucky.

I have always found it impossible to write into the abyss, without having an expectant reader on the other side of the screen. My colleague Tamara Nopper has proved just that, helping me to see around the corners of my thinking, surprising me with critical insights about topics that I thought I understood.

Huge shout-out to the dynamic duo Aliya Ram and Sarika Ram (no relation, which is how we know it was meant to be!), whose research and editorial support proved invaluable over many months and until the very last endnote was formatted and every citation recovered.

Likewise, my brilliant friend Liz Dwyer stepped in at a critical phase and helped push the final revisions over the finish line. I can't wait until we are old and gray, Liz, so we can cackle away about Wu-Tang "Klan." You are *a friend of my mind*, as Toni put it, *you gather me, the pieces I am, and give them back to me in all the right order.*

I am forever indebted to my writing group—Rina Bliss, Bettina Judd, Keisha-Khan Perry, Ashanté Reese, and Bianca Williams. Here's to the power of virtual copresence. Thank you for your daily accountability and encouragement. I am also grateful to my aunty Beverlee and the Cedarburg crew for their invaluable feedback after I read excerpts from an early draft.

I am fortunate to work with so many amazing students in the Ida B. Wells Just Data Lab, especially the "viral justice team"—Cameron, Kakuyon, Katrina, Leyla, and Maya—who excavated stories for a viral justice digital repository that will be publicly available. May our lab motto, *Be careful with each other, so we can be dangerous together*, live on!

Enormous thanks to the lab's associate director, Cierra Robson, and creative content director, Payton Croskey, for being such wonderful stewards of this "beautiful experiment." Our work in the lab would not be possible without major support from Princeton's Office of Information Technology in addition to other campus supporters.

At Princeton, I am also immensely grateful for the friendship of Rashidah Andrews, Angel Gardener, Janet Vertesi, and Meredith Martin (shout-out to the entire team at the Center for Digital Humanities). Thanks, also, to the Center for Health and Wellbeing for supporting this project with funds for research assistance and editing.

Early in the writing of this book, I received a 2020 Inaugural Freedom Scholar Award from the Marguerite Casey Foundation and Group Health Foundation, which provided me time and resources to dedicate to this project. Just as crucial, the magnificent community of Freedom Scholars continues to remind me why any of us do what we do. *A luta continua!*

Finally, none of this would be possible without the love and support of Shawn Benjamin, who knows precisely when to give me a side-eye for not practicing what I preach about rest; my mom, Behin, and brother, Jamal, who graciously allowed me to recount their stories; and Malachi and Khalil, whose indecipherable sibling banter is my love language.

NOTES

Author's Note

Page

ix   **The Siamese crocodiles,** "The Siamese Crocodile," Dr. Monk (blog), January 27, 2017, https://www.drmonk.org/blogarticle/64/the-siamese -crocodile.

Introduction

Page

1   **out of slavery.** During this same period on the other side of the world, my maternal grandparents had taken flight in response to religious persecution, leaving the province of Yazd in their native Iran to settle in Maharashtra, India, where my mother (and eventually I) was born. But this is not an autobiography, so I'll save that story and many others for another space and time.

1   **were "the Whites."** I never met my paternal grandfather, Truitt White Sr., who died before I was born.

5   **her own home."** Errin Haines, "Family Seeks Answers in Fatal Shooting of Louisville Woman in Her Apartment," *Washington Post*, May 11, 2020, https://www.washingtonpost.com/nation/2020/05/11/family-seeks -answers-fatal-police-shooting-louisville-woman-her-apartment/.

6   **anticipation of discrimination."** Margaret T. Hicken et al., "'Every Shut Eye, Ain't Sleep': The Role of Racism-Related Vigilance in Racial/Ethnic Disparities in Sleep Difficulty," *Race and Social Problems* 5, no. 2 (2013): 100–112, https://doi.org/10.1007/s12552-013-9095-9, p. 101.

7   **for me.** "Feeling Good," Nina Simone, 1965.

7   **researcher Arline Geronimus.** Arline T. Geronimus, "The Weathering Hypothesis and the Health of African-American Women and Infants: Evidence and Speculations," *Ethnicity and Disease* 2, no. 3 (1992): 207–21.

8   **income whites received.** Note on language: All racial-ethnic labels are political—reflecting a historic relationship to structures of power, shifting over time, and across borders and regions. Classifications are often imposed

by the state, but are also contested and crafted by social movements. Racial-ethnic labels do not name a fixed essence or homogeneous group identity, and they are definitely *not* stable biological or genetic classifications.

Throughout the text, I opt to use the more expansive "Black" rather than "African American," unless my point applies specifically to descendants of enslaved Africans in the United States. I also opt to capitalize the *B* in "black" when it refers to people with a shared sense of identity, history, and community in the context of global white supremacy.

When it comes to white Americans, I choose to use lowercase. I agree with those, like historian Nell Painter and sociologist Eve L. Ewing, who argue that using the lowercase *w* can reinforce the invisibility of white identity and white power. But I think naming whiteness *period*, without adopting the naming practices of white supremacist groups (who use a capital *W*), still compels white Americans to reckon with whiteness—"where it comes from, how it operates, or what it does"—rather than "maintain the fiction that race is other people's problem, that they are mere observers in a centuries-long stage play in which they have, in fact, been the producers, directors, and central actors." Source: Eve L. Ewing, "I'm a Black Scholar Who Studies Race. Here's Why I Capitalize 'White," *Zora* July 2, 2020. Even so, I believe thoughtful people committed to racial justice can come to different conclusions.

Throughout the text, I also opt to use the more gender-inclusive "Latinx" unless I am quoting a source that uses another designation. Debate among Latinx scholars and activists about whether Latinx should take the place of "Latino/a" is ongoing. Again, thoughtful people disagree. Some critics charge "Latinx" with being an imperialist imposition, championed by gringos and out-of-touch academics. In response, those who adopt "Latinx" point out that when the term "Latino" was first introduced as an alternative to "Hispanic," there was similar pushback.

In deciding which term to use, I turned to the work of trusted colleagues, including Lorgia García Peña and Arlene Dávila, whose commitment to combatting anti-Blackness and other forms of exclusion within Latinadad informs their language use. They advocate the use of "Latinx" (or "Latine" in Spanish) as part of the larger struggle against racism *within* Latinx communities—not to settle or win a classification debate, but to open up important questions about racial and gender inclusion. "Latinx," they remind us, is not a racial label—there are *Black* Latinx, *Asian* Latinx, *Indigenous* Latinx, and *white* Latinx, despite the frequent erasure of those who are not white. A recent *Los Angeles Times* story, for example, described a "woman defending Black lives on the border," saying, "She can pass as Latina. But she identifies as Black" (December 27, 2021), as if the two were mutually exclusive. Finally, for those who argue that the *x* in Latinx is hard to pronounce in Spanish, García Peña points to "Taxi. Boxeo. Sexo. Saxofón. Alex. If you can say these words. You can say Latinx." (@lorgia_pena, Twitter post, May 20, 2021, 6:21pm), https://twitter.com/lorgia_pena/status/1395505008628621322.

8   **has actually increased.** Don Beyer, *The Economic State of Black America in 2020* (Joint Economic Committee, February 14, 2020), https://www.jec .senate.gov/public/_cache/files/ccf4dbe2-810a-44f8-b3e7-14f7e5143ba6 /economic-state-of-black-america-2020.pdf; Eduardo Porter, "Black Workers Stopped Making Progress on Pay. Is It Racism?," *New York Times*, June 28, 2021, https://www.nytimes.com/2021/06/28/business/economy /black-workers-racial-pay-gap.html.

8   **real estate industry.** Richard Rothstein, *The Color of Law: A Forgotten History of How Our Government Segregated America* (New York: Liveright, 2018); Keeanga-Yamahtta Taylor, *Race for Profit: How Banks and the Real Estate Industry Undermined Black Homeownership* (Chapel Hill: University of North Carolina Press, 2021).

8   **as an opportunity."** Louise Seamster, "Black Debt, White Debt," *Contexts* 18, no. 1 (2019): 30–35, https://doi.org/10.1177/1536504219830674, p. 32

8   **these subprime loans."** Seamster, "Black Debt, White Debt," p. 34.

9   **everything is interdependent."** James Baldwin, "The World I Never Made," filmed December 10, 1986, at the National Press Club, Washington, DC, video, 55:56, https://www.youtube.com/watch?v=7_1ZEYgtijk.

9   **a nationwide "reinvention."** Somini Sengupta, "Chile Writes Its Constitution, Confronting Climate Change Head On," *New York Times*, December 28, 2021, https://www.nytimes.com/2021/12/28/climate/chile -constitution-climate-change.html.

9   **and ecological emergency."** Sengupta, "Chile Writes Its Constitution . . ."

10   **about future generations?"** Sengupta, "Chile Writes Its Constitution . . ."

10   **imposing a singularity.** Arturo Escobar, *Designs for the Pluriverse: Radical Interdependence, Autonomy, and the Making of Worlds* (Durham: Duke University Press, 2018).

10   **all be watching."** Greg Carr (@AfricanaCarr), Twitter post, December 29, 2021, 4:43 p.m., https://mobile.twitter.com/AfricanaCarr/status/1476307947 059826693.

10   **before he died.** Baldwin, "The World I Never Made."

11   **the coronavirus pandemic."** Eric Klinenberg, "We Need Social Solidarity, Not Just Social Distancing," March 14, 2020, https://www.nytimes.com /2020/03/14/opinion/coronavirus-social-distancing.html.

11   **those deemed disposable.** See the People's Vaccine Campaign, https:// peoplesvaccine.org. Note also, medical "progress" has always tied some people down so others could race forward. See, Hannah McLane, "A Disturbing Medical Consensus Is Growing. Here's What It Could Mean for Black Patients with Coronavirus," *WHYY*, April 10, 2020, https://whyy.org /articles/a-disturbing-medical-consensus-is-growing-heres-what-it-could -mean-for-black-patients-with-coronavirus/.

11   **and learn from?** Even when it comes to literal viruses, there are many that have beneficial properties for their hosts, and there's even an entire field called virotherapy. See Mario Mietzsch et al., "The Good That Viruses

Do," *Annual Review of Virology* 4, no. 1 (2017): iii–v, https://doi.org/10.1146/annurev-vi-04-071217-100011.

12 **racism enshrines it."** Kenton Card, dir., *Geographies of Racial Capitalism with Ruth Wilson Gilmore* (2020; Antipode Foundation, 2002), video, 16:18, https://www.youtube.com/watch?v=2CS627aKrJI.

12 **2019–20 school year.** "New Data Show Number of NYC Students Who Are Homeless Topped 100,000 for Fifth Consecutive Year," Advocates for Children of New York, January 3, 2020, https://advocatesforchildren.org/node/1675.

12 **that we need.** Kumar Rao, "The High Cost of Policing," *New York Times*, January 18, 2020, https://www.nytimes.com/2018/01/18/opinion/policing.html.

12 **the hard way."** Bayard Rustin, interview by Phil Zwickler, Phil Zwickler Papers, 1986, video, https://rmc.library.cornell.edu/hsclegacy/zwickler/Rustin_interview.htm.

13 **the dominant species.** Erik Olin Wright, *How to Be an Anticapitalist in the Twenty-First Century* (London: Verso Books, 2019).

13 **of all kinds.** Peter A. Kropotkin, *Mutual Aid: A Factor of Evolution* (Boston: Porter Sargent, 1988).

13 **Mutual Aid NYC.** Mariame Kaba et al., "Mutual Aid: Building Communities of Care during Crisis and Beyond," virtual panel discussion, May 22, 2020, video, 1:36:55, https://www.youtube.com/watch?v=ZTVLYPdF0x0.

14 **to be served."** Jaya Saxena, "'The Community Still Makes Me Feel We All Belong to Each Other,'" *Eater*, May 24, 2021, https://www.eater.com/22441013/gandhi-mahal-restaurant-minneapolis-protests-burned-ruhel-islam-interview.

14 **be with everyone."** Gandhi Mahal Restaurant—Minneapolis MN (@GandhiMahalRestaurant), "Hello everyone! Thank you to everyone for checking in. Sadly Gandhi Mahal has caught fire and has been damaged. We won't loose [*sic*] hope though," Facebook post, May 29, 2020, https://www.facebook.com/GandhiMahalRestaurant/posts/3030378453725259.

14 **and essential workers.** "PPE for the People," GoFundMe, last modified August 23, 2020, https://www.gofundme.com/f/p5gba3-ppe-for-the-people.

14 **Big Door Brigade.** Mariame Kaba and Dean Spade, "Solidarity Not Charity: Mutual Aid & How to Organize in the Age of Coronavirus," interview by Amy Goodman, *War and Peace Report, Democracy Now!*, March 20, 2020, video, 59:02, https://www.democracynow.org/2020/3/20/coronavirus_community_response_mutual_aid.

14 **participation, and solidarity.** Dean Spade, "Solidarity Not Charity," *Social Text* 38, no. 1 (2020): 131–51, https://doi.org/10.1215/01642472-7971139.

14 **like everybody else."** Sigal Samuel, "Ecuador Legalized Gangs. Murder Rates Plummeted," *Vox*, March 26, 2019, https://www.vox.com/future-perfect/2019/3/26/18281325/ecuador-legalize-gangs.

15   **to build up."** Samuel, "Ecuador Legalized Gangs. Murder Rates Plummeted."

15   **poet Mary Oliver.** Mary Oliver, "Lead," in *New and Selected Poems 2* (Boston: Beacon, 2007), p. 54.

15   **want to live."** Dean Spade, Mariame Kaba, and Ejeris Dixon, "We Keep Each Other Safe: Mutual Aid for Survival and Solidarity," virtual discussion, Barnard Center for Research on Women, November 12, 2020, video, 1:36:36, https://bcrw.barnard.edu/event/we-keep-each-other-safe/.

16   **choose to be."** Octavia E. Butler, "A Few Rules for Predicting the Future," *Essence*, May 2000, https://antiableistcomposition.files.wordpress.com /2020/07/octavia_e._butler_a_few_rules_.pdf.

17   **and public commitments.** In making explicit the way life experiences have shaped my work, I follow a long line of scholars, many of whom work in a Black feminist tradition, including bell hooks (*Remembered Rapture*), Gabeba Baderoon (*The History of Intimacy*), Imani Perry (*Breathe*), Patricia J. Williams (*The Alchemy of Race & Rights*), Saidiya Hartman (*Lose Your Mother*), Sara Ahmed (*Living a Feminist Life*), and Zimitri Erasmus (*Race Otherwise*).

17   **over the other."** Bahá'u'lláh, *The Hidden Words of Baha'u'llah* (London: Bahá'í Publishing Trust, 1975), p. 41. This work consists of short passages that distill spiritual guidance revealed by the founder of the Bahá'í faith in Persian and Arabic in 1857–58, translated by his grandson Shoghi Effendi, and published by the US Bahá'í Publishing Trust, available online: https:// www.bahaibookstore.com/Hidden-Words-Free-ePub-P9352.aspx.

17   **before thine eyes."** Bahá'u'lláh, *The Hidden Words of Baha'u'llah*, pp. 14-15. See also, Robin S. Chandler, ed., *Transformative Change: 10 Essays on Race & Spirituality* (Boston: RM Chandler Consultants LLC, 2021).

18   **order of things.** One of the central teachings of the Bahá'í faith is the *independent investigation of truth*; therefore, the views I share throughout the text have grown out of my personal understanding and should not be construed as an authoritative or official "Bahá'í view" on any of the subjects explored.

18   **a newfangled phenomenon.** Viral justice connects to a long-standing appeal to "prefigurative politics," a term often credited to political scientist Carl Boggs, although the notion was already in circulation among anarchist, feminist, antiauthoritarian Leftist thinkers before his coinage. By "prefigurative," Boggs was describing "the embodiment, within the ongoing political practice of a movement, of those forms of social relations, decision-making, culture, and human experience that are the ultimate goal." Craig Jeffrey and Jane Dyson, "Geographies of the Future: Prefigurative Politics," *Progress in Human Geography* 45, no. 4, published ahead of print, May 27, 2020, https://doi.org/10.1177/0309132520926569, p. 643.

    Occupy and the alter-globalization movements against the World Trade Organization in Seattle are just two recent efforts to "prefigure" a radically different world by experimenting with more egalitarian social relations and decision-making as part of protest. The other major way prefigurative politics takes shape is in creating alternative institutions and initiatives, or "real utopias," to borrow Erik Olin Wright's formulation.

For more on the distinction between prefiguration as "either a way of doing mobilisation where the 'means reflect the ends'" or "an alternative or parallel project," see Luke Yates, "Rethinking Prefiguration: Alternatives, Micropolitics and Goals in Social Movements," *Social Movement Studies* 14, no. 1 (2014): 1–21, https://doi.org/10.1080/14742837.2013.870883, p. 4.; Carl Boggs, "Marxism, Prefigurative Communism, and the Problem of Workers' Control," *Radical America* 11, no. 6 (1977): 99–122; Erik Olin Wright, *Envisioning Real Utopias* (London: Verso, 2010).

19 **often localized, actions.** There is ongoing debate and disagreement about how or even whether prefigurative politics contributes to social transformation. As Yates explains in his survey of these concerns, some argue that prefigurative politics are "too localised, small-scale and focused on the present . . . insufficiently ambitious . . . fetishizing process . . . alienating newcomers and being too closely associated with identity and self-expression." Luke Yates, "Prefigurative Politics and Social Movement Strategy: The Roles of Prefiguration in the Reproduction, Mobilisation and Coordination of Movements," *Political Studies* 69, no. 4 (2020): 1033–52, https://doi.org/10.1177/0032321720936046, p. 1042.

19 **be the goal.** There are many historical and contemporary mass movements that focus on policy change and grassroots organizing. For example, the Third Reconstruction, organized by the Poor People's Campaign: A National Call for Moral Revival, with fourteen policy priorities and a comprehensive action plan, offers a bold and revolutionary vision of what must change and how. See Poor People's Campaign, homepage, accessed January 13, 2022, https://www.poorpeoplescampaign.org/.

But there is also a long tradition of Black anarchism that does not look to the state for redress or reform. "Surviving this all is one thing, but moving beyond that to claim our right to be liberated and safe is another . . . So why not embrace the darkness we're in, the darkness we are, and organize through it and with it? Use the conditions that the state has placed on us to inform our most radical incursions, rather than asking the state to change, when we should know by now that it certainly won't. The state is not for us. This sort of work, making do and building from exactly where we are has always been a Black skill, but the world around us demands we do this with more revolutionary intentions." William C. Anderson, *The Nation on No Map* (Chico, CA: AK Press 2021), p. 35. See also Zoé Samduzi and William C. Anderson, *As Black As Resistance: Finding the Conditions of Liberation* (Chico, CA: AK Press, 2018).

19 **circles of care.** Saidiya Hartman, "Foreword," in *The Nation on No Map* by William C. Anderson (Chico, CA: AK Press 2021), p. xvii.

19 **that is sought."** Jeffrey and Dyson, "Geographies of the Future: Prefigurative Politics."

19   **of the uprooter.** Octavia E. Butler, *Parable of the Sower* (New York: Grand Central, 2020).

19   **are still here."** Saidiya Hartman, *Wayward Lives, Beautiful Experiments: Intimate Histories of Riotous Black Girls, Troublesome Women, and Queer Radicals* (New York: W. W. Norton & Company, 2019), p. 30.

19   **animates Black life.** Hartman, *Wayward Lives,* p. 60.

19   **utopia, but *ustopia.*** "Ustopia" is a term coined by Margaret Atwood: "Historically, Ustopia has not been a happy story. High hopes have been dashed, time and time again. The best intentions have indeed paved many roads to Hell. Does that mean we should never try to rectify our mistakes, reverse our disaster-bent courses, clean up our cesspools or ameliorate the many miseries of many lives? Surely not: if we don't do maintenance work and minor improvements on whatever we actually have, things will go downhill very fast. So of course, we should try to make things better, insofar as it lies within our power. But we should probably not try to make things perfect, especially not ourselves, for that path leads to mass graves." Margaret Atwood, "Margaret Atwood: The Road to Ustopia," *Guardian,* October 14, 2011, https://www.theguardian.com /books/2011/oct/14/margaret-atwood-road-to-ustopia.

19   **demanding *why wait?*** Prefigurative politics has a long and complex history. Most recently, philosopher Amia Srinivasan writes that "taken too far, a prefigurative politics—a politics that insists individuals act as if they were already in the world to come—not only alienates those who do not conform, but also becomes an end in itself for those who do. At worst, prefigurative politics allows its practitioners to substitute individual personal transformation for collective political transfiguration. It becomes, in other words, a liberal politics. But the same is true of a politics that refuses prefiguration. What does it mean to say that we want to transform the political world—but that we ourselves will remain unchanged?" Amia Srinivasan, *The Right to Sex: Feminism in the Twenty-First Century* (New York: Farrar, Straus and Giroux, 2021), p. 102.

20   **the whole system."** adrienne maree brown, *Emergent Strategy: Shaping Change, Changing Worlds* (Chico, CA: AK Press, 2021), pp. 6, 55.

21   **of social transformation.** Imani Perry, *More Beautiful and More Terrible: The Embrace and Transcendence of Racial Inequality in the United States* (New York: New York University Press, 2011), p. 1.

21   **'structural' racism folks."** Imani Perry (@imaniperry), Twitter post, April 8, 2020, 3:17 p.m., https://twitter.com/imaniperry/status /1247966877537767425?lang=he.

22   **harm and violence."** Mia Mingus, "The Four Parts of Accountability: How to Give a Genuine Apology Part 1," *Leaving Evidence* (blog), December 18, 2019, https://leavingevidence.wordpress.com/2019/12/18/how-to-give-a -good-apology-part-1-the-four-parts-of-accountability/.

22   **justice for all."** Stephanie D. Keene, "Kneel, Donate, or Burn It All Down? Decarceration and 5 Types of Justice Work," *Medium,* June 22, 2020,

https://medium.com/@StephanieDKeene/kneel-donate-or-burn-it-all
-down-decarceration-and-5-types-of-justice-work-2a817620cb04.

22   **is your plot?** The "plot" has a long history as a site of resistance and world-building for enslaved and unfree laborers on plantations globally. Speaking of enslaved Africans in the Americas, Jamaican philosopher Sylvia Wynter writes, "But from early, the planters gave the slaves plots of land on which to grow food to feed themselves in order to maximize profits. We suggest that this plot system, was . . . the focus of resistance to the market system and market values . . . Around the growing of yam, of food for survival, [African peasants] created on the plot a folk culture—the basis of a social order—in three hundred years . . . This folk culture became a source of cultural guerilla resistance to the plantation system." Sylvia Wynter, "Novel and History, Plot and Plantation," *Savacou*, no. 5 (June 1971): 95–102, p. 99. Also see Mythri Jegathesan, "Black Feminist Plots before the Plantationocene and Anthropology's 'Regional Closets,'" *Feminist Anthropology* 2, no. 1 (2021): 78–93, https://doi.org/10.1002/fea2.12037; and Katherine McKittrick, "Plantation Futures," *Small Axe* 17, no. 3 (2013): 1–15, https://muse.jhu.edu/article/532740.

24   **educator Paolo Freire.** Paulo Freire, *Pedagogy of the Oppressed*, trans. Myra Bergman Ramos, with an introduction by Donaldo Macedo (New York: Continuum, 1993), 72.

25   **that looks like."** *American Climate Rebels*, episode 11, "Cooperation Jackson: Building a Social and Solidarity Economy," aired September 10, 2018, on ReelNews, https://www.youtube.com/watch?v=_Nt9Z2P7mPY&t=1807s.

26   **many worlds fit."** This is a Zapatismo invitation, *Un Mundo Donde Caben Muchos Mundos*, which emphasizes "the dignity of 'others,' belonging, and common struggle, as well as the importance of laughter, dancing, and nourishing children." https://globalsocialtheory.org/topics/zapatism; see also, Marisol de la Cadena and Mario Blaser, *A World of Many Worlds* (Durham: Duke University Press, 2018).

Chapter One

Page

27   **of her father.** Bruce Britt, "The Tragic Loss of Erica Garner," The Undefeated, January 1, 2018, https://theundefeated.com/features/the-tragic-loss-of-erica-garner/.

27   **then," she said.** Elizabeth Day, "Erica Garner-Snipes: 'I Believe in Justice. It Will Take a Long Time but It's Gonna Come,'" *Guardian*, January 24, 2015, https://www.theguardian.com/us-news/2015/jan/25/eric-garner-erica-garner-snipes-justice-will-take-a-long-time-police-violence.

27   **four full siblings.** Erica was the eldest of four biological children that her dad had with her mother, Esaw. Esaw had two other children from a prior relationship that she and Eric Garner raised as their own.

28 **stroller and crib.** For details about Erica and her relationship with her father and his murder, see Day, "Erica Garner-Snipes."

28 **swollen with affection.** Toni Morrison, *Beloved* (New York: Knopf Doubleday Publishing Group, 2007 [originally published 1987]), p. 193. Contrary to the stereotype of the absent Black father, research indicates that "African-American fathers, when compared with other ethnic groups, have greater or similar levels of involvement with their children (Cabrera, Ryan, Mitchell, Shannon and Tamis-Lemonda, 2008; King, Heard, & Harris, 2004)." Shauna M. Cooper, "Reframing the Discussion on African-American Fathers: Implications for Positive Development of African American Boys," American Psychological Association, August 2015, https://www.apa.org/pi/families/resources/newsletter/2015/08/african -american-fathers.

28 **fighting to breathe.** Day, "Erica Garner-Snipes."

28 **to her son.** Christina Carrega and Thomas Tracy, "Eric Garner's Daughter Erica Declared Brain Dead after Heart Attack," *Los Angeles Times*, December 28, 2017, https://www.latimes.com/nation/la-na-erica-garner -brain-dead-20171228-story.html.

28 **born, Erica died.** Amy Russo and Gwynne Hogan, "Daughter of Black Lives Matter Icon Eric Garner Dies at 27," *New York Post*, December 30, 2017, https://nypost.com/2017/12/30/erica-garner-dies-after-suffering-major -heart-attack/.

28 **twice-weekly protests.** Davina Sutton, "Erica Garner Will Not Stop Marching," NBC News, March 30, 2015, https://www.nbcnews.com/news /nbcblk/erica-garner-will-not-stop-marching-n327941; Amanda Holpuch, "Erica Garner Leads Protests in Staten Island in Memory of Her Father," *Guardian*, December 12, 2014, https://www.theguardian.com/us-news /2014/dec/12/erica-garner-leads-protests-eric.

28 **to police reform.** Britt, "Tragic Loss of Erica Garner."

28 **for due process."** Britt, "Tragic Loss of Erica Garner."

29 **called her dad.** Day, "Erica Garner-Snipes."

29 **of economic precarity.** Likewise, due to his asthma, Eric Garner couldn't work most jobs because dust and other pollutants were debilitating, which may explain the context of his murder; the police harassed him for allegedly selling single cigarettes outside a bodega.

29 **and premature death.** Arline T. Geronimus, "The Weathering Hypothesis and the Health of African-American Women and Infants: Evidence and Speculations," *Ethnicity and Disease* 2, no. 3 (1992): 207–21.

29 **of our environments."** Christina Sharpe, "The Weather," *New Inquiry*, January 19, 2017, https://thenewinquiry.com/the-weather/.

30 **the United Kingdom.** Kevin Rawlinson, "Windrush: 11 People Wrongly Deported from UK Have Died—Javid," *Guardian*, November 12, 2018, https://www.theguardian.com/uk-news/2018/nov/12/windrush-11-people -wrongly-deported-from-uk-have-died-sajid-javid.

31   **will not tell."** Nancy Krieger, "Embodiment: A Conceptual Glossary for Epidemiology," *Journal of Epidemiology and Community Health* 59, no. 5 (2005): 350–55, https://doi.org/10.1136/jech.2004.024562, p. 350.

31   **high school diplomas.** Jasmine D. Johnson et al., "Racial Disparities in Prematurity Persist among Women of High Socioeconomic Status," *American Journal of Obstetrics and Gynecology MFM* 2, no. 3 (2020): 100104, https://doi.org/10.1016/j.ajogmf.2020.100104.

31   **counterparts in Bangladesh.** "Black Men in America Are Living Almost as Long as White Men," *Economist,* June 15, 2019, https://www.economist.com/united-states/2019/06/15/black-men-in-america-are-living-almost-as-long-as-white-men.

31   **each subsequent generation.** William A. Vega, Michael A. Rodriguez, and Elisabeth Gruskin, "Health Disparities in the Latino Population," *Epidemiologic Reviews* 31, no. 1 (2009): 99–112, https://doi.org/10.1093/epirev/mxp008.

31   **across racial groups.** Ellis P. Monk, "The Cost of Color: Skin Color, Discrimination, and Health among African-Americans," *American Journal of Sociology* 121, no. 2 (2015): 396–444, https://doi.org/10.1086/682162; Ellis P. Monk, "Colorism and Physical Health: Evidence from a National Survey," *Journal of Health and Social Behavior* 62, no. 1 (2021): 37–52, https://doi.org/10.1177/0022146520979645.

32   **and Korean adults.** Alexander C. Adia, Jennifer Nazareno, Don Operario, and Ninez A. Ponce, "Health Conditions, Outcomes, and Service Access Among Filipino, Vietnamese, Chinese, Japanese, and Korean Adults in California, 2011–2017," *American Journal of Public Health* 110 (2020): 520–526, https://doi.org/10.2105/AJPH.2019.305523.

32   **flatten social reality.** By contrast, there is a rich literature that deepens the stories we tell about racial health disparities, including Lundy Braun, *Breathing Race into the Machine* (Minneapolis: University of Minnesota Press, 2014); James Doucet-Battle, *Sweetness in the Blood: Race, Risk, and Type 2 Diabetes* (Minneapolis: University of Minnesota Press, 2021); Nadine Ehlers and Shiloh R. Krupar, *Deadly Biocultures: The Ethics of Life-Making* (Minneapolis: University of Minnesota Press, 2020); Nadine Ehlers and Leslie R. Hinkson, *Subprime Health: Debt and Race in U.S. Medicine* (Minneapolis: University of Minnesota Press, 2017); Anthony Ryan Hatch, *Blood Sugar: Racial Pharmacology and Food Justice in Black America* (Minneapolis: University of Minnesota Press, 2016); Nancy Krieger, *Ecosocial Theory, Embodied Truths, and the People's Health* (New York: Oxford University Press, 2021); and Anne Pollock, *Sickening: Anti-Black Racism and Health Disparities in the United States* (Minneapolis: University of Minnesota Press, 2021).

33   **Is a Lie."** Philip Bump, "Your Generational Identity Is a Lie," *Washington Post,* April 1, 2015, https://www.washingtonpost.com/news/the-fix/wp/2015/04/01/your-generational-identity-is-a-lie/.

33 **rash character judgment."** Philip N. Cohen, "Generation Labels Mean Nothing. It's Time to Retire Them," *Washington Post*, July 17, 2021, https://www.washingtonpost.com/opinions/2021/07/07/generation-labels-mean-nothing-retire-them/.

33 **in its surveys.** Philip N. Cohen, "Open Letter to the Pew Research Center on Generation Labels," *Family Inequality* (blog), May 26, 2021, https://familyinequality.wordpress.com/2021/05/26/open-letter-to-the-pew-research-center-on-generation-labels/.

33 **in the body.** Alissa Greenberg, "How the Stress of Racism Can Harm Your Health—and What That Has to Do with Covid-19," PBS, July 14, 2020, https://www.pbs.org/wgbh/nova/article/racism-stress-covid-allostatic-load/.

34 **began in 2000.** Amy Weaver, "Study Finds Increasing Racism Linked to Cell Aging in African Americans," Auburn University, January 13, 2020, http://ocm.auburn.edu/newsroom/news_articles/2020/01/131635-study-racism-cell-aging.php.

34 **Black women's skin.** Arline T. Geronimus et al., "Do Us Black Women Experience Stress-Related Accelerated Biological Aging?," *Human Nature* 21, no. 1 (2010): 19–38, https://doi.org/10.1007/s12110-010-9078-0.

34 **to know today?"** Toni Cade Bambara, *Those Bones Are Not My Child: A Novel* (New York: Vintage Books, 1999), 168.

34 **loss harms DNA."** Colter Mitchell et al., "Father Loss and Child Telomere Length," *Pediatrics* 140, no. 2 (2017): e20163245, https://doi.org/10.1542/peds.2016-3245.

35 **development of children."** Mitchell et al., "Father Loss."

35 **of parental incarceration."** Mitchell et al., "Father Loss."

35 **an incarcerated parent?** Sentencing Project, *Parents in Prison* (Washington, DC: Sentencing Project, 2021), https://www.sentencingproject.org/publications/parents-in-prison/.

35 **them or not.** Anna Crawford-Roberts et al., "George Floyd's Autopsy and the Structural Gaslighting of America," *Scientific American*, June 6, 2020, https://blogs.scientificamerican.com/voices/george-floyds-autopsy-and-the-structural-gaslighting-of-america/.

36 **to his death.** Rocco Parascandola and Thomas Tracy, "NYPD Chief Surgeon Determined Officer Pantaleo Didn't Put Eric Garner in Chokehold: Attorney," *New York Daily News*, April 4, 2019, https://www.nydailynews.com/new-york/nyc-crime/ny-nypd-chief-surgeon-doesnt-see-chokehold-20190404-matpyvan3vbgbjqnuut6ghdamu-story.html; Michael R. Sisak, "Medical Examiner: Chokehold Triggered Eric Garner's Death," Associated Press, May 15, 2019, https://apnews.com/article/1903161fb60848a7851e68b25167f73b.

36 **and economic challenges."** New Jersey Department of Children and Families, *NJ ACES Statewide Action Plan* (Trenton: New Jersey Office of Resilience, 2021), https://www.nj.gov/dcf/documents/NJ.ACEs.Action.Plan.2021.pdf, p. i.

36   **healing centered state."** New Jersey Department of Children and Families, *NJ Aces*, p. 16.

37   **of childhood trauma."** New Jersey Department of Children and Families, *NJ Aces*, p. 4.

37   **and white supremacy."** New Jersey Department of Children and Families, *NJ Aces*, p. i.

37   **the first place.** Dorothy E. Roberts, *Torn Apart: How the Child Welfare System Destroys Black Families—and How Abolition Can Build a Safer World* (New York: Basic Books, 2022).

38   **much to bear."** Cheryl I. Harris, "Whiteness as Property," *Harvard Law Review* 106, no. 8 (August 31, 2006): 1707–91, p. 1711.

38   **Harris puts it.** Cheryl I. Harris, "Whiteness as Property," p. 1711.

38   **happens that day."** Joe R. Feagin, "The Continuing Significance of Race: Antiblack Discrimination in Public Places," *American Sociological Review* 56, no. 1 (1991): 101, https://doi.org/10.2307/2095676.

39   **and sexist stereotypes."** Tanisha C. Ford, "SNCC Women, Denim, and the Politics of Dress," *Journal of Southern History* 79, no. 3 (2013): 625–58, http://www.jstor.org/stable/23795090, p. 630.

39   **and sartorial elegance."** Tanisha C. Ford, *Liberated Threads: Black Women, Style, and the Global Politics of Soul* (Chapel Hill: University of North Carolina Press, 2017), p. 70.

40   **prison industrial complex."** Dána-Ain Davis, "'The Bone Collectors' Comments for Sorrow as Artifact: Black Radical Mothering in Times of Terror," *Transforming Anthropology* 24, no. 1 (2016): 8–16, https://doi.org/10.1111/traa.12056, p. 8-9.

40   **long, dirty toenails."** Theresa Waldrop, "Defense Lawyer Prompts Outrage for Bringing Up Ahmaud Arbery's Toenails," CNN, November 24, 2021, https://www.cnn.com/2021/11/22/us/ahmaud-arbery-trial-toenails-comment-outrage/index.html.

40   **of the jurors."** Waldrop, "Defense Lawyer Prompts Outrage for Bringing Up Ahmaud Arbery's Toenails."

40   **anxiety over grooming.** Dawn Marie Dow, *Mothering While Black: Boundaries and Burdens of Middle-Class Parenthood* (Oakland: University of California Press, 2019).

41   **as homogeneously white.** Elijah Anderson, "'The White Space,'" *Sociology of Race and Ethnicity* 1, no. 1 (2015): 10–21, https://doi.org/10.1177/2332649214561306, p. 14-15.

41   **ID on them.** Ari Shapiro, "Sociologist on How Black Men Try to Appear Non-threatening as a Defense Mechanism," NPR, May 7, 2020, https://www.npr.org/2020/05/07/852319565/sociologist-on-how-black-men-try-to-appear-non-threatening-as-a-defense-mechanism.

42   **home! Go home!"** Anderson, "'The White Space,'" p. 14.

43   **resident Aaron Thomas.** Aaron Thomas (@Aaron_TheThomas), Twitter post, April 4, 2020, 1:43 p.m., https://twitter.com/aaron_thethomas/status/1246493711032356866?lang=en.

43   **by an officer.** Ashleigh Atwell, "Video: Cop Follows Two Black Men around Illinois Walmart for Allegedly Wearing Surgical Masks, Asks Them for ID," *Atlanta Black Star*, March 27, 2020, https://atlantablackstar.com /2020/03/27/video-cop-follows-two-black-men-around-illinois-walmart -for-allegedly-wearing-surgical-masks-asks-them-for-id/.

43   **wearing a mask.** Chas Danner, "Philly Police Drag Man from Bus for Not Wearing a Face Mask," *New York Magazine*, April 10, 2020, https://nymag .com/intelligencer/2020/04/philly-police-drag-man-from-bus-for-not -wearing-a-face-mask.html.

43   **and social services.** Jonathan Metzl, *Dying of Whiteness: How the Politics of Racial Resentment Is Killing America's Heartland* (New York: Basic Books, 2019).

44   **this distorted outlook.** John Wayne, "Some of the Best John Wayne Quotes and Words of Wisdom," Country Thang Daily, April 27 (no year), https:// www.countrythangdaily.com/john-wayne-quotes/.

44   **during an interview.** Metzl, *Dying of Whiteness*, p. 3.

44   **and welfare queens."** Metzl, *Dying of Whiteness*, p. 3.

44   **immigrants deemed "essential."** Miriam Jordan, "Farmworkers, Mostly Undocumented, Become 'Essential' during Pandemic," *New York Times*, April 2, 2020, https://www.nytimes.com/2020/04/02/us/coronavirus -undocumented-immigrant-farmworkers-agriculture.html.

45   **1970s and '80s.** Roge Karma, "'Deaths of Despair': The Deadly Epidemic That Predated Coronavirus," *Vox*, April 15, 2020, https://www.vox.com /2020/4/15/21214734/deaths-of-despair-coronavirus-covid-19-angus -deaton-anne-case-americans-deaths.

46   **governing everyday life.** Carol Anderson, *White Rage: The Unspoken Truth of Our Racial Divide* (New York: Bloomsbury, 2016).

46   **James Baldwin's words.** James Baldwin, "Take This Hammer," aired February 4, 1962, on KQED Channel 9, San Francisco, video, 44:14, https:// diva.sfsu.edu/bundles/187041.

46   **disadvantaged Black businesses.** Ben Popken, "Why Are So Many Black-Owned Small Businesses Shut Out of PPP Loans?," NBC News, April 29, 2020, https://www.nbcnews.com/business/business-news/why-are-so -many-black-owned-small-businesses-shut-out-n1195291.

46   **the upper hand.** Popken, "Why Are So Many Black-Owned Small Businesses Shut Out of PPP Loans?"

47   **so-called n*gger programs.** Wayne Flynt, *Dixie's Forgotten People: The South's Poor Whites*, new ed. (Bloomington: Indiana University Press, 2006).

47   **your manly privilege."** Lois Beckett, "'Dying of Whiteness': Why Racism Is at the Heart of America's Gun Inaction," *Guardian*, August 9, 2019, https:// www.theguardian.com/us-news/2019/aug/08/racism-gun-control-dying -of-whiteness.

47   **and class too.** Jennifer Carlson, "Covid & Guns: A Conversation with Jenny Carlson," interview by Darrell A. H. Miller, Center for Firearms Law at Duke

University School of Law, May 19, 2020, video, 12:50, https://www.youtube
.com/watch?v=ZRurj07ptvI.

47   **put down uprisings.** Connie Hassett-Walker, "How You Start Is How You
Finish? The Slave Patrol and Jim Crow Origins of Policing," American Bar
Association, January 11, 2021, https://www.americanbar.org/groups/crsj
/publications/human_rights_magazine_home/civil-rights-reimagining
-policing/how-you-start-is-how-you-finish/.

47   **to patrol Blackness.** W.E.B. Du Bois, *Black Reconstruction in America,
1860–1880* (New York: Atheneum, 1969).

47   **well-being *for all*.** That is why we must abandon the "zero sum model
of freedom built on slavery," according to writer Heather McGhee. "The
narrative that white people should see the well-being of people of color as
a threat to their own is one of the most powerful subterranean stories in
America," she writes in *The Sum of Us*. "Until we destroy the idea, opponents
of progress can always unearth it and use it to block any collective action
that benefits us all." Heather McGhee, *The Sum of Us: What Racism Costs
Everyone and How We Can Prosper Together* (New York: One World, 2021),
p. 15.

47   **due to COVID-19.** Kathleen Gray, "In Michigan, a Dress Rehearsal for the
Chaos at the Capitol on Wednesday," *New York Times*, January 9, 2021;
Abigail Censky, "Heavily Armed Protesters Gather Again at Michigan
Capitol to Decry Stay-at-Home Order," NPR, May 14, 2020, https://www
.npr.org/2020/05/14/855918852/heavily-armed-protesters-gather-again-at
-michigans-capitol-denouncing-home-order.

48   **of other groups?** Everytown, *Firearm Suicide in the United States* (New
York: Everytown, 2021), https://everytownresearch.org/report/firearm
-suicide-in-the-united-states/.

49   **dark and menacing.** George Lipsitz, The *Possessive Investment in Whiteness:
How White People Profit from Identity Politics* (Philadelphia: Temple
University Press, 2006).

49   **17-year-old Trayvon Martin.** Brandon Hunter-Pazzara, "The Possessive
Investment in Guns: Towards a Material, Social, and Racial Analysis of Guns."
Palgrave Communications 6, no. 79 (2020): 1-10, https://doi.org/10.1057
/s41599-020-0464-x

49   **to her son.** Zimmerman auctioned it on UnitedGunGroup.com after
another website, GunBroker, refused to let him list it. See "Trayvon Martin
Death: Zimmerman Handgun 'Auction Reaches $65m,'" BBC, May 13, 2016,
https://www.bbc.com/news/world-us-canada-36281438.

49   **of "profound neurosis."** Toni Morrison, interview by Charlie Rose, *Charlie
Rose*, PBS, May 7, 1993, video, 55:11, https://charlierose.com/videos/18778.

49   **do about it."** Inae Oh, "Watch Toni Morrison Explain the 'Profound Neurosis'
of Racism," *Mother Jones*, August 6, 2019, https://www.motherjones.com
/politics/2019/08/watch-toni-morrison-explain-the-profound-neurosis-of
-racism/.

49   **in the mirror.** In the early days of the COVID-19 pandemic, gun sales skyrocketed, with about two million sold in March 2020 alone, as people feared civil unrest. The numbers are higher still because this doesn't account for all gun sales in states, such as Kansas, where background checks are not required. The only other times sales were this high were in the aftermath of Barack Obama's reelection and after the Sandy Hook Elementary School shooting, both in 2012.

       Many public health professionals are worried about our recent spike because new gun ownership is linked to a higher risk of suicide. Add to that rising unemployment and anxieties around the virus itself, and we're already seeing a spike in gun violence, where, in some areas, the rate has doubled from the previous year. While some local officials have proposed that gun stores should be closed temporarily during the pandemic, the Trump administration has said that they are essential businesses likes gas stations and grocers and should remain open. See Keith Collins and David Yaffe-Bellany, "About 2 Million Guns Were Sold in the U.S. as Virus Fears Spread," *New York Times*, April 1, 2020; and Zusha Elinson, "Gun Stores Ruled Essential Businesses during Coronavirus Shutdowns," *Wall Street Journal*, March 30, 2020, https://www.wsj.com/articles/gun-stores-ruled-essential-businesses-during-coronavirus-shutdowns-11585601189.

50   **but shared happiness.** David Scott, "The Re-enchancement of Humanism: An Interview with Sylvia Wynter," *Small Axe* 8 (September 2000): 119–207.

50   **with social domination.** John Garvey and Noel Ignatiev, "The New Abolitionism," *Minnesota Review* 47 (1996): 105–8.

50   **your own hide?"** "Questions for: Noel Ignatiev," *New York Times*, February 16, 1997, https://www.nytimes.com/1997/02/16/magazine/questions-for-noel-ignatiev.html.

50   **to explode it."** "Questions for: Noel Ignatiev."

51   **a moral choice.** Maria Popova, "James Baldwin and Chinua Achebe's Forgotten Conversation about Beauty, Morality and the Political Power of Art," *Marginalian*, September 21, 2016; James Baldwin and Fred L. Standley, *Conversations with James Baldwin* (Jackson: University Press of Mississippi, 1996), p. 218.

51   **for residents only."** Jean-Marie Baland, Pranab Bardhan, and Samuel Bowles, eds., *Inequality, Cooperation, and Environmental Sustainability* (Princeton, NJ: Princeton University Press, 2007); Samuel Kling and Lucas Stephens, "The Right to the Shoreline: Race, Exclusion, and Public Beaches in Metropolitan Chicago," Chicago Council on Global Affairs, September 22, 2020, https://www.thechicagocouncil.org/research/working-paper/right-shoreline-race-exclusion-and-public-beaches-metropolitan-chicago.

51   **pimped as 'freedom.'"** Maria Popova, "Arts of the Possible: Adrienne Rich on Writing, Capitalism, Freedom, and How Silence Fertilizes the Human Imagination," *Marginalian*, May 19, 2015; Adrienne Rich, *Arts of the Possible: Essays and Conversations* (New York: W. W. Norton, 2002), p. 147.

51 **a collective good.** These deadly fault lines determine who lives and who dies, in what the philosopher Charles Mills calls a *racial contract* between the state and the individual. It turns out the racial contract is also killing those it was designed to serve. See Charles W. Mills, *The Racial Contract* (Ithaca, NY: Cornell University Press, 2014).

52 **for rural America.** John M. Eason, "Why Prison Building Will Continue Booming in Rural America," The Conversation, March 12, 2017, https:// theconversation.com/why-prison-building-will-continue-booming-in -rural-america-71920.

52 **like the U.S.** Kenneth Rapoza, "China Quits Recycling U.S. Trash as Sustainable Start-Up Makes Strides," *Forbes*, January 10, 2021, https://www .forbes.com/sites/kenrapoza/2021/01/10/china-quits-recycling-us-trash -as-sustainable-start-up-makes-strides/?sh=74c184705a56; Ciarra Torres-Spelliscy, "Blood on Your Handset," *Slate*, September 20, 2013, https:// slate.com/news-and-politics/2013/09/conflict-minerals-from-the-congo -is-your-cellphone-made-with-them.html; Moritz Riesewieck and Hans Block, dirs., *The Cleaners* (PBS, 2018); Sarah T. Roberts, *Behind the Screen: Content Moderation in the Shadows of Social Media* (New Haven, CT: Yale University Press, 2021); Siddharth Suri and Mary L. Gray, *Ghost Work: How to Stop Silicon Valley from Building a New Global Underclass* (Boston: Houghton Mifflin Harcourt, 2019).

52 **angry he looked."** Jamelle Bouie, "Michael Brown Wasn't a Superhuman Demon," *Slate*, November 26, 2014, https://slate.com/news-and-politics /2014/11/darren-wilsons-racial-portrayal-of-michael-brown-as-a -superhuman-demon-the-ferguson-police-officers-account-is-a-common -projection-of-racial-fears.html.

53 **go," she insisted.** "Gwen Carr," SWHelper, accessed January 14, 2022, https://globalsocialwelfaresummit.com/speaker/gwen-carr/.

53 **spend my life.** Gwen Carr and Dave Smitherman, *This Stops Today: Eric Garner's Mother Seeks Justice after Losing Her Son* (Lanham, MD: Rowman and Littlefield, 2018), p. 175.

53 **young people's work.** Rita Omokha, "'She's Become a Symbol of a Movement': Gwen Carr, Political Powerhouse, Is a Force to Be Reckoned With," *Vanity Fair*, August 12, 2021, https://www.vanityfair.com/news/2021 /08/political-powerhouse-gwen-carr-is-a-force-to-be-reckoned-with.

54 **that's capitalism speaking."** Jia Tolentino, "What Mutual Aid Can Do during a Pandemic," *New Yorker*, May 11, 2020, https://www.newyorker.com /magazine/2020/05/18/what-mutual-aid-can-do-during-a-pandemic.

55 **of my house."** Ron Finley, "A Guerrilla Gardener in South Central LA," filmed February 2013 at TED conference, Long Beach, CA, video, 10:09, https:// www.ted.com/talks/ron_finley_a_guerrilla_gardener_in_south_central_la /details?language=en.

55 **jaded you are."** UPROXX Studio, "Ron Finley: Urban Gangsta Gardener in South Central LA," video, 5:11, December 16, 2015, https://www.youtube .com/watch?v=7t-NbF77ceM&t=3s.

56 **of each other."** "Love—BLM—Take Care of Each Other," street art, July 7, 2020, Saint Paul, MN, Urban Art Mapping Research Project, https:// georgefloydstreetart.omeka.net/items/show/1249.

57 **impacts of racism.** Jenna Wortham, "How a New Wave of Black Activists Changed the Conversation," *New York Times*, August 25, 2020, https://www .nytimes.com/2020/08/25/magazine/black-visions-collective.html.

57 **Floyd was murdered.** Dionne Searcey and John Eligon, "Minneapolis Will Dismantle Its Police Force, Council Members Pledge," *New York Times*, June 7, 2020, https://www.nytimes.com/2020/06/07/us/minneapolis -police-abolish.html.

57 **for several years.** Lois Beckett, "Minneapolis Public School Board Votes to Terminate Its Contract with Police," *Guardian*, June 2, 2020, https://www .theguardian.com/us-news/2020/jun/01/minneapolis-public-school-end -police-contract.

57 **and corrections officers.** Mark Keierleber, "Exclusive: Minneapolis Hires Specialists for Revamped School Safety Beat Following George Floyd's Death. Job Finalists Called the Change 'Cosmetic,'" The 74, September 20, 2020, https://www.the74million.org/article/minnesota-police-school -security-hiring/.

57 **in criminal justice."** Mark Keierleber, "After Ending Police Contract, Minneapolis Schools Consider Former Cops for Revamped School Safety Role—and Activists Fear a 'Dangerous' National Trend,'" *MinnPost*, August 24, 2020, https://www.minnpost.com/education/2020/08/after -ending-police-contract-minneapolis-schools-consider-former-cops-for -revamped-school-safety-role-and-activists-fear-a-dangerous-national -trend/.

58 **who's doing it."** Alliance for Educational Justice (@4EdJustice), Twitter post, August 13, 2020, 5:36 p.m., https://twitter.com/4edjustice/status /1294025136488800262.

58 **felt like, *wow*."** "Erica Garner," video, 4:12, Marshall Project, 2017, https:// www.themarshallproject.org/witnesses?page=erica.

Chapter Two

Page

60 **for many years."** Officer A. Cab, "Confessions of a Former Bastard Cop," Medium, June 6, 2020, https://medium.com/@OfcrACab/confessions-of-a -former-bastard-cop-bb14d17bc759.

60 **police misconduct claims.** Scott Calvert and Dan Frosch, "Police Rethink Policies as Cities Pay Millions to Settle Misconduct Claims," *Wall Street Journal*, October 22, 2020, https://www.wsj.com/articles/police-rethink -policies-as-cities-pay-millions-to-settle-misconduct-claims-11603368002.

60 **its ignoble offspring.** Still, according to Gallup's "Confidence in Institutions" survey, public confidence in policing is at a thirty-year low, though, not

surprisingly, there is a huge racial gap—56 percent of white adults have "a great deal" or "quite a lot" of confidence in the police, compared with 19 percent of Black adults. See Tommy Beer, "Poll: U.S. Confidence in Police Plummets to All-Time Low," *Forbes*, August 12, 2020, https://www.forbes.com/sites /tommybeer/2020/08/12/poll-us-confidence-in-police-plummets-to-all -time-low/?sh=6e5c42c63cb0.

61   ***punishment and suffering?*** Mariame Kaba, "Against Punishment; A Resource by Project Nia and Interrupting Criminalization," December 2, 2020, https://issuu.com/projectnia/docs/against_punishment_curriculum _final.

61   **on his wall.** In the racial calculus of this nation, there are no second chances. For many Black folks, even *first* chances are hard to come by. Meanwhile, whiteness confers a world of second chances, wiped clean again and again to kill with impunity. See Ruha Benjamin, "Black AfterLives Matter," *Boston Review*, July 11, 2018, http://bostonreview.net/race/ruha-benjamin-black -afterlives-matter.

62   **mental health facility."** "Twin Towers Correctional Facility Home Page," Los Angeles County Sheriff's Department, accessed February 10, 2022, http://shq.lasdnews.net/pages/PageDetail.aspx?id=1404. As sociologist Anthony Hatch writes, "The great contradiction of total institutions lies in the tension between their professed goals (e.g. caring for the mentally and physically ill, protecting the aged or vulnerable, guarding the dangerous) and their undeclared use as dumping grounds." Anthony Hatch, *Silent Cells: The Secret Drugging of Captive America* (Minneapolis: University of Minnesota Press, 2019), p. 13.

62   **of Los Angeles."** James Ridgeway and Jean Casella, "The Abu Ghraib of Los Angeles?," *Mother Jones*, January 19, 2012, https://www.motherjones .com/politics/2012/01/abu-ghraib-los-angeles-county-jail-abuses; see also Andrew Dilts, *Punishment and Inclusion* (New York: Fordham University Press, 2014).

62   **line into torture."** Jean Casella and James Ridgeway, "Abu Ghraib, California: Report Shows Brutal Abuse of Prisoners in LA County Jails," Solitary Watch, September 29, 2011, https://solitarywatch.org/2011/09/29/abu-ghraib -california-report-shows-brutal-abuse-of-prisoners-in-la-county-jails/.

62   **maximum-security prisons.** James Ridgeway and Jean Casella, "The Abu Ghraib of Los Angeles?," *Mother Jones*, January 19, 2012, https://www .motherjones.com/politics/2012/01/abu-ghraib-los-angeles-county-jail -abuses/.

62   **patterns of violence."** Sarah Liebowitz et al., *Cruel and Usual Punishment: How a Savage Gang of Deputies Controls LA County Jails* (ACLU, September 2011), https://www.aclu.org/report/report-cruel-and-usual -punishment-how-savage-gang-deputies-controls-la-county-jails?redirect =prisoners-rights/report-cruel-and-usual-punishment-how-savage-gang -deputies-controls-la-county-jails, p. 1.

63   **modern-day brand?** Devah Pager, "The Mark of a Criminal Record," *American Journal of Sociology* 108, no. 5 (2003): 937–975.

63   **into its gates."** Abigail [Alyasah] A. Sewell and Kevin A. Jefferson, "Collateral Damage: The Health Effects of Invasive Police Encounters in New York City," *Journal of Urban Health* 93, no. S1 (2016): 42–67, https://doi.org/10.1007/s11524-015-0016-7, p. S55.

63   **individual-level, trauma.** When a person is locked up, his or her entire family can feel trapped. Walking by a loved one's room, seeing his or her clothes hanging in the closet, shoes sitting by the door, might evoke the same feelings as they would in the aftermath of death. But in this case, the individual is buried alive, a civic death. As sociologist Loïc Wacquant describes it, "Just as bondage effected the 'social death' of imported African captives and their descendants on American soil, mass incarceration also induces the civic death of those it ensnares by extruding them from the social compact." Loic Wacquant, "From Slavery to Mass Incarceration: Rethinking the 'Race Question' in the US," in *Race, Law and Society*, ed. Ian Haney López (London: Routledge, 2017), 277–96, p. 293

64   **in a group."** "How Does Hunting Affect Non-target Animals?," RSPCA, last updated August 19, 2019, https://kb.rspca.org.au/knowledge-base/how-does-hunting-affect-non-target-animals/.

64   **be more visible.** "Hunting," Animal Ethics, accessed January 18, 2022, https://www.animal-ethics.org/hunting/.

64   **NBC South Florida.** Mc Nelly Torres and Willard Shepard, "Family Outraged after North Miami Beach Police Use Mug Shots as Shooting Targets," NBC Miami, January 15, 2015, https://www.nbcmiami.com/news/local/family-outraged-after-north-miami-beach-police-use-criminal-photos-as-shooting-targets/57613/.

64   **would be reprimanded.** Oliver Laughland, "Florida Police on Defense after Black Men's Mugshots Used for Target Practice," *Guardian*, January 16, 2015, https://www.theguardian.com/us-news/2015/jan/16/police-black-mens-mugshots-target-practice.

65   **attention to this."** Elahe Izadi, "Florida Police Use Mugshots of Black Men for Target Practice. Clergy Responded: #UseMeInstead," *Washington Post*, January 25, 2015, https://www.washingtonpost.com/news/morning-mix/wp/2015/01/25/florida-police-used-mugshots-of-black-men-for-target-practice-clergy-responded-usemeinstead/.

65   **for target practice.** Carli Teproff, "Angry Residents Lash Out at North Miami Beach Police over Use of Mugshots in Target Practice," *Miami Herald*, January 21, 2015, https://www.miamiherald.com/news/local/community/miami-dade/north-miami/article7836504.html.

66   **nine to five."** Laughland, "Florida Police on Defense."

66   **for her kids."** Christie Thompson, "Deporting 'Felons, Not Families,'" Marshall Project, November 21, 2014, https://www.themarshallproject.org/2014/11/21/deporting-felons-not-families.

67 **for determining dangerousness.** Emphasis added. Ruth Wilson Gilmore, "The Worrying State of the Anti-prison Movement," *Social Justice*, February 23, 2015, http://www.socialjusticejournal.org/the-worrying-state -of-the-anti-prison-movement/.

67 **ensure Donna's participation.** Donna Hylton, *Little Piece of Light: A Memoir of Hope, Prison, and a Life Unbound* (New York: Hachette Books, 2019).

67 **that desperate situation.** Hylton, *Little Piece of Light*, p. xiii.

67 **coercion and threat.** Hylton, *Little Piece of Light*, p. x.

67 **not often vicious.** Beth Richie, *Arrested Justice: Black Women, Violence, and America's Prison Nation* (New York: New York University Press, 2012).

68 **people in power."** Alec Karakatsanis (@equalityAlec), Twitter post, June 10, 2021 3:55p.m.; https://twitter.com/equalityAlec/status/14030 78372620656641. Alec Karakatsanis, *Usual Cruelty: The Complicity of Lawyers in the Criminal Injustice System* (New York: New Press, 2019).

68 **whichever was more!"** Alec Karakatsanis (@equalityAlec), Twitter post, July 6, 2021, 8:08 a.m., https://twitter.com/equalityalec/status /1412428330792542209.

68 **of force 'disappeared.'"** Samuel Peterson et al., *Understanding Subgroups within the Los Angeles County Sheriff's Department: Community and Department Perceptions with Recommendations for Change* (Santa Monica, CA: RAND, 2021), https://www.rand.org/pubs/research_reports/RRA616-1.html, p. 116.

68 **and raped children."** Andrea J. Ritchie, "How Some Cops Use the Badge to Commit Sex Crimes," *Washington Post*, January 12, 2018, https://www .washingtonpost.com/outlook/how-some-cops-use-the-badge-to-commit -sex-crimes/2018/01/11/5606fb26-eff3-11e7-b390-a36dc3fa2842_story.html.

69 **willing to admit.** Ritchie, "How Some Cops Use the Badge to Commit Sex Crimes."

69 **police for help?** According to RAINN, "Only 310 out of every 1,000 sexual assaults are reported." Of the people who didn't report being assaulted, 20 percent of victims said they didn't reach out to law enforcement because they fear retaliation, and 13 percent said they believe police, prosecutors, and prisons won't help. See "The Criminal Justice System: Statistics," Rape, Abuse, and Incest National Network, accessed January 18, 2022, https:// www.rainn.org/statistics/criminal-justice-system.

69 **betrayed the code."** Cab, "Confessions."

69 **involved in a crime."** "Asset Forfeiture Abuse," ACLU, accessed January 18, 2022, https://www.aclu.org/issues/criminal-law-reform/reforming-police /asset-forfeiture-abuse.

69 **are also essential.** Cab, "Confessions."

69 **life is precious."** Rachel Kushner, "Is Prison Necessary? Ruth Wilson Gilmore Might Change Your Mind," *New York Times*, April 17, 2019, https://www.nytimes.com/2019/04/17/magazine/prison-abolition-ruth -wilson-gilmore.html. Also see Reuben J. Miller, *Halfway Home: Race,*

Punishment, and the Afterlife of Mass Incarceration (New York: Little, Brown, and Company, 2021).

70 **as a class.** Ruth Wilson Gilmore, "Fatal Couplings of Power and Difference: Notes on Racism and Geography," *Professional Geographer* 54, no. 1 (2002): 15–24, https://doi.org/10.1111/0033-0124.00310.

70 **the carceral system.** Ruth Wilson Gilmore, "Pierce the Future for Hope: Mothers and Prisoners in the Post-Keynesian California Landscape," in *Global Lockdown: Race, Gender, and the Prison-Industrial Complex*, ed. Julia Sudbury (New York: Routledge, 2014): p. 29. See also, Ruth Wilson Gilmore, *Golden Gulag: Prisons, Surplus, Crisis, and Opposition in Globalizing California* (Berkeley: University of California Press, 2007).

71 **or exaggerated charges.** Mothers Reclaiming Our Children, homepage, May 16, 2019, https://mothersroc.home.blog/.

71 **are not alienable."** Gilmore, *Golden Gulag*, p. 238.

71 **the prison system."** Gilmore, *Golden Gulag*, p. 236. As Gilmore explains, the "insistence on the rights of mothers to children and children to mothers was not a defense of traditional domesticity as a separate sphere; rather it represented political activation around rising awareness of the specific ways that the contemporary working-class household is a site saturated by the neoliberal racial state." Gilmore, p. 239.

72 **[a police] occupation."** Gilmore, *Golden Gulag*, p. 238.

72 **3,000 had died.** "Covid-19's Impact on People in Prison," Equal Justice Initiative, April 16, 2021, https://eji.org/news/covid-19s-impact-on-people-in -prison/.

72 **Muldrow: 'Pretty much.'"** Eileen Guo, "'Obsessed with Staying Alive': Inmates Describe a Prison's Piecemeal Response to a Fatal Covid-19 Outbreak," STAT, June 12, 2020, https://www.statnews.com/2020/06/12 /california-institution-for-men-covid19-outbreak/.

72 **larger body politic.** As public health policy expert Kenyon Farrow notes, "The disproportionate impact of Covid-19 in carceral settings, the incomplete reporting of data, and the minimal public health and health care standards being uniformly implemented is no surprise to anyone who has been inside a facility, has a loved one who is or was imprisoned, or works as staff. Prisons, jails, and detention centers themselves are well known to be incubators of infectious disease outbreaks. This is not the fault of those confined in carceral settings, but rather is a result of how societies view people whom they send to such places of forced confinement. To condemn one to such a facility is to judge not just their actions, but their *person*." Kenyon Farrow, "Prisons Are a Public Health Crisis—and the Cure Is Right in Front of Us," Medium, October 14, 2020, https://level.medium .com/prisons-are-a-public-health-crisis-and-the-cure-is-right-in-front-of -us-aecd54b442c3.

72 **working for good."** Vanessa Northington Gamble, "'There Wasn't a Lot of Comforts in Those Days': African Americans, Public Health, and the 1918

Influenza Epidemic," *Public Health Reports* 125, no. 3, supplement (2010): 113–22, https://doi.org/10.1177/00333549101250s314.

72 **became coronavirus hotspots.** "Coronavirus in the U.S.: Latest Map and Case Count," *New York Times*, https://www.nytimes.com/interactive/2020/us/coronavirus-us-cases.html#clusters.

73 **and future epidemics."** Farrow, "Prisons."

73 **of Park Slope."** Ashley Southall, "Scrutiny of Social-Distance Policing as 35 of 40 Arrested are Black," *New York Times*, May 7, 2020. https://www.nytimes.com/2020/05/07/nyregion/nypd-social-distancing-race-coronavirus.html.

73 **percent were white.** Southall, "Scrutiny of Social-Distance Policing as 35 of 40 Arrested Are Black."

73 **were bogus charges.** Fariha Karim and John Simpson, "Woman Fined £660 for Crime That Doesn't Exist," *Times*, April 2, 2020, https://www.thetimes.co.uk/article/police-fine-woman-660-for-breaching-coronavirus-lockdown-laws-at-train-station-5ftr9ql0f

74 **New Jim Code."** Ruha Benjamin, *Race After Technology: Abolitionist Tools for the New Jim Code* (Cambridge, UK: Polity, 2019).

74 **and feel connected."** Lil Kalish, "How Long Until Citizen Gets Someone Killed?," *Mother Jones*, June 28, 2021, https://www.motherjones.com/crime-justice/2021/06/how-long-until-citizen-gets-someone-killed/.

75 **in your skull."** George Orwell, *1984*, with a foreword by Thomas Pynchon and an afterword by Erich Fromm (New York: Berkley, 2016), p. 28.

75 **free white persons."** Beth Lew-Williams, *The Chinese Must Go: Violence, Exclusion, and the Making of the Alien in America* (Cambridge, MA: Harvard University Press, 2021).

75 **of Black protest."** Kalish, "How Long?"

75 **Store's news section.** Jacob Silverman, "The Citizen App's Gamification of Vigilantism," *New Republic*, June 15, 2021, https://newrepublic.com/article/162747/citizen-app-crime-stats-private-security.

76 **for contact tracing.** Jenny Gross, "Citizen App Falsely Accused Man of Starting Los Angeles Wildfire," *New York Times*, May 18, 2021, https://www.nytimes.com/2021/05/18/business/citizen-app-arson-wildfire-devin-hilton.html.

76 **and asylum seekers.** "Palantir Played Key Role in Arresting Families for Deportation, Document Shows," Mijente, May 2, 2019, https://mijente.net/2019/05/palantir-arresting-families/.

76 **service' called Protect."** Silverman, "Citizen App's Gamification."

76 **"democratizing" public safety.** Silverman, "Citizen App's Gamification."

76 **the live search.** Joseph Cox and Jason Koebler, "'FIND THIS FUCK': Inside Citizen's Dangerous Effort to Cash In on Vigilantism," *Vice*, May 27, 2021, https://www.vice.com/en/article/y3dpyw/inside-crime-app-citizen-vigilante.

77 **Bel-Air home.** Cox and Koebler, "'FIND THIS FUCK'."

77 **all of la.** Cox and Koebler, "'FIND THIS FUCK'."

77 **guy EVERY DAY.** Kalish, "How Long?"

77 **an unhoused man.** Cox and Koebler, "'FIND THIS FUCK'."

77 **up user numbers.** Cox and Koebler, "'FIND THIS FUCK'."

77 **after this debacle.** "L.A. County and City Leaders Join Forces with Citizen to Launch Safepass Partnership," County of Los Angeles, accessed January 18, 2022, https://covid19.lacounty.gov/covid19-news/la-county-city-leaders-join-forces-citizen-launch-safepass-partnership/.

77 **refuse to intervene."** Sid Simpson and Chris Lay, "White Bear and Criminal Punishment," in *"Black Mirror" and Philosophy: Dark Reflections*, ed. David Kyle Johnson (Hoboken, NJ: John Wiley and Sons, 2019), 50–58, p. 50.

78 **feel morally justified."** Simpson and Lay, "White Bear," p. 58.

78 **cohesive about it."** Simpson and Lay, "White Bear," p. 56.

79 **toward the camera.** Breanna Edwards, "Missouri Waitress Fired over 'N-Word Hunting' Video Swears She Isn't Racist, Claims to Have Black Friends," *Root*, June 12, 2018, https://www.theroot.com/missouri-waitress-fired-after-n-word-hunting-video-swea-1826765082. Although the video has been taken down, it can be seen on the Facebook page for Real STL News.

79 **being videoed. Checkmate.** Edwards, "Missouri Waitress Fired over 'N-Word Hunting' Video Swears She Isn't Racist, Claims to Have Black Friends."

79 **of white supremacy.** "Historian Stephanie Jones-Rogers writes in *They Were Her Property* that white women in the United States were enthusiastic in their cruelty as owners of enslaved people on plantations. White women throughout colonialism have wielded power over subjugated people, as Vron Ware writes in her book *Beyond the Pale*." Jessie Daniels, *Nice White Ladies: The Truth about White Supremacy, Our Role in It, and How We Can Help Dismantle It* (New York: Seal, 2021), p. 16.

79 **to endanger others.** This term is used in a different context by Chuck DeGroat, professor of counseling at the Western Theological Seminary, in a critique of pastors. See Kylie Beach, "'Fauxnerability' a Growing Phenomenon among Narcissistic Pastors, Leaders," Eternity, June 8, 2021, https://www.eternitynews.com.au/in-depth/fauxnerability-a-growing-phenomenon-among-narcissistic-pastors-leaders/.

79 **on black people."** Justin Louis Mann, "What's Your Emergency? White Women and the Policing of Public Space," *Feminist Studies* 44, no. 3 (2018): 766–75, https://doi.org/10.15767/feministstudies.44.3.0766, p. 768.

80 **of black people."** Mann, "What's Your emergency?"

80 **and whole communities."** Daniels, *Nice White Ladies*, p. 22–23.

81 **the cops immediately!"** "Central Park Birdwatching Incident," Wikipedia, last edited January 11, 2022, https://en.wikipedia.org/wiki/Central_Park_birdwatching_incident.

81 **devastating police violence."** Katrina Feldkamp and S. Rebecca Neusteter, "The Little Known, Racist History of the 911 Emergency Call System," *In These Times*, January 26, 2021, https://inthesetimes.com/article/911-emergency

-service-racist-history-civil-rights. Feldkamp and Neusteter note, "Tellingly, in the [Kerner] report's 'Supplement on Control of Disorder' —a section left out of nearly all published copies of the report but eventually converted into a training program administered by the Department of Justice—the Commission recommends expanding police capacity to suppress protests. The section advises state and federal law enforcement to intervene in civil disorders, recommends local police departments adopt militaristic riot control training and equipment (including tear gas) and encourages police departments to infiltrate Black communities."

81 **about unhoused people.** Feldkamp and Neusteter, "The Little Known, Racist History."

81 **take swift action.** Feldkamp and Neusteter, "The Little Known, Racist History."

81 **do end lives."** Daniels, *Nice White Ladies*, p. 35.

81 **ourselves or others."** Peter Szekely, "Charge Dropped against Woman Who Made False Claim to Cops about Black Man in Central Park," Reuters, February 16, 2021, https://www.reuters.com/article/us-global-race-usa -new-york-idUSKBN2AG1Y7.

82 **with Amy Cooper."** Chelsey Sanchez, "Why Christian Cooper Refuses to Cooperate with Prosecution against Amy Cooper," *Harper's Bazaar*, July 9, 2020, https://www.harpersbazaar.com/culture/politics/a33261790/christian -cooper-refuses-to-cooperate-with-prosecution-against-amy-cooper/.

82 **told NBC News.** Caroline Radnofsky and Rima Abdelkader, "Disabled, Black and Searching for Justice," NBC News, July 3, 2020, https://www .nbcnews.com/news/nbcblk/disabled-black-searching-justice-n1232204.

83 **and assume criminality."** Radnofsky and Rima Abdelkader, "Disabled, Black and Searching for Justice."

83 **white disabled counterparts.** Also note, "a person's inability to hear and react appropriately to an officer's commands can be misread as the person being difficult. Those with an awkward gait pattern due to cerebral palsy can be erroneously thought of as being under the influence and subjected to questioning or arrest. Autistic people who are not able to maintain eye contact or repeat the statements given to them may be perceived as displaying hostile or uncooperative behaviors. Individuals in mental or physical crisis who are unable to communicate clearly or express themselves may be read as threatening or lacking self-control and, subsequently, may experience unnecessary force because they cannot understand or follow an officer's orders." Vilissa Thompson, "Understanding the Policing of Black, Disabled Bodies," Center for American Progress, February 10, 2021, https:// www.americanprogress.org/issues/disability/news/2021/02/10/495668 /understanding-policing-black-disabled-bodies/.

83 **of police brutality."** James Tracy, "Nothing about Us, without Us!— Interview with Leroy Moore," *Left Turn*, October 1, 2007, http://leftturn.org /nothing-about-us-without-us-interview-leroy-moore/.

85 **civil rights movement.** Jonathan Lykes and Fresco Steez, *The Black Joy Experience Resource Guide* (Chicago: Black Youth Project 100, 2017), https://media.milanote.com/p/files/1KeYZr1wO1gf60/c6I/The-Black-Joy -Experience-Resource-Guide-.pdf.

85 **was so rare.** Breanna Edward, "Black Youths Attending Princeton Conference Pulled Over by Police, Then This Happened," *Root*, March 18, 2014, https://www.theroot.com/black-youths-attending-princeton-con ference-pulled-over-1790874989.

85 **for me, guys."** Kevin Shea, "Gunman in Panera Begged Cops to Shoot Him for Hours. State Says They Were Justified When They Had To," *NJ .com*, November 9, 2018, https://www.nj.com/news/2018/11/gunman_in _princeton_panera_begged_police_for_hours.html.

85 **don't weaponize distress.** Ari Shapiro, "Sociologist on How Black Men Try to Appear Non-threatening as a Defense Mechanism," NPR, May 7, 2020, https://www.npr.org/2020/05/07/852319565/sociologist-on-how -black-men-try-to-appear-non-threatening-as-a-defense-mechanism.

86 **departments and communities.** Dan Kopf, "The Fining of Black America," June 24, 2016, *Priceonomics*, https://priceonomics.com/the-fining-of-black -america/.

86 **citizens to protect."** Kopf, "The Fining of Black America."

87 **dismantled," Rice says.** Imani Perry, "Stop Hustling Black Death," *Cut*, May 24, 2021, https://www.thecut.com/article/samaria-rice-profile.html.

87 **our families? communities?"** Derecka Purnell (@dereckapurnell), Twitter post, April 19, 2021, 1:46 p.m.; https://twitter.com/dereckapurnell/status /1384201740258447360; see also, Derecka Purnell, *Becoming Abolitionists: Police, Protests, and the Pursuit of Freedom* (New York: Astra House, 2021).

88 **times," she insisted.** Erica Thompson, "Ma'Khia Bryant Death: Teachers, Social Workers Discuss How They Defuse Conflicts, Avoid Tragedies," *Columbus Dispatch*, May 5, 2021, https://www.dispatch.com/story/news /2021/05/05/makhia-bryant-death-social-workers-teachers-de-escalation /7355508002/.

89 **courage and creativity.** Creative Interventions, *Creative Interventions Toolkit: A Practical Guide to Stop Interpersonal Violence* (Creative Inter- ventions, 2012), https://www.creative-interventions.org/toolkit/.

89 **a "power project."** "Process," Oakland Power Projects, accessed January 18, 2022, https://oaklandpowerprojects.org/process.

89 **when seeking healthcare.** "Healthcare," Oakland Power Projects, accessed January 18, 2022, https://oaklandpowerprojects.org/healthcare.

90 **on our bodies.** One Million Experiments, homepage, accessed January 18, 2022, https://millionexperiments.com.

90 **solve the problem."** Jeremy Scahill, "Scholar Robin D. G. Kelley on How Today's Abolitionist Movement Can Fundamentally Change the Country," *Intercept*, June 27, 2020, https://theintercept.com/2020/06/27/robin-dg -kelley-intercepted/.

90   **domestic violence significantly."** Scahill, "Scholar Robin D. G. Kelley on How Today's Abolitionist Movement Can Fundamentally Change the Country."

91   **calls "healing justice."** "Programs," Audre Lorde Project, accessed January 18, 2022, https://alp.org/programs.

91   **on the planet."** "About the Project," Solitary Gardens, accessed January 18, 2022, https://solitarygardens.org/about.

91   **punishment and suffering?"** Mariame Kaba, "Against Punishment; A Resource by Project Nia and Interrupting Criminalization," December 2, 2020, https://issuu.com/projectnia/docs/against_punishment_curriculum_final.

92   **on juvenile incarceration.** For data on per-student spending, see "Oakland Unified," Education Data Partnership, accessed January 18, 2022, http://www.ed-data.org/district/Alameda/Oakland-Unified. Click the "Financial Data" tab, then "General Fund: Expenditures," and then "Current Expense of Education per ADA 2019–20." For data on juvenile incarceration, see Jill Tucker and Joaquin Palomino, "Juvenile Hall Costs Skyrocket," *San Francisco Chronicle*, April 26, 2019, https://www.sfchronicle.com/news/article/Vanishing-Violence-Cost-of-locking-up-a-youth-in-13793488.php.

92   **poverty, abuse, neglect."** "A Brief but Spectacular Take on Giving Incarcerated Youth a Voice," *PBS Newshour*, August 30, 2019, video, 3:16, https://www.youtube.com/watch?time_continue=7&v=Rjy0ntl5XLM&feature=emb_logo.

92   **was your kid?"** "Brief but Spectacular."

93   **our own locale.** "Tools for Action," Project NIA, accessed January 18, 2022, https://project-nia.org/tools-for-action.

93   **healing and accountability.** "Building Transformative Justice Responses to Child Sexual Abuse," Bay Area Transformative Justice Collective, accessed January 18, 2022, https://batjc.wordpress.com.

93   **from calling 911?** Layel Camargo, "Transformative Justice Has Been a Struggle Lately," Bay Area Transformative Justice Collective, July 26, 2018, https://batjc.wordpress.com/2018/07/26/transformative-justice-has-been-a-struggle-lately/.

94   **that for myself."** Camargo, "Transformative Justice."

95   **advocate for change.** "Healing to Advocacy Program," Essie Justice Group, accessed January 18, 2022, https://essiejusticegroup.org/healing-to-advocacy-program/.

Chapter Three

Page

99   **to see me."** Ralph Ellison, *Invisible Man* (New York: The Modern Library, 1994), p. 3.

100 **make it easier.** "The Greatest Love of All" composed & produced by Michael Masser, lyrics by Linda Creed, 1977.

101 **an assembly line."** Grace Lee Boggs, *The Next American Revolution: Sustainable Activism for the Twenty-First Century*, with Scott Kurashige (Berkeley: University of California Press, 2012), p. 137.

101 **what they *are.***" Friedrich Wilhelm Nietzsche, *The Gay Science: Or, the Joyful Wisdom*, edited by Bill Chapko, translated by Thomas Common, originally published in 1910 (Dumfries & Galloway, Scotland: Anodos Books, 2019), p. 42, emphasis added.

102 **pathologizes young people.** Victor Rios, "From 'At-Risk' to 'At-Promise': Supporting Teens to Overcome Adversity," TEDxUCSB, Santa Barbara, CA, May 15, 2012, video, 13:21, https://www.youtube.com/watch?v=JZ5D_Je8tvo.

102 **Black Students. Art."** Brit M. Williams (@DrBritWilliams), Twitter post, January 20, 2021, 12:37 p.m., https://twitter.com/DrBritWilliams/status /1351947029535141894.

102 **by their parents.** But there is also a growing movement to break these cycles of intergenerational trauma. As just one example, see Latinx Parenting, homepage, accessed January 20, 2022, https://latinxparenting.org/. Also, read everything by bell hooks, starting with *All about Love*: "For years I lived my life suspended, trapped by the past, unable to move into the future. Like every wounded child I just wanted turn back time and be in that paradise again, in that moment of remembered rapture where I felt loved, where I felt a sense of belonging. We can never go back. I know that now. We can go forward. We can find the love our hearts long for, but not until we let go grief about the love we lost long ago, when we were little and had no voice to speak the heart's longing." bell books, *All about Love: New Visions* (New York: William Morrow, 2018), p. x.

103 **things into being.** Ian Hacking, "Making Up People," *London Review of Books*, August 17, 2006.

103 **even enjoy it."** Patricia Williams, "Spirit-Murdering the Messenger: The Discourse of Fingerpointing as the Law's Response to Racism," *University of Miami Law Review* 42 (September 1, 1987): 127–57, p. 103.

103 **to be educated."** Bettina L. Love, *We Want to Do More Than Survive: Abolitionist Teaching and the Pursuit of Educational Freedom* (Boston: Beacon, 2019), p. 38.

104 **than an athlete."** Bettina Love et al., "Abolitionist Teaching and the Future of Our Schools," virtual panel discussion, Haymarket Books and Schomburg Center for Research in Black Culture, June 23, 2020, video, 1:31:51, https://www.youtube.com/watch?v=uJZ3RPJ2rNc.

104 **us to say.** Joy DeGruy, *Post Traumatic Slave Syndrome: America's Legacy of Enduring Injury and Healing*, with a foreword by Randall Robinson (Portland, OR: Joy DeGruy Publications, 2018).

104 **to control you.** Patricia Hill Collins, *Black Feminist Thought: Knowledge, Consciousness, and the Politics of Empowerment* (New York: Routledge, 2009).

104 **historical redlining practices.** Sarah Mervosh, "How Much Wealthier Are White School Districts Than Nonwhite Ones? $23 Billion, Report Says,"

New York Times, February 27, 2019, https://www.nytimes.com/2019/02/27/education/school-districts-funding-white-minorities.html.

105 **for having nothing."** Eve Ottenberg, "Gentrification, School Closings, and Displacement in Chicago," *American Prospect*, March 14, 2019, https://prospect.org/education/gentrification-school-closings-displacement-chicago/.

105 **purpose and plans.'"** Grace Lee Boggs and Scott Kurashige, *The Next American Revolution: Sustainable Activism for the 21st Century* (Berkeley: University of California Press, 2012), p. 90.

105 **glorify the hunter."** Annalisa Quinn, "Chinua Achebe and the Bravery of Lions," NPR, March 22, 2013, https://www.npr.org/sections/thetwo-way/2013/03/22/175046327/chinua-achebe-and-the-bravery-of-lions.

105 **in the world.** Bill Bigelow, "From Johannesburg to Tucson," *Rethinking Schools*, Summer 2012, https://rethinkingschools.org/articles/from-johannesburg-to-tucson/.

105 **are too controversial."** Liz Dwyer, "Here's What the Parthenon Would Look Like If It Were Made Out of 100,000 Banned Books," Good, August 13, 2017, https://www.good.is/education/parthenon-banned-books-learning-about-democracy.

106 **and worked there.** Jeremy Cook and Jason Long, "How the Tulsa Race Massacre Caused Decades of Harm," *Atlantic*, May 24, 2021, https://www.theatlantic.com/ideas/archive/2021/05/1921-tulsa-race-massacre-economic-census-survivors/618968/.

107 **than to affirm."** J. Douglas Allen-Taylor, "Septima Clark: Teacher to a Movement," Safero, accessed January 20, 2022, http://www.safero.org/articles/septima.html.

107 **civil rights activists.** "Highlander Folk School," Digital SNCC Gateway, accessed January 20, 2022, https://snccdigital.org/inside-sncc/alliances-relationships/highlander/.

107 **of infectious disease.** Indigenous communities have also sustained traditions of healing and mutual aid for centuries, which we can and must learn from: "This looks like a small crew coordinating their relatives or friends to chop wood and distribute to elders. It looks like traditional medicine herbal clinics or sexual health supply distribution. It looks like community water hauling efforts or large scale supply runs to ensure elders have enough to make it through harsh winters." "About," Indigenous Mutual Aid, accessed January 20, 2022, https://www.indigenousmutualaid.org/about/.

107 **the enslaved population.** Jennifer L. Morgan, *Laboring Women: Reproduction and Gender in New World Slavery* (Philadelphia: University of Pennsylvania Press, 2004).

108 **hell of slavery.** Laura Isensee, "Why Calling Slaves 'Workers' Is More Than an Editing Error," NPR, October 23, 2015, https://www.npr.org/sections/ed/2015/10/23/450826208/why-calling-slaves-workers-is-more-than-an-editing-error.

108 **1939 to 1945.** Meanwhile, Aktion T4 regime killed seventy thousand mentally and physically disabled people during World War II. See "T4—Memorial and Information Centre for the Victims of the Nazi Euthanasia Programme," Visit Berlin, accessed January 20, 2022, https://www.visitberlin.de/en/t4 -memorial-and-information-centre-victims-nazi-euthanasia-programme.

108 **Arendt put it.** Hannah Arendt, "Eichmann in Jerusalem—I," *New Yorker*, February 8, 1963, https://www.newyorker.com/magazine/1963/02/16 /eichmann-in-jerusalem-i.

108 **with Aktion T4."** Photograph of plaque taken by author on September 24, 2015.

109 **business as usual.** Peter Morgan, "Bureaucracy of Evil," *Index on Censorship* 28, no. 2 (1999), 73-76, https://doi.org/10.1080/03064229908536547.

109 **Death" at Auschwitz.** David Turner, "Foundations of Holocaust: American Eugenics and the Nazi Connection," *Jerusalem Post*, December 30, 2012, https://www.jpost.com/blogs/the-jewish-problem—from-anti-judaism-to -anti-semitism/foundations-of-holocaust-american-eugenics-and-the-nazi -connection-364998.

109 **the American South.** James Q. Whitman, *Hitler's American Model: The United States and the Making of Nazi Race Law* (Princeton: Princeton University Press, 2017).; Ira Katznelson, "What America Taught the Nazis," *Atlantic*, November 2017, https://www.theatlantic.com/magazine/archive /2017/11/what-america-taught-the-nazis/540630/.

109 **chancellors, and professors.** Human Betterment Foundation, *Human Sterilization Today* (Pasadena, CA: Human Betterment Foundation, 1938), 6. https://www.loc.gov/resource/rbpe.0020380g/?q=Human+Betterment +Foundation+&sp=6&st=text.

110 **of racial improvement.** Ayah Nuriddin, "The Black Politics of Eugenics," *Nursing Clio* (blog), June 1, 2017, https://nursingclio.org/2017/06/01/the -black-politics-of-eugenics.

110 **their own defense.** "Buck v Bell, One of the Supreme Court's Worst Mistakes," Bioethics Research Library at the Kennedy Institute of Ethics, accessed January 20, 2022, https://bioethics.georgetown.edu/2016/02 /buck-v-bell-one-of-the-supreme-courts-worst-mistakes/.

110 **imbeciles are enough."** "BUCK V. BELL, Superintendent of State Colony Epileptics and Feeble Minded," Legal Information Institute, accessed January 20, 2022, https://www.law.cornell.edu/supremecourt/text/274 /200.

110 **philosophy and program.** maya finoh, "Allegations of Forced Sterilization in ICE Detention Evoke a Long Legacy of Eugenics in the United States," Center for Constitutional Rights, September 18, 2020, https://ccrjustice .org/home/blog/2020/09/18/allegations-forced-sterilization-ice-detention -evoke-long-legacy-eugenics.

110 **unfit to procreate.** Adam Cohen, "The Supreme Court Ruling That Led to 70,000 Forced Sterilizations," interview by Terry Gross, *Fresh Air*, NPR,

March 7, 2016, audio, 37:40, https://www.npr.org/sections/health-shots/2016/03/07/469478098/the-supreme-court-ruling-that-led-to-70-000-forced-sterilizations.

110 **Virginia until 2013.** Caroline Lyster, "West Virginia Sterilization Law Repealed," Eugenics Archives, March 25, 2013, https://eugenicsarchive.ca/discover/timeline/550054e7cc8b722e0400000e.

110 **the twentieth century.** Cohen, "Supreme Court Ruling."

110 **59 percent higher rates.** Nicole L. Novak and Natalie Lira, "California Once Targeted Latinas for Forced Sterilization," *Smithsonian Magazine*, March 22, 2018, https://www.smithsonianmag.com/history/california-targeted-latinas-forced-sterilization-180968567/.

110 **allowed to survive.** Rosemarie Garland-Thomson, "Eugenic World-Building and Disability: The Strange World of Kazuo Ishiguro's Never Let Me Go," *Journal of Medical Humanities,* 38, no. 2 (2017), 133–145, 10.1007/s10912-015-9368-y.

111 **College, among others.** Teresa Watanabe and Tomás Mier, "USC Removes Name of Rufus von KleinSmid, a Eugenics Leader, from Prominent Building," *Los Angeles Times*, June 11, 2020, https://www.latimes.com/california/story/2020-06-11/usc-removes-name-of-former-president-rufus-von-kleinsmid-a-supporter-of-eugenics-from-prominent-building; Teresa Watanabe, "Caltech to Remove Name of Founding President, a Eugenics Supporter, from Buildings," *Los Angeles Times*, January 16, 2021, https://www.latimes.com/california/story/2021-01-16/caltech-to-remove-name-of-founding-president-and-eugenics-supporter-from-campus-buildings; Chris Peacock, "Stanford Will Rename Campus Spaces Named for David Starr Jordan and Relocate Statue Depicting Louis Agassiz," *Stanford News*, October 7, 2020, https://news.stanford.edu/2020/10/07/jordan-agassiz/.

111 **gift in 1975.** Teresa Watanabe and Nina Agrawal, "New Blow to SAT Empire Shows California's Key Role in Diminishing College Admissions Tests," *Los Angeles Times*, January 20, 2021, https://www.latimes.com/california/story/2021-01-20/sat-test-diminish-california-key-role.

111 **to know today?"** Toni Cade Bambara, *Those Bones Are Not My Child: A Novel* (New York: Vintage Books, 1999), 168.

111 **in California prisons.** Bill Chappell, "California's Prison Sterilizations Reportedly Echo Eugenics Era," NPR, July 9, 2013, https://www.npr.org/sections/thetwo-way/2013/07/09/200444613/californias-prison-sterilizations-reportedly-echoes-eugenics-era.

111 **my Spelman classmate.** Kid Tafesse, "What the 'Mississippi Appendectomy' Says about the Regard of the State towards the Agency of Black Women's Bodies," Movement for Black Women's Lives, May 1, 2019, https://blackwomenintheblackfreedomstruggle.voices.wooster.edu/2019/05/01/what-the-mississippi-appendectomy-says-about-the-regard-of-the-state-towards-the-agency-of-black-womens-bodies/.

112   *Madrigal v. Quilligan.* "A Latinx Resource Guide: Civil Rights Cases and Events in the United States," Library of Congress, accessed January 20, 2022, https://guides.loc.gov/latinx-civil-rights/madrigal-v-quilligan.

112   **middle of labor.** Antonia Hernandez, "Chicanas and the Issue of Involuntary Sterilization: Reforms Needed to Protect Informed Consent," *Chicana/o Latina/o Law Review* 3 (1976): 3–37, https://doi.org/10.5070/c730020919.

112   **"environment for abuse."** Jessica Wolf, "UCLA Professor's Film Documents Forced Sterilization of Mexican Women in Late '60s and Early '70s L.A.," UCLA Newsroom, October 23, 2017, https://newsroom.ucla.edu /stories/ucla-professor-s-film-documents-forced-sterilization-of-mexican -women-in-late-60s-l-a.

112   **"I.Q. of 46."** Kimberly Lawson, "California's Dark History of Forcibly Sterilizing Latinas," *Vice*, August 16, 2018, https://www.vice.com/en/article /gy339b/california-forced-sterilizations-latina-women-history; Alexandra Minna Stern, "Remembering Sara Rosas Garcia," *Process: A Blog for American History*, February 7, 2017, http://www.processhistory.org/sara -rosas-garcia/.

112   **had any children."** Lawson, "California's Dark History of Forcibly Sterilizing Latinas."

113   **and moral health.** Molly Ladd-Taylor, "Fitter Family Contests," Eugenics Archive, April 29, 2014, https://eugenicsarchive.ca/discover/connections /535eebfb7095aa0000000228.

113   **"good mothering strategies."** Francine Uenuma, "'Better Babies' Contests Pushed for Much-Needed Infant Health but Also Played into the Eugenics Movement," *Smithsonian Magazine*, January 17, 2019, https:// www.smithsonianmag.com/history/better-babies-contests-pushed-infant -health-also-played-eugenics-movement-180971288/.

113   **into the curriculum.** Jonathan Chernoguz, "High School Students for the Incorporation of the History of Eugenics into California Curricula," Change.org, 2013, https://www.change.org/p/high-school-students-for -the-incorporation-of-the-history-of-eugenics-into-california-curricula; see also San Francisco Youth Commission, "File No. Resolution No. 1213," March 29, 2013, https://sfgov.org/youthcommission/sites/default/files /FileCenter/Documents/44952-1213--15--Recommending%20the%20 Inclusion%20of%20California%27s%20History%20of%20Eugenics%20 into%20the%20California%20High%20School%20Curriculum.pdf

114   **make them matter."** Joy James, "Black Lives: Between Grief and Action," interview by George Yancy, *New York Times*, December 23, 2014, https:// sites.williams.edu/jjames/files/2019/06/BlackGriefNYT2014-1.pdf.

114   **public health measures.** Although the Trump administration disbanded the pandemic response team, some of the team members were reassigned to roles that included pandemic response. See Reuters Staff, "Partly False Claim: Trump Fired Entire Pandemic Response Team in 2018," Reuters, March 25, 2020, https://www.reuters.com/article/uk-factcheck-trump

-fired-pandemic-team/partly-false-claim-trump-fired-entire-pandemic
-response-team-in-2018-idUSKBN21C32M.

115 **what it takes."** Shamus Rahman Khan, *Privilege: The Making of an Adolescent Elite at St. Paul's School* (Princeton, NJ: Princeton University Press, 2013), p. 193.

116 **work and talent."** Khan, *Privilege*, p. 186.

116 **for Black students.** Savannah Shange, *Progressive Dystopia: Abolition, Antiblackness, and Schooling in San Francisco* (Durham, NC: Duke University Press, 2019).

116 **a uniform incorrectly.** "Zero Tolerance," Law Library—American Law and Legal Information, accessed January 20, 2022, https://law.jrank.org/pages /11439/Zero-Tolerance.html; "Zero Tolerance," School Discipline Support Initiative, accessed January 20, 2022, https://supportiveschooldiscipline .org/zero-tolerance-policy.

116 **discouraged you become."** Catherine Winter, "Spare the Rod: Amid Zero Tolerance Doesn't Work, Schools Reverse Themselves," APM Reports, August 26, 2016, https://www.apmreports.org/episode/2016/08/25 /reforming-school-discipline.

117 **and talking 'unladylike.'"** Dorothy E. Hines and Jennifer M. Wilmot, "From Spirit-Murdering to Spirit-Healing: Addressing Anti-Black Aggressions and the Inhumane Discipline of Black Children," *Multicultural Perspectives* 20, no. 2 (2018): 62–69, https://doi.org/10.1080/15210960.2018.1447064.

117 **white female students.** Kayla Patrick, "How Many Girls of Color Are Really Pushed out of School? It Could Be More Than We Thought," National Women's Law Center, July 19, 2017, https://nwlc.org/blog/how-many-girls-of-color -are-really-pushed-out-of-school-it-could-be-more-than-we-thought/.

117 **perpetuated racial inequities.** Laurie Stern, "Restorative Justice: A New Approach to Discipline," APM Reports, August 25, 2016, https://www .apmreports.org/story/2016/08/25/restorative-justice-school-discipline.

117 **calm and loving.** Ella Torres and Karma Allen, "Video Shows Oregon Coach Disarming Student Then Embracing Him Before Police Arrive," ABC News, October 20, 2019, https://abcnews.go.com/US/video-shows-oregon -coach-disarming-student-embracing-police/story?id=66389192.

118 **'pacify' the situation."** "Meet Calvin Terrell of Social Centric in Central," Voyage Phoenix, March 5, 2020, http://voyagephoenix.com/interview /meet-social-centric-central.

118 **and better community.** Social Centric Institute website, https://www .socialcentric.com/socialcentricneighborhoods, accessed on February 18, 2022.

118 **for evolving relations.** Calvin Terrell website, https://www.calvinterrell .com/speaker, accessed February 18, 2022.

118 **practices in schools.** Stern, "Restorative Justice."

118 **of Black disingenuity."** Bruce Sinclair, ed. *Technology and the African-American Experience: Needs and Opportunities for Study* (Cambridge, MA: MIT Press, 2004).

119 **stop repelling them!** Chonda Prescod-Weirstein, *The Disordered Cosmos: A Journey into Dark Matter, Spacetime, and Dreams Deferred* (New York: Bold Type Books, 2021).

119 **education-related resources."** R. L'Heureux Lewis-McCoy, *Inequality in the Promised Land: Race, Resources, and Suburban Schooling* (Stanford, CA: Stanford University Press, 2014), p. 23.

120 **a greater degree."** Eric Kiefer, "South Orange–Maplewood Ponders $127M Plan to Integrate Schools," Patch, May 17, 2018, https://patch.com /new-jersey/maplewood/south-orange-maplewood-ponders-127m-plan -integrate-schools.

120 **her son's classroom.** Whitney Pirtle, "The Other Kind of School Segregation," Route Fifty, April 24, 2019, https://www.route-fifty.com/management /2019/04/gifted-talented-school-segregation/156518/.

120 **nothing would change."** Nikole Hannah-Jones, "Choosing a School for My Daughter in a Segregated City," *New York Times*, June 9, 2016, https://www .nytimes.com/2016/06/12/magazine/choosing-a-school-for-my-daughter -in-a-segregated-city.html.

121 **race and class."** Christopher Robbins, "Upper West Side Uproar as City Tries to Diversify Schools," Gothamist, May 1, 2018, https://gothamist.com /news/upper-west-side-uproar-as-city-tries-to-diversify-schools; Christina Veiga, "Push to Curb Academic Segregation on the Upper West Side Generates a Backlash—and Support," Chalkbeat, April 25, 2018, https://ny .chalkbeat.org/2018/4/25/21104968/push-to-curb-academic-segregation -on-the-upper-west-side-generates-a-backlash-and-support.

121 **the eugenics movement.** Valerie Strauss, "The Rise of the Anti–Standardized Testing Movement," *Washington Post*, October 30, 2014, https://www .washingtonpost.com/news/answer-sheet/wp/2014/10/30/the-rise-of-the -anti-standardized-testing-movement/. "Rosner, of the Princeton Review Foundation, said he plans to begin raising another potentially explosive issue about the SAT: Its founder, Carl Brigham, was a Princeton professor and supporter of the eugenics movement . . . He believes the origins of the test cannot be dismissed." Watanabe and Agrawal, "New Blow to SAT."

121 **for fall 2022.** Giulia McDonnell Nieto del Rio, "University of California Will No Longer Consider SAT and ACT Scores," *New York Times*, May 15, 2021, https://www.nytimes.com/2021/05/15/us/SAT-scores-uc-university-of -california.html; "1,400+ U.S. Four-Year Colleges and Universities Will Not Require ACT/SAT Scores for Fall 2022 Entry," FairTest, April 28, 2021, https://www.fairtest.org/1400-us-fouryear-colleges-and-universities-will-no.

122 **engage in class."** Phillip Palmer, "LAUSD Program Helping Black Students Achieve Personal, Academic Goals," ABC7, December 29, 2021, https://abc7 .com/lausd-black-students-student-achievement-plan-education/11402389/.

122 **really concerted effort."** Palmer, "LAUSD Program Helping Black Students Achieve Personal, Academic Goals."

124 ***The Time Machine.*** "Radio Free Hillman," IMDb, accessed January 21, 2022, https://www.imdb.com/title/tt0560194/; "Radio Free Hillman,"

Different World Wiki, accessed January 21, 2022, https://differentworld .fandom.com/wiki/Radio_Free_Hillman.

124 **that we have."** "Rosalind Cash," interview by S. Pearl Sharp, *Lead In*, BET, 1981, video, 9:41, https://www.youtube.com/watch?v=lPw-jHt6RjQ.

125 **hateful, unpleasant; odious."** Online Etymology Dictionary, s.v. "heinous," accessed January 21, 2022, https://www.etymonline.com/word/heinous.

125 **for "acting white."** Indianz Com, "My Brother's Keeper Town Hall," July 21, 2014, video, 7:55, https://www.youtube.com/watch?v=iYhsnLdUiUs/.

125 **other model minorities.** Signithia Fordham and John U. Ogbu, "Black Students' School Success: Coping with the 'Burden of 'Acting White,'" *Urban Review* 18, no. 3 (1986): 176–206, https://doi.org/10.1007/bf01112192, p. 181.

126 **of academic success."** Signithia Fordham, "Beyond Capital High: On Dual Citizenship and the Strange Career of 'Acting White,'" *Anthropology and Education Quarterly* 39, no. 3 (2008): 227–46, http://www.jstor.org/stable /25166666, p. 232.

126 **becoming academically successful."** Fordham, "Beyond Capital High," p. 243.

126 **strategy for survival.** Angel L. Harris, *Kids Don't Want to Fail: Oppositional Culture and the Black-White Achievement Gap* (Cambridge, MA: Harvard University Press, 2011), p. ix.

126 **of social inequality."** Carla Shedd, *Unequal City: Race, Schools, and Perceptions of Injustice* (New York: Russell Sage Foundation, 2015), p. 5.

126 **cheated," she says.** Shedd, *Unequal City*, p. 2.

126 **supremacist, capitalist patriarchy,"** Media Education Foundation Transcript (1997), https://www.mediaed.org/transcripts/Bell-Hooks -Transcript.pdf; In the same interview, hooks explains, "I wanted to have some language that would actually remind us continually of the interlocking systems of domination that define our reality and not to just have one thing be like, you know, gender is the important issue, race is the important issue, but for me the use of that particular jargonistic phrase was a way, a sort of short cut way of saying all of these things actually are functioning simultaneously at all times in our lives . . ."

126 **soul-sucking status quo.** For example, Hailey Denise Colborn (@ hailoswailo), TikTok post, December 7, 2021, https://www.tiktok.com/@ hailoswailo/video/7039061815430712622; Clare Brown (@clarabellecwb), TikTok post, December 10, 2021, https://www.tiktok.com/@clarabellecwb /video/7043811487617436975; and Erynn Chambers (@rynnstar), TikTok post, June 3, 2020, https://www.tiktok.com/@rynnstar/video /6834208444824734981.

127 **spirit ans swagger.** "New PHS Courses on Racial Literacy and Harmony Join Curriculum for Coming Year," *Town Topics*, July 19, 2017, http://www .towntopics.com/wordpress/2017/07/19/new-phs-courses-on-racial -literacy-and-harmony-join-curriculum-for-coming-year/.

127 **of people's lives.** Zack Beauchamp, "The Unbearable Whiteness of Social Networks," *Vox*, August 22, 2014, https://www.vox.com/xpress/2014/8/22/6056835/white-black-social-networks-ferguson.

128 **Black students live."** Clara Totenberg Green, "The Latest in School Segregation: Private Pandemic 'Pods,'" *New York Times*, July 22, 2020, https://www.nytimes.com/2020/07/22/opinion/pandemic-pods-sschools.html.

128 **of their pods.** "Health Equity Considerations and Racial and Ethnic Minority Groups," Centers for Disease Control and Prevention, November 30, 2021, https://www.cdc.gov/coronavirus/2019-ncov/community/health-equity/race-ethnicity.html.

128 **the late 1960s."** Green, "Latest in School Segregation."

128 **more desirable alternatives.** Christopher Bonastia, "Why the Racist History of the Charter School Movement Is Never Discussed," *Facing South*, March 16, 2012, https://www.facingsouth.org/2012/03/why-the-racist-history-of-the-charter-school-movement-is-never-discussed.html.

129 **for all children."** Green, "Latest in School Segregation."

129 **in the state.** "Disconnected in Maryland," Abell Foundation, January 2021, https://abell.org/publications/disconnected-maryland.

129 **for the program.** Donna St. George, "'Equity Hubs' Giving Families Struggling Financially a Chance at Pandemic Pods," *Washington Post*, December 25, 2020, https://www.washingtonpost.com/local/education/pandemic-learning-pod-montgomery-county/2020/12/25/9216f7c4-2de9-11eb-860d-f7999599cbc2_story.html.

129 **for vulnerable families."** St. George, "Equity Hubs."

130 **on, eliciting "boos."** Anne Levin, "Black Mothers Rising Group Holds Dialogue with Police," *Town Topics*, June 10, 2020, http://www.towntopics.com/wordpress/2020/06/10/black-mothers-rising-group-holds-dialogue-with-police/; Marissa Michaels, "'It Has to End': Protestors in Princeton Demand Justice for Floyd's Death," *Daily Princetonian*, June 3, 2020, https://www.dailyprincetonian.com/article/2020/06/george-floyd-protest-princeton; Angelina Chen, "Princeton Protests the Death of George Floyd," *Tower*, June 12, 2020, https://thetowerphs.com/2020/06/news/princeton-protests-the-death-of-george-floyd/?pdf=14114.

132 **be born thus."** Malcolm X, *The Autobiography of Malcolm X*, with Alex Haley (New York: Ballantine Books, 1992), p. 5.

132 **her dark complexion.** *Merriam-Webster*, s.v. "colorism," accessed January 21, 2022, https://www.merriam-webster.com/dictionary/colorism.

132 **and, yes, education.** Margaret Hunter, "The Consequences of Colorism," in *The Melanin Millennium: Skin Color as 21st Century International Discourse*, ed. Ronald E. Hall (Dordrecht: Springer, 2012), 247–56, https://doi.org/10.1007/978-94-007-4608-4_16; Margaret Hunter, "The Persistent Problem of Colorism: Skin Tone, Status, and Inequality," *Sociology Compass* 1, no. 1 (2007): 237–54, https://doi.org/10.1111/j.1751-9020.2007.00006.x;

Margaret L. Hunter, *Race, Gender, and the Politics of Skin Tone* (New York: Routledge, 2007).

132   **darker-skinned counterparts.** Margaret L. Hunter, "'If You're Light You're Alright': Light Skin Color as Social Capital for Women of Color," *Gender and Society* 16, no. 2 (2002): 175–93, http://www.jstor.org/stable /3081860.

132   **play in this.** Margaret Hunter, "Colorism in the Classroom: How Skin Tone Stratifies African American and Latina/o Students," *Theory into Practice* 55, no. 1 (2015): 54–61, https://doi.org/10.1080/00405841.2016.1119019. P. 54.

132   **of other characteristics."** Hunter, "Colorism in the Classroom," p. 56.

133   **favored, evaluated, *celebrated*.** Sean N. Talamas, Kenneth I. Mavor, David I. Perrett, "Blinded by Beauty: Attractiveness Bias and Accurate Perceptions of Academic Performance," PLoS ONE 11, no. 2 (2016): 1–18, https://doi.org/10.1371/journal.pone.0148284.

133   **[her] in academia."** Tressie McMillan Cottom, *Thick and Other Essays* (New York: New Press, 2019).

133   **an academic. Whew."** Tressie McMillan Cottom (@tressiemcphd), Twitter post, March 31, 2021, 12:14 p.m., https://twitter.com/tressiemcphd/status /1377338581832720385.

134   **for a conductor.** Pierre Bourdieu, *Outline of a Theory of Practice*, translated by Richard Nice, (Cambridge: Cambridge University Press, 1972, translation (1977).

134   **for science-related content.** Erika Delgado, "How a Movie Gig Inspired '13 Reasons Why' Star Derek Luke to Give Back through Hip-Hop," Showbiz CheatSheet, June 8, 2020, https://www.cheatsheet.com/entertainment /how-a-movie-gig-inspired-13-reasons-why-star-derek-luke-to-give-back -through-hip-hop.html/.

135   **at the time.** Candace King, "Beats, Rhymes, & Bunsen Burners: Using Hip Hop as Teaching Tool," NBC News, June 13, 2016, https://www.nbcnews .com/news/nbcblk/beats-rhymes-bunsen-burners-using-hip-hop-teaching -tool-n581646.

135   **senior Peter Simms.** King, "Beats, Rhymes, & Bunsen Burners: Using Hip Hop as Teaching Tool."

135   **Jamaica, and more.** "Science Genius," HipHopEd, accessed January 21, 2022, https://hiphoped.com/science-genius/; Mary Getaneh, "Hip-Hop Helping Calgary Students Get Schooled in Science," *Star*, May 31, 2018, https://www.thestar.com/calgary/2018/05/31/hip-hop-helping-calgary -students-get-schooled-in-science.html; "Science Genius Jamaica," JN Foundation, accessed January 21, 2022, https://www.jnfoundation.com /science-genius-jamaica/; "Hip Hop Education Turns Young Rapper into a Science Genius," HipHopEd, February 25, 2021, https://hiphoped.com/hip -hop-education-turns-young-rapper-into-a-science-genius/; Tina Khan, "*The Science Genius B.A.T.T.L.E.S.*: The Toronto Experience," in *#HipHopEd: The Compilation on Hip-Hop Education*, vol. 1, *Hip-Hop as Education,*

Philosophy, and Practice, ed. Christopher Emdin and Edmund Adjapong (Leiden: Brill, 2018), 66–73, https://doi.org/10.1163/9789004371873_009.

135 **success with them."** Gloria Ladson-Billings, "Culturally Relevant Pedagogy 2.0: a.k.a. the Remix," *Harvard Educational Review* 84, no. 1 (Spring 2014): 74–84, https://www.cue.pitt.edu/sites/default/files/images/Source%20 5%20-%20ladson-billings%20culturally%20relevant%20pedagogy%20 -%20the%20remix.pdf, p. 74.

135 **to the student."** Christopher Emdin, *For White Folks Who Teach in the Hood . . . and the Rest of Y'all Too: Reality Pedagogy and Urban Education* (Boston: Beacon, 2017), p. 206.

135 **of Black children.** Hines and Wilmot, "From Spirit-Murdering."

136 **lies within them."** Gholdy Muhammad, *Cultivating Genius: An Equity Framework for Culturally and Historically Responsive Literacy* (London: Scholastic, 2021), p. 14.

136 **was not evaluating."** Jill DiSanto, "Penn GSE Student Uses Humor to Create Change," Penn Today, April 2, 2012, https://penntoday.upenn.edu /news/penn-gse-student-uses-humor-create-change.

137 **more equitable one."** DiSanto, "Penn GSE Student."

137 **of young people.** "The Demands," BLM at School, accessed January 21, 2022, https://www.blacklivesmatteratschool.com/the-demands.html.

138 **Ainu (Indigenous people).** Ellie Cobb, "Japan's Forgotten Indigenous People," BBC, May 20, 2020, https://www.bbc.com/travel/article/20200519 -japans-forgotten-indigenous-people.

138 **and *kurokoge* (blackburn).** Joel Assogba, "Fighting against Racism/ Bullying and Promoting Diversity in Schools and Communities in Japan," in *Human Rights Education in Asia-Pacific* (Osaka: Asia-Pacific Human Rights Information Center, 2010), 1:156–70; For examples of "Japanese Only" signs on business establishments, see "The Rogues' Gallery," Debito.org, last updated April 2014, http://www.debito.org/roguesgallery.html.

138 **and institutionalized racism.** The *koseki* family registry system is a database of every Japanese household maintained by local governments, which includes an individual's age; date and place of birth and death; details about marriage, divorce, and adoption; and all previous addresses. The registry is used to verify citizenship status and allocate rights and benefits, such as national health insurance and public-school enrollment. In practice, anyone can access the koseki of others for a small fee, using it to trace people's backgrounds, and knowing a person's former address in a Burakumin neighborhood is enough to elicit stigma. In the context of employment and housing applications, and before marriage, results from a koseki search enable discrimination against those with ties to a racially marked community. And in recent years, the personal information of Burakumin people has been posted online to make harassment even easier. See "'There Is No Discrimination in Japan': Survey Results Show Statement Is Far from True," *Mainichi*, February 21, 2021, https://mainichi

.jp/english/articles/20210220/p2a/00m/0na/015000c; and FRANCE 24 English, "Japan's Pariah Descendants Fight Present-Day Discrimination," YouTube, February 2, 2017, video, 9:03, https://www.youtube.com/watch?v=upE7BNG5N1w.

138   **termed "stereotype lift."** Claude S. Fischer et al., *Inequality by Design: Cracking the Bell Curve Myth* (Princeton, NJ: Princeton University Press, 2021).

138   **mainstream Japanese schools.** Human Rights Association for Korean Residents in Japan, *Discrimination against Minority Children in Japan in the Provision of Educational Opportunities—Focusing on Children Attending Korean Schools in Japan* (Tokyo: Human Rights Association for Korean Residents in Japan, 2017), https://www.upr-info.org/sites/default/files/general-document/pdf/factsheet2_discrimination_against_minority_children_japan_2017.pdf.

139   **harassment and violence.** It is no wonder that racially stigmatized people in Japan who have the ability to camouflage their identity attempt to assimilate by using a *tsumei*, or "pass name." However, there is always the risk that their "impure" ethnic ancestry could come to light through official forms of state surveillance or through unofficial forms of online outing, such as the recent publication of addresses of Burakumin people intended to make discrimination more user-friendly. The Burakumin Liberation League has been working to get the list taken down, an action that might help mitigate harassment in the short term but doesn't address why many people in Japan, including children, are so invested in reinforcing racist hierarchies in the first place. See Human Rights Association for Korean Residents in Japan, *Discrimination against Minority Children.*

139   **contribution to make."** Assogba, "Fighting against Racism/Bullying," p. 169.

140   **his white laborers.** Gene L. Howard, *Death at Cross Plains: An Alabama Reconstruction Tragedy* (Tuscaloosa: University of Alabama Press, 2015).

140   **educational practices today.** Jarvis R. Givens, *Fugitive Pedagogy: Carter G. Woodson and the Art of Black Teaching* (Cambridge, MA: Harvard University Press 2021).

140   **them ironed out."** "Septima Clark," SNCC Digital Gateway, https://snccdigital.org/people/septima-clark/, accessed on February 15, 2022.

Chapter Four

Page

144   **canceling student debt.** You can learn more about the growing community of debtors organizing to cancel debts and build financial and political power on the Debt Collective website, https://debtcollective.org/.

144   **and disability accommodations.** Baby bonds are a "prospective policy aimed at endowing everybody at birth independent of their race, gender,

or other characteristic with at least a capital foundation," according to Darrick Hamilton. Pete Buttigieg, "The Deciding Decade: Professor Darrick Hamilton on 'Baby Bonds' and the Future of Our Economy Post-COVID," *Medium*, October 21, 2020, https://buttigieg.medium.com/the-deciding -decade-professor-darrick-hamilton-on-baby-bonds-and-the-future-of -our-economy-3e942848a566; Mark Paul, William Darity Jr., and Darrick Hamilton, "Why We Need a Federal Job Guarantee," *Jacobin*, February 4, 2017, https://www.jacobinmag.com/2017/02/federal-job-guarantee -universal-basic-income-investment-jobs-unemployment/.

144 **ancestors were enslaved.** William A. Darity and A. Kirsten Mullen, *From Here to Equality: Reparations for Black Americans in the Twenty-First Century* (Chapel Hill: University of North Carolina Press, 2020).

146 **Lyft, and Postmates.** Amir Khafagy, "Black Lives Matter on the Picket Line," *Discourse Blog*, August 27, 2020, https://discourseblog.substack.com /p/black-lives-matter-on-the-picket.

147 **of future employment.** Stephen Pegula and Matt Gunter, "Fatal Occupational Injuries to Independent Workers," U.S. Bureau of Labor Statistics, August 2019, https://www.bls.gov/opub/btn/volume-8/fatal -occupational-injuries-to-independent-workers.htm.

148 **professor Julia Ticona.** Julia Ticona, "Essential and Untrusted," *Dissent* (Fall 2020) https://www.dissentmagazine.org/article/essential-and-untrusted. Moreover, undocumented workers are often paid less for more strenuous or risky work compared with citizens and legal residents, because their employers can use their legal status against them. See Shannon Gleeson, *Precarious Claims: The Promise and Failure of Workplace Protections in the United States* (Oakland: University of California Press, 2017); Shannon Gleeson, *Conflicting Commitments: The Politics of Enforcing Immigrant Worker Rights in San Jose and Houston* (Ithaca, NY: ILR Press, 2013); and Rhacel Salazar Parreñas, *Servants of Globalization: Migration and Domestic Work* (Stanford, CA: Stanford University Press, 2015).

148 **types of work.** Julia Ticona, Alexandra Mateescu, and Alex Rosenblat, *Beyond Disruption: How Tech Shapes Labor across Domestic Work and Ridehailing* (New York: Data and Society, 2018).

148 **are "constantly watched."** "'We Were Constantly Watched. It Felt Like We Were in Prison,'" BBC, July 5, 2019, https://www.bbc.com/worklife /article/20190705-we-were-constantly-watched-it-felt-like-we-were-in -prison.

148 **of social control."** Ticona, "Essential and Untrusted"; Funda Ustek-Spilda et al., "COVID-19, the Gig Economy, and the Hunger for Surveillance," Ada Lovelace Institute, December 8, 2020, https://www.adalovelaceinstitute.org /blog/covid-19-gig-economy-hunger-for-surveillance/; see also, Simone Browne, *Dark Matters: On the Surveillance of Blackness* (Durham, NC: Duke University Press, 2015).

148 **by tech platforms.** Matthew Lavietes and Michael McCoy, "Waiting for Work: Pandemic Leaves U.S. Gig Workers Clamoring for Jobs," Reuters,

October 19, 2020, https://www.reuters.com/article/us-biggerpicture -health-coronavirus-gigw/waiting-for-work-pandemic-leaves-u-s-gig -workers-clamoring-for-jobs-idUSKBN2741DM.

149 **had fewer hours.** Srikanth Karra, "The Gig or Permanent Worker: Who Will Dominate the Post-pandemic Workforce?," *Forbes*, May 13, 2021, https://www.forbes.com/sites/forbeshumanresourcescouncil/2021/05/13 /the-gig-or-permanent-worker-who-will-dominate-the-post-pandemic -workforce/?sh=7c56b82b3cdc.

149 **all-time high).** "Uber Q2 Mobility Bookings Fell 75%, Delivery Bookings up 106%," Yahoo Sports, August 6, 2020, https://sports.yahoo.com/uber-q2 -mobility-bookings-fell-211939551.html.

149 **grocery store themselves.** Lavietes and McCoy, "Waiting for Work."

149 **money they make.** Lavietes and McCoy, "Waiting for Work."

150 **first and foremost.** Ticona, Mateescu, and Rosenblat, *Beyond Disruption*, p. 45.

150 **potential wage theft."** Ticona, Mateescu, and Rosenblat, *Beyond Disruption*, p. 46.

150 **solve collective problems."** Ticona, Mateescu, and Rosenblat, p. 7.

150 **rating, and more.** Eliza Levinson, "Meet the Gig Workers Collective: 11 Women Who Organize Nationwide Strikes but Have Never Met," *Next City*, May 21, 2020, https://nextcity.org/urbanist-news/meet-gig-workers -collective-11-women-organize-nationwide-strikes-never-met.

151 **among other things.** Levinson, "Meet the Gig Workers Collective."

151 **improve working conditions."** "About NLRB," National Labor Relations Board, accessed January 24, 2022, https://www.nlrb.gov/resources/faq/nlrb.

151 **and worker compensation.** Tina Bellon, "Uber, Lyft Spend Big in California to Oppose Even Costlier Gig-Worker Law," Reuters, October 5, 2020, https://www.reuters.com/article/uber-california/uber-lyft-spend-big-in -california-to-oppose-even-costlier-gig-worker-law-idUSKBN26Q2LX.

151 **the United States.** Gig Workers Collective, "Proposition 22," Medium, November 4, 2020, https://gigworkerscollective.medium.com/proposition -22-c5927b11e599.

151 **as contract workers.** Rebecca Lake, "California Assembly Bill 5 (AB5)," Investopedia, August 29, 2021, https://www.investopedia.com/california -assembly-bill-5-ab5-4773201.

151 **business in California.** Gig Workers Collective, "Proposition 22."

152 **discuss with riders.** Tom Spiggle, "Gig Workers as Employees: Why America Won't Follow the U.K. Anytime Soon," *Forbes*, February 26, 2021, https:// www.forbes.com/sites/tomspiggle/2021/02/26/gig-workers-as-employees -why-america-wont-follow-the-uk-anytime-soon/?sh=fb8576a1db85.

152 **misclassified as self-employed.** Jennifer Rankin, "Gig Economy Workers to Get Employee Rights under EU Proposals," *Guardian*, December 9, 2021, https://www.theguardian.com/business/2021/dec/09/gig-economy -workers-to-get-employee-rights-under-eu-proposals.

152   **basic legal rights.** Bama Athreya, "Gig Workers Are in the Driver's Seat in Europe. Is There Hope for the US?" December 13, 2021, https://inequality .org/research/gig-workers-rights-europe.

152   **in the U.S.** Dough Mann, "The University as Feudal State: The Abysmal Failure of Interdisciplinarity in Higher Education," Western University, accessed January 24, 2022, https://publish.uwo.ca/~dmann/feudal.htm.

153   **observer put it.** Mann, "The University as Feudal State."

153   **in his fiefdom.** Mann, "The University as Feudal State."

153   **among other things.** One of the most pressing areas of concern, which was laid bare during the pandemic, is how disability is routinely ignored and dismissed in most workplaces, including academia. Seemingly overnight, massive, institution-wide accommodations were put in place so that students, faculty, and staff could work remotely during the pandemic— accommodations that disabled people have long advocated for. Only after the pandemic put schools at risk of closure did employers make an institution-wide shift. And still the shift was marked by a demand for productivity and compliance regardless of circumstances. The ableism of academia affects adjunct professors especially hard because, rather than lose contract work, they will be forced to return to campus.

154   **or ethical violations.** "Tenure," American Association of University Professors, accessed January 24, 2022, https://www.aaup.org/issues /tenure.

155   **publisher Walter Hussman.** Haleluya Hadero, Glenn Gamboa, and Associated Press, "Backed by $20 Million in Donations, Nikole Hannah-Jones Establishes Her Future at Howard," *Fortune*, July 17, 2021, https://fortune .com/2021/07/07/nikole-hannah-jones-20-million-donation-philanthropic -journalism-howard/; Brooke Cain, "Hussman's Letter to UNC Chancellor on Nikole Hannah-Jones Tenure Debate," *News and Observer*, July 16, 2020, https://www.newsobserver.com/news/local/education/article252789883 .html.

155   **up as well."** Laurel Wamsley, "After Tenure Controversy, Nikole Hannah-Jones Will Join Howard Faculty Instead of UNC," NPR, July 6, 2021, https:// www.npr.org/2021/07/06/1013315775/after-tenure-controversy-nikole -hannah-jones-will-join-howard-faculty-instead-of.

156   **Washington, DC, earns.** Imani Light, "An Open Letter to Nikole Hannah-Jones from a Howard Faculty Member," Medium, July 12, 2021, https:// howardprof.medium.com/an-open-letter-to-nikole-hannah-jones-from-a -howard-faculty-member-ad1fb3f9c05b.

156   **goodbye," explains Light.** Light, "An Open Letter to Nikole Hannah-Jones."

156   **and collective bargaining."** Light, "An Open Letter to Nikole Hannah-Jones."

157   **observer put it.** Laura Finley, "Adjunct Professors and Worker's Rights," *CounterPunch* July 27, 2015, https://www.counterpunch.org/2015/07/27 /adjunct-professors-and-workers-rights.

157   **on the table.** Light, "An Open Letter to Nikole Hannah-Jones."

157 **since the 1980s.** This injustice has ripple effects because professors who are deciding between buying food and buying medicine would reasonably find it difficult to provide the best instruction for students, and a lecturer whose contract is not renewed would not be available to mentor or write recommendation letters for their students the following year. Justice for adjuncts in the form of well-paying, stable employment would directly benefit students and families who are paying more and more each year in tuition. But even without this win-win scenario, they deserve better.

157 **and livable wage.** Adam Andrzejewski, "Ballooning Ivy League Endowment Forecasted to Top $1 Trillion by 2048," *Forbes*, October 31, 2021, https://www .forbes.com/sites/adamandrzejewski/2021/10/31/ballooning-ivy-league -endowment-forecasted-to-top-1-trillion-by-2048/?sh=1c1c052c3a37.

157 *to live on?* Alissa Quart, "Professors Are Selling Their Plasma to Pay Bills. Let's Hold Colleges' Feet to the Fire," *Guardian*, November 27, 2018, https:// www.theguardian.com/inequality/2018/nov/27/professors-are-selling-their -plasma-to-pay-bills-lets-hold-colleges-feet-to-the-fire?CMP=share_btn_tw.

157 **paid wage laborers."** Hadas Thier, "The Working Class Is the Vast Majority of Society," *Jacobin*, September 13, 2020, https://jacobinmag.com/2020/09 /working-class-peoples-guide-capitalism-marxist-economics.

157 **guilty as hell.** A report by the American Federation of Teachers, *An Army of Temps*, confirms that many adjunct lecturers make less than $3,500 a course and are thus forced to teach at multiple institutions, take on many more classes than they can manage, or supplement their income with other work to piece together a subsistence living. Even then, a quarter of contingent faculty rely on public assistance and 40 percent, according to the report, struggle to make ends meet. See Colleen Flaherty, "Barely Getting By," *Inside Higher Ed*, April 20, 2020, https://www.insidehighered.com/news/2020/04/20/new -report-says-many-adjuncts-make-less-3500-course-and-25000-year.

157 **already existing inequities."** Laura Krantz, "In Higher Education, the Pandemic Has Been Especially Cruel to Adjunct Professors," *Boston Globe*, September 20, 2020, https://www.bostonglobe.com/2020/09/20/metro /pandemic-deepens-great-divide-academia/; Emily Chua, "POV: BU Should Go Fully Online This Fall," *BU Today*, July 9, 2020, https://www.bu .edu/articles/2020/why-bu-should-go-fully-online-this-fall/.

158 **staff in Canada.** *In Search of Professor Precarious*" (2020), directed by Gerry Potter, Red Heeler Media, https://professorprecarious.com.

158 **of college instructors.** "Facts about Adjuncts," New Faculty Majority, accessed January 24, 2022, https://www.newfacultymajority.info/facts -about-adjuncts/.

158 **professional development funds.** "Our Impact," SEIU Faculty Forward, accessed January 24, 2022, http://seiufacultyforward.org/faculty/our -impact/.

158 **position in jeopardy.** BU Today Staff, "Part-Time Faculty Will Vote on Unionization in January," *BU Today*, November 17, 2014, http://www.bu .edu/articles/2014/part-time-faculty-will-vote-on-unionization-in-january.

158   **children's *learning* conditions.** Diane Ravitch, "Did Albert Shanker Say That?," May 30, 2012, https://dianeravitch.net/2012/05/30/did-albert -shanker-say-that; Also, the Delphi Project on the Changing Faculty and Student Success addresses the fundamental shift in the American academic workforce from tenurable to contingent faculty and focuses on the effects of that shift on student learning. See "The Delphi Project on the Changing Faculty and Student Success," Pullias Center for Higher Education, University of Southern California, accessed January 24, 2022, http://pullias .usc.edu/delphi/; and Eric Hirsch and Scott Emerick, *Teaching Working Conditions Are Student Learning Conditions: A Report on the 2006 North Carolina Teacher Working Conditions Survey* (Chapel Hill, NC: Center for Teacher Quality, 2007), https://eric.ed.gov/?id=ED498770.

159   **in the *Guardian*.** Claire Sosienski Smith, "As Students, We Support Our Striking Lecturers in Their Fight for Education," *Guardian*, February 20, 2020, https://www.theguardian.com/education/2020/feb/20/as-students -we-support-our-striking-lecturers-in-their-fight-for-education.

159   **not fully secure.** "I and all my tenured colleagues received notice this evening that our employment is being terminated as of June 30, 2023. There was no warning. 'Financial constraints' of course," tweeted a professor of Hebrew scriptures at St. Andrew's College in Saskatoon, Canada. Christine Mitchell (@CMitchellSask), Twitter post, March 3, 2021, 7:30 p.m., https:// twitter.com/CMitchellSask/status/1367316587095597057. In New Jersey, tenured faculty at Centenary University were let go in 2019, including the president and vice president of the faculty union, leading them to sue the institution for wrongful termination. See Lori Comstock, "Centenary University Sued by Professors Who Say They Were 'Illegally Targeted' by School," *New Jersey Herald*, February 8, 2021, https://www.njherald.com /story/news/local/2021/02/08/centenary-university-sued-by-professors -say-dismissals-violated-tenure/4439554001/.

159   **to replace them.** As one observer put it, "Academics don't want tenure because they think they're better or smarter than you. Academics, whether they have it or not, want some form of tenure to exist to protect the integrity of the knowledge that is produced, preserved, and disseminated . . . If professors are not protected from disagreeing with the agenda of their 'bosses'—whether that be Dow Chemical, Gov. Walker, or President Trump—the consequences will go far beyond one person's paycheck." Rebecca Schuman, "The End of Research in Wisconsin," *Slate*, March 21, 2016, https://slate.com/human-interest/2016/03/university-of-wisconsin -and-the-aftermath-of-destroying-professor-tenure.html.

159   **maddeningly vague criteria."** Schuman, "The End of Research in Wisconsin."

159   **degrades us all."** "Our Mission," Tenure for the Common Good, accessed January 24, 2022, https://tenureforthecommongood.org.

159   **hiring and employment."** "What We Do," Tenure for the Common Good, accessed January 24, 2022, https://tenureforthecommongood.org /initiatives.

160   **lucrative 'shelter' economy."** Davarian L. Baldwin, *In the Shadow of the Ivory Tower: How Universities Are Plundering Our Cities* (New York: Bold Type Books, 2021), p. 13.

160   **the Ivory Tower."** Baldwin, *In the Shadow of the Ivory Tower.*

161   **and fire services.** At the time, Princeton was paying approximately $11 million in property taxes, and the lawyer representing the residents said that "Princeton's tax bill would be in the $30–40 million range if it paid taxes on all of its property." Rick Seltzer, "Deferring a Key Battle for Wealthy Universities," *Inside Higher Ed*, October 21, 2016, https://www.insidehighered.com/news/2016/10/21/princeton-settlement-leaves-door-open-future-tax-exemption-challenges; Kate King, "Princeton University Settles Tax Suit Filed by Local Homeowners," *Wall Street Journal*, October 17, 2016, https://www.wsj.com/articles/princeton-university-settles-tax-suit-filed-by-local-homeowners-1476742298.

161   **provide government services.** Elaine S. Povich, "Princeton Settles Nonprofit Property Tax Suit for $18 Million," Pew Charitable Trusts, https://www.pewtrusts.org/en/research-and-analysis/blogs/stateline/2016/10/17/princeton-settles-nonprofit-property-tax-suit-for-18-million.

161   **in commercial royalties."** Baldwin, *In the Shadow of the Ivory Tower*, p. 13.

161   **a profit-making entity.** Elise Young, "Princeton's Neighbors Say to Heck with Freebies—We Want Cash," Bloomberg, May 2, 2016, https://www.bloomberg.com/news/articles/2016-05-02/princeton-s-neighbors-say-to-heck-with-freebies-we-want-cash.

161   **underfunding public institutions.** Maddie Hanna, "Penn Professors Call for University to Pay Taxes to Support Philly Schools," *Philadelphia Inquirer*, July 8, 2020, https://www.inquirer.com/education/university-of-pennsylvania-pilot-taxes-schools-petition-20200708.html; Penn for PILOTs, homepage, accessed January 24, 2022, https://www.pennforpilots.org.

162   **to the city."** Baldwin, *In the Shadow*, p. 205.

162   **in an Uber?"** Aliya Ram, personal correspondence with author, July 22, 2021.

163   **the multi-conglomerate corporation."** Iordanis Passas, "Graphic Designers Have Always Loved Minimalism. But at What Cost?," Iordanis Passas Design, accessed January 24, 2022, https://ipassas.com/graphic_design_and_typography/graphic-designers-have-always-loved-minimalism-but-at-what-cost/; see also Kyle Chayka, *The Longing for Less: Living with Minimalism* (New York: Bloomsbury Publishing, 2020).

163   **the holiday season.** Michael Sainato, "'We Are Not Robots': Amazon Warehouse Employees Push to Unionize," *Guardian*, January 1, 2019, https://www.theguardian.com/technology/2019/jan/01/amazon-fulfillment-center-warehouse-employees-union-new-york-minnesota.

163   **of racial capitalism.** Matthew Gault, "Amazon Introduces Tiny 'ZenBooths' for Stressed-Out Warehouse Workers," *Vice*, May 27, 2021, https://www.vice

.com/amp/en/article/wx5nmw/amazon-introduces-tiny-zenbooths-for
-stressed-out-warehouse-workers?__twitter_impression=true.

163 **the warehouse floor.** Nantina Vgontzas, "Toward Degrowth: Worker
Power, Surveillance Abolition, and Climate Justice at Amazon," *New Global
Studies* (2021), 1–26. SSRN: https://ssrn.com/abstract=3981869, accessed
August 9, 2021.

164 **just a warning.** Spencer Soper, Michael Tobin, and Michael Smith,
"'Keep Driving': Amazon Dispatcher Texts Show Chaos amid Twisters,"
Bloomberg, December 16, 2021, https://www.bloomberg.com/news
/features/2021-12-17/amazon-tornado-aftermath-workers-say-they-lacked
-emergency-training.

164 **their fulfillment centers.** Sainato, "'We Are Not Robots.'"

164 **amount of time."** Frances Wallace, "Interview with Bessemer Amazon
Worker: 'It Feels the Same as Most of the BLM Protests," interview by Left
Voice, March 27, 2021, video, 21:14, https://www.youtube.com/watch?v
=5mZZSnk1Bl0.

165 **said Frances Wallace.** Wallace, "Interview with Bessemer Amazon Worker."

166 **comfortable in life."** "It just feels like they'll work you to death if they
can . . . They don't actually care about anything but getting their product
out. They don't care about anything but making their money . . . Amazon
hires so many people on each week, that they just think, *Oh, well, if you leave,
we can just find somebody to replace you.* And so they find no value in their
actual workers." Wallace, "Interview with Bessemer Amazon Worker."

166 **the internal battery."** Gault, "Amazon Introduces Tiny 'ZenBooths.'"

166 **humans, not robots."** Sainato, "'We Are Not Robots.'"

166 **labor" or "servitude."** Benjamin, *Race After Technology*, p. 55.

166 **Amazon computer screen?"** Gault, "Amazon Introduces Tiny
'ZenBooths.'"

167 **for operations employees."** Amazon Staff, "Meet Employees behind
Amazon's New Health and Wellness Program," Amazon, May 17, 2021,
https://www.aboutamazon.com/news/workplace/meet-employees-behind
-amazons-new-health-and-wellness-program.

167 **lives back #WorkingClassSolidarity.** @decolonizethisplace, "That's why
no bosses • no landlords • no prisons • no borders," Instagram post, July 10,
2021, https://www.instagram.com/p/CRJt0cighuB/?utm_medium=copy
_link.

168 **"*artificial* artificial intelligence."** M. Six Silberman and Lilly Irani,
"Operating an Employer Reputation System: Lessons from Turkopticon,
2008–2015," *Comparative Labor Law and Policy Journal*, vol 37, 3 (2016):
pp.505–542, available at: https://wtf.tw/pubs/silberman_irani_2016
_operating_an_employer_reputation_system_preprint.pdf.

168 **do those tasks."** Lilly C. Irani and M. Six Silberman, "Turkopticon:
Interrupting Worker Invisibility in Amazon Mechanical Turk," in *CHI
'13: Proceedings of the SIGCHI Conference on Human Factors in Computing*

Systems (New York: Association for Computing Machinery, 2013), 611–20, p.612. https://doi.org/10.1145/2470654.2470742.

168 **on the platform.** Silberman and Irani, "Operating an Employer Reputation System," p. 506.

168 **~$2 an hour."** Kotaro Haro et al., "A Data-Driven Analysis of Workers' Earnings on Amazon Mechanical Turk," in *CHI '18: Proceedings of the 2018 CHI Conference on Human Factors in Computing Systems* (New York: Association for Computing Machinery, 2018), 1–14, https://doi.org/10.1145/3173574.3174023; p. 1; see also Mary L. Gray and Siddharth Suri, *Ghost Work: How to Stop Silicon Valley from Building a New Global Underclass* (Boston: Houghton Mifflin Harcourt, 2019); Sarah T. Roberts, *Behind the Screen: Content Moderation in the Shadows of Social Media* (New Haven, CT: Yale University Press, 2019).

168 **behind a screen.** Jaron Lanier, *Who Owns the Future?* (New York: Simon and Schuster, 2014), p. 177.

168 **collaboration with Turkers.** Irani and Silberman, "Turkopticon."

168 **seems to be."** "About," Turkopticon, accessed January 24, 2022, https://turkopticon.net; "About Us," Turkopticon, accessed January 24, 2022, https://blog.turkopticon.net.

169 **level of communicativeness.** Irani and Silberman, "Turkopticon," p. 614.

169 **'neutral' or 'bad.'"** Silberman and Irani, "Operating an Employer Reputation System."

169 **harassment and abuse.** Silberman and Irani, "Operating an Employer Reputation System."

169 **before his murder.** "Since emancipation, racism has underwritten black economic hardship. That hardship is expressed through the concentration of African-Americans in low-wage jobs—many of which are now ironically designated 'essential.'" Keeanga-Yamahtta Taylor, "The Black Plague," *New Yorker*, April 16, 2020, https://www.newyorker.com/news/our-columnists/the-black-plague.

170 **with our kids."** Khafagy, "Black Lives Matter."

170 **a labor dispute.** "The practice of using convict labor to break strikes dates back to the early 1890s when mine owners attempted to subvert striking mineworkers' union efforts during the Coal Creek Wars in eastern Tennessee. The mine owners replaced the striking miners with convict laborers leased out by the Tennessee state prison system. Enraged, striking miners attacked the state prison stockades, freed hundreds of prison laborers, and set mine properties ablaze. The conflict led the Tennessee state government to abolish its convict leasing system—making Tennessee the first southern state to end the practice, in 1894." Khafagy, "Black Lives Matter."

171 **make ends meet.** "How I learned to be a better boss: I was a bad CEO. 7 years ago, I found a McDonald's training handbook on the desk of an employee named Rosita. Turns out she was training to become a manager there because she couldn't survive on the income I paid here. I called her to my office . . ." Dan Price (@DanPriceSeattle), Twitter post, July 29, 2021, 4:24 p.m., https://twitter.com/DanPriceSeattle/status/1420842784853012480.

171 **on social media.** Paul Keegan, "Here's What Really Happened at That Company That Set a $70,000 Minimum Wage," *Inc*, November 2015, https://www.inc.com /magazine/201511/paul-keegan/does-more-pay-mean-more-growth.html.

171 **going to fail."** Carla Sinclair, "CEO Gets the Last Laugh after Fox News Called Him a 'Lunatic' for Paying All Employees $70k," *BoingBoing*, April 14, 2021, https://boingboing.net/2021/04/14/ceo-gets-the-last-laugh-after-fox -news-called-him-a-lunatic-for-paying-all-employees-70k.html, accessed February 12, 2022.

171 **to 95 percent.** Keegan, "Here's What Really Happened."

171 **have remained stagnant.** WTF Happened in 1971?, homepage, accessed January 24, 2022, https://wtfhappenedin1971.com/.

171 **system is fair?"** Dan Price (@DanPriceSeattle), Twitter post, July 7, 2021, 1:35 p.m., https://twitter.com/DanPriceSeattle/status/1412872800847683591.

171 **$0 in taxes."** Dan Price (@DanPriceSeattle), Twitter post, July 12, 2021, 8:38 p.m., https://twitter.com/danpriceseattle/status/1414791218697998341. Also see Dan Price (@DanPriceSeattle), "Remember kids: if you study hard, get good grades, go to a good college, get a job, work hard, never take a sick day, live within your means and do what you're told . . . then one day your boss might go to space," Twitter post, July 11, 2021, 5:20 p.m., https://twitter .com/danpriceseattle/status/1414379001334976517.

172 **than any CEO.** Dan Price (@DanPriceSeattle), Twitter post, July 7, 2021, 12:33 p.m., https://twitter.com/DanPriceSeattle/status/1412812058610044929.

172 **factory in Vietnam."** Keegan, "Here's What Really Happened."

172 **the "wage bomb."** Keegan, "Here's What Really Happened."

173 **a flourishing life."** Erik Olin Wright, *How to Be an Anticapitalist in the Twenty-First Century* (London: Verso Books, 2019), p. 10.

173 **and society overall."** "About Us," Cooperation Jackson, accessed January 24, 2022, https://cooperationjackson.org/intro.

173 **in Black Jackson.** patricia torres (@la_pati), "A Brief Black History of Cooperatives," Instagram post, December 21, 2020, https://www.instagram .com/p/CJE7H42gZQl/?igshid=1fan4c7puewz4.

173 **things," reflected Akuno.** "Mutual Aid: Building Communities of Care during Crisis and Beyond," virtual panel discussion, May 22, 2020, video, 1:36:55, https://www.youtube.com/watch?v=ZTVLYPdF0x0.

173 **that looks like."** *American Climate Rebels*, episode 11, "Cooperation Jackson: Building a Social and Solidarity Economy," aired September 10, 2018, on ReelNews, https://www.youtube.com/watch?v=_Nt9Z2P7mPY&t=1807s.

174 **of our ancestors.** *Farming While Black: Soul Fire Farm's Practical Guide to Liberation on the Land* (White River Junction, VT: Chelsea Green Publishing, 2018), p. 7–8.

174 **of service hours).** Kali Akuno, "Building a Solidarity Economy," Cooperation Jackson, October 10, 2019, https://cooperationjackson.org/blog/2019 /10/10/building-a-solidarity-economy-in-jackson-mississippi.

175 **wasteful mega-developments . . . ?"** Daniel Wortel-London, "The Tax Trap," *Dissent*, (Winter 2021) https://www.dissentmagazine.org/article/the-tax-trap.

175 **a job guarantee.** "By subsidizing and creating jobs around green energy and transit, we can begin to shift our economy off its current earth-destroying path. By serving as a generous employer of last resort, the government can also bolster the wage floor, shop conditions, and bargaining power of every worker." Wortel-London, "The Tax Trap."

175 **say in spending.** "What Is PB?," Participatory Budgeting Project, accessed January 24, 2022, https://www.participatorybudgeting.org/what-is-pb/.

175 **over eight years.** Brian Wampler and Mike Touchton, "Brazil Let Its Citizens Make Decisions about City Budgets. Here's What Happened," *Washington Post*, January 22, 2014, https://www.washingtonpost.com/news/monkey -cage/wp/2014/01/22/brazil-let-its-citizens-make-decisions-about-city -budgets-heres-what-happened/.

175 **and other institutions."** "What Is PB?," Participatory Budgeting Project.

175 **people in China.** Will Flagle, "Participatory Budgeting," Next System Project, June 11, 2019, https://thenextsystem.org/learn/stories/participatory -budgeting.

175 **involving 402,000 participants.** "PB's Impacts," Participatory Budgeting Project, accessed January 24, 2022, https://www.participatorybudgeting .org/impacts/.

176 **running the show.** Tressie McMillan Cottom, "The Hustle Economy," *Dissent*, (Fall 2020), https://www.dissentmagazine.org/article/the-hustle -economy.

176 **more ragtag upstarts.** Moises Mendez II, "'Wish I Could Unsee Every Second of This': People Can't Believe This 16-Person 'Entrepreneur House' in NYC," Daily Dot, July 9, 2021, https://www.dailydot.com/unclick/16 -person-entrepreneur-house-new-york-city-tiktok/.

176 **organizers, put it.** Cache McClay, "Why Black TikTok Creators Have Gone on Strike," BBC, July 15, 2021, https://www.bbc.com/news/world -us-canada-57841055.

177 **songs go viral.** Alessandro Bogliari, "Four Ways Influencers Can Make Money on TikTok," *Forbes*, June 19, 2019, https://www.forbes.com/sites /forbesagencycouncil/2019/06/19/four-ways-influencers-can-make -money-on-tiktok/?sh=d1d8fa919ea5.

177 **for the fund.** Kaitlyn Wylde, "How the TikTok Creator Fund Works, According to Users," *Bustle*, October 23, 2020, https://www.bustle.com/life /how-tiktok-creator-fund-works-users.

177 **supported the strike.** McClay, "Why Black TikTok Creators."

178 **greater Atlanta area.** McClay, "Why Black TikTok Creators."

178 **of these things."** Sharon Pruitt-Young, "Black TikTok Creators Are on Strike to Protest a Lack of Credit for Their Work," NPR, July 1, 2021, https:// www.npr.org/2021/07/01/1011899328/black-tiktok-creators-are-on-strike -to-protest-a-lack-of-credit-for-their-work; Sarah J. Jackson, Moya Bailey, and Brooke Foucault Welles, *#HashtagActivism: Networks of Race and Gender Justice* (Cambridge, MA: MIT Press, 2020); Radhika Gajjala and Yeon Ju Oh, eds., *Cyberfeminism 2.0* (New York: Peter Lang, 2012).

178   **by the harvesters.**" Deanna MacDonald, "Jean-François Millet: *The Gleaners*—1857," Great Works of Western Art, accessed January 24, 2022, http://www.worldsbestpaintings.net/artistsandpaintings/painting/103/.

178   **movement was spreading.** *The Gleaners*, Wikipedia, last edited January 21, 2022, https://en.wikipedia.org/wiki/The_Gleaners.

179   **smokes a cigarette.** "*Agency Job*, Banksy," WikiArt, added February 1, 2017, https://www.wikiart.org/en/banksy/agency-job.

179   **by Western values.**" Mikeisha Dache Vaughn, "Rest as Resistance: Why Nap Ministry and Others Want Black People to Sleep," Yahoo Money, May 20, 2021, https://money.yahoo.com/rest-resistance-why-nap-ministry-194500712.html.

180   **sake of it.** Vaughn, "Rest as Resistance."

Chapter Five

Page

184   **the parking lot.** Jason Braverman, "Formerly Known as 'Murder' Kroger, Brand New '725 Ponce' Kroger Set to Open This Week," 11 Alive, October 14, 2019, https://conifer.rhizome.org/Biosthmors/murder-kroger/20191016130013/; https://www.11alive.com/article/news/local/725-ponce-kroger-murder-kroger-beltline-atlanta/85-3ffe37fc-2850-43e4-ac5c-598539a5d790.

184   **store's nickname endure.** Dan Whisenhunt, "With Second Reboot Kroger on Beltline Looks to Shed 'Murder' from Store's Moniker," Decaturish, October 15, 2019, https://decaturish.com/2019/10/with-second-reboot-kroger-on-beltline-looks-to-shed-murder-from-stores-moniker/.

185   **cannot live within**"? James Baldwin. *The Fire Next Time.* (New York: The Modern Library, 2021 [1962]), p. 78.

186   **daring and growth.** Baldwin, *The Fire Next Time*, p. 78.

186   **how to learn.**" Toni Morrison, *Paradise* (New York: Knopf, 1998), pp. 141–42.

186   **but not exposed.** Over time, I have even come to think of love as a kind of technology that we exert, not only feel: "the unique power that bindeth together the divers elements of this material world, the supreme magnetic force that directeth the movements of the spheres in the celestial realms." 'Abdu'l-Bahá, *Selections from the Writings of 'Abdu'l-Bahá*, accessed February 13, 2022: https://www.bahai.org/library/authoritative-texts/abdul-baha/selections-writings-abdul-baha.

186   **in the air.** Even as late as 2005, *Time* magazine ran a story with the headline "Children Having Children: Teen Pregnancies Are Corroding America's Social Fabric." Claudia Wallis, "Children Having Children: Teen Pregnancies Are Corroding American's Social Fabric," *Time*, June 21, 2005, http://content.time.com/time/subscriber/article/0,33009,1074861,00.html.

186   **were clamoring about.** Kristin Luker, *Dubious Conceptions: The Politics of Teenage Pregnancy* (Cambridge, MA: Harvard University Press, 1996).

187 **of these facts.** Gene Demby, "Making the Case That Discrimination Is Bad for Your Health," NPR, January 14, 2018, https://www.npr.org/sections /codeswitch/2018/01/14/577664626/making-the-case-that-discrimination -is-bad-for-your-health.

187 **we're upset about.** Toni Morrison, "The Pain of Being Black," interview by Bonnie Angelo, *Time*, May 22, 1989, http://content.time.com/time /magazine/article/0,9171,957724,00.html.

188 **of Black womanhood.** Deirdre Clemente, *Dress Casual: How College Students Redefined American Style* (Chapel Hill: University of North Carolina Press, 2016).

188 **Spelman's "puritanical atmosphere."** David Bradley, "Novelist Alice Walker Telling the Black Woman's Story," *New York Times*, January 8, 1984, https://archive.nytimes.com/www.nytimes.com/books/98/10/04/specials /walker-story.html.

190 **income and education.** Jamila Taylor et al., *Eliminating Racial Disparities in Maternal and Infant Mortality* (Washington, DC: Center for American Progress, 2019); Michael R. Kramer et al., "Preconceptional Stress and Racial Disparities in Preterm Birth: An Overview," *Acta Obstetricia et Gynecologica Scandinavica* 90, no. 12 (2011): 1307–16, https://doi.org/10.1111/j.1600-0412 .2011.01136.x; Emma Kasprzak, "Why Are Black Mothers at More Risk of Dying?," BBC, April 12, 2019, https://www.bbc.com/news/uk-england -47115305.

190 **graduate high school.** Samuel H. Fishman et al., "Race/Ethnicity, Maternal Educational Attainment, and Infant Mortality in the United States," *Biodemography and Social Biology* 66, no. 1 (2020): 1–26, https:// doi.org/10.1080/19485565.2020.1793659, p. 1. As anthroplogist Dána-Ain Davis notes, "[T]he distance between poor, low-income, and middle-class and professional Black women's birth outcomes is a short one. The class structure in US society is ostensibly a strategy for accessing sets of privilege that supposedly transcend race and racism. Of course, we know that is not the case." Dána-Ain Davis, *Reproductive Injustice: Racism, Pregnancy, and Premature Birth* (New York: NYU Press, 2019), p. 202.

190 **would have died.** "The nurse thought her pain medicine might be making her confused. But Serena insisted, and soon enough a doctor was performing an ultrasound of her legs. 'I was like, a Doppler? I told you, I need a CT scan and a heparin drip,' she remembers telling the team. The ultrasound revealed nothing, so they sent her for the CT, and sure enough, several small blood clots had settled in her lungs. Minutes later she was on the drip. 'I was like, listen to Dr. Williams!'" Rob Haskell, "Serena Williams on Motherhood, Marriage, and Making Her Comeback," *Vogue*, January 10, 2018, https:// www.vogue.com/article/serena-williams-vogue-cover-interview-february -2018.

190 **synonym for pain."** Jennifer C. Nash, *Birthing Black Mothers* (Durham, NC: Duke University Press, 2021), p. 4.

190 **to obstetric violence.** Jennifer C. Nash, *Birthing Black Mothers* (Durham, NC: Duke University Press, 2021), p. 4; Khiara M. Bridges, *Reproducing Race: An Ethnography of Pregnancy as a Site of Racialization* (Berkeley: University of California Press, 2011).

190 **people and babies.** According to practicing midwives P. Mimi Niles and Michelle Drew, "Midwifery is one of the most ancient of traditions and professions in the world, with roots that can be traced back to the healing traditions of Babylonia, Egypt, Ancient Greece, Vedic India, and the Aztecs." P. Mimi Niles and Michelle Drew, "Constructing the Modern American Midwife: White Supremacy and White Feminism Collide," *Nursing Clio* (blog), October 22, 2020, https://nursingclio.org/2020/10/22/constructing-the -modern-american-midwife-white-supremacy-and-white-feminism-collide/.

191 **thrive in life?"** Serena Williams, "Serena Williams: What My Life-Threatening Experience Taught Me about Giving Birth," CNN, February 20, 2018, https://www.cnn.com/2018/02/20/opinions/protect-mother-pregnancy -williams-opinion/index.html.

191 **impact one another."** "Reproductive Justice," SisterSong, accessed January 25, 2022, https://www.sistersong.net/reproductive-justice; Laura Briggs, *How All Politics Became Reproductive Politics: From Welfare Reform to Foreclosure to Trump* (Oakland: University of California Press, 2018).

191 **schedule takes priority.** Steven L. Clark et al., "Association of Obstetric Intervention with Temporal Patterns of Childbirth," *Obstetrics and Gynecology* 124, no. 5 (2014): 873–80, https://doi.org/10.1097/aog.00000000000 00485.

192 **considered major surgery.** Erin Johnson and M. Marit Rehavi, "Physicians Treating Physicians: Information and Incentives in Childbirth" *American Economic Journal: Economic Policy* 8, no. 1 (2016): 115–141, DOI: 10.1257/ pol.20140160. Emily Oster and W. Spencer McClelland, "Why the C-Section Rate Is So High," *Atlantic*, October 17, 2019, https://www.theatlantic.com /ideas/archive/2019/10/c-section-rate-high/600172/.

192 **funded healthcare systems.** Luz Gibbons et al., *The Global Numbers and Costs of Additionally Needed and Unnecessary Caesarean Sections Performed per Year: Overuse as a Barrier to Universal Coverage* (Geneva: World Health Organization, 2010).

192 **capita on healthcare.** Roosa Tikkanen and Melinda K. Abrams, "U.S. Health Care from a Global Perspective, 2019: Higher Spending, Worse Outcomes?," Commonwealth Fund, January 30, 2020, https://www.commonwealthfund .org/publications/issue-briefs/2020/jan/us-health-care-global-perspective -2019.

192 **for preventable causes.** Tikkanen and Abrams, "U.S. health Care."

192 **C-sections went down.** Katy B. Kozhimannil et al., "Cesarean Delivery Rates and Costs of Childbirth in a State Medicaid Program after Implementation of a Blended Payment Policy," *Medical Care* 56, no. 8 (2018): 658–64, https:// doi.org/10.1097/mlr.0000000000000937.

192 **to elect surgery.** Johnson and Rehavi, "Physicians Treating Physicians."

192 **economist Erin Johnson.** Shankar Vedantam, "Money May Be Motivating Doctors to Do More C-Sections," NPR, August 30, 2013, https://www.npr.org /sections/health-shots/2013/08/30/216479305/money-may-be-motivating -doctors-to-do-more-c-sections.

192 **in the U.S.** Marco Huesch and Jason N. Doctor, "Factors Associated with Increased Cesarean Risk among African American Women: Evidence from California, 2010," *American Journal of Public Health* 105, no. 5 (2015): 956–62, https://doi.org/10.2105/ajph.2014.302381.

193 **of the team?"** Fran Kritz, "A New Campaign to Reduce C-Sections Is Especially Critical for African-American Mothers and Babies," California Health Report, August 10, 2018, https://www.calhealthreport.org/2018/08 /10/new-campaign-reduce-c-sections-especially-critical-african-american -mothers-babies/.

193 **poorer birth outcomes."** *Unnatural Causes*, episode 2, "When the Bough Breaks," dir. Tracy Heather Strain, aired 2009, PBS, https://unnaturalcauses .org/assets/uploads/file/UC_Transcript_2.pdf.

193 **to summarize it."** *Unnatural Causes*, "When the Bough Breaks."

194 **(and still is).** "Three-quarters of the country's states allow licenses for midwives to practice out-of-hospital deliveries, including home births. Some states, like West Virginia and Georgia, do not offer licenses, making midwifery essentially illegal. Home births themselves are not illegal." Kimiko de Freytas-Tamura, "Pregnant and Scared of 'Covid Hospitals,' They're Giving Birth at Home," *New York Times*, April 21, 2020, https:// www.nytimes.com/2020/04/21/nyregion/coronavirus-home-births.html.

195 **length of stay.** Hillary Hoffower and Jenny Cheng, "Kate Middleton's Delivery of Her Third Baby Probably Cost Less Than a Typical Birth in the US," *Insider*, April 23, 2018, https://www.businessinsider.com/kate -middleton-royal-baby-lindo-wing-st-marys-delivery-cost-2018-4?r =US&IR=T.

195 **experimentation and criminalization.** Dorothy Roberts. *Killing the Black Body: Race, Reproduction, and the Meaning of Liberty* (New York: Vintage Books, 2014), originally published by Pantheon Books (1997).

197 **mid-1940s (55 percent).** Pam England and Rob I. Horowitz, *Birthing from Within: An Extra-ordinary Guide to Childbirth Preparation* (London: Souvenir, 2007), p. 106. "In the last twenty years, most babies in the Western world were born drugged, in an electronic, clinical environment, and separated from their mothers." But this must make things safer, right? *Nope.* "This turnaround was motivated by a concern for safety, yet paradoxically there is mounting evidence that birth complications rise as the utilization of routine technology increases." It turns out that the drop in overall maternal mortality since the 1930s is attributable not to hospital births but to antibiotics and the overall improved health of prospective parents. See England and Horowitz, p. 106.

197　**with a midwife.** Nora Ellman, *Community-Based Doulas and Midwives* (Washington, DC: Center for American Progress, 2020).

197　**and earning power.** Rose Weitz and Deborah A. Sullivan, "The Politics of Childbirth: The Re-emergence of Midwifery in Arizona," *Social Problems* 33, no. 3 (1986): 163–75, https://doi.org/10.2307/800702.

197　**untrained, incompetent women."** Annalisa Merelli, "The Reason Childbirth Is Over-medicalized in America Has Its Roots in Racial Segregation," Quartz, December 1, 2017, https://qz.com/1119699/how-racial-segregation-led -childbirth-in-america-to-be-over-medicalized/.

197　**the safer bet.** Barbara Ehrenreich and Deirdre English, *Witches, Midwives, and Nurses: A History of Women Healers* (Olympia, WA: Last Work, 2016).

197　**from their ranks.** "So the question in a country whose foundations remain rooted in white supremacy is whether midwives are ready for a reckoning. Can midwifery uproot themselves from its ties to misogyny and white supremacy in a workforce that currently identifies as 90% white . . . ?" Niles and Drew, "Constructing."

197　**neonatologist Richard David.** *Unnatural Causes,* "When the Bough Breaks."

198　**about almost immediately.** Not only do the baths warm and nourish the womb, which is "cold" after giving birth, according to traditional medicine, the special attention offsets postpartum exhaustion and loneliness.

198　**Emerson put it.** Ralph Waldo Emerson, *The Complete Works of Ralph Waldo Emerson,* with a biographical introduction and notes by Edward Waldo Emerson (New York: AMS, 1979).

198　**their inner strength."** From Rothman's website, http://www.barbara katzrothman.com. She also writes, "For a long time I've been thinking about going beyond what my colleagues in sociology now routinely call 'the biomedical industrial complex,' and asking us to think of Biomedicine as an Imperial power, having not only enormous financial resources but also the almost-religious belief system and the governmental power of any empire. People 'believe' in aspects of medicine; and your citizenship, your personhood, depends on medical approval."

199　**they save money.** Ellman, *Community-Based Doulas and Midwives.*

200　**low-birthweight baby.** Kenneth J. Gruber, Susan H. Cupito, and Christina F. Dobson. "Impact of Doulas on Healthy Birth Outcomes," *Journal of Perinatal Education* 22, no. 1 (2013): 49–58, https://doi.org/10.1891/1058-1243.22.1 .49.

200　**develop depressive symptoms.** Meghan A. Bohren et al., "Continuous Support for Women during Childbirth," *Cochrane Database of Systematic Reviews* 2017, no. 8 (2017), https://doi.org/10.1002/14651858.cd003766 .pub6.

200　**could turn risky.** Rebecca Dekker, "Evidence On: Doulas," Evidence Based Birth, May 4, 2019, https://evidencebasedbirth.com/the-evidence-for -doulas/.

201 **to begin with."** Irin Carmon, "Midwives Are Swamped with Home-Birth Requests," Cut, March 26, 2020, https://www.thecut.com/2020/03/midwives-are-swamped-with-home-birth-requests.html.

201 **percent of Asians.** "Pregnant Black and Hispanic Women Five Times More Likely to Be Exposed to Coronavirus," Penn Medicine News, July 29, 2020, https://www.pennmedicine.org/news/news-releases/2020/july/pregnant-black-and-hispanic-women-five-times-more-likely-to-be-exposed-to-coronavirus.

201 **said Scott Hensley.** Katherine J. Wu, "Study of Coronavirus in Pregnant Women Finds Striking Racial Differences," *New York Times*, July 10, 2020, https://www.nytimes.com/2020/07/10/health/coronavirus-race-pregnancy.html.

202 **Florida, called it.** From Commonsense Childbirth website, https://commonsensechildbirth.org/jjway/; see also, Sugar Heal Gang based in Los Angeles, https://www.sugarheal.com.

202 **and immigration status.** Ellman, *Community-Based Doulas and Midwives.*

202 **training and accountability.** "Momnibus Act of 2020," website of United States Congresswoman Alma Adams, accessed January 25, 2022, https://adams.house.gov/momnibus-act-2020.

202 **in "perfect health."** Kristi Pahr, " 'My Wife's Legacy Gives a Voice to the Voiceless': Charles Johnson's Loss Launched a Maternal Health Revolution," *Parents*, April 10, 2020, https://www.parents.com/pregnancy/giving-birth/stories/my-wifes-legacy-gives-a-voice-to-the-voiceless-charles-johnsons-loss-launched-a-maternal-health-revolution/.

202 **priority right now."** Pahr, "My Wife's Legacy."

204 **parent-child visitation sessions.** Ashoka Contributors, "The Drama of Pregnant Women in Prison—and the Woman on a Mission to Fix It," *Forbes*, October 25, 2018, https://www.forbes.com/sites/ashoka/2018/10/25/the-drama-of-pregnant-women-in-prison-and-the-woman-on-a-mission-to-fix-it/?sh=33a9a043948c.

204 **prisons each year.** Alysia Santo, "For Most Women Who Give Birth in Prison, 'the Separation' Soon Follows," PBS, May 6, 2020, https://www.pbs.org/wgbh/frontline/article/for-most-women-who-give-birth-in-prison-the-separation-soon-follows/.

205 **with the babies.** Alysia Santo, "The Separation," Marshall Project, May 6, 2020, https://www.themarshallproject.org/2020/05/06/the-separation.

205 **could most benefit.** "New York State Doula Pilot Program," New York State Department of Health, revised December 2021, https://www.health.ny.gov/health_care/medicaid/redesign/doulapilot/index.htm.

205 **to Jennifer Nash.** Nash, *Birthing Black Mothers*, 71.

205 **to attend births.** "Prison Doula Services," Ancient Song Doula Services, accessed January 25, 2022, https://www.ancientsongdoulaservices.com/prison-doula-services.

206 **grief," Perez said.** Elizabeth Perez, "Help Elizabeth Become a Death Doula," GoFundMe, last modified July 23, 2020, https://www.gofundme.com/f/help-elizabeth-become-a-death-doula; Demby, "Making the Case."

206   **through the process.** Julian Milo, "Death Doula Training Program,"
       September 17, 2018, video, 4:11, https://www.youtube.com/watch?v=kXDCA
       axvtYk&t=118s.

206   **to do afterward."** Milo "Death Doula."

206   **$12,000 on average.** "How Much Does a Funeral Cost?," Lincoln Heritage
       Funeral Advantage, accessed January 25, 2022, https://www.lhlic.com
       /consumer-resources/average-funeral-cost/; "United States Death Care
       Market Report 2018–2023: Market Is Estimated to Reach Revenues of around
       $68 Billion," PR Newswire, November 27, 2018, https://www.prnewswire.com
       /news-releases/united-states-death-care-market-report-2018-2023-market-is
       -estimated-to-reach-revenues-of-around-68-billion-300755813.html.

207   **many unclaimed bodies.** W. J. Hennigan, "Lost in the Pandemic: Inside
       New York City's Mass Graveyard on Hart Island," *Time*, November 18, 2020,
       https://time.com/5913151/hart-island-covid/.

208   **journalist Jody Rosen.** Jody Rosen, "How Covid-19 Has Forced Us to Look
       at the Unthinkable," *New York Times Magazine*, April 29, 2020, https://www
       .nytimes.com/2020/04/29/magazine/covid-hart-island.html.

208   **pothole," wrote Rosen.** Rosen.

208   **of suspected coronavirus.** Sara Dorn, "Woman Slams de Blasio after
       Relative's Body Left at Home for Hours," *New York Post*, April 18, 2020,
       https://nypost.com/2020/04/18/nyc-woman-slams-de-blasio-after-relatives
       -body-left-at-home/.

208   **of funeral homes.** Dorn, "Woman Slams de Blasio after Relative's Body
       Left at Home for Hours."

209   **on this earth.** Munchies, "Harlem's Seafood Queen Takes on Coronavirus
       | Street Food Icons," May 14, 2020, video, 7:31, https://www.youtube.com
       /watch?v=FA5Vivq9ryA.

209   **been done before.** Octavia E. Butler, *Parable of the Talents* (London:
       Headline, 2019), p. 167.

209   **1968 and 1973.** Alondra Nelson, *Body and Soul: The Black Panther Party
       and the Fight against Medical Discrimination* (Minneapolis: University of
       Minnesota Press, 2011), 6; Mary T. Bassett, "No Justice, No Health: The
       Black Panther Party's Fight for Health in Boston and Beyond," *Journal of
       African American Studies* 23, no. 4 (2019): 352–63, https://doi.org/10.1007
       /s12111-019-09450-w.

210   **more extensive treatment."** Nelson, *Body and Soul*, p. 6.

210   **to BPP activism.** Alfredo Morabia, "Unveiling the Black Panther Party
       Legacy to Public Health," *American Journal of Public Health* 106, no. 10
       (2016): 1732–33, https://doi.org/10.2105/ajph.2016.303405.

210   **you have FREEDOM!"** Bassett, "No Justice, No Health" p. 354.

210   **of the country."** "Hoover and the F.B.I.," PBS, accessed January 25, 2022,
       https://www.pbs.org/hueypnewton/people/people_hoover.html; see
       also Suzanne Cope, *Power Hungry: Women of the Black Panther Party and
       Freedom Summer and Their Fight to Feed a Movement* (Chicago: Lawrence
       Hill Books, 2022).

211 **destined for greatness.** Noreen Iftikhar, "What Is an En Caul Birth?," Healthline, December 20, 2019, https://www.healthline.com/health /pregnancy/en-caul-birth#what-happens-at-birth.

212 **perfect condition. £5."** Genevieve Carlton, "The Caul: History's Strangest Protective Charm," Weird History Ranker, October 6, 2017, https://www .ranker.com/list/caul-superstitions/genevieve-carlton; Thomas R. Forbes, "The Social History of the Caul," *Yale Journal of Biology and Medicine* 25, no. 6 (1953): 495–508.

213 **thicker than whites'.** Kali Holloway, "Medical Racism and the Ignoring of Black Pain," AlterNet, April 23, 2016, https://www.alternet.org/2016/04 /medical-racism-and-ignoring-black-pain/.

214 **are systematically undertreated."** Keith Wailoo, "Keith Wailoo on the Pain Gap: Why Doctors Offer Less Relief to Black Patients," Princeton University Department of History News, April 11, 2016, https://history.princeton.edu /news-events/news/pain-gap-why-doctors-offer-less-relief-black-patients.

214 **other than human."** Holloway, "Medical Racism."

214 **healthcare per capita.** "Current Health Expenditure per Capita (Current US$)," World Bank, accessed January 25, 2022, https://data.worldbank.org /indicator/SH.XPD.CHEX.PC.CD.

214 **a family doctor.** Temma Ehrenfeld, "Cuba Does It. Why Can't the U.S. Provide Healthcare for Its Poor?," *Healthline*, October 16, 2017, https:// www.healthline.com/health-news/why-cant-us-provide-healthcare-for -poor#Pregnancy-related-mortality.

214 **once they return.** Anakwa Dwamena, "Why African-American Doctors Are Choosing to Study Medicine in Cuba," *New Yorker*, June 6, 2018, https:// www.newyorker.com/science/elements/why-african-american-doctors -are-choosing-to-study-medicine-in-cuba.

215 **with her patients.** Dwamena, "Why African-American Doctors Are Choosing to Study Medicine in Cuba."

215 **of U.S. embargoes.** Andrés Cárdenas O'Farrill, "How Cuba Became a Biopharma Juggernaut," Institute for New Economic Thinking, March 5, 2018, https://www.ineteconomics.org/perspectives/blog/how-cuba-became -a-biopharma-juggernaut.

215 **cases since 1992.** Ehrenfeld, "Cuba Does It"; "Measles Cases and Outbreaks," Centers for Disease Control and Prevention, last updated November 19, 2021, https://www.cdc.gov/measles/cases-outbreaks.html.

215 **and diplomatic tool.** Ciara Nugent, "How Doctors Became Cuba's Biggest Export," *Time*, November 30, 2018, https://time.com/5467742/cuba-doctors -export-brazil/.

215 **and other reasons.** Ever since food rationing eased and the country allowed people to start their own businesses, diabetes and heart disease have increased along with the spread of fast-food stands on every corner. But in addition to consultorios (community-based clinics), small-scale gardens and bicycling are also common, helping to keep Cuba's rates of chronic

illness down compared with the U.S. See Ciara Nugent, "How Doctors Became Cuba's Biggest Export," *Time*, November 30, 2018, https://time .com/5467742/cuba-doctors-export-brazil/; and Ehrenfeld, "Cuba Does It."

215 **in the streets.** María Luisa Paúl, "'A Powder Keg About to Explode': Long Marginalized Afro Cubans at Forefront of Island's Unrest," *Washington Post*, July 19, 2021, https://www.washingtonpost.com/world/2021/07/19/cuba -protests-afro-cubans/.

215 **for many islanders.** Paúl, "A Powder Keg."

216 **the prison systems."** Amalia Dache, "Afro-Cubans Come Out in Droves to Protest Government," interview by Lulu Garcia Navarro, *Weekend Edition Sunday*, NPR, July 25, 2021, audio, 5:25, https://www.npr.org/2021/07/25 /1020342843/afro-cubans-come-out-in-droves-to-protest-government.

216 **death toll down.** Sarah Marsh, "Cuba Credits Two Drugs with Slashing Coronavirus Death Toll," Reuters, May 22, 2020, https://www.reuters.com /article/us-health-coronavirus-cuba/cuba-credits-two-drugs-with-slashing -coronavirus-death-toll-idUSKBN22Y2Y4; Hannah Ritchie et al., "Cuba: Coronavirus Pandemic Country Profile," Our World in Data, 2020, https:// ourworldindata.org/coronavirus/country/cuba.

216 **medical brigades' arrival.** The U.S. international response to COVID-19 has mainly been in the form of foreign aid and the assertion of "soft power" around the world. See John Kirk, "2021 Nobel Peace Prize Nomination for the Cuban Henry Reeve Brigade's Remarkable International Health Work, Particularly during the Global COVID-19 Pandemic," Council of Canadians, September 14, 2020, https://canadians.org/sites/default/files/2020-11/2021-nobel-peace -prize-for-cuban-medics.pdf; "Foreign Assistance for Coronavirus (COVID- 19)," U.S. Department of State, accessed January 25, 2022, https://www.state .gov/foreign-assistance-for-coronavirus-covid-19/; "Covid-19: Italy Bids Farewell to Cuban Doctors," *Wanted in Rome*, June 9, 2020, https://www .wantedinrome.com/news/covid-19-italy-bids-farewell-to-cuban-doctors .html.

216 **of "human trafficking."** Ellen Wulfhorst, "U.S. Says Cuban Medical Missions Are Trafficking Doctors," Reuters, September 26, 2019, https:// www.reuters.com/article/us-usa-cuba-trafficking-idUSKBN1WC00X; Maria Werlau et al., "The Repressive Nature of Cuba's Medical Brigades," virtual panel discussion, Oslo Freedom Forum, September 24, 2020, video, 1:25:25, https://www.youtube.com/watch?v=bnNVES3QtUc.

216 **want to participate.** Peter Beaumont and Ed Augustin, "Trump Puts Cuban Doctors in Firing Line as Heat Turned Up on Island Economy," *Guardian*, February 11, 2020, https://www.theguardian.com/global-development /2020/feb/11/trump-puts-cuban-doctors-in-firing-line-as-heat-turned-up -on-island-economy/.

216 **during the pandemic.** "Panama Abandons Cuban Doctors Plan under US Pressure," France 24, August 27, 2020, https://www.france24.com/en /20200827-panama-abandons-cuban-doctors-plan-under-us-pressure.

216 **to be stopped."** Ed Augustin, "Cuba Has Sent 2,000 Doctors and Nurses Overseas to Fight Covid-19," *Nation*, May 22, 2020, https://www.thenation .com/article/world/cuba-doctors-covid-19/.

217 **that kills you.** Bridges, *Reproducing Race.*

217 **public health emergency.** "Racism Is a Public Health Crisis," American Public Health Association, accessed January 25, 2022, https://www.apha.org /topics-and-issues/health-equity/racism-and-health/racism-declarations.

217 **police in 2014.** White Coats for Black Lives, homepage, accessed January 25, 2022, https://whitecoats4blacklives.org.

218 **by faculty members.** Mara Gordon, "Racism, Hazing and Other Abuse Taints Medical Training, Students Say," NPR, June 16, 2020, https://www .npr.org/sections/health-shots/2020/06/16/876279025/racism-hazing-and -other-abuse-taints-medical-training-students-say.

218 **Indigenous, or queer.** Katherine A. Hill et al., "Assessment of the Prevalence of Medical Student Mistreatment by Sex, Race/Ethnicity, and Sexual Orientation," *JAMA Internal Medicine* 180, no. 5 (2020): 653, https:// doi.org/10.1001/jamainternmed.2020.0030.

218 **by other experts.** Amanda Davis, "Flint Is Slowly Getting Better, Says Scientists Who Exposed Water Crisis," *Sierra*, August 26, 2017, https:// www.sierraclub.org/sierra/flint-slowly-getting-better-say-scientists-who -exposed-water-crisis.

218 **that," she tweeted.** Uché Blackstock (@uche_blackstock), Twitter post, August 12, 2020, 9:06 p.m., https://twitter.com/uche_blackstock/status /1293715476716105729.

218 **in urgent care.** Uché Blackstock, "Why Black Doctors Like Me Are Leaving Faculty Positions in Academic Medical Centers," *Stat News*, January 16, 2020, https://www.statnews.com/2020/01/16/black-doctors-leaving -faculty-positions-academic-medical-centers/.

219 **doctors are Black.** "Diversity in Medicine: Facts and Figures 2019," Association of American Medical Colleges, accessed January 25, 2022, https://www.aamc.org/data-reports/workforce/interactive-data/figure -18-percentage-all-active-physicians-race/ethnicity-2018.

219 **babies are delivered.** Rob Picheta, "Black Newborns More Likely to Die When Looked After by White Doctors," CNN, August 20, 2020, https:// edition.cnn.com/2020/08/18/health/black-babies-mortality-rate-doctors -study-wellness-scli-intl/index.html.

220 **India in 1948.** Henry Louis Gates, Jr. "Who Designed the March on Washington?" PBS.org, https://www.pbs.org/wnet/african-americans -many-rivers-to-cross/history/100-amazing-facts/who-designed-the -march-on-washington/; accessed on February 13, 2022.

223 **of each TRI-k.** Kathleen M. Blee, *Women of the Klan: Racism and Gender in the 1920s* (Berkeley: University of California Press, 2009), p. 159.

224 **last ambulance ride.** Payton Guion, "Tamir Rice Shooting: Cleveland Mayor Apologizes for Ambulance Bill Sent to Rice Family," *Independent*, February 11, 2016, https://www.independent.co.uk/news/world/americas

/tamir-rice-shooting-family-sued-over-unpaid-ambulance-bill-of-son-shot
-dead-by-cleveland-police-a6866896.html.

224 **twenty years old.** Sheila Dewan and Richard A. Oppel Jr. "In Tamir Rice Case, Many Errors by Cleveland Police, The a Fatal One,: *New York Times*, January 22, 2015, https://www.nytimes.com/2015/01/23/us/in-tamir-rice-shooting-in-cleveland-many-errors-by-police-then-a-fatal-one.html.

Chapter Six

Page

225 **Museum for Decades."** Maya Kassutto, "Remains of Children Killed in MOVE Bombing Sat in a Box at Penn Museum for Decades," Billy Penn, April 21, 2021, https://billypenn.com/2021/04/21/move-bombing-penn-museum-bones-remains-princeton-africa/.

225 **in the process.** Lindsey Norward, "The Day Philadelphia Bombed Its Own People," *Vox*, August 15, 2019, https://www.vox.com/the-highlight/2019/8/8/20747198/philadelphia-bombing-1985-move.

225 **in the house.** Ed Pilkington, "The Day Police Bombed a City Street: Can Scars of 1985 Move Atrocity Be Healed?," *Guardian*, May 20, 2020, https://www.theguardian.com/us-news/2020/may/10/move-1985-bombing-reconciliation-philadelphia.

225 **be stagnant, dead."** Robert Longley, "MOVE Philadelphia Bombing History and Fallout," ThoughtCo, October 2, 2021, https://www.thoughtco.com/move-philadelphia-bombing-4175986.

225 **Delisha and Tree.** The *New Yorker* says this: "Tree and Netta's mother, Consuewella Africa, was also imprisoned when her daughters were killed." Heather Ann Thompson, "Saying Her Name," *New Yorker*, May 16, 2021, https://www.newyorker.com/news/essay/saying-her-name.

226 **age of sixty-seven.** Oona Goodin-Smith and Mensah M. Dean, "Consuewella Dotson Africa, Longtime MOVE Member, Dies at 67," *Philadelphia Inquirer*, June 16, 2021, https://www.inquirer.com/obituaries/consuewella-dotson-africa-dead-move-philadelphia-20210616.html.

226 **because of stress."** Goodin-Smith and Dean, "Consuewella Dotson Africa, Longtime MOVE Member, Dies at 67."

226 **tore her down."** Goodin-Smith and Dean, "Consuewella Dotson Africa, Longtime MOVE Member, Dies at 67."

226 **important to reveal."** Malcolm Burnley, "Former MOVE Members Are Speaking Out about Abusive Behavior within the Organization," Billy Penn, August 4, 2021, https://billypenn.com/2021/08/04/move-philadelphia-abusive-behavior-child-marriage-leaving-members/.

226 **for any wrongdoing.** William K. Stevens, "Grand Jury Clears Everyone in Fatal Philadelphia Siege," *New York Times*, May 4, 1998, https://www.nytimes.com/1988/05/04/us/grand-jury-clears-everyone-in-fatal-philadelphia-siege.html.

226 **they belonged to.** Teo Armus, "A Philly Museum Kept the Bones of a Black Child Killed in a Police Bombing. Decades Later, It's Apologizing," *Washington Post*, August 30, 2021, https://www.washingtonpost.com/nation /2021/04/30/philadelphia-move-bombing-bones-upenn/.

227 **Mike Africa Jr.** Michael Levenson, "Decades after Police Bombing, Philadelphians 'Sickened' by Handling of Victim's Bones," *New York Times*, April 24, 2021, https://www.nytimes.com/2021/04/24/us/move-rowhouse -bombing-victim-remains.html.

227 **keep their bones."** Kassutto, "Remains of Children Killed."

227 **of white supremacy.** Mishal S. Khan et al., "Rethinking Vaccine Hesitancy among Minority Groups," *Lancet* 397, no. 10288 (2021): 1863–65, https://doi .org/10.1016/s0140-6736(21)00938-7.

228 **by their government.** However, a Penn-commissioned investigation following the revelations said it was not certain that the remains were those of Tree Africa or that the remains of Delisha Africa were ever housed at the Penn Museum. See Conor Murray, "Investigation Finds Penn Profs. Demonstrated 'Gross Insensitivity' in Handling MOVE Remains," *Daily Pennsylvanian*, August 25, 2021, https://www.thedp.com/article/2021/08 /penn-musem-investigation-move-bombing-africa-family.

228 **in Forensic Anthropology.** Ed Pilkington, "Bones of Black Children Killed in Police Bombing Used in Ivy League Anthropology Course," *Guardian*, April 23, 2021, https://www.theguardian.com/us-news/2021/apr/22/move -bombing-black-children-bones-philadelphia-princeton-pennsylvania.

228 **an older-style grease."** Pilkington, "Bones of Black Children."

229 **by federal law.** "Western research has prioritized the quest for knowledge above all else. And in doing so, human bodies have been treated as research subjects, as objects to extract data from. The use of human bodies, in this case, is an ethical failure." Sage Alexander, "Grave Robbing at UC Berkeley: A History of Failed Repatriation," *Weekender*, December 7, 2020, https:// www.dailycal.org/2020/12/05/grave-robbing-at-uc-berkeley-a-history-of -failed-repatriation/.

229 **through the media.** Alfred Lubrano, "Mothers of Children Who Died in MOVE Bombing Find No Comfort in City Discovery That Human Remains Were Not Destroyed," *Philadelphia Inquirer*, May 15, 2021, https://www .inquirer.com/news/move-bombing-remains-farley-mumia-abu-jamal -children-20210515.html.

229 **1,300 human skulls.** Suzanne Rowan Kelleher, "How a Museum's Human Skull Collection Sparked a Racial Reckoning," *Forbes*, April 16, 2021, https:// www.forbes.com/sites/suzannerowankelleher/2021/04/16/penn-museum -samuel-morton-human-skull-collection-black-slaves-repatriation/.

229 **ground in Cuba.** Paul Wolff Mitchell, "Black Philadelphians in the Samuel George Mortion Cranial Collection," Penn Program on Race, Science & Society, February 15, 2021, https://prss.sas.upenn.edu/penn-medicines-role /black-philadelphians-samuel-george-morton-cranial-collection.

231 **"launched his career."** Bettina Judd, "Gynecology Was Built on the Backs of Black Women, Anyway," interview by Phillip Williams, Race Baiter, July 7, 2015, https://racebaitr.com/2015/07/07/gynecology-was-built-on -the-backs-of-black-women-anyway-an-interview-with-bettina-judd/.

231 **finally brought down.** Nadja Sayej, "J Marion Sims: Controversial Statue Taken Down but Debate Still Rages," *Guardian*, April 21, 2018, https:// www.theguardian.com/artanddesign/2018/apr/21/j-marion-sims-statue -removed-new-york-city-black-women.

231 **"mothers of gynecology."** More Up Campus, homepage, accessed January 27, 2022, https://www.anarchalucybetsey.org.

231 **mid-nineteenth century.** Deirdre Cooper Owens, *Medical Bondage: Race, Gender, and the Origins of American Gynecology* (Athens: University of Georgia Press, 2017), p. 2.

231 **were experimented on."** Kirsten Fiscus, "'Mothers of Gynecology' Anarcha, Lucy and Betsey to Get Their Own Monument in Montgomery," *Montgomery Advertiser*, December 8, 2020, https://eu.montgomeryadvertiser.com /story/news/2020/12/08/enslaved-women-operated-j-marion-sims-get -monument-montgomery/3814683001/.

231 **invent the wincing."** Bettina Judd. "Betsey Invents the Speculum," in *Patient* (Black Lawrence Press 2014), p. 32.

231 **crowded my bed.** Bettina Judd, "Sapphire as Praxis: Toward a Methodology of Anger," *Feminist Studies* 45, no. 1 (2019): 178. https://doi.org/10.15767 /feministstudies.45.1.0178.

232 **a cervical biopsy.** "The Legacy of Henrietta Lacks," Johns Hopkins Medicine, https://www.hopkinsmedicine.org/henriettalacks/.

232 **an economic entity.** Hannah Landecker, *Culturing Life: How Cells Became Technologies* (Cambridge, MA: Harvard University Press, 2010), p. 3.

232 **heirs and descendants."** Karla F. C. Holloway, *Private Bodies, Public Texts: Race, Gender, and a Cultural Bioethics* (Durham, NC: Duke University Press, 2011).

232 **thousand scientific papers.** Robin McKie, "Henrietta Lacks's Cells Were Priceless, but Her Family Can't Afford a Hospital," *Guardian*, April 3, 2019, https://www.theguardian.com/world/2010/apr/04/henrietta-lacks-cancer -cells.

232 **other medical breakthroughs.** Timothy Turner, "Development of the Polio Vaccine: A Historical Perspective of Tuskegee University's Role in Mass Production and Distribution of Hela Cells," *Journal of Health Care for the Poor and Underserved* 23, no. 4a (2012): 5–10, https://doi.org/10.1353 /hpu.2012.0151.

232 **a COVID-19 vaccine.** Collins mentions this fact in the CELLebrate panel discussion mentioned later in the chapter. See also, Faroque Ahmad Khan, review of *The Immortal Life of Henrietta Lacks*, by Rebecca Skloot, *Journal of the Islamic Medical Association of North America* 43, no. 2 (2011), https://doi .org/10.5915/43-2-8609.

232 **get health insurance?"** Rebecca Skloot, *The Immortal Life of Henrietta Lacks* (New York: Gale/Cengage, 2010), p. 168.

233 **talk by Skloot.** "Family Recognition, Community Awards, and Author Highlight Henrietta Lacks Memorial Lecture 2010," Johns Hopkins Institute for Clinical and Translational Research, accessed January 27, 2022, https://ictr.johnshopkins.edu/community/community-involvement/the-henrietta-lacks-memorial-lecture/family-recognition-community-awards-and-author-highlight-henrietta-lacks-memorial-lecture-2010/.

233 **health and medicine?"** "Professor Ruha Benjamin Delivers the Johns Hopkins Henrietta Lacks Memorial Lecture," Princeton University Department of African American Studies, March 15, 2017, https://aas.princeton.edu/news/professor-ruha-benjamin-delivers-johns-hopkins-henrietta-lacks-memorial-lecture.

234 **to rest easy.** "Professor Ruha Benjamin."

234 **simply reproduces them?"** "Professor Ruha Benjamin."

234 **got to go!"** "Professor Ruha Benjamin."

234 **according to Judd.** Bettina Judd, "Sapphire as Praxis: Toward a Methodology of Anger," *Feminist Studies* 45, no. 1 (2019): 178–208. https://doi.org/10.15767/feministstudies.45.1.0178, p. 196.

235 **scars are produced.** Although Hopkins researchers, like others around the world, rely on HeLa cells for research of all kinds, the university is quick to remind the public that Hopkins does not technically own the rights to them, nor does the university directly sell them for profit (although researchers profit from their use in other ways). See Andrea K. McDaniels, "Henrietta Lacks' Family Wants Compensation for Her Cells," *Baltimore Sun*, February 15, 2017, https://www.baltimoresun.com/health/bs-hs-henrietta-lacks-johns-hopkins-20170213-story.html.

235 **mostly Black families.** Siddhartha Mitter, "Gentrify or Die? Inside a University's Controversial Plan for Baltimore," *Guardian*, April 18, 2018, https://www.theguardian.com/cities/2018/apr/18/gentrify-or-die-inside-a-universitys-controversial-plan-for-baltimore.

235 **of Black Baltimore.** Greg Rienzi, "The Changing Face of East Baltimore," *Gazette*, January 2013, https://hub.jhu.edu/gazette/2013/january/east-baltimore-changes-development/.

235 **everything around it."** Jacob Took, "How Do HopkinsLocal Investments Impact the City?," *Johns Hopkins News-letter*, February 28, 2019, https://www.jhunewsletter.com/article/2019/02/how-do-hopkinslocal-investments-impact-the-city.

236 **just a fact."** Cameron Jenkins, "Fauci Addresses Americans' Vaccine Concerns: This Was 'Developed by an African American Woman,'" *The Hill*, December 11, 2020, https://thehill.com/homenews/news/529841-fauci-addresses-black-americans-vaccine-concerns-this-was-developed-by-an.

237 **40 YEARS!!! #fuckouttahere.** Comments on Black Gotham Experience (@blackgotham), "Fauci wants people to know that one of lead scientists

who developed the Covid-19 vaccine is a Black woman," Instagram post, December 9, 2020, https://www.instagram.com/p/CImaPGxF2ir/?igshid =1cl1x9xq47k30.

237 **better termed suspicion.** Nicole Charles, *Suspicion: Vaccines, Hesitancy, and the Affective Politics of Protection in Barbados* (Durham, NC: Duke University Press, 2021).

237 **in the U.S.** Juana Summers, "Little Difference in Vaccine Hesitancy among White and Black Americans, Poll Finds," NPR, March 12, 2021, https://www .npr.org/sections/coronavirus-live-updates/2021/03/12/976172586/little -difference-in-vaccine-hesitancy-among-white-and-black-americans-poll-find.

237 **trusted its effectiveness.** Harmeet Kaur, "Fauci Wants People to Know That One of the Lead Scientists Who Developed the Covid-19 Vaccine Is a Black Woman," CNN, December 10, 2020, https://www.cnn.com/2020/12 /09/us/african-american-scientists-vaccine-development-trnd/index.html.

237 **Center in Queens.** Jonathan Allen and Gabriella Borter, "'Race against Time': First Americans Vaccinated as U.S. Death Toll Passes 300,000," Reuters, December 14, 2020, https://www.reuters.com/article/health -coronavirus-vaccines-distribution/healing-is-coming-first-americans -vaccinated-as-u-s-death-toll-passes-300000-idUSKBN28O1TQ.

238 **lead abatement methods.** David Rosner and Gerald Markowitz, "With the Best Intentions: Lead Research and the Challenge to Public Health," *American Journal of Public Health* 102, no. 11 (2012): e19–e33, https://doi .org/10.2105/ajph.2012.301004.

238 **advocate in Baltimore.** Lawrence T. Brown, *The Black Butterfly: The Harmful Politics of Race and Space in America* (Baltimore: Johns Hopkins University Press, 2021), 159.

238 **lead prevention program.** Aria Bendix, "Why Lead Paint Still Haunts Industrial Cities in the U.S.," Bloomberg, July 29, 2016, https://www .bloomberg.com/news/articles/2016-07-29/why-lead-paint-still-haunts -industrial-cities-in-the-u-s; Tracey Ross, Chelsea Parsons, and Rebecca Vallas, *Creating Safe and Healthy Environments for Low-Income Families* (Washington, DC: Center for American Progress, 2016), https://cdn .americanprogress.org/wp-content/uploads/2016/07/14065816/SafeAnd HealthyHomes-report.pdf.

239 **$20,000 or more.** Richard Morse, "Grimes v. Kennedy Krieger Institute: Nontherapeutic Research with Children," *AMA Journal of Ethics* 5, no. 11 (2003): 383–85, https://doi.org/10.1001/virtualmentor.2003.5.11.hlawl -0311; Timothy B. Wheeler and Meredith Cohn, "Lead-Paint Lawsuits Dog Kennedy Krieger," *Baltimore Sun*, June 7, 2014, https://www.baltimoresun .com/health/bs-hs-lead-lawsuit-new-20140607-story.html.

239 **with governmental requirements.** Manuel Roig-Franzia, "Probe Opens on Study Tied to Johns Hopkins," *Washington Post*, August 23, 2001, https:// www.washingtonpost.com/archive/local/2001/08/23/probe-opens-on -study-tied-to-johns-hopkins/2fbe602d-777b-425f-acfc-8ce0e7c332a3/;

Nash Jenkins, "Lawsuit Filed Due to Kennedy-Krieger Study," *Johns Hopkins News-letter*, October 12, 2011, https://www.jhunewsletter.com/article/2011/10/lawsuit-filed-due-to-kennedy-krieger-study-85421.

239 **or study objectives.** Rosner and Markowitz, "With the Best Intentions."

239 **R. Cathell wrote.** Manuel Roig-Franzia and Rick Weiss, "Md. Appeals Court Slams Researchers," *Washington Post*, August 21, 2001, https://www.washingtonpost.com/archive/local/2001/08/21/md-appeals-court-slams-researchers/cfc8a73c-8333-467d-ae3e-31905b580243/.

239 **the long run.** Wheeler and Cohn, "Lead-Paint Lawsuits."

240 **and other damage."** Armstrong v. Kennedy Krieger Inst., Inc. (Circuit Court for Baltimore City, September 15, 2011), https://www.documentcloud.org/documents/249648-armstrong-vs-kennedy-krieger-class-action.html.

240 *Homes et al.* "Baltimore Jury Awards $1.2 Million Lead Paint Verdict," Law Office of Evan K. Thalenberg, September 18, 2019, https://ektlaw.com/news/2019/09/baltimore-jury-awards-1-2-million-lead-paint-verdict/.

240 **and Korryn Gaines.** Catherine Jampel, "Intersections of Disability Justice, Racial Justice and Environmental Justice," *Environmental Sociology* 4, no. 1 (2018): 122–35, https://doi.org/10.1080/23251042.2018.1424497.

240 **Baltimore public housing.** Baynard Woods, "'Rough Ride': Practice Linked to Freddie Gray's Death at the Center of Latest Trial," *Guardian*, June 9, 2016, https://www.theguardian.com/us-news/2016/jun/09/freddie-gray-death-trial-rough-ride-baltimore-police; Jannell Ross, "Why You Should Know What Happened in Freddie Gray's Life—Long before His Death," *Washington Post*, December 19, 2015, https://www.washingtonpost.com/news/the-fix/wp/2015/12/19/why-you-should-know-what-happened-in-freddie-grays-life-long-before-his-death/.

240 **in special education."** Terrence McCoy, "Freddie Gray's Life a Study on the Effects of Lead Paint on Poor Blacks," *Washington Post*, April 29, 2015, https://www.washingtonpost.com/local/freddie-grays-life-a-study-in-the-sad-effects-of-lead-paint-on-poor-blacks/2015/04/29/0be898e6-eea8-11e4-8abc-d6aa3bad79dd_story.html.

240 **of the police.** Ed Williams, "Criminalizing Disability: Special-Needs Kids Who Don't Get Help in School Are Winding Up in Jail," New Mexico Political Report, May 10, 2019, https://nmpoliticalreport.com/2019/05/10/criminalizing-disability-special-needs-kids-who-dont-get-help-in-school-are-winding-up-in-jail/.

240 **years in jail.** McCoy, "Freddie Gray's Life."

241 **poisoned me wit."** Baynard Woods, "Korryn Gaines: Police Killing Highlights Baltimore's Lead Poisoning Crisis," *Guardian*, August 5, 2016, https://www.theguardian.com/us-news/2016/aug/05/korryn-gaines-baltimore-lead-poisoning-crisis.

241 **Baltimore's "toxic legacy."** Scott Dance, "Number of Maryland Children Tested Positive for Lead Poisoning Fell 11% in 2018," *Baltimore Sun*, October 23, 2019, https://www.baltimoresun.com/health/bs-hs-lead-poisoning-20191023-uey3q4yddnffrpgpykmd7eud7i-story.html.

241 **at today's levels.** See Dance, "Number of Maryland Children"; and Terrence McCoy, "Lead Poisoning Is 'Toxic Legacy' That Still Haunts Freddie Gray's Baltimore," *Washington Post*, May 1, 2015, http://www.liu .edu/~/media/RedesignFiles/LIU%20Main%20Page/Polk/2015_Regional _TheWashingtonPost.pdf.

241 **bodies each year.** On the number of housing units with lead paint, the U.S. Department of Housing and Urban Development finds thirty-seven million. See "Housing with Lead Risk," America's Health Rankings, accessed January 27, 2022, https://www.americashealthrankings.org/explore/health -of-women-and-children/measure/housing_leadrisk/state/ALL; Sam P. K. Collins, "Before the Police, Freddie Gray Was Attacked by His Own Walls," ThinkProgress, April 27, 2015, https://archive.thinkprogress.org/before-the -police-freddie-gray-was-attacked-by-his-own-walls-d74b3c1cd405/; U.S. Department of Housing and Urban Development and Office of Healthy Homes and Lead Hazard Control, *American Healthy Homes Survey: Lead and Arsenic Findings* (Washington, DC: U.S. Department of Housing and Urban Development and Office of Healthy Homes and Lead Hazard Control, 2011), https://www.hud.gov/sites/documents/AHHS_REPORT.PDF; and Committee on Environment and Public Works, *Hearing Transcript, Lead and Children's Health: Hearing before the Committee on Environment and Public Works*, Senate Hearing 110-1234 (2007).

241 **would be lead."** "Quotation of the Day," *New York Times*, January 30, 2016, https://www.nytimes.com/2016/01/30/todayspaper/quotation-of-the-day .html.

241 **on her door."** Woods, "Korryn Gaines."

242 **of "innate inferiority."** Harriet A. Washington, *A Terrible Thing to Waste: Environmental Racism and Its Assault on the American Mind* (New York: Little, Brown Spark, 2019) p. 87; see also Harriet A. Washington, "How Environmental Racism Is Fueling the Coronavirus Pandemic," *Nature*, May 19, 2020, https://www.nature.com/articles/d41586-020-01453-y.

242 **in their mouths."** Harriet A. Washington, *A Terrible Thing to Waste: Environmental Racism and Its Assault on the American Mind* (New York: Little, Brown Spark, 2020), p. 2.

243 **knowledge or permission.** "NIH, Lacks Family Reach Understanding to Share Genomic Data of HeLa Cells," National Institutes of Health, August 7, 2013, https://www.nih.gov/news-events/news-releases/nih-lacks-family -reach-understanding-share-genomic-data-hela-cells; Paul Harris, "Final Twist of Henrietta Lacks, the Woman Whose Cells Helped the Fight against Cancer," *Guardian*, March 30, 2013, https://www.theguardian.com/world /2013/mar/31/henrietta-lacks-cancer-research-genome.

243 **without our consent."** Rebecca Skloot, "The Immortal Life of Henrietta Lacks, the Sequel," *New York Times*, March 23, 2013, https://www.nytimes .com/2013/03/24/opinion/sunday/the-immortal-life-of-henrietta-lacks -the-sequel.html.

243 **questions about consent."** Skloot, "The Immortal Life."

244 **to catch up."** Skloot, "The Immortal Life."

244 **at the table.** Sally Rockey, "NIH and the Lacks Family Announce a HeLa Genome Data Sharing and Use Agreement," National Institutes of Health Office of Extramural Research, August 8, 2013, https://nexus.od.nih.gov /all/2013/08/08/nih-and-the-lacks-family-announce-a-hela-genome-data -sharing-and-use-agreement/.

244 **to public unveiling."** Holloway, *Private Bodies, Public Texts*, 9.

245 **for darker-skinned individuals.** Amy Moran-Thomas, "How a Popular Medical Device Encodes Racial Bias," *Boston Review*, August 2, 2020, http:// bostonreview.net/science-nature-race/amy-moran-thomas-how-popular -medical-device-encodes-racial-bias.

246 **send them home."** Dakin Andone, "A Black Doctor Died of Covid-19 Weeks after Accusing Hospital Staff of Racist Treatment," CNN, December 25, 2020, https://www.cnn.com/2020/12/24/us/black-doctor-susan-moore -covid-19/index.html.

246 **as a patient?** Ruha Benjamin, *People's Science: Bodies and Rights on the Stem Cell Frontier* (Palo Alto, CA: Stanford University Press, 2013), p. 113.

247 **Hospital in Paris.** Reuters Staff, "French Doctor Apologises for Suggesting Covid-19 Treatment be Tested in Africa," *Reuters*, April 3, 2020, https:// www.reuters.com/article/us-health-coronavirus-africa-apology/french -doctor-apologises-for-suggesting-covid-19-treatment-be-tested-in-africa -idUSKBN21L2MS.

247 **racists [sic] words."** Didier Drogba (@didierdrogba), Twitter post, April 2, 2020, 3:40 p.m., https://twitter.com/didierdrogba/status /1245798251720314880?lang=en.

247 **White Savior flag.** Harriet A. Washington, *Medical Apartheid: The Dark History of Medical Experimentation on Black Americans from Colonial Times to the Present* (New York: Anchor Books, 2008); Helen Tilley, *Africa as a Living Laboratory: Empire, Development and the Problem of Scientific Knowledge, 1870–1950* (Chicago: University of Chicago Press, 2016); Judith A. Scully, "Black Women and the Development of International Reproductive Health Norms," in *Black Women and International Law: Deliberate Interactions, Movements and Actions*, ed. Jeremy I. Levitt (Cambridge: Cambridge University Press, 2015), pp. 225–49, https://doi.org/10.1017/cbo9781139108751 .013.

248 **cost effective" alternatives.** Kim Dalton, "AZT Trials in the Third World: Tuskegee Redux or Cheap Shot?," *21stC* 3, no. 3 (Fall 1998), http://www .columbia.edu/cu/21stC/issue-3.3/dalton.html.

248 **fatal, side effects."** Sara Lowes and Eduardo Montero, "The Legacy of Colonial Medicine in Central Africa," *American Economic Review* 111, no. 4 (2021): 1284–314, https://doi.org/10.1257/aer.20180284, p. 1284.

248 **many people realize.** "The U.S. Public Health Service Syphilis Study at Tuskegee," Centers for Disease Control and Prevention, last revised April 22, 2021, https://www.cdc.gov/tuskegee/timeline.htm; "About the

USPHS Syphilis Study," Tuskegee University, accessed January 28, 2022, https://www.tuskegee.edu/about-us/centers-of-excellence/bioethics -center/about-the-usphs-syphilis-study.

248 **mind," Temple said.** Angel Jennings, "'We Want to Study You.' For Black Angelenos, Coronavirus Triggers Fear of Another Tuskegee," *Los Angeles Times*, May 10, 2020, https://www.latimes.com/california/story/2020-05 -10/coronavirus-tuskegee-experiment-black-patients-trust-health-care.

249 **in offshore research.** Adriana Petryna, *When Experiments Travel: Clinical Trials and the Global Search for Human Subjects* (Princeton, NJ: Princeton University Press, 2009), 17–18.

249 **in different subgroups.** Investigational New Drug Applications and New Drug Applications, 63 Fed. Reg. 6854 (February 11, 1998), https://www .fda.gov/science-research/clinical-trials-and-human-subject-protection /investigational-new-drug-applications-and-new-drug-applications -2111998.

249 **time-consuming body hunt."** Steven Epstein, "The Rise of 'Recruit-mentology,'" *Social Studies of Science* 38, no. 5 (2008): 806, https://doi.org /10.1177/0306312708091930.

249 **standard safety tests.** Petryna, *When Experiments Travel*, p. 17.

249 **get that far.** "Pfizer and BioNTech Conclude Phase 3 Study of COVID-19 Vaccine Candidate, Meeting All Primary Efficacy Endpoints," Pfizer, November 18, 2020, https://www.pfizer.com/news/press-release/press -release-detail/pfizer-and-biontech-conclude-phase-3-study-covid-19 -vaccine; "Covid: Vaccines Running Out in Poorer Nations, WHO Says," BBC, June 21, 2021, https://www.bbc.com/news/world-57558401; Owen Dyer, "Covid-19: Many Poor Countries Will See Almost No Vaccine Next Year, Aid Groups Warn," *BMJ* 371 (2020): m4809, https://doi.org/10.1136 /bmj.m4809; Michael Safi, "Most Poor Nations 'Will Take Until 2024 to Achieve Mass Covid-19 Immunisation,'" *Guardian*, January 26, 2021, https://www.theguardian.com/society/2021/jan/27/most-poor-nations -will-take-until-2024-to-achieve-mass-covid-19-immunisation.

249 **of the research.** Sharon Lerner, "World Faces COVID-19 'Vaccine Apartheid,'" *Intercept*, December 31, 2020, https://theintercept.com/2020 /12/31/covid-vaccine-countries-scarcity-access/.

250 **recommended treatment plans.** Katrina Armstrong et al., "Racial/Ethnic Differences in Physician Distrust in the United States," *American Journal of Public Health* 97, no. 7 (2007): 1283–89, https://doi.org/10.2105/ajph .2005.080762; L. Ebony Boulware et al., "Race and Trust in the Health Care System," *Public Health Reports* 118, no. 4 (2003): 358–65, https://doi .org/10.1016/s0033-3549(04)50262-5; Rodolfo A. Bulatao and Norman B. Anderson, eds., *Understanding Racial and Ethnic Differences in Health in Late Life: A Research Agenda*, National Research Council Panel on Race, Ethnicity, and Health in Later Life (Washington, DC: National Academies Press, 2004); Adolfo Cuevas, "Exploring Four Barriers Experienced by

African Americans in Healthcare: Perceived Discrimination, Medical Mistrust, Race Discordance, and Poor Communication" (master's thesis, Portland State University, 2013), https://doi.org/10.15760/etd.615.

251 **help save lives."** Louis Farrakhan, "Don't Take Their Vaccine!," *The Final Call*, September 15, 2020, p. 1.

251 **and broader level?"** Farrakhan, "Don't Take Their Vaccine!, p. 20.

251 **prostate cancer education.** Alton Hart et al., "Recruiting African-American Barbershops for Prostate Cancer Education," *Journal of the National Medical Association* 100, no. 9 (2008): 1012–20, https://doi.org/10.1016/s0027-9684(15)31437-1.

251 **existing, community infrastructures."** Bill J. Releford, Stanley K. Frencher Jr., and Antronette K. Yancey, "Health Promotion in Barbershops: Balancing Outreach and Research in African American Communities," *Ethnicity and Disease* 20, no. 2 (2010): 185–88, p. 186.

251 **community-based organizations.** See "Events," Black Emotional and Mental Health Collective, accessed January 28, 2022, https://www.beam.community/events; Yolo Akili (@YoloAkili), "Black hairstylists and Barbers in Los Angeles! BEAM has paid scholarships for you to join us for our Black Mental Health & Healing Peer Support Certificate Training! Email contact on flyer for scholarship," Twitter post, February 17, 2021, 4:38 p.m., https://twitter.com/YoloAkili/status/1362154595208761345?s=20.

251 **as a result.** Sarah L. Krein, Mary E. Madigan, and Linda Smith-Wheelock, "Healthy Hair Starts with a Healthy Body: Hair Stylists as Lay Health Advisors to Prevent Chronic Kidney Disease," *Preventing Chronic Disease* 4, no. 3 (2007): A64.

252 **as welcoming spaces.** Miranda Whittington, "Charlotte Barbershop Wins Human Rights Campaign & SHOWTIME's Queer to Stay LGBTQ Business Preservation Funding," Spectrum News 1, September 21, 2020, https://spectrumlocalnews.com/nc/charlotte/news/2020/09/22/charlotte-barbershop-wins-human-rights-campaign---showtime-s-queer-to-stay-lgbtq-business-preservation-funding-; Ryan Benk, "Barbershops Can Be Fraught for People Who Aren't Straight Cis Men. These Women Want to Change That," DCist, June 17, 2019, https://dcist.com/story/19/06/17/barbershops-can-be-fraught-for-people-who-arent-straight-cis-men-these-women-want-to-change-that/; Aaron Rundle, "When a Haircut Is More Than Just a Haircut," *New York Times*, March 11, 2020, https://www.nytimes.com/2020/03/11/nyregion/nyc-queer-black-barbershops.html.

252 **our 'country club.'"** Releford, Frencher, and Yancey, "Health Promotion in Barbershops," p. 187.

252 **is catching on.** "The Black Barbershop," accessed January 28, 2022, https://www.blackbarbershop.org/.

252 **from prostate cancer.** "Man Up! Brings Health and Haircuts to Men in South LA," MLK Community Healthcare, accessed January 28, 2022, https://www.mlkch.org/ManUp.

253 **a brick-by-brick fashion."** Kaur, "Fauci Wants People."

253 **speed of trust."** adrienne maree brown, "From the Freedom Side," adrienne maree brown's blog, July 22, 2016, https://adriennemareebrown.net/2016/07/22/from-the-freedom-side/.

254 **so self-evident.** See *The Panola Project* documentary, directed by Jeremy S. Levine and Rachel DeCruz for the *New Yorker*, see also "One Woman's Mission to Get Vaccines to Her Rural Alabama Town," YouTube, August 11, 2021, https://www.youtube.com/watch?v=j1wI4T9SKGA.

254 **goods and services.** Ruth Wilson Gilmore, "What Is to Be Done?" *American Quarterly* 63, no. 2 (2011): 245–65. http://www.jstor.org/stable/41237545, p. 257.

255 **them to attend.** Uché Blackstock (@uche_blackstock), "Thanks everyone for engaging with my live tweeting today. I'm really worried. Based on what I'm seeing at work this morning, people still plan to travel to see their loved ones next week," Twitter post, November 20, 2020, 11:33 a.m., https://twitter.com/uche_blackstock/status/1329825255188262912.

255 **it with love."** Uché Blackstock (@uche_blackstock), Twitter post, November 19, 2020, 2:50 p.m., https://twitter.com/uche_blackstock/status/1329512355315806212?lang=en.

255 **like they care."** Joe Sparkman (@JoeSparkman), Twitter post, November 19, 2020, 3:15 p.m., https://twitter.com/JoeSparkman7/status/1329518620230246416.

255 **clinical and detached."** Karen Killian (@LadyLevite03), Twitter post, November 19, 2020, 3:31 p.m., https://twitter.com/LadyLevite03/status/1329522717188517888.

255 **short, context matters.** Monica McLemore, an acclaimed professor of family healthcare nursing, retweeted a *Washington Post* article with the headline "Coronovirus Vaccines Face Trust Gap in Black and Latino Communities, Study Finds." McLemore responded to the headline by reminding her followers, "Acts of individuals do not garner trust. We (healthcare & public health) are not trustworthy!! Our team hopes to hear from folx to help understand what actions & steps are necessary to build & create trust." Monica McLemore (@mclemoremr), Twitter post, November 24, 2020, 9:18 a.m., https://twitter.com/mclemoremr/status/1331240788492050432. There is no formula or quick fix, and some of the most brilliant and committed health justice advocates are still searching for answers.

256 **our attention now."** "Racism Is an Ongoing Public Health Crisis That Needs Our Attention Now," American Public Health Association, May 29, 2020, https://www.apha.org/news-and-media/news-releases/apha-news-releases/2020/racism-is-a-public-health-crisis.

256 **$215,900—"worth it."** Melanie Hanson, "Average Medical School Debt," Education Data Initiative, December 9, 2021, https://educationdata.org/average-medical-school-debt.

256 **disincentivizes preventative care.** Victoria Knight, "American Medical Students Less Likely to Choose to Become Primary Care Doctors," KHN,

July 3, 2019, https://khn.org/news/american-medical-students-less-likely-to-choose-to-become-primary-care-doctors/; Jared Ortaliza et al., "COVID-19 Preventable Mortality and Leading Cause of Death Ranking," Peterson-KFF Health System Tracker, December 10, 2021, https://www.healthsystemtracker.org/brief/covid19-and-other-leading-causes-of-death-in-the-us/.

256 **in the world"?** "Morality Rate, Under-5 (per 1,000 Live Births)—Cuba," World Bank, accessed January 28, 2022, https://data.worldbank.org/indicator/SH.DYN.MORT?locations=CU; "Mortality Rate, Under-5 (per 1,000 Live Births)—United States," World Bank, accessed January 28, 2022, https://data.worldbank.org/indicator/SH.DYN.MORT?locations=US.

256 **am I patient?** Judd, *Patient*, p. 1.

257 **them no justice."** Judd, "Sapphire as Praxis," p. 198.

257 **bodies with care."** Derek Ayeh, "The Case for Medical Reparations," *The New Inquiry*, November 4, 2016, https://thenewinquiry.com/the-case-for-medical-reparations/.

257 **in the community."** Derek Ayeyh, "The Case for Medical Reparations," *The New Inquiry*, November 4, 2016, https://thenewinquiry.com/the-case-for-medical-reparations.

257 **us without us."** James I. Charlton, *Nothing about Us without Us: Disability Oppression and Empowerment* (Berkeley: University of California Press, 2004).

258 **material, and more.** Carla May Dhillon, "Using Citizen Science in Environmental Justice: Participation and Decision-Making in a Southern California Waste Facility Siting Conflict," *Local Environment* 22, no. 12 (2017): 1479–96, https://doi.org/10.1080/13549839.2017.1360263; Leona F. Davis and Mónica D. Ramírez-Andreotta, "Participatory Research for Environmental Justice: A Critical Interpretive Synthesis," *Environmental Health Perspectives* 129, no. 2 (2021): 026001, https://doi.org/10.1289/ehp6274.

258 **and hard work."** Davis and Ramírez-Andreotta, "Participatory Research for Environmental Justice."

258 **Edwards described it.** Goldman Environmental Prize, "LeeAnne Walters, 2018 Goldman Environmental Prize, United States," April 23, 2018, video, 4:58, https://www.youtube.com/watch?v=hpFNG8DDTrs.

259 **the water supply."** Goldman Environmental Prize, "LeeAnne Walters, 2018 Goldman Environmental Prize, United States."

259 **across racial differences.** On "conspire" (*to breathe together*) "as an analytic to rethink coalition and solidarity in the contemporary moment," see Kimberly Bain, "On Black Breath" (PhD diss., Princeton University, 2021), p. 29.

259 **wait for help."** Sonia Saraiya, "TV Review: Lifetime's 'Flint' Starring Queen Latifah," *Variety*, October 27, 2017, https://variety.com/2017/tv/reviews/flint-review-queen-latifah-lifetime-1202600467/.

260 **disseminate the results."** "Citizen Science Project Explores Causes, Solutions to COVID-19 Vaccine Hesitancy," UIC Today, June 2, 2021, https://today.uic.edu/citizen-science-project-explores-causes-solutions -to-covid-19-vaccine-hesitancy.

260 **public health concerns."** "Citizen Science Project Explores Causes, Solutions to COVID-19 Vaccine Hesitancy," UIC Today, June 2, 2021, https://today.uic.edu/citizen-science-project-explores-causes-solutions -to-covid-19-vaccine-hesitancy.

260 **blood and leave."** Patricia A. Cochran et al., "Indigenous Ways of Knowing: Implications for Participatory Research and Community," *American Journal of Public Health* 98, no. 1 (2008): 22–27, https://doi.org/10.2105/ajph.2006 .093641, p. 22.

261 **samples and data.** Lizzie Wade, "To Overcome Decades of Mistrust, a Workshop Aims to Train Indigenous Researchers to Be Their Own Genome Experts," *Science Magazine*, September 27, 2018, https://www.sciencemag .org/news/2018/09/overcome-decades-mistrust-workshop-aims-train -indigenous-researchers-be-their-own.

261 **and that trust."** Kelly Boutsalis, "Weaving Indigenous and Western Knowledge," University Affairs, April 27, 2021, https://www.universityaffairs .ca/features/feature-article/weaving-indigenous-and-western-knowledge/.

261 **Saskatchewan Polytechnic said.** "Cowessess First Nation and Saskatchewan Polytechnic Search for Unmarked and Unidentified Graves," Saskatchewan Polytechnic, July 2021, https://saskpolytech.ca/news/posts /2021/cowessess-frst-nation-and-sask-polytech-search-for-unmarked-and -unidentified-graves.aspx/%22.

262 **to other authorities."** Wade, "To Overcome Decades."

262 **make lifelong relations."** Wade, "To Overcome Decades."

262 **do the same.** Amy Dockser Marcus, "Henrietta Lacks and Her Remarkable Cells Will Finally See Some Payback," *Wall Street Journal*, August 1, 2020, https://www.wsj.com/articles/henrietta-lacks-and-her-remarkable-cells -will-finally-see-some-payback-11596295285#; Samara Reck-Peterson et al., "Call to Action," Henrietta Lacks Foundation, August 1, 2020, http:// henriettalacksfoundation.org/wp-content/uploads/2020/08/UCSD -CalltoAction-8-1-20.pdf.

262 **minorities," he said.** Marcus, "Henrietta Lacks."

262 **her book royalties.** Steve Hendrix, "On the Eve of an Oprah Movie about Henrietta Lacks, an Ugly Feud Consumes the Family," *Washington Post*, March 29, 2017, https://www.washingtonpost.com/local/on-the-eve-of -an-oprah-movie-about-henrietta-lacks-an-ugly-feud-consumes-the-family /2017/03/28/d33d3418-1248-11e7-ada0-1489b735b3a3_story.html.

263 **take as scientists."** Reck-Peterson et al., "Call to Action."

263 **are really equitable."** Alexandra Witze, "Wealthy Funder Pays Reparations for Use of HeLa Cells," *Nature*, October 29, 2020, https://www.nature.com /articles/d41586-020-03042-5.

264 **repair and restitution.** Guest contributors, "Princeton Owes the Families of the MOVE Bombing Victims Answers," *Daily Princetonian*, April 26, 2021, https://www.dailyprincetonian.com/article/2021/04/princeton-university -move-families-bombing-victims-philadelphia.

264 **and research objects."** "MOVE Children Deserve to Rest in Peace! Return Our Family's Remains NOW!," Action Network, accessed January 28, 2022, https://actionnetwork.org/petitions/move-children-deserve-to-rest-in -peace?source=direct_link.

264 **going through that."** Lubrano, "Mothers of Children."

264 **Frackville, Pennsylvannia.** Lubrano, "Mothers of Children."

264 **officer Daniel Faulkner.** Bobby Allyn, "Mumia Abu-Jamal Granted Right of Appeal after Decades in Prison," NPR, December 28, 2018, https://www .npr.org/2018/12/28/680781150/mumia-abu-jamal-granted-right-of-appeal -after-decades-in-prison.

265 **thirteen American colonies.** As professor of global health and social medicine Anne Pollock illustrates, where we locate scientific knowledge and whom we imagine as scientists shape future possibilities. See, Anne Pollock, *Synthesizing Hope: Matter, Knowledge, and Place in South African Drug Discovery* (Chicago: University of Chicago Press, 2019).

265 **trials, Cotton Mather.** Walker, "Cotton Mather."

265 **in a Drop."** Ted Widmer, "How an African Slave Helped Boston Fight Smallpox," *Boston Globe*, October 17, 2014, https://www.bostonglobe.com /ideas/2014/10/17/how-african-slave-helped-boston-fight-smallpox /XFhsMMvTGCeV62YP0XhhZI/story.html.

265 **build up immunity.** Rene F. Najera, "Black History Month: Onesimus Spreads Wisdom That Saves Lives of Bostonians during a Smallpox Epidemic," History of Vaccines, February 3, 2019, https://www.historyofvaccines.org /content/blog/onesimus-smallpox-boston-cotton-mather.

265 **for smallpox, variola.** "History of Smallpox," Centers for Disease Control and Prevention, last revised February 20, 2021, https://www.cdc.gov /smallpox/history/history.html.

266 **his 'Negroish' thinking)."** Najera, "Black History Month."

266 **was a lifesaver.** Vaccination today is a much safer method than variolation because the former uses a weakened version of the pathogen from cows (Latin *vacca*). Variolation, by contrast, used pus directly from people infected with smallpox and thus posed a greater risk to the inoculated patient, who could also spread the disease to others.

Chapter Seven

Page

267 **would put it.** Cornel West, *Brother West: Living and Loving Out Loud: A Memoir*, with David Ritz (New York: SmileyBooks, 2010), 4.

269 **spoken-word piece.** Lucas Rivera, "a love poem."

270 **all the time."** Angela Davis, speech at Southern Illinois University Carbondale, February 13, 2014, video, 56:45, https://www.youtube.com/watch?v=6s8QCucFADc; McKenzie Jean-Philippe, "9 Essential Angela Davis Books to Add to Your Shelf," *Oprah Daily*, June 8, 2020, https://www.oprahdaily.com/entertainment/books/g32803115/angela-davis-books/.

271 **invented every day."** Eddie S. Glaude, *Begin Again: James Baldwin's America and Its Urgent Lessons for Our Own* (New York: Crown, 2021), p. 145.

272 **human rights lawyer.** Tasha Wibawa, "Black Lives Matter Protests Spark Reminder of 'Deeply Rooted' Racial Injustice towards West Papuans," ABC News, June 11, 2020, https://www.abc.net.au/news/2020-06-12/black-lives-matter-protests-debate-over-racism-papuans-indonesia/12331580.

272 **"divisive" and political").** Mike Rosen, "NFL Fumbles Black National Anthem Policy," *Colorado Springs Gazette*, August 4, 2021, https://gazette.com/opinion/column-nfl-fumbles-black-national-anthem-policy-mike-rosen/article_20f98442-f46a-11eb-8704-03ed799ee5cf.html; Leandra Bernstein, "Reported NFL Decision to Play Black National Anthem before Games Faces Pushback," ABC13 News, August 2, 2021, https://wset.com/news/nation-world/nfl-decision-to-play-black-national-anthem-before-games-faces-pushback.

273 **enjoys pancakes sometimes.** "Quaker Oats Replaces Historically Racist Aunt Jemima Mascot With Black Female Lawyer Who Enjoys Pancakes Sometimes," *The Onion*, June 12, 2020, https://www.theonion.com/quaker-oats-replaces-historically-racist-aunt-jemima-ma-1844015205.

273 **toward racial equality."** Daniel Kreps, "Quaker Oats to End Aunt Jemima Brand to 'Make Progress Toward Racial Equality'" *Rolling Stone*, June 17, 2020, https://www.rollingstone.com/culture/culture-news/quaker-oats-ends-aunt-jemima-brand-1016380/.

273 **corporate solidarity statements.** Amber M. Hamilton, "What's Missing from Corporate Statements on Racial Injustice? The Real Cause of Racism," *MIT Technology Review*, September 5, 2020, https://www.technologyreview.com/2020/09/05/1008187/racial-injustice-statements-tech-companies-racism-racecraft-opinion/.

274 **to heal trauma."** James Rainey, Dakota Smith, and Cindy Chang, "Growing the LAPD Was Gospel at City Hall. George Floyd Changed that," *Los Angeles Times*, June 5, 2020, https://www.latimes.com/california/story/2020-06-05/eric-garcetti-lapd-budget-cuts-10000-officers-protests.

274 **ignoring our demands."** Nicholas Wu, "'Black Lives Matter' Painted in 50-Foot Yellow Letters Near White House to Honor George Floyd Protesters," *USA Today*, June 5, 2020, https://www.usatoday.com/story/news/politics/2020/06/05/black-lives-matter-mural-painted-near-white-house-mayors-behest/3153364001/.

274 **home ownership smh.** F. Thot FitzBearald (@tmrwlandiz2good), Twitter post, June 27, 2020, 2:12 p.m., https://twitter.com/tmrwlandiz2good/status/1276941399913459712.

274 **them to do.** Rosalyn Denise Campbell (@DrRosalynDenise), Twitter post, June 27, 2020, 6:39 a.m., https://twitter.com/DrRosalynDenise/status /1276827469509726208.

274 **racially steering them.** Lisa Rice (@ItsLisaRice), Twitter post, June 20, 2020, 2:48 p.m. https://twitter.com/ItsLisaRice/status/1276950633753575427.

274 **not as much."** Gloria Bigelow (@gloriabigelow), Twitter post, June 27, 2020, 1:08 a.m., https://twitter.com/gloriabigelow/status/12767442 14429052928.

274 **the police people.** Yolo Akili (@YoloAkili), Twitter post, June 27, 2020, 2:40 a.m., https://twitter.com/YoloAkili/status/1276767353989029893.

275 **of the work."** Mariame Kaba, "Join the Abolitionist Movement with Mariame Kaba," interview by Liz, *Rebel Steps*, Channel Zero Network, audio, 39:34, https://rebelsteps.com/episodes/abolition-with-mariame -kaba/.

275 **all its forms."** The email was later published; see Christopher L. Eisgruber, "Statement on the School of Public and International Affairs and Wilson College," June 27, 2020, https://president.princeton.edu/blogs/statement -school-public-and-international-affairs-and-wilson-college.

275 **refuted that characterization.** In a public statement following Princeton's announcement, the Black Justice League wrote, "With frankness and candor, Christopher Eisgruber et. al, we denounce your actions as woefully inadequate. Such symbolic gestures—absent a more substantive reckoning with lasting traditions perpetuating anti-blackness that our full list of demands addressed—reflect the University's ongoing failure to confront deep-rooted issues that allow the racist status quo to remain intact under the guise of progress . . . The nature of Princeton's response is illustrative of a tried-and-true strategy of using symbolic gestures to palliate student demands." Black Justice League, "A Statement from the Black Justice League in Response to the Removal of the Wilson Name," Medium, June 28, 2020, https://medium.com/@blackjusticeleague15/a-statement-from-the -black-justice-league-in-response-to-the-removal-of-the-wilson-name -853153b6c12f.

275 **policy of exclusion.** April C. Armstrong, "Erased Pasts and Altered Legacies: Princeton's First African American Students." *Princeton & Slavery*, https://slavery.princeton.edu/stories/erased-pasts-and-altered-legacies -princetons-first-african-american-students,,accessed February 15, 2022.

276 **in the country."** Jeffrey Barg, "A Year after Decision to Capitalize 'Black,' Shades of Gray Remain for Readers," *Philadelphia Inquirer*, July 21, 2021, https://www.inquirer.com/opinion/capital-b-black-ap-style-language -20210721.html.

276 **statement of solidarity.** Monica Cox (@DrMonicaCox), Twitter post, July 8, 2021, 10:00 a.m.

276 **or viral publicity?** In many instances, so-called progress (such as Wal-Mart announcing it would no longer lock up "multicultural" products typically

purchased by Black customers) just revealed how backward things have been. So now we are where we should have been.

277 **a flourishing life."** Erik Olin Wright, *How to Be an Anticapitalist in the Twenty-First Century* (London: Verso Books, 2019), p. 9.

277 **a *radio* imagination.** Octavia Butler, Marilyn Mehaffy, and AnaLouise Keating. "'Radio Imagination': Octavia Butler on the Poetics of Narrative Embodiment." *MELUS* 26, no. 1 (2001): 45–76, https://doi.org/10.2307 /3185496.

279 **you are, right?"** Directed by C. A. Griffith and H. L. T. Quan, *Mountains That Take Wing* (2010), Quad Productions, http://www.quadproductions .org/our-films/mountains-that-take-wing, accessed February 15, 2022.

280 **with 'critical connections.'"** Grace Lee Boggs, *The Next American Revolution: Sustainable Activism for the Twenty-First Century*, with Scott Kurashige (Berkeley: University of California Press, 2012), p. 14.

281 **part out loud.** Emily Stewart, "How 9/11 Convinced Americans to Buy, Buy, Buy," *Vox*, September 9, 2021, https://www.vox.com/the-goods/22662889 /september-11-anniversary-bush-spend-economy.

281 **to follow it."** Ruth Wilson Gilmore, personal communication.

281 **we *do* need."** Seattle Solidarity Budget "Post-election Update," November 9, 2021, https://www.seattlesolidaritybudget.com/news/solidarity-budget -update.

282 ***what* we value."** Seattle Solidarity Budget, "Post-election Update," accessed January 31, 2022, https://www.seattlesolidaritybudget.com/news/solidarity -budget-update; J. M. Wong, "Opinion: Which Side Are You On?," *South Seattle Emerald*, November 22, 2021, https://southseattleemerald.com/2021 /11/22/opinion-which-side-are-you-on/.

282 **which is *everything*."** Ruth Wilson Gilmore, "Making Abolition Geography in California's Central Valley," *Funambulist*, December 20, 2018, https:// thefunambulist.net/magazine/21-space-activism/interview-making -abolition-geography-california-central-valley-ruth-wilson-gilmore.

283 **code is blue."** Nelson Makamo, "Art as Activism—a Conversation with Nelson Makamo," Harvard University Center for African Studies, Cambridge, MA, December 7, 2021. Nelson Makamo writes, "We work tirelessly to create new structures; structures that encourage, nurture, and house our genius expressions, moving from a place of lack to a place of abundance. We are the only ones that can deliberately administer change within ourselves and our communities, no one else!"

283 **everything went right.** "Septima Clark," SNCC Digital Gateway, https:// snccdigital.org/people/septima-clark/, accessed on February 15, 2022.

283 **worthy of poetry."** NPR Interview, "Rita Dove on New Anthology, Advice for Young Poets," January 2, 2012, https://www.npr.org/2012/01/02/144491211 /-rita-dove-on-new-anthology-advice-for-young-poets.

INDEX

A NOTE ON THE TYPE

This book has been composed in Adobe Text and Gotham. Adobe Text, designed by Robert Slimbach for Adobe, bridges the gap between fifteenth- and sixteenth-century calligraphic and eighteenth-century Modern styles. Gotham, inspired by New York street signs, was designed by Tobias Frere-Jones for Hoefler & Co.